lonely planet

MOSCOW

Mara Vorhees
Ryan Ver Berkmoes

LONELY PLANET PUBLICATIONS
Melbourne • Oakland • London • Paris

Moscow
2nd edition – March 2003
First published – August 2000

Published by
Lonely Planet Publications Pty Ltd ABN 36 005 607 983
90 Maribyrnong St, Footscray, Victoria 3011, Australia

Lonely Planet offices
Australia Locked Bag 1, Footscray, Victoria 3011
USA 150 Linden St, Oakland, CA 94607
UK 10a Spring Place, London NW5 3BH
France 1 rue du Dahomey, 75011 Paris

Photographs
Many of the images in this guide are available for licensing from
Lonely Planet Images.
ⓦ www.lonelyplanetimages.com

Front cover photograph
Part of the vast Moscow metro system (Kim Steele, PhotoDisc)

ISBN 1 86450 359 9

text & maps © Lonely Planet Publications Pty Ltd 2003
photos © photographers as indicated 2003

Printed by SNP SPrint (M) Sdn Bhd
Printed in Malaysia

Contents – Text

PLACES TO EAT 149

ENTERTAINMENT 162

SHOPPING 169

EXCURSIONS 175

LANGUAGE 215

GLOSSARY 225

THANKS 227

INDEX 234

COLOUR MAPS SEE BACK PAGES

MAP LEGEND BACK PAGE

METRIC CONVERSION INSIDE BACK COVER

Contents – Maps

MOSCOW WALKS

THE KREMLIN

THINGS TO SEE & DO

EXCURSIONS

COLOUR MAPS

The Authors

Mara Vorhees

Mara was born and raised in St Clair Shores, Michigan. Her fascination with world cultures and her penchant for good deeds led her into the field of international development and she set out to assist Russia in its economic transition. After two years in the field, mainly spent fighting with the tax police (and losing), she resorted to seeing and saving the world by some other means. The pen-wielding traveller has since worked on Lonely Planet's *Trans-Siberian Railway*, *Eastern Europe* and *Russia & Belarus*. When not traipsing around the former Soviet bloc, she resides in Somerville, Massachusetts with her husband and her cat. She still dabbles in international development.

Ryan Ver Berkmoes

In addition to writing the first edition of *Moscow*, Ryan authored *Chicago*, co-wrote *Texas*, *Canada* and *Western Europe*, and coordinated *Russia, Ukraine & Belarus*, *Great Lakes*, *Out to Eat London*, *Netherlands* and *England*. Based in San Francisco, he is the publisher of Lonely Planet's country titles.

From the Author

Mara Vorhees I am especially grateful to Liz Filleul, who brought me into the LP fold, and whom I will miss now that she has moved on to bigger and better things. Fortunately, she left this project in the capable hands of Imogen Franks, whose hard work and encouragement have been much appreciated.

Thanks also to Ryan Ver Berkmoes and Alevtina Chernorukova for their efforts on the 1st edition of *Moscow*. On the ground in Moscow, I received valuable support from Viktor Orekhov and Natasha Lodyasova. Alexandra Lanskaya of Dom Patriarshy Tours and Nikita Ivanov of www.gay.ru were more than forthcoming with information and tips.

I am ever indebted to friends and family back home, for keeping in touch while I'm on the road; to Theo Panayotou and Rob Faris at CID, for letting me go (again); and especially to my parents, for never tiring of *russkie suveniri* (or at least for pretending). Most of all, to Gerald Easter – who may lose patience with Russia, but never seems to lose it with me – спасибо и целую.

This Book

The 1st edition of this book was written by Ryan Ver Berkmoes.

From the Publisher

The coordinating editor of this book was Craig MacKenzie. The coordinating designer of this book was Jack Gavran. Craig was assisted by Sally O'Brien. Jack was assisted by Jarrad Needham and Ed Pickard. Belinda Campbell took the book through layout. Thanks also to Eoin Dunlevy, Imogen Franks, Mark Griffiths, Kerryn Burgess, Kate McDonald, Mark Germanchis, Csanád Csutoros and LPI Images. A special thanks to David Burnett for Cyrillic support. Simon Bracken produced the cover and Jim Jenkin and Quentin Frayne produced the Language chapter.

THANKS
Many thanks to the travellers who used the last edition and wrote to us with helpful hints, advice and interesting anecdotes. Your names appear in the back of this book.

Foreword

ABOUT LONELY PLANET GUIDEBOOKS

The story begins with a classic travel adventure: Tony and Maureen Wheeler's 1972 journey across Europe and Asia to Australia. There was no useful information about the overland trail then, so Tony and Maureen published the first Lonely Planet guidebook to meet a growing need.

From a kitchen table, Lonely Planet has grown to become the largest independent travel publisher in the world, with offices in Melbourne (Australia), Oakland (USA), London (UK) and Paris (France).

Today Lonely Planet guidebooks cover the globe. There is an ever-growing list of books and information in a variety of media. Some things haven't changed. The main aim is still to make it possible for adventurous travellers to get out there – to explore and better understand the world.

At Lonely Planet we believe travellers can make a positive contribution to the countries they visit – if they respect their host communities and spend their money wisely. Since 1986 a percentage of the income from each book has been donated to aid projects and human rights campaigns, and, more recently, to wildlife conservation.

Although inclusion in a guidebook usually implies a recommendation we cannot list every good place. Exclusion does not necessarily imply criticism. In fact there are a number of reasons why we might exclude a place – sometimes it is simply inappropriate to encourage an influx of travellers.

UPDATES & READER FEEDBACK

Things change – prices go up, schedules change, good places go bad and bad places go bankrupt. Nothing stays the same. So, if you find things better or worse, recently opened or long-since closed, please tell us and help make the next edition even more accurate and useful.

Lonely Planet thoroughly updates each guidebook as often as possible – usually every two years, although for some destinations the gap can be longer. Between editions, up-to-date information is available in our free, monthly email bulletin *Comet* (ⓦ www.lonelyplanet.com/newsletters). You can also check out the *Thorn Tree* bulletin board and *Postcards* section of our website, which carry unverified, but fascinating, reports from travellers.

Tell us about it! We genuinely value your feedback. A well-travelled team at Lonely Planet reads and acknowledges every email and letter we receive and ensures that every morsel of information finds its way to the relevant authors, editors and cartographers.

Everyone who writes to us will find their name listed in the next edition of the appropriate guidebook. The very best contributions will be rewarded with a free guidebook.

We may edit, reproduce and incorporate your comments in Lonely Planet products such as guidebooks, websites and digital products, so let us know if you don't want your comments reproduced or your name acknowledged.

How to contact Lonely Planet:
Online: ⓔ talk2us@lonelyplanet.com.au, ⓦ www.lonelyplanet.com
Australia: Locked Bag 1, Footscray, Victoria 3011
UK: 10a Spring Place, London NW5 3BH
USA: 150 Linden St, Oakland, CA 94607

Introduction

How many times in my sorrowful separation,
In my wandering fate,
Have I thought of you, O Moscow!
Moscow…how much there is in that sound
That flows together for the heart of the Russian.
A Pushkin, from *Yevgeny Onegin*

Some people love Moscow. Some hate it. Most do both. It's glittering and grey, beautiful and bleak, pious and hedonistic.

Moscow is the epicentre of the 'New Russia' and everything that represents. Its commerce and culture are characteristics that most provincial Russians can still only dream about. Plagued by soaring prices, riddled with corruption, and spattered with beggars, it also epitomises the seamier side of postcommunist Russia.

Nowhere are Russia's contrasts more apparent than in Moscow, where ancient monasteries and ultra-modern monoliths stand side by side, and where New Russian millionaires and poverty-stricken pensioners walk the same streets. This one city captures much of Russian history, culture and contemporary life.

Russia's medieval roots are here, and in the surrounding towns of the Golden Ring. The Kremlin still shows off the splendour of Muscovy's grand princes; St Basil's Cathedral still recounts the defeat of the Tatars. Yet this place also recalls Russia's more recent history, still fresh in our memories. On Red Square, the founder of the Soviet state lies embalmed. And only a few kilometres away, his heir heroically defied the army – leading to the demise of the same state.

Moscow has always been known for the diversity of its population and the richness of its culture. Today, more than ever, visitors and residents alike can enjoy events ranging from the classic to the progressive. Whether a Tchaikovsky opera or an Ostrovsky drama, classical performing arts in Moscow are among the best – and cheapest – in the world. The Tretyakov Gallery and Pushkin Fine Arts Museum house internationally famous collections of Russian and impressionist art.

Of course, New Russia comes with new forms of art and entertainment. This bohemian side of Moscow – be it a beatnik band at an underground club, or an avant-garde exhibit at the Moscow Museum of Contemporary Art – provides a glimpse of Russia's future. Sometimes intellectual and inspiring, sometimes debauched and depraved, it is *always* eye-opening.

Despite all its present-day sophistication, Moscow began its life in 1147 as a provincial outpost of the Vladimir-Suzdal princedom. From the Kremlin, which was its heart, the city expanded in all directions. The new settlements developed distinct identities depending on their inhabitants. Kitai Gorod, home of craftspeople and merchants, was the centre of trade; Zamoskvorechie was the locale of quarters servicing the royal court; Zauzie developed around a blacksmith guild in the 17th century. The streets around Tverskoy attracted 18th-century nobility, while the Arbat claimed the artists and writers who were the intellectual elite of the 19th century.

Modern-day Moscow reflects this development. It is a network of neighbourhoods, each with its own flavour. Each street, courtyard and staircase has its own character. Moscow has always been a living city – thus its spirit stems from its inhabitants. As you admire the crumbling architecture on a quiet corner, watch the playful children in a leafy park, barter for beets at a farmers' market…there you will find the heart and soul of Moscow.

7

Facts about Moscow

HISTORY

Today, the red brick towers and sturdy stone walls of the Kremlin occupy the founding site of Moscow. Perched atop the Borovitsky Hills, the location overlooked a strategic bend in the Moskva River at the intersection of a network of waterways feeding the Upper Volga and Oka Rivers.

Medieval Muscovy

Early Settlement & Founding The hilly terrain of the region has supported human inhabitants for at least 5000 years. Its earliest occupants were forest-dwelling hunter-gatherer tribes, who lived off the plentiful bounty of the woodlands and waters. More than 2500 years ago, small agricultural settlements started sprouting up along the many rivers and lakes in the region. These first farmers were relatives of the Ugro-Finnic tribes that long ago populated the northern Eurasian forests.

Around the 10th century, eastern Slav tribes began to migrate to the region, eventually assimilating or displacing the earlier inhabitants.

The Krivich tribe settled in the northern section, while the Vyatich tribe relocated to the south. They came to cultivate hardy cereal crops in the abundant arable lands and to escape the political volatility of the fractious Kyivan (Kievan) Rus principality.

Present-day Moscow grew up on the Vyatich side as a trading post between these two Slav tribes, near the confluence of the Moskva and Yauza Rivers. For a brief time, these outlying communities enjoyed an autonomous existence away from the political and religious powers that were in the medieval Kyivan Rus state.

Anxious to secure his claim of sovereignty over all the eastern Slavs, Vladimir I, Grand Prince of Kyivan Rus, made his son Yaroslavl the regional vicelord, who oversaw the collection of tribute and undertook the conversion of pagans. Upon his death, in 1015, Vladimir's realm was divided among his sons, leading to a protracted and often violent period of family feuds. In this competition, the descendants of Yaroslavl inherited the northeastern territories of the realm, wherein they established a Golden Ring of towns, fortresses and monasteries.

Political power gradually shifted eastward. Under Vladimir Monomakh, the grandson of Yaroslavl, the Vladimir-Suzdal principality became a formidable rival within the medieval Russian realm. When Vladimir ascended to the throne of the Grand Prince, he appointed his youngest son, Yury Dolgorukhy, to look after the region.

Legend has it that Prince Yury stopped at Moscow on his way back to Vladimir from Kyiv (Kiev). Believing that Moscow's Prince Kuchka had not paid him sufficient homage, Yury put the impudent *boyar* (high-ranking noble) to death and placed Moscow under his direct rule.

Moscow is first mentioned in the historic chronicles in 1147, when Yury invited his allies to a banquet there: 'Come to me, brother, please come to Moscow.' Moscow's strategic importance prompted Yury to construct a moat-ringed wooden palisade on the hilltop and install his personal vassal on site. With its convenient access to riverways and roads, Moscow soon blossomed into a regional economic centre, attracting traders and artisans to the merchant rows just outside the Kremlin's walls. In the early 13th century, Moscow became the capital of a small independent principality, though it remained a contested prize by successive generations of boyar princes.

Mongol Yoke & the Rise of Muscovy

Beginning in 1236, Eastern Europe was overwhelmed by the marauding Golden Horde, a Mongol-led army of nomadic tribesmen, who appeared out of the eastern Eurasian steppes and were led by Jenghis Khan's grandson, Batu.

The ferocity of the Golden Horde raids was unprecedented and quickly Russia's ruling princes acknowledged the region's new overlord. The Golden Horde Khan would constrain Russian sovereignty for the next two centuries, demanding tribute and allegiance from his Slav hosts.

The Mongols introduced themselves to Moscow by burning the city to the ground and killing its governor. This menacing new presence levelled the political playing field in the region, thereby creating an opportunity for the small Muscovite principality.

The years of Mongol domination coincided with the rise of medieval Muscovy in a marriage of power and money. After Novgorod's Alexander Nevsky thwarted a Swedish invasion from the west, Batu Khan appointed him Grand Prince of Rus, but moved his throne to Vladimir, where he could be watched more closely.

Meanwhile, Alexander's brother, Mikhail, was charged with looking after Moscow. The Golden Horde was mainly interested in tribute, and Moscow was more conveniently situated to monitor the river trade and road traffic. With Mongol backing, Muscovite officials soon emerged as the chief tax collectors in the region.

As Moscow prospered economically, its political fortunes rose as well. In the late 13th century, a new dynasty was created in Moscow under Prince Daniil. His son Yury Danilovich won the Khan's favour and in the early 14th century, Moscow – for the first time – held the seat of the Grand Prince. Yury's brother, Ivan Danilovich, earned the moniker of Moneybags (Kalita) because of his remarkable revenue-raising abilities.

Ivan Kalita used his good relations with the Khan to manoeuvre Moscow into a position of dominance in relation to his rival princes. By the middle of the 14th century, Moscow had absorbed its erstwhile patrons, Vladimir and Suzdal.

Soon Moscow became a nemesis rather than a supplicant to the Mongols. In the 1380 Battle of Kulikovo, Moscow's Grand Prince Dmitry, Kalita's grandson, led a coalition of Slav princes to a rare victory over the Golden Horde on the banks of the Don River. He was thereafter immortalised as Dmitry Donskoy. This feat did not break the Mongols, however, who retaliated by setting Moscow ablaze only two years later. From this time, however, Moscow acted as champion of the Russian cause.

Toward the end of the 15th century, Moscow's ambitions were realised as the once diminutive duchy evolved into an expanding autocratic state. Under the long reign of Grand Prince Ivan III (the Great), the eastern Slav independent principalities were forcibly consolidated into a single territorial entity. The growing influence of the Polish-Lithuanian Commonwealth in the west forced Ivan to take action. In 1478, after a seven-year assault, Ivan's army finally subdued the prosperous merchant principality of Novgorod and evicted the Hansa trading league.

After Novgorod's fall, the 'gathering of the lands' picked up pace as the young Muscovite state annexed Tver, Vyatka, Ryazan, Smolensk and Pskov. In 1480, Poland-Lithuania's King Casimer conspired with the Golden Horde to join forces in an attack on Muscovy from the south. Casimer, however, became preoccupied with other matters and Ivan's army faced down the Mongols at the Ugra River without a fight. Ivan now refused outright to pay tribute or deference to the Golden Horde and the 200-year Mongol yoke was lifted. A triumphant Ivan had himself crowned 'Ruler of all Russia' in a solemn Byzantine-style ceremony.

Ivan the Terrible At the time of Ivan III's death, the borders of Muscovy stretched from the Baltic region in the west to the Ural Mountains in the east and the Barents Sea in the north. The south was still the domain of hostile steppe tribes of the Golden Horde. In the 16th century, however, the Golden Horde fragmented into the Khanates of Crimea, Astrakhan, Kazan and Sibir, from where they controlled vital river networks and continued to raid Russian settlements.

At this time, Ivan III's grandson, Ivan IV (the Terrible), led the further expansion and consolidation of the upstart Muscovy state. In the 1550s, Moscow conquered the Kazan and Astrakhan Khanates, thus securing control over the Volga River. Two decades later, a Cossack army commissioned by Ivan defeated the Khan of Sibir, opening up a vast wilderness east of the Urals. Ivan was less successful against the Crimean Tatars, who dominated the southern access routes to the Black Sea.

On the home front, Ivan IV's reign stirred tumult for Moscow city. Ivan IV took the throne in 1533 at age three with his mother as regent, though she died only five years later. Upon reaching adulthood, 13 years later, he was crowned 'Tsar of all the Russias'. (The Russian word 'tsar' is derived from the Latin term 'caesar'.) Ivan IV's marriage to Anastasia, a member of the Romanov boyar family, was a happy one, unlike the five that followed her early death.

In 1547, the city was consumed by fire. The tragedy provoked hysteria when a crowd became convinced that the inferno was the work of Ivan's grandmother, a suspected witch. The mob stormed the Kremlin and killed Ivan's uncle.

1560, the year in which his beloved Anastasia died, marked a turning point. Believing her to have been poisoned, he started a reign of terror against the ever-intriguing and jealous boyars, earning himself the sobriquet *grozny* (literally 'dreadfully serious' but in his case translated as 'terrible'). Later, in a fit of rage, he even killed his eldest son and heir to the throne.

Ivan suffered from a fused spine and took mercury treatments to ease the intense pain. The cure, however, was worse than the ailment, as it gradually made him insane.

The last years of Ivan's reign proved ruinous for Moscow. In 1571, Crimean Tatars set the city to the torch, burning most of it to the ground. Ivan's volatile temperament made matters worse by creating political instability. At one point he vacated the throne and concealed himself in a monastery.

Upon his death, power was passed to his feeble-minded son Feodor. For a short time, Feodor's brother-in-law and able prime minister, Boris Godunov, succeeded in restoring order to the realm. By the beginning of the 17th century, however, Boris was dead, Polish invaders occupied the Kremlin and Russia slipped into a 'Time of Troubles'. Finally, the Cossack soldiers relieved Moscow of its uninvited Polish guests and political stability was achieved with the selection of Mikhail as tsar, inaugurating the Romanov dynasty.

Social & Cultural Life With the rise of the Muscovy state, Moscow city underwent its own impressive development. The city's defence structures were upgraded. Yury Dolgorukhy's first Kremlin, a simple wooden fort on the hill above the Moskva, was refortified and expanded. Dmitry Donskoy replaced the wooden walls with a more durable limestone edifice.

To celebrate his successes, Ivan III imported a team of Italian artisans and masons for a complete renovation of the fortress. The Kremlin's famous thick brick walls and imposing watchtowers were constructed at this time. Next to the Kremlin, traders and artisans set up shop in Kitai Gorod. After the Crimean Tatars devastated the city in 1571, a stone wall was erected around these commercial quarters.

The city developed in concentric rings outward from this centre. A 16km earthen rampart was also built around the city to establish a forward line of defence.

As it emerged as a political capital, Moscow also took on the role of religious centre. Relations between the Church and the Grand Prince were always closely intertwined. In the 1320s, Metropolitan Pyotr, head of the Russian episcopate, departed from Vladimir and moved into the Kremlin.

In the mid-15th century, a separate Russian Orthodox Church was organised, independent of the Greek Church. In the 1450s, when Constantinople fell to heathen Turks, the Metropolitan declared Moscow to be the 'Third Rome', the rightful heir of Christendom. Ivan III vowed to make Moscow a stronghold of spirituality. Under Ivan IV, the city earned the nickname of 'Gold-Domed Moscow' because of the multitude of monastery fortresses and magnificent churches constructed within.

As Moscow prospered, the once-small village grew into an urban centre. By the early 15th century, Moscow was the largest town among the Russian lands, with a population surpassing 50,000 people. Contemporary visitors said Moscow was 'awesome', 'brilliant' and 'dirty', comparable to Prague or Florence, and twice as large.

Outside the Kremlin walls, the city's inhabitants were mostly clergy, merchants, artisans and labourers. The city was ringed by noble estates, monastery holdings and small farms. The town recovered quickly from fire, famine and fighting; its population topped 100,000 and then 200,000. In the early 17th century, Moscow was the largest city in the world.

Imperial Moscow
Peter the Great & the Spurned Capital
Peter I, known as 'the Great' for his commanding frame (reaching over 2m) and equally commanding victory over the Swedes, dragged Russia kicking and screaming into modern Europe. Born to Tsar Alexey's second wife in 1672, Peter spent much of his youth in royal residences in the Moscow countryside, organising his playmates in war games. Energetic and inquisitive, he was eager to learn about the outside world. As a boy, he spent hours in Moscow's European district; as a young man, he spent months travelling in the West. In fact, he was Russia's first ruler to venture abroad. Peter briefly shared the throne with his half-brother, before taking sole possession in 1696.

Peter wilfully imposed modernisation on Moscow. He ordered the boyars to shave their beards, imported European advisers and craftsmen, and rationalised state administration. He built Moscow's tallest structure, the 90m-high Sukharev Tower, and next to it founded a College of Mathematics and Navigation.

Yet, Peter always despised Moscow for its scheming boyars and archaic traditions. In 1712, he startled the country by announcing the relocation of the capital to a swampland, recently acquired from Sweden in the Great Northern War. St Petersburg would be Russia's 'Window on the West', and everything that Moscow was not –

modern, scientific and cultured. Alexander Pushkin later wrote that 'Peter I had no love for Moscow, where, with every step he took, he ran into remembrances of mutinies and executions, inveterate antiquity and the obstinate resistance of superstition and prejudice.'

The spurned ex-capital quickly fell into decline. With the aristocratic elite and administrative staff departing for marshier digs, the population fell by more than a quarter by 1725. The city suffered further from severe fires, a situation exacerbated by Peter's mandate to direct all construction materials to St Petersburg.

In the 1770s, Moscow was devastated by an outbreak of bubonic plague, which claimed more than 50,000 lives. It was decreed that the dead had to be buried outside the city limits. Vast cemeteries, including Danilovskoye and Vagankovskoye, were the result. The situation was so desperate that residents went on a riotous looting spree that was violently put down by the army. Empress Catherine II (the Great) responded to the crisis by ordering a new sanitary code to clean up the urban environment and silencing the Kremlin alarm bell that had set off the riots. By 1780, St Petersburg's population surpassed that of Moscow.

By the turn of the 19th century, Moscow had recovered from its gloom. The population climbed back to over 200,000, its previous high point. Peter's exit had not caused a complete rupture. The city retained the ceremonial title of 'first-throned capital', where coronations were held. When Peter's grandson, Peter III, relieved the nobles of obligatory state service in 1762, many returned home to Moscow. Moreover, many of the merchants never left and, after the initial shock, their patronage and wealth became visible again throughout the city.

The late 18th century saw the construction of the first embankments along the Moscow (Moskva) River, which were followed by bridges. In the 1750s, Russia's first university, museum and newspaper were started in Moscow. This new intellectual and literary scene would soon give rise to a nationalist-inspired cultural movement, which would embrace those features of Russia that were distinctively different from the West.

Napoleon & the Battle of Moscow In 1807 Tsar Alexander I negotiated the Treaty of Tilsit. It left Napoleon in charge as Emperor of the West and Alexander as Emperor of the East, united (in theory) against England. The alliance lasted until 1810, when Russia resumed trade with England. A furious Napoleon decided to crush the tsar with his Grand Army of 700,000, the largest force the world had ever seen for a single military operation.

The vastly outnumbered Russian forces then retreated across their own countryside throughout the summer of 1812, scorching the earth in an attempt to deny the French sustenance, and fighting some successful rearguard actions.

Napoleon set his sights on Moscow. In September, with the lack of provisions beginning to bite the French, Russian general Mikhail Kutuzov finally decided to turn and fight at Borodino, 130km from Moscow. The battle was extremely bloody, but inconclusive, with the Russians withdrawing in good order. More than 100,000 soldiers lay dead at the end of a one-day battle.

Before the month was out, Napoleon entered a deserted city. Defiant Muscovites burned down two-thirds of the city rather than see it occupied by the French invaders. French soldiers tried to topple the formidable Kremlin, but its sturdy walls and towers withstood the force. Alexander, meanwhile, ignored Napoleon's overtures to negotiate.

With winter coming and supply lines overextended, Napoleon declared victory and retreated. His badly weakened troops stumbled westward out of the city, falling to starvation, disease or Russian snipers. Only one in 20 made it back to the relative safety of Poland. The tsar's army pursued Napoleon all the way to Paris, which Russian forces briefly occupied in 1814.

The 19th Century Moscow was feverishly rebuilt in just a few years following the war. Monuments were erected to commemorate Russia's hard-fought victory and Alexander's

'proudest moment' – a Triumphal Arch, inspired by their former French hosts, was placed at the top of Tverskaya ulitsa on the road to St Petersburg. The sculpture of Minin and Pozharsky, who had liberated Moscow from a previous foreign foe, alighted Red Square.

And, the immensely grandiose Cathedral of Christ the Redeemer, which took almost 50 years to complete, went up along the river embankment outside the Kremlin.

The building frenzy did not stop with national memorials. In the centre, engineers diverted the Neglinnaya River to an underground canal and created two new urban spaces: the Alexandrovsky Garden, running alongside the Kremlin's western wall; and Theatre Square, featuring the glittering Bolshoi Theatre and later the opulent Metropol Hotel. The rebuilt Manezh, the 180m-long imperial stables, provided a touch of neoclassical grandeur to the scene. Meanwhile, the city's two outer defensive rings were replaced with the tree-lined Boulevard Ring and Garden Ring roads.

The Garden Ring became an informal social boundary line: on the inside were the abodes and amenities of the merchants, intellectuals, civil servants and foreigners; on the outside were the factories and flophouses of the toiling, the loitering and the destitute.

A post-war economic boom changed the city forever. The robust recovery was at first led by the big merchants, long the mainstay of the city's economy. In the 1830s, they organised the Moscow Commodity Exchange. By mid-century, industry began to overtake commerce as the city's economic driving force. Moscow became the hub of a network of new railroad construction, connecting the raw materials of the East to the manufacturers of the West. With a steady supply of cotton from Central Asia, Moscow became a leader in the textile industry. By 1890, more than 300 of the city's 660 factories were engaged in cloth production and the city was known as 'Calico Moscow'. While St Petersburg's industrial development was financed largely by foreign capital, Moscow drew upon its own resources. The Moscow Merchant Bank, founded in 1866, was the country's second largest bank by century's end.

The affluent and self-assured business elite extended its influence over the city. The eclectic tastes of the nouveaux riches were reflected in the multiform architectural styles of their mansions, salons and hotels. The business elite eventually secured direct control over the city government, removing the remnants of the old boyar aristocracy. In 1876, Sergei Tretyakov, artful entrepreneur and art patron, started a political trend when he became the first mayor who could not claim noble lineage.

The increase in economic opportunity in the city occurred simultaneously with a decline of agriculture and the emancipation of the serfs. As a result, the city's population surged. By 1890, Moscow could claim over one million inhabitants. That number would increase by another 50% in less than 20 years. Moscow still ranked second to St Petersburg in population, however, unlike the capital, Moscow was a thoroughly Russian city – its population was 95% ethnic Russian.

The steep rise in numbers was driven by an influx of rural job seekers. By 1900, more than 50% of the city's inhabitants were first-generation peasant migrants. Some stayed for only short stints in between the planting and harvesting seasons, others adjusted to the unfamiliar rhythm of industrial society and became permanent residents. They settled in the factory tenements outside the Garden Ring and south of the river in the Zamoskvoreche district.

The influx of indigents overwhelmed the city's meagre social services and affordable accommodation. At the beginning of the 20th century, Moscow's teeming slums were a breeding ground for disease and discontent. The disparity of wealth among the population grew to extremes. Lacking a voice, the city's less fortunate turned an ear to the outlawed radicals.

Socialist Moscow

Moscow in Revolution The tsarist autocracy staggered into the new century. In 1904, the impressionable and irresolute Tsar Nicolas II was talked into declaring war on Japan over some forestland in the Far East. His imperial forces suffered a decisive and embarrassing defeat, touching off a nationwide wave of unrest.

Taking their cue from St Petersburg, Moscow's workers and students staged a series of demonstrations, culminating in the October 1905 general strike, forcing political concessions from a reluctant Nicolas. In December, the attempt by city authorities to arrest leading radicals provoked a new round of confrontation, which ended in a night of bloodshed on hastily erected barricades in the city's Presnya district.

Vladimir Ilich Ulyanov (Lenin) called the failed 1905 Revolution the 'dress rehearsal for 1917', vowing that next time Russia's rulers would not escape the revolutionary scourge. Exhausted by three years of a losing war, the tsarist autocracy meekly succumbed to a mob of St Petersburg workers in February 1917. Unwilling to end the war and unable to restore order, the provisional government was itself overthrown in a bloodless palace coup, orchestrated by Lenin's Bolshevik Party (which was eventually renamed the Communist Party). In Moscow, regime change was not so easy, as a week of street fighting left more than 1000 dead. Radical socialism had come to power in Russia.

Fearing a German assault, Lenin ordered that the capital return to Moscow. In March 1918, Lenin set up shop in the Kremlin and the new Soviet government expropriated the nicer downtown hotels and townhouses to conduct affairs. The move unleashed a steady stream of favour-seeking sycophants on the city. The new communist-run city government authorised the redistribution of housing space, as scores of thousands of workers upgraded to the dispossessed digs of the bourgeoisie.

The revolution and ensuing civil war, however, took its toll on Moscow. Political turmoil fostered an economic crisis. In 1921, the city's factories were operating at only 10% of their prewar levels of production. Food and fuel were in short supply. Hunger and disease stalked the darkened city. The population dropped precipitously from two million in 1917 to just one million in 1920. Wearied workers returned to the villages in search of respite, while the old elite packed up its belongings and moved beyond the reach of a vengeful new regime.

Stalin's Moscow In May 1922, Lenin suffered the first of a series of paralysing strokes that removed him from effective control of the Party and government. He died, aged 54, in January 1924. His embalmed remains were put on display in Moscow, Petrograd was renamed Leningrad in his honour, and a personality cult was built around him – all orchestrated by Josef Stalin.

The most unlikely of successors, Stalin outwitted his rivals and manoeuvred himself into the top post of the Communist Party. Ever paranoid, Stalin later launched a reign of terror against his former Party rivals, which eventually consumed nearly the entire first generation of Soviet officialdom. Hundreds of thousands of Muscovites were systematically executed and secretly interred on the ancient grounds of the old monasteries.

In the early 1930s, Stalin launched Soviet Russia on a hell-bent industrialisation campaign. The campaign cost millions of lives, but by 1939 only the USA and Germany had higher levels of industrial output. Moscow set the pace for this rapid development. Political prisoners became slave labourers. The building of the Moscow-Volga Canal was overseen by the secret police, who forced several hundred thousand 'class enemies' to dig the 125km-long ditch.

The brutal tactics employed by the state to collectivise the countryside created a new wave of peasant inmigrants to Moscow. Around the city, work camps and bare barracks were erected to shelter the huddling hordes who shouldered Stalin's industrial revolution. At the other end, Moscow also became a centre of a heavily subsidised military industry, whose engineers and technicians enjoyed a larger slice of the proletarian pie. The Party elite, meanwhile, moved into new spacious accommodation, like the Dom Naberezhnya (House of the Embankment), across the river from the Kremlin.

Under Stalin, one of the world's first comprehensive urban plans was devised for Moscow. On paper, it appeared as a neatly organised garden city; unfortunately, it was implemented with a sledgehammer. Historic cathedrals and bell towers were demolished in the middle of the night. The Kitai Gorod wall was dismantled for being 'a relic of medieval times'. Alexander's Triumphal Arch and Peter's Sukharev Tower likewise fell victim to unsympathetic city planners, eager to wrench Moscow into a proletarian future.

New monuments marking the epochal transition to socialism went up in place of the old. The first line of the marble-bedecked metro was completed in 1935. The enormous Cathedral of Christ the Saviour was razed, with the expectation of erecting the world's tallest building, upon which would stand an exalted 90m statute of Lenin. This scheme was later abandoned and the foundation hole instead became the world's biggest municipal swimming pool. Broad thoroughfares were created and neo-Gothic skyscrapers girded the city's outer ring.

In the 1930s, Stalin's overtures to enter into an anti-Nazi collective security agreement were rebuffed by England and France. Vowing that the Soviet Union would not be pulling their 'chestnuts out of the fire', Stalin signed a nonaggression pact with Hitler instead.

Thus, when Hitler launched 'Operation Barbarossa' in June 1941, Stalin was caught by surprise and did not come out of his room for three days.

The ill-prepared Red Army was no match for the Nazi war machine, which advanced on three fronts. By December, the Germans were just outside Moscow, within 30km of the Kremlin. Only an early, severe winter halted the advance. A monument now marks the spot, near the entrance road to Sheremetevo airport, where the Nazis were stopped in their tracks. Staging a brilliant counteroffensive, Soviet war hero General Zhukov staved off the attack and pushed the invaders back.

Post-Stalinist Moscow Stalin died in March 1953. His funeral procession brought out so many gawkers that a riot ensued and scores of mourners were trampled to death. The system he built, however, lived on, with a few changes.

First, Nikita Khrushchev, a former mayor of Moscow, tried a different approach to ruling. He curbed the powers of the secret police, released political prisoners, introduced wide-ranging reforms and promised to improve living conditions. Huge housing estates grew up round the outskirts of Moscow; many of the hastily constructed low-rise projects were nicknamed *khrushchoby*, after *trushchoby* (slums). Khrushchev's populism and unpredictability made the ruling elite a bit too nervous and he was ousted in 1964.

Next came the long reign of Leonid Brezhnev. From atop Lenin's mausoleum, he presided over the rise of a military superpower. Brezhnev provided long sought-after political stability and material security. Most Russians, even today, say that their living standard was higher in Brezhnev's time.

During these years, the Cold War shaped Moscow's development as the Soviet Union enthusiastically competed with the USA in arms and space races. The aerospace, radio-electronics and nuclear weapons ministries operated factories, research laboratories and design institutes in and around the capital. By 1980, as much as one-third of the city's industrial production and one-quarter of its labour force were connected to the defence industry. Moscow city officials were not privy to what went on in these secretly managed facilities. As a matter of national security, the KGB discreetly constructed a second subway system, Metro-2, under the city.

Still, the centrally planned economy could not keep pace with rising consumer demands. While the elite lived in privilege, ordinary Muscovites stood in line for scarce goods. For the Communist Party, things became a bit too comfortable. Under Brezhnev, the political elite grew elderly and corrupt, while the economic system slid into a slow, irreversible decline. And the goal of turning Moscow into a showcase socialist city was quietly abandoned.

Nonetheless, Moscow enjoyed a postwar economic boom. The city underwent further expansion, accommodating more and more buildings and residents. Brezhnev showed a penchant for brawny displays of modern architecture. Cavernous concrete-and-glass slabs, such as the Hotel Rossiya and the Kremlin's Palace of Congresses, were constructed to show the world the modern face of the Soviet Union. The cement pouring reached a frenzy in the build-up to the 1980 Summer Olympics. However, the invasion of Afghanistan caused many nations to boycott the Games and the facilities stood empty.

Appreciation for Moscow's past, however, began to creep back into city planning. Most notably, Alexander's Triumphal Arch was reconstructed, though plans to re-erect Peter's tall tower were not realised. Residential life continued to move farther away from the city centre, which was increasingly occupied by the governing elite. Shoddy high-rise apartments went up on the periphery and metro lines were extended outward.

The attraction for Russians to relocate in Moscow in these years was, and continues to be, very strong. City officials tried desperately to enforce the residency permit system, but to no avail. In 1960, the population topped six million, and, by 1980, it surpassed eight million. The spillover led to the rapid growth of Moscow's suburbs. While industry, especially military industry, provided the city's economic foundation, many new jobs were created in science, education and public administration. The city became more ethnically diverse, particularly with the arrival of petty-market traders from Central Asia and the Caucasus.

Transitional Moscow
The Communist Collapse The Soviet leadership showed it was not immune to change. Mikhail Gorbachev came to power in March 1985, with a mandate to revitalise the ailing socialist system. Gorbachev soon launched a multifaceted programme of reform under the catchphrase *'perestroika'*

(restructuring). Gorbachev recognised that it would take more than the bureaucratic re-organisations and stern warnings to reverse economic decline. He believed that the root of the economic crisis was society's alienation from the socialist system. Thus, he sought to break down the barrier between 'us and them'.

His reforms were meant to engage the population and stimulate initiative. *Glasnost*, or openness, gave new voice to a moribund popular culture and stifled media. Democratisation introduced multicandidate elections and new deliberative legislative bodies. Cooperatives brought the first experiments in market economics in over 50 years. Gorbachev's plan was to lead a gradual transition to reform socialism, but in practice, events ran ahead of him. Moscow set the pace.

In 1985, Gorbachev promoted Boris Yeltsin from his Urals bailiwick into the central leadership as new head of Moscow. Yeltsin was given the assignment of cleaning up the corrupt Moscow Party machine and responded by sacking hundreds of officials. His populist touch made him an instant success with Muscovites, who were often startled to encounter him riding public transport or berating a shopkeeper for not displaying his sausage. During Gorbachev's ill-advised anti-alcohol campaign, Yeltsin saved Moscow's largest brewery from having to close its doors.

More importantly, Yeltsin embraced the more open political atmosphere. He allowed 'informal' groups, unsanctioned by the Communist Party, to organise and express themselves in public. Soon Moscow streets, such as the Arbat, were hosting demonstrations by democrats, nationalists, reds and greens. Yeltsin's renegade style one by one ticked off the entire Party leadership. He was summarily dismissed by Gorbachev in October 1987, though he would be heard from again.

Gorbachev's political reforms included elections to reformed local assemblies in the spring of 1990. By this time, communism had already fallen in Eastern Europe and events in the Soviet Union were becoming increasingly radical. In their first free election in 88 years, Muscovites turned out in large numbers at the polls and voted a bloc of democratic reformers into office.

The new mayor was economist Gavril Popov and the vice-mayor was Yury Luzhkov. Popov immediately embarked on the 'decommunisation' of the city, selling off housing and state businesses and restoring prerevolutionary street names. He clashed repeatedly with the Soviet leadership over the management of city affairs. Popov soon acquired a key ally when Yeltsin made a political comeback as the elected head of the new Russian Supreme Soviet.

On 18 August 1991, the city awoke to find a column of tanks in the street and a 'Committee for the State of Emergency' claiming to be in charge. This committee was composed of leaders from the Communist Party, the KGB and the military. They had already detained Gorbachev at his Crimean dacha and issued directives to arrest Yeltsin and the Moscow city leadership.

But the ill-conceived coup quickly went awry and confusion ensued. Yeltsin, Popov and Luzhkov made it to the Russian parliament building, the so-called White House, to rally opposition. Crowds gathered at the White House, persuaded some of the tank crews to switch sides, and started to build barricades. Yeltsin climbed on a tank to declare the coup illegal and call for a general strike. He dared the snipers to shoot him, and when they didn't, the coup was over.

The following day, huge crowds opposed to the coup gathered in Moscow. Coup leaders lost their nerve, one committed suicide, some fell ill and the others simply got drunk. On 21 August, the tanks withdrew; the coup was foiled. Gorbachev flew back to Moscow to resume command, but his time was up as well. On 23 August, Yeltsin banned the Communist Party in Russia.

Gorbachev embarked on a last-ditch bid to save the Soviet Union with proposals for a looser union of independent states. Yeltsin, however, was steadily transferring control over everything that mattered from Soviet hands into Russian ones. On 8 December, Yeltsin and the leaders of Ukraine and Belarus, after several rounds of vodka toasts, announced that the USSR no longer existed. They proclaimed a new Commonwealth of Independent States (CIS), a vague alliance of fully independent states with no central authority. Gorbachev, a president without a country, formally resigned on 25 December, the day the white, blue and red Russian flag replaced the Soviet red flag over the Kremlin.

Painful Rebirth of Russian Politics

Buoyed by his success over Gorbachev and coup plotters, Yeltsin (now Russia's president) was granted extraordinary powers by the parliament to find a way out of the Soviet wreckage. Yeltsin used these powers, however, to launch radical economic reforms and rapprochement with the West. In so doing, he polarised the political elite. As Yeltsin's team of economic reformers began to dismantle the protected and subsidised command economy, in early 1992 the parliament finally acted to seize power back from the president. A stalemate ensued that lasted for a year and a half.

The executive-legislative conflict at the national level was played out in Moscow politics as well. After the Soviet fall, the democratic bloc that had brought Popov to power came apart. In Moscow, a property boom began, as buildings and land with no real owners changed hands at a dizzying rate with dubious legality. Increasingly, the mayor's office was at odds with the city council, as well as the new federal government. Popov began feuding with Yeltsin, just as he had previously with Gorbachev.

In June 1992, the impulsive Popov resigned his office in a huff. Without pausing to ask him to reconsider, Vice-Mayor Yuri Luzhkov readily affixed himself to the mayor's seat. The city council passed a vote of no confidence in Luzhkov and called for new elections, but the new mayor opted simply to ignore the resolution (see the boxed text 'The Mayor in the Cap' later in this chapter).

Throughout 1993, the conflict between President Yeltsin and the Russian parliament intensified. Eight different constitutional drafts were put forward and rejected. In September 1993, parliament convened with plans to remove many of the president's powers. Before it could act, Yeltsin issued a decree that shut down the parliament and called for new elections.

Events turned violent. Yeltsin sent troops to blockade the White House, ordering the members to leave it by 4 October. Many did, but on 2 and 3 October, a National Salvation Front appeared, in an attempt to stir popular insurrection against the president. They clashed with the troops around the White House and tried to seize Moscow's Ostankino TV centre.

The army, which until this time had sought to remain neutral, intervened on the president's side and blasted the parliament into submission. In all, 145 people were killed and another 700 wounded – the worst such incident of bloodshed in the city since the Bolshevik takeover in 1917. The 1993 constitution created a new political system organised around strong executive power.

'New' Moscow: The Party after the Party

While the rest of Russia struggled to survive the collapse of the command economy, Moscow emerged quickly as an enclave of affluence and dynamism. By the mid-1990s Moscow was replete with all the things Russians had expected capitalism to bring, but which had yet to trickle down to the provinces: banks, shops, restaurants, casinos, BMWs, bright lights and nightlife.

Before all else, Moscow remains a centre of power – the seat of the president, government and legislature. While it may be true, in general, that power and wealth tend to find each other, this is especially the case in post-communist Russia, where politicians have enormous control over the redistribution of economic resources. The hallways of the Duma (see Government & Politics later in this chapter) and the offices of the White House magnetically attract favour seekers and fortune hunters.

Throughout the 1990s, Yeltsin suffered increasingly from heart disease. Come 1996, however, he was not prepared to step down from his throne. Insider deals reached a

The Capital Meets the Caucasus

The 1990s marked the revival of a war that is more than two hundred years old. In the late 18th century, Catherine the Great expanded the Russian empire southward into the Caucasus. The Chechens, a fiercely independent, Muslim, mountain tribe, refused to recognize Russian rule.

In the 19th century, Russia sought to consolidate its claim on the Caucasus to maintain access to southern sea routes, to thwart British expansion into the region and to protect Russian settlers. The tsar ordered General Yermolov, a veteran of the Napoleonic Wars, to pacify the mountain peoples. An intense 30-year conflict ensued between Russians and Chechens, with displays of wanton savagery by both sides. The leader of the Chechen resistance, Imam Shamil, who evaded Russian capture and eventually journeyed to Mecca and retirement in Medina, became a larger-than-life folk hero and the inspiration for today's separatist fighters.

Chechnya was tenuously incorporated into the empire through deals that Russia struck with more cooperative Chechen clans, but separatist sentiments remained strong. Under Soviet rule, a Chechen independence revolt broke out during the Nazi invasion. After WWII, Stalin wreaked his revenge terrorising villages and deporting nearly a half-million Chechens to remote areas of Central Asia and Siberia. After Stalin's death, survivors were finally allowed to return to their homes after almost two decades. In 1969, the statue of General Yermolov in Grozny was dynamited.

National separatists declared Chechnya independent in 1992. President Yeltsin tried unsuccessfully to cajole, buy off and threaten Chechnya into submission. In 1994, he unleashed a military assault on the renegade republic. By 1996, fighting had subsided as Russian troops were contained to a few pockets of influence, while rebel gangs ruled the mountainous countryside in a condition of de facto independence.

In September 1999, a series of mysterious explosions in Moscow left more than 200 people dead. There was widespread belief, although unproven, that Chechen terrorists were responsible for the bombings. Further provoked by the incursion of Chechen rebels into neighbouring Dagestan, the Russian military recommenced hostilities with a vengeance.

Though the Caucasus seem a far way off, the repercussions of war continue to reach Moscow. Chechen residents of the capital city have endured increased harassment, both officially and unofficially. Meanwhile, in 2002, Chechen rebels wired with explosives seized a popular Moscow theatre, demanding independence. Nearly 800 theatre employees and patrons were held hostage for three days. Russian troops responded by flooding the theatre with immobilising toxic gas, disabling hostage-takers and hostages alike and preventing the worst-case scenario. The victims' unexpectedly severe reaction to the gas and a lack of available medical facilities resulted in 120 deaths and hundreds of illnesses.

The incident refuelled Russia's relentless and ruthless campaign to force capitulation. Yet prospects for a negotiated peace appear all but nonexistent.

peak in the 1996 presidential election. Russia's newly rich financiers, who backed Yeltsin's campaign, were rewarded with prized state-owned assets in rigged privatisation auctions and policy-making positions in the government. In a scene reminiscent of the medieval boyars, the power grabs of these 'oligarchs' became more brazen during Yeltsin's prolonged illness.

At the end of 1999, Yeltsin surprisingly resigned and named Vladimir Putin to replace him as president. His succession was reconfirmed in the 2000 election. And one Mayor Luzhkov saw his dreams of the presidency evaporate, while Putin succeeded in restoring a semblance of political stability.

In the New Russia, wealth is concentrated in Moscow. The city provides nearly 25% of all tax revenues collected by the federal government. Commercial banks, commodity exchanges, big businesses and high-end retailers have all set up headquarters in the capital. Since the mid-1990s, Moscow has become one of the most expensive cities in the world.

When the government defaulted on its debts and devalued the currency in 1998, it appeared that the boom had gone bust. But as the panic subsided, it became clear that it was less a crisis and more a correction for a badly overvalued rouble. Russian firms have become more competitive and productive with the new exchange rate. Wages are being paid and consumption is up. The economy has registered positive growth since 1999.

The new economy has spawned a small group of 'New Russians', who are routinely derided for their garish displays of wealth. Outside this elite, Russia's transition to the market economy has come at enormous social cost. The formerly subsidised sectors of the economy, such as education, science and healthcare, have been devastated. For many dedicated professionals, it is now close to impossible to eke out a living in their chosen profession. More sadly, many of the older generation, whose hard-earned pensions are now worth a pittance, paid the price for this transformation. They have been reduced to begging and scrimping at the margins of Moscow's new marketplace.

Following decades of an austere and prudish Soviet regime, Muscovites are revelling in their new-found freedom. Liberation, libation, defiance and indulgence are all on open display. Those reared in a simpler time are no doubt shocked by the immodesty of a younger generation. In the 21st century, however, the rhythms of the city seemed to have steadied. Decadence is still for sale, but it has become more corporate. Espresso coffees have replaced five-for-one drink specials. Moscow, however, remains the most freewheeling city in Russia; for the cynics there are no surprises, and for the ambitious there are no limits.

GEOGRAPHY

Moscow is in the middle of European Russia and at the northwest corner of its most densely developed and populated region. The Moscow River, a tributary of the Volga, crosses through the middle of the city. A smaller offshoot, the Yauza, wanders off in the southeast corner of the city. The Moscow River is responsible for the broad, shallow and almost flat valley that the city occupies. The one city area with any elevation is in the southwest, where the river has cut into Cretaceous rock, creating cliffs known as the Sparrow Hills.

ECOLOGY & ENVIRONMENT

The Soviet Union's neglect of environmental issues caused significant damage in Moscow, as throughout the country. The capital was particularly effected, perhaps due to high concentrations of industry and people. Since the Soviet collapse, local authorities are more aware of these issues, which does not mean they have the cash to do anything about them.

Ground water is largely polluted as a result of industrial dumping, leaking sewage pipes and poor drainage. Unregulated disposal and construction continue to impede clean-up efforts. Moscow once got most of its drinking water from deep artesian wells; due to overuse and pollution, however, the city now has to rely on treated river water.

None of the ponds or reservoirs around the city meets the fishing industry's health standards, although the Moscow River is actually relatively clean. While the Soviet Union's Five-Year Plans were never big on environmental policy, a major effort commenced in the 1960s to control pollution of the river. Apparently, a visiting delegation's complaints about the stink from the river caught somebody's attention. Fortunately, raw sewage is no longer dumped into the river, but industrial waste continues to be a source of pollution.

Despite improvements, fish caught in the Moscow River are not safe for consumption due to high levels of chemicals and toxins. Drinking water is drawn from the river far to the north of the city, where the waters are fairly clean as they are above Moscow's industrial belt.

Other environmental problems include air and noise pollution from both industrial and private sources. The increase in automobile

The Mayor in the Cap

Within the Moscow city government, the election of Yuri Luzhkov as mayor in 1992 set the stage for the creation of a big-city boss in the grandest of traditions. Through a web of financial arrangements, ownership deals and real-estate holdings, Luzhkov is as much a CEO as he is mayor. His interests range from the media to manufacturing and from five-star hotels to shopping malls.

When Luzhkov was first elected in June 1992, Moscow was exempted from the privatisation process then sweeping the country. This allowed the city government to retain ownership of land and property. In addition, hardly a business venture of any size receives approval from the authorities without the government as a partner. Most of the large Western hotels can boast the Moscow government as an investor, an arrangement that obviously has its advantages when city inspectors come calling.

But Luzhkov also plays the role of populist with genuine aplomb, cleaning streets and planting trees. He consistently supports patriotic causes and identifies himself with nationalist themes. He has been generous with the city's money in the restoration of the long-neglected churches and historic monuments. His 'bread and circus' strategy has included hosting spectacular city celebrations, such as 1997's over-the-top 850th anniversary fete. Luzhkov also made crime prevention a priority, a policy appreciated by voters, who put personal safety ahead of concepts like human rights.

Say what you will, his politicking has paid off: Luzhkov secured sound victories in each of Moscow's mayoral elections, winning 90% of the vote in 1996, and 71.5% in 1999.

traffic over the past 10 years has exacerbated both problems, and air quality certainly does not benefit from the widespread use of leaded fuels and uncontrolled emissions by vehicles.

As of 1994, the city has implemented an Integrated Environmental Action Plan, which includes measures such as automobile inspections, industrial regulations and local neighbourhood clean-up efforts.

GOVERNMENT & POLITICS

Russia is governed by an executive president and a two-house parliament *(duma)*. This system, ushered in by the new constitution of 1993, has potential flaws in that the president and the parliament can both (and do) make laws and can effectively block each other's actions. In practice, though, the president can usually get his way by issuing presidential decrees – in Yeltsin's time this happened often, however, Putin has worked harmoniously with the Duma.

The president is the head of state and has broad powers. He or she appoints all government ministers, including the prime minister, who is effectively number two and would assume the presidency should the president die or become incapacitated. The Duma has to approve the president's appointees, which has led to showdowns. Presidential elections are held every four years – the next one is due in 2004, but is likely to occur earlier.

The Duma's upper house, the Federation Council (Soviet Federatsii), has 178 seats, occupied by two representatives from each of Russia's 89 administrative districts. Representatives are the top officials from these areas and, as such, are not elected to this body.

The lower house, the State Duma (Gosudarstvennaya Duma), oversees all legislation. Its 450 members are equally divided between representatives elected from single-member districts and those elected from political party lists.

Although the Communist Party received the largest single share of the vote (24%) in the 1999 elections, it was not a convincing victory, being only 1% more than the hastily formed pro-Putin Unity party received. The third-placed Fatherland-All Russia party – headed by the trio of ex-premier Yevgeniy Primakov, Moscow mayor Luzhkov and Tatarstan president Mentimer – was in opposition to Putin at the time of elections, when Primakov was still deemed one of the main presidential hopefuls. But after Putin became president, it reconciled with Unity. In early 2002, these movements merged to form the United Russia party.

Moscow is divided up into political districts called *rayony*. At present there are 32, a number that grows with the population. Each elects its own representative to the city council. In recent years this body has proved to be a rubber stamp for Mayor Luzhkov as the members enjoy the fruits of his success.

ECONOMY

Moscow is the undisputed economic heart of Russia. Since the economic collapse of 1998, the city's economy – as the rest of the country – is looking comparatively healthy. In 2001, Russia saw its third consecutive year of real growth, with GDP up by 5%, fuelled mainly by high oil prices. Inflation, rampant in the 1990s, is now under control with a consequent stabilisation of the rouble. In Moscow, there is evidence of a burgeoning middle class, with the economic trappings to match.

The details of Moscow's real economic conditions are hazy, and financial reporting is, to say the least, not widespread. In a city of around 10 million people, only 182,000 individuals bothered to file tax returns in 1999. Most of the revenue collected comes from a 20% value-added tax (VAT), an ever-rising sales tax (now 5%) and huge taxes levied on industry and commerce.

Although tax revenues suffered after the economic collapse, the city has made repaying its international loans a priority. In early 2000, Moscow held over US$1 billion in bonds backed by European governments.

The average Muscovite earns about US$6000 a year, far in excess of the average US$1200 in annual earnings elsewhere in the country. However, this figure is misleading, as huge portions of society are on fixed wages and pensions that may not top US$50 a month.

Figures for unemployment are unknown. Scores of people work off the books for tax purposes, others work on a barter system and others – lacking residency permits – are officially not counted.

Much of Moscow's commerce at a personal level is conducted by an immense barter system that is a way around the lack of cash. Factories pay workers in the products they produce, and the workers trade those products for food. Local governments trade tax credits with the electric company for power, and on and on it goes. The result is a false economy without capital or taxes to pay for investment or services.

In its mix of commerce and industry, Moscow mirrors trends in the West. The 80% cut in military procurement spending in 1992, and further cuts after that, helped to devastate the traditional heavy industrial factories ringing the city. Much of the employment growth has been in the service sectors of retail and banking.

POPULATION & PEOPLE

Moscow's official population is nine million, but many estimates put it closer to 12 million. Part of the discrepancy stems from the fact that many people in the city have not been able to obtain the residency permit needed to gain work. Russian courts have declared this document illegal, but the local

Return to Reading, 'Riting & 'Rithmatic

Education was among the Soviet Union's greatest achievements. Prerevolutionary Russia was an agrarian society in which literacy was limited to the few in the upper classes. However, the USSR achieved a literacy rate of 98%, among the best in the world. Russia continues to benefit from this legacy and the literacy rate has been maintained.

Since the Soviet collapse, mandatory schooling has fallen from 11 to eight years. This change is, in part, attributed to the fact that a full 25% of coursework under the Soviet system involved ideological subjects such as Marxism and the History of the Communist Party.

police do not seem to be aware of this fact. The capital's advantageous economic conditions lead to permit-less Muscovites tolerating frequent police document inspections and pocket-emptying bribes.

The overwhelming majority (over 80%) of Muscovites are Russian. There are small percentages – less than 3% – of Jews, Ukrainians, Belarusians and Tatars. People from the southern republics such as Georgia, Kazakhstan and Armenia each make up about 1% of the population.

Russian Orthodox Church

After decades of church closure, confiscation of property and harassment of believers under the Soviet regime, the Russian Orthodox Church (Russkaya Pravoslavnaya Tserkov) is enjoying a remarkable revival. By 1991, it already had an estimated 50 million members. The rise in churchgoers has been linked to the growth of Russian nationalism, as Orthodoxy for many people is an intimate part of what it means to be Russian.

After the revolution, Lenin adopted Marx's view of religion as 'the opium of the people' and the Bolsheviks commenced a systematic seizure of church property. Stalin increased the level of persecution by harassing and even arresting the more outspoken believers. In 1941, however, he decided that the war effort would benefit from the patriotism that religion could stir up, and softened the policy. Khrushchev recommenced a harsh crackdown on the Church in the 1950s. He closed about 15,000 churches, some of which became museums of atheism.

Today, closed and neglected churches are being restored all over the country and especially in Moscow. There are now close to 25,000 active churches in the country, compared to fewer than 7000 in 1988. This seems like an impressive comeback, until you discover that Russia had over 50,000 churches in 1917.

History & Hierarchy Prince Vladimir of Kyiv effectively founded the Russian Orthodox Church in 988 by adopting Christianity from Constantinople. From this point, the head of the Church moved as the capital moved, from Kyiv to Vladimir to Moscow.

Today, Patriarch Alexy of Moscow and All Russia is head of the Church. The Patriarch's residence is the Danilov Monastery, though some Church business is still conducted at the Trinity Monastery of St Sergius at Sergiev Posad. The Yelokhovsky Cathedral is currently the senior church in Moscow.

Beliefs & Practice Russian Orthodoxy is highly traditional, and the atmosphere inside a church is both formal and solemn: priests dress imposingly, the smell of candles and incense permeates the air, and old women bustle about sweeping and polishing. Churches have no seats, no music (only melodic chanting) and no statues. What they do have are icons (see Architecture later in this chapter), before which the faithful pray, cross themselves and even kiss the ground. The Virgin Mary (Bogomater – Mother of God) is especially revered.

The language of the liturgy is 'Church Slavonic', the old Bulgarian dialect into which the Bible was first translated for Slavs. Easter (Paskha) is the focus of the Church year, with festive midnight services to launch Easter Day. Christmas (Rozhdestvo) falls on 7 January because the Church still uses the Julian calendar that the Soviet state abandoned in 1918.

In most churches, Divine Liturgy (Bozhestvennaya Liturgia) lasts about two hours. It is usually held at 8am, 9am or 10am Monday to Saturday, and at 7am and 10am on Sunday and festival days. Most churches also hold services at 5pm or 6pm daily. Some of these include an akathistos (akafist), a series of chants to the Virgin or saints.

Other Religions

Russia has small numbers of Roman Catholics, and Lutheran and Baptist Protestants, mostly among the German and other non-Russian ethnic groups. Other groups, such as the Mormons and Seventh-Day Adventists, are sending hordes of missionaries. Courts have tried to use the 1997 religion law to ban some of these missionaries, including the Pentecostalist Church, Jehovah's Witnesses and other evangelisers seen as threats by the Russian Orthodox Church. All of the above churches have at least one church or centre in Moscow.

European Russia has about 12 million active and nominal Muslims, mainly among the Tatars, Bashkirs and several of the Caucasian ethnic groups. Islam has, just like Christianity, enjoyed growth since the mid-1980s. Some of the Muslim minorities – notably the Chechens and Tatars – have been the most resistant of Russia's minorities to joining the Russian national fold since 1991. Moscow's Muslim population is estimated at 100,000, but their overall percentage of the population is about 1%. Russians are often distrustful of Muslims, especially since the war in Chechnya began.

For information on the Jewish religion, see the boxed text 'Judaism in Moscow' in the Things to See & Do chapter.

SCIENCE & PHILOSOPHY

When the Age of Enlightenment came to Russia, it came in the form of social criticism first, with science and scholarship a distant second. The relatively liberal reign of Catherine the Great spawned various forward-thinking movements advocating freedom of the serfs, among other ideas. The Freemasons, based at the University of Moscow, expounded on the importance of individual contemplation and self-perfection, as well as on one's obligations to social activism. Alexander Radishchev (1749–1802) was the most outspoken proponent of ending serfdom. His scathing condemnation of the institution, *A Journey from Petersburg to Moscow*, earned him 10 years at a Siberian labour camp.

Mikhail Lomonosov (1711–65), for whom Moscow State University is now named, was the greatest scientist of the 18th century. By no means a specialist, his most outstanding achievements were in the fields of chemistry and physics, including the discovery of the law of the preservation of matter and energy, as well as groundbreaking theories on electricity, heat and optics.

Despite the autocratic rule of the 19th century, this period witnessed an expansion of higher education and achievements in science and scholarship. Most notably, the noted mathematician Nicholas Lobachevsky (1793–1856) developed a noteworthy form of non-Euclidian geometry.

Frederick Struve utilised the new observatory facilities at Pulkovo to make advances in astronomy, including developing methods to count and weigh stars. In 1869, the celebrated chemist Dmitrii Mendeleev (1834–1907) categorised all of the known elements into the periodic table. Ivan Pavlov (1849–1936) and his famous dogs developed theories on conditioned reflexes, which contributed to both physiology and behavioural psychology.

The evolution of Russian social and philosophical ideas in the 19th century is even more striking, especially considering the outcome. A new radical spirit found expression in the nihilist movement, embodied in Turgenev's *Fathers and Sons*. The related populist movement, championed by Herzen and Bakunin, preached the glory of the peasant commune. Nicholas Chernyshevsky (1828–89) was among the most influential proponents of a utilitarian socialist revolution, which he advocated in his popular novel *What is to be done?*

Of course, Marxism was another branch of radicalism – this one without the populist twist. While often compared to a religion, Marxism was actually considered a 'science' by its adherents. The revolution was supposed to be an inevitable result of economic laws and social cycles, and did not depend on popular support.

By the end of the 19th century, a significant sector of Russian intellectuals were mellowing from this radical stance and arguing for a return to metaphysics and religion. Many of the writers and artists were retreating from politics altogether. While not particularly influential during his lifetime, the philosopher and theologian Vladimir Soloviev (1853–1900) gained followers at the turn of the 20th century. His prominent work, *A Justification of the Good*, was a scathing critique of the radical intelligentsia.

In 1909, seven authors – including the former Marxist Nicholas Berdiaev – contributed to *Signposts*, which attacked the intelligentsia for disregarding truth, religion and law.

The Russian Revolution put a sudden stop to much of this intellectual debate, as thinkers were forced to adopt the Party line. Once the new regime was in place, Soviet society became increasingly conservative, especially in the 1930s. This break from revolutionary ideals – known as the 'great retreat' – emphasised such bourgeois matters as family life and social manners. Some scholars such as Pitirim Sorokin even argued that society would become more democratic. Alas, this was not to be.

By contrast, the sciences flourished during the Soviet regime, which devoted disproportionate resources to this indispensable field. Scientific achievements were most evident in space: Sputnik I and II were the first satellites to orbit the earth in 1957; two years later, the Soviets obtained the first photographs of the far side of the moon; most notably, Yury Gagarin was the first man in space in 1961.

Post-Soviet Russia has become a bit of a vacuum as far as science and philosophy are concerned.

The state no longer has funds to support scientific research. Society, whether still recovering from Marxism-Leninism or simply overwhelmed by excessive capitalism, seems unable to generate innovative philosophical thinking. The only trend worth noting is Russia's growing nationalism, which is manifested by the resurgence of Russian Orthodoxy and the more dangerous development of fascist movements.

ARTS
Ballet
Russian ballet grew out of dance schools set up in 18th-century Moscow and St Petersburg. Being a dancer was originally a low-status position, and the Moscow ballerinas, called *devki*, were actually recruited from orphanages. Their performances, however, were patronised by the tsars.

In the 19th century, French and Italian teachers and dancers brought new techniques,

The Politics of Dancing

Many leading dancers went to the West after the revolution, but Soviet ballet maintained its technical standards and applied them to new social and political themes. New Socialist Realist works with dramatic storylines included *The Red Poppy* (1927) and Prokofiev's *Romeo and Juliet* (1946). The first outstanding dancers of the Soviet period were Galina Ulanova and Maya Plisetskaya, both of whom rose to prominence at Moscow's Bolshoi ballet and went on to teach another generation of dancers. In the 1950s, the Bolshoi made its first triumphant tours of the West.

In 1964, Yuri Grigorovich emerged as its bright new choreographer, with *Spartacus*, *Ivan the Terrible* and other successes. He directed the theatre for 30 years, but not without controversy. In the late 1980s, Grigorovich came to loggerheads with some of his leading dancers. Stars such as Maya Plisetskaya, Ekaterina Maximova and Vladimir Vasiliev resigned, accusing Grigorovich of being 'brutal' and 'Stalinist'. With encouragement from President Yeltsin, Grigorovich finally resigned in 1995, prompting loyal dancers to stage the Bolshoi's first-ever strike.

Under artistic director Vladimir Vasiliev, the Bolshoi commenced a turnaround. During these years, his new productions included *Swan Lake* and *Giselle*, starring dancers such as Nina Anaiashvili, Dmitri Belogolovtsev, Sergei Filin and Svetlana Lunkina. Reviews were initially positive, but trouble was brewing. Politics and finances made Vasiliev's task near impossible, and he soon came under fire for mismanagement.

In 2000, President Putin replaced the entire theatre administration. A power struggle ensued, but Yuri Grigorovich has emerged – yet again – as the most prominent figure in the Bolshoi ballet.

and ballet was far more prestigious in Russia than in Western Europe. During this time, ballet in Moscow and St Petersburg developed distinctive styles, embodied in each city's primary theatres: the Bolshoi emphasised melodrama and romance, while St Petersburg's Kirov focused on elegance and movement.

Music

Classical As the cultural heart of Russia, Moscow was a natural draw for generations of composers. Its rich cultural life drew talent from throughout Russia, even during the years in which St Petersburg was the capital.

Moscow-born Mikhail Glinka (1804–57) was the first to merge religious chants and folk songs with Western forms in operas that include *Ivan Susanin* (or *A Life for the Tsar*) and *Ruslan and Lyudmila*. He influenced composers, known as the Mighty Handful, who lacked formal musical training until adulthood and were concerned with exploring their Slav roots.

Their orchestral works include *Pictures at an Exhibition* by Modest Mussorgsky (1839–81) and *Scheherazade* by Nikolai Rimsky-Korsakov (1844–1908). *Boris Godunov* by Mussorgsky and *Prince Igor* by Alexander Borodin (1833–87) are two of the best-loved Russian operas.

Pyotr Tchaikovsky (1840–93) also used folk motifs but was more similar to Western tradition. His music first received widespread recognition when it was performed at the then-new Conservatory in 1866. His *1812 Overture*, his concertos and symphonies, the ballets *Swan Lake*, *The Sleeping Beauty* and *The Nutcracker*, and his opera *Yevgeny Onegin* are still among the world's most popular works. All were written in Moscow.

The next generation included the great bass singer and pianist Fyodor Chaliapin (1873–1938), pianist-composer Alexander Scriaban (1872–1915), Romantic composer Sergey Rachmaninov (1873–1943) and innovator Igor Stravinsky (1882–1971). Scriaban was born in Moscow and spent the most productive years of his life in a small apartment near ulitsa Arbat. The last two fled the revolution. Sergey Prokofiev (1891–1953), who also left but returned in 1934, wrote the scores for Sergey Eisenstein's films *Alexander Nevsky* and *Ivan the Terrible*, the ballet *Romeo and Juliet*, and *Peter and the Wolf*. His work was condemned for 'formalism' towards the end of his life.

Dmitry Shostakovich (1906–75) won international acclaim for his symphonies while working in Moscow (not without conflict). Other innovative composers were silenced. Major performers to emerge in the Soviet era (though some left for the West) included violinist David Oystrakh (1908–74), pianist Svyatoslav Richter (born 1914), the cellist/conductor Mstislav Rostropovich (born 1927) and pianist/conductor Vladimir Ashkenazy.

Progressive new music surfaced slowly in the post-Stalin era, with outside contacts limited. Alfred Schnittke's *First Symphony*, probably the most important work of this experimental modern Russian composer, was premiered in the provincial city of Gorky (now Nizhny Novgorod) in 1974. It wasn't played in Moscow till 1986.

Among the best of Moscow's recent composers have been Andrey Volkonsky, Sofia Gubaydulina, Edison Denisov, Valentin Silvestrov and, in the most recent generation, Edward Artemov, Vladimir Martinov, and husband-and-wife team Dmitry Smirnov and Yelena Firsova.

Rock This musical form developed underground, starved of decent equipment and the chance to record or perform to big audiences, but gathered a huge following among the disaffected, distrustful youth of the 1970s and '80s. Moscow's sheer size allowed underground clubs to flourish in relative obscurity.

Initially inspired by Western groups like the 'bourgeois' Beatles, Russian rock bands eventually developed a home-grown style, in which lyrics often reflected social issues. Russian *klassik rok* greats include Boris Grebenshikov, with his band Akvarium (Aquarium), and Mashina Vremeni (Time Machine), headed up by Andrei Makarevich. Both are up there with the Beatles and the Stones on Moscow's classic rock stations' play lists.

Music was circulated by illegal tapes which were known as *magizdat*, the musical equivalent of *samizdat* (underground publishing); concerts were held, if at all, in remote halls in Moscow's suburbs and attendance was risky.

Punk and heavy metal came into fashion in the early 1980s, followed by New Wave music, fashionable from about the mid-1980s. The tone of many groups of the 1980s was one of protest (or gloomy resignation) at the frustration and alienation of Soviet life. Examples include the tortured dronings of Viktor Tsoy and the chunky riffs of his band Kino, or the punk-influenced Va Bank. One of the brightest New Wave stars of the 1980s, Vasily Shumov and his band Center, still have an avid fan base in their new home of California.

With the onset of glasnost, authorities allowed the true voice of youth to sound out. Two decades after a jazz show had been the first sanctioned nonclassical public show in the nation, Moscow was hosting giant, outdoor concerts. The state record company, Melodia, began producing albums by previously unacceptable groups. The industry today is flourishing.

The latest popular rock groups in Moscow include Nautilus Pompilus, Mummy Troll, Nogu Svelo, Obermaneken (now based in New York) and Splin. The airwaves and dance halls are also often filled with Euro techno pop, which has its fair share of Russian imitators. Russia has not escaped the Western phenomenon of teenie-bop bands, evidenced by groups such as Na-Na. All of the above acts can be found at different times performing at some of Moscow's 30 concert halls and ever-changing roster of over 200 clubs and bars.

Literature & Drama

19th Century The poet Alexander Pushkin (1799–1837) is revered as the father of Russian literature. *Yevgeny Onegin*, a verse novel, was Pushkin's major work. Almost every step he took – and he travelled *very* widely around tsarist Russia – is marked by a monument or museum. However, it is with Moscow that he is most closely linked. Here he spent many of his most productive years and also enjoyed a dissipative lifestyle, even while under the constant surveillance of the

secret police. For the 200th anniversary of his birth, Moscow engaged in an orgy of Pushkin-mania that included decrees mandating the display of pictures of the writer in all store windows.

Other major Russian writers lived at least part of their lives in Moscow. The first, and probably shortest, important Russian novel, *A Hero of Our Time* by Mikhail Lermontov (1814–41), makes a great travelling companion in the Caucasus, where it's set. Its cynical antihero, Pechorin, is an indirect comment on the climate of the times. Pushkin and Lermontov launched a long tradition of conflict between writers and the state, and both died in duels widely perceived as having been set up by the authorities. The satirical *The Government Inspector* by Nikolai Gogol (1809–52), who also wrote the novel *Dead Souls*, was the first major Russian play.

Ivan Turgenev (1818–83), the first of the three great novelists of the second half of the 19th century, wrote his first works as a young man living in Moscow. Bazarov, hero of his *Fathers and Sons*, became a symbol for the antitsarist nihilist movement.

The Possessed by Fyodor Dostoevsky (1821–81) is both a satire of provincial society and an analysis of political violence. Like his other great works – *Crime and Punishment*, *The Idiot* and *The Brothers Karamazov* – it combines profound treatment of questions of morality and faith with deep psychological probing.

War and Peace by Moscow-born Leo Tolstoy (1828–1910) is a panorama of Russia during the Napoleonic Wars. It's at the pinnacle of world literature, but it won't leave you much time for seeing today's Russia if you read it while you're there. On a slightly smaller scale, *Anna Karenina* is the tragedy of a woman who violates the rigid sexual code of her time.

Chekhov & Gorky Anton Chekhov (1860–1904) first practised as a doctor in Moscow before turning to writing. His plays – *The Seagull, Three Sisters, The Cherry Orchard,* and *Uncle Vanya* – look tragicomically at the angst of the stagnating provincial middle class in the late 19th century. They owed much of their early success to 'realist' productions at the Moscow Art Theatre directed by Konstantin Stanislavsky, which aimed to show life as it really was (see the boxed text 'Stanislavsky's Methods' in the Entertainment chapter). Even though Chekhov in his later years refused to live in Moscow, he still insisted that his plays be staged first by Stanislavsky.

Maxim Gorky (1868–1936) painted a graphic picture of urban poverty and brutality from the same era in his autobiographical *My Childhood* and in the play *The Lower Depths*. He spent the last years of his life living in Moscow, the unofficial state scribe for Stalin. He is buried in the Kremlin Wall.

Revolutionary Period The futurist poets who emerged as the revolution approached used shock tactics – slang, eroticism, abrupt switches of tack – to stir people out of complacency. Though many supported the revolution, their lives often ended in tragedy. Vladimir Mayakovsky (1893–1930), practically the revolution's official bard, committed suicide, as did Sergei Yesenin (1895–1925).

Boris Pasternak (1890–1960) was another persecuted futurist poet, best known in the West for his novel *Dr Zhivago*. He gave poetry readings in Moscow before he fell out of favour with the authorities.

Soviet Era In 1932 the Party officially demanded Socialist Realism from art and literature. This meant 'concrete representation of reality in its revolutionary development…in accordance with…ideological training of the workers in the spirit of Socialism'. Writers had to convey the Party's messages – and please Stalin.

Alexei Tolstoy is known primarily for his novels about the Civil War and the revolution, the most famous being the trilogy *The Ordeal*. Mikhail Sholokhov, with his sagas of revolution and war among the Don Cossacks, *And Quiet Flows the Don* and *The Don Flows Home to the Sea*, was another one of the few decent writers to win approval.

The Master and Margarita, by the great satirist Mikhail Bulgakov (1891–1940), was banned for ages. It's a darkly comic novel, in which the devil turns up in Moscow to cause all manner of anarchy and make idiots of the system and its lackeys.

The Khrushchev thaw saw the emergence of poets like Yevgeny Yevtushenko and Andrey Voznesensky, who managed to remain on the right side of the authorities, and the Nobel Prize-winning novelist Alexander Solzhenitsyn, who didn't. *One Day in the Life of Ivan Denisovich*, a short tale of brutal Gulag life, was published in the USSR in 1962, but Solzhenitsyn fell foul of the Brezhnev clampdown and was exiled in 1974. He went to the USA and finally returned to Russia in 1994. His *Cancer Ward* and *The First Circle*, both written before his departure, are powerful accounts of the 1930s, but *The Gulag Archipelago* is his major work.

Glasnost brought forth a flood of writing previously suppressed. Anatoly Rybakov wrote *Children of the Arbat*, which traces his Moscow childhood. *On the Golden Porch*, a collection of stories about big souls in little Moscow flats, made Tatyana Tolstaya an international name when published in the West in 1989.

Post-Soviet Era Recent years have seen a flowering of Russian publishing and the traditional Russian love of books seems as strong as ever. Just note the number of people reading novels to wile away the minutes on the Moscow metro. Viktor Dotsenko sells almost one million of his crime fiction novels a year. Other authors, such as Irina Ratushinskaya, have earned international acclaim and sales. Her *Fictions and Lies* (1999) shows a cast of characters held hostage by the sly methods of the KGB. Viktor Pelevin's novels, such as *The Yellow Arrow* (1997), have been widely translated and he has been compared to the great Mikhail Bulgakov.

The crisis and decline of Moscow theatres, predicted by theatre critics after state funding nearly stopped, did not happen. Not only did the existing theatres manage to survive, but many new ones have appeared (see Theatre in the Entertainment chapter).

Inside the Church

Churches are decorated with frescoes, mosaics and icons with the aim of conveying Christian teachings and assisting veneration. Different subjects are assigned traditional places in the church (the *Last Judgment*, for instance, appears on the western wall). An often elaborately decorated iconostasis (icon stand) divides the main body of the church from the sanctuary, or altar area, at the eastern end, which is off-limits to all but the priest. During a service, the priest comes and goes through the Holy or Royal Door, an opening in the middle of the iconostasis.

The iconostasis is composed of up to six tiers of icons. The biggest is the deesis row *(deisusnyy ryad)*, whose central group of icons, known as the deesis, consists of Christ enthroned as the judge of the world, with the Virgin and John the Baptist interceding for humanity on either side. Archangels, apostles and Eastern Church fathers may also appear on this row.

Below the deesis row are one or two rows of smaller icons – the bottom one is the local row *(mestnyy ryad)* showing saints with local links. Above the deesis row are the festival row *(prazdnichnyy ryad)* showing the annual festivals of the Church, the prophet row *(prorocheskiy ryad)* showing Old Testament prophets, and sometimes a further patriarch row *(praotechesky ryad)* showing Old Testament patriarchs.

Normally, a traditional menu of Russian and foreign classics is accompanied by a long list of contemporary plays. The most popular playwrights are Nikolay Kolyada and Alexander Galin, who offer tragicomic reflections of the present Russian reality. Nina Sadur gives new interpretations of Russian classics. Among theatre directors the noticeable figures are Alexander Zhitinkin, Roman Viktyuk and Pyotr Fomenko.

Architecture

The *izba*, or single-storey wooden cottage still fairly common in the countryside, was the typical Moscow dwelling up until the Soviet period. Stone and brick were usually the preserves of the Church, royalty and nobility.

Medieval Period The earliest Russian architecture was by the Kyivan Rus who adopted the 'cross in square' church plan developed in Byzantium in the 9th century. At its simplest, this consisted of three aisles, each with an eastern apse (semicircular end), a dome or 'cupola' over the central aisle next to its apse, and high vaulted roofs forming a crucifix shape centred on the dome. As Russian culture moved north, Novgorod, Pskov and Vladimir-Suzdal developed their own variations on the pattern in the 11th and 12th centuries. Roofs grew steeper to prevent heavy northern snows collecting and crushing them, and windows grew narrower to keep the cold out.

Moscow in the 15th century looked to these earlier centres for inspiration in its grand building programme. Though the architects of two of the Kremlin's three great cathedrals, built between 1475 and 1510, were Italian, they took Vladimir-Suzdal's churches as their models; the third cathedral was erected by builders from Pskov.

16th to 19th Centuries Later in the 16th century, many of the north Russian wooden church features, such as the tent roof *(shatyor)* and the onion dome on a tall drum, were translated into brick. This change added up to a new, uniquely Russian architecture, more vertical in effect than the Byzantine shape. St Basil's Cathedral, the Ivan the Great Bell Tower in the Moscow Kremlin, and the Ascension Church at Kolomenskoe are three highlights of this era.

In the 17th century, builders in Moscow added tiers of *kokoshniki*, colourful tiles and brick patterning to create jolly, merchant-financed churches such as St Nicholas of the Weavers and the Trinity in Nikitniki. In the middle of the century, Patriarch Nikon outlawed such frippery, but elaboration returned later with the Western-influenced Moscow baroque. This style featured ornate white detailing against red-brick walls, such as at the Church of the Intercession at Fili.

In 1714, it all came to a halt. Peter the Great's edict banned stone construction in Moscow and anywhere else in Russia, as all the resources were needed for the new city of St Petersburg. But frequent fires and a general outcry from Moscow's wealthy elite meant that the order was rescinded in 1722.

In the later 18th century, the grandiose Russian Empire style developed under Tsar Alexander. Moscow abounds with Empire-style buildings, since much of the city had to be rebuilt after the fire of 1812. The flamboyant decorations of earlier times were used on huge new buildings erected to proclaim Russia's importance.

A series of architectural revivals, notably of early Russian styles, began in the late 19th century. The first, a pseudo-Russian phase, produced the GUM (Gosudarstvenny Univermag), or state department store, the State History Museum and the Leningrad Station in Moscow. The early-20th-century neo-Russian movement brought forth the extraordinary Kazan Station, which imitates no fewer than seven earlier styles; Style Moderne (Russian Art Nouveau) yielded the bizarre Yaroslavl Station across the square.

Soviet & Post-Soviet Eras The revolution gave rein to young Constructivist architects, who rejected superficial decoration in favour of buildings whose appearance was a direct function of their uses and materials – a new architecture for a new society. They used lots of glass and concrete in uncompromising geometric forms.

Konstantin Melnikov was probably the most famous Constructivist and his own house off ulitsa Arbat is one of the most interesting examples of the style. The *Pravda* and *Izvestia* offices are others. In the 1930s the Constructivists were denounced. Yet another revival, monumental classicism, inspired a 400m-high design for Stalin's pet project, a Palace of Soviets, which (mercifully) never got off the ground.

Stalin favoured neoclassical architecture, which echoed ancient Athens ('the only culture of the past to approach the ideal', according to Anatoly Lunacharsky, the first Soviet Commissar of Education). Stalin also favoured a gigantic scale to underline the might of the Soviet state. Often, convict labour was used, with a high death toll, to create enormous structures around the country. They reached their apogee in Stalin's 'Seven Sisters' – seven skyscrapers, Gothic in effect, which popped up around Moscow soon after WWII (see the boxed text 'Stalin's Seven Sisters' in this chapter).

In 1955, a schizophrenic decree ordered architects to avoid 'excesses'. A bland International Modern style – Constructivism without the spark, you might say – was then often used for prestigious buildings, while drab blocks of cramped flats sprouted seemingly everywhere to house the people. These tower flats, not unlike those constructed for masses in other cities around the world, were ugly then and have not improved since.

The bright side of recent architectural efforts is the restoration of decrepit churches and monasteries. The dark side is also widely apparent in the bright metals, mirrored glass and gargantuan size of some of the modern monstrosities.

Icons These are images that are supposed to embody the holy subjects they depict; as such, they are sometimes believed to be able to grant luck, wishes or miracles. Although icons were the primary form of art up until the time of Peter the Great, they were actually chiefly objects of worship, and considered 'works of art' only in the 20th century. They're most commonly found on the iconostasis of a church, a large screen in front of the east-end sanctuary.

The churches of the Kremlin are a festival of icons and some of the best in Russia are found there.

Originally, only monks could paint icons. Byzantine rules decreed that only Christ, the Virgin, the angels, saints and scriptural events could be depicted. All were supposed to be copies of a limited number of approved prototype images. Christ images include the Pantokrator (All-Ruler) and the Mandilion. The latter has the subtitle 'not made by hand' because it supposedly came from the imprint of Christ's face on St Veronica's handkerchief.

Stalin's Seven Sisters

The foundations for seven large skyscrapers were laid in 1947 to mark Moscow's 800th anniversary. Stalin had decided that Moscow suffered from a 'skyscraper gap' when compared to the USA and ordered the construction of these seven behemoths to jump-start the city's skyline.

One of the main architects, Vyacheslav Oltarzhevsky, had worked in New York during that city's skyscraper boom of the 1930s and his experience proved essential. (Fortunately he'd been released from a Gulag in time to help.)

With their widely scattered sites, the towers provide a unique visual look and reference for Moscow. Their official name in Russia is *vystony dom* (high-rise) as opposed to *neboskryob* (foreign skyscraper). They have been nicknamed variously 'Seven Sisters', 'wedding cakes', 'Stalin's sisters' and more.

The buildings, with their dates of completion and details, are:

Apartment block *(Map 2; Kudrinskaya ploshchad 1)* 1954, 160m high; a popular place with government officials
Apartment block *(Map 5; Kotelnicheskaya nab 17/1)* 1952; very ornate with multiple towers, turrets and pinnacles
Transport Ministry *(Map 3; ul Sadovaya-Spasskaya)* 1953, 133m high
Foreign Affairs Ministry *(Map 4; Smolenskaya-Sennaya ploshchad 32/34)* 1952, 27 floors; the pylons and entrance portals are polished granite and the facade has the USSR coat of arms
Hotel Ukrainia *(Map 2; Kutuzovsky pr 2/1)* 1957, 200m high with 29 floors
Hotel Leningradskaya *(Map 3; ul Kalanchevskaya 21/40)* 1954; the smallest of the group
Moscow State University *(Outer South Moscow map; Universitetskaya ploshchad 1)* 1953, 36 floors, 236m high with four huge wings

Icons were traditionally painted in tempera (inorganic pigment mixed with a binder such as egg yolk) on wood. When they faded they were often touched up, obscuring the original work.

The earliest outstanding painter was Theophanes the Greek (Feofan Grek, about 1340–1405), who worked in Byzantium, Novgorod and Moscow, and brought a new delicacy and grace to the form. His finest works are in the Annunciation Cathedral of the Moscow Kremlin.

Andrey Rublyov (born 1360), a monk at the Trinity Monastery of St Sergius and the Andronikov Monastery, was the greatest Russian icon painter. His most famous work is the fantastic *Old Testament Trinity*, in Moscow's Tretyakov Gallery.

The layman Dionysius, the leading late-15th-century painter, elongated his figures and refined the use of colour. Sixteenth-century icons grew ever smaller and more crowded, their figures more realistic and Russian-looking. In 17th-century Moscow, Simon Ushakov moved towards Western religious painting with the use of perspective and architectural backgrounds.

Peredvizhniki The major artistic force of the 19th century was the Peredvizhniki (Wanderers) movement, which saw art as a vehicle for national awareness and social change. The movement, named for its 'wandering' exhibitions, was patronised by the industrialists Savva Mamontov and Pavel Tretyakov. Artists included Vasily Surikov, who painted some vivid Russian historical scenes, Nikolai Ge (biblical and historical scenes), and Ilya Repin, perhaps the best loved of all Russian artists. Repin's work ranged from social criticism *(Volga Bargemen)* to history *(Zaporozhie Cossacks Writing a Letter to the Turkish Sultan)* to portraits.

End-of-the-19th-century genius Mikhail Vrubel inspired by sparkling Byzantine and Venetian mosaics, showed early traces of Western influence. His panels on the sides of Hotel Metropol are some of his best work (see the boxed text 'Mamontov's Metropol' in the Places to Stay chapter).

Futurism From about 1905 Russian art became a maelstrom of groups, styles and 'isms', as it absorbed decades of European change in a few years. It finally gave birth to its own avant-garde futurist movements, which in turn helped Western art go head over heels.

Mikhail Larionov and Natalia Goncharova were the centre of the Cézanne-influenced Knave of Diamonds group (with which Vasily Kandinsky was associated) before developing neoprimitivism, based on popular arts and primitive icons.

In 1915, Kazimir Malevich announced the arrival of Suprematism. His utterly abstract geometrical shapes (with the black square representing the ultimate 'zero form') finally freed art from having to depict the material world and made it a doorway to higher realities. Another famed futurist, who managed to escape subordinate isms, was Vladimir Mayakovsky, who was also a poet. Both Malevich and Mayakovsky taught art in Moscow.

Soviet Era Futurists now turned to the needs of the revolution – education, posters, banners – with enthusiasm. They had a chance to act on their theories of how art shapes society. But at the end of the 1920s, Formalist (abstract) art fell out of favour. The Communist Party wanted Socialist Realism (see Literature & Drama earlier in this chapter): images of striving workers, heroic soldiers and inspiring leaders took over; two million sculptures of Lenin and Stalin dotted the country; Malevich ended up painting portraits (penetrating ones) and doing designs for Red Square parades; and Mayakovsky committed suicide.

After Stalin, an avant-garde 'Conceptualist' underground was allowed to form.

Ilya Kabakov painted, or sometimes just arranged, the debris of everyday life, to show the gap between the promises and realities of Soviet existence. Erik Bulatov's 'Sotsart' pointed to the devaluation of language by ironically reproducing Soviet slogans or depicting words disappearing over the horizon. In 1962 the authorities set up a show of such 'unofficial' art at the Moscow Manezh; Khrushchev's response unequivocally sent it back underground.

Eventually a thaw set in and the avant-garde became international big business. In 1988, *A Fundamental Lexicon* by Grisha Bruskin, a multipanelled iconostasis-like work satirising Soviet propaganda and the Church, was sold for UK£242,000 at a Sotheby's sale in Moscow.

The most popular painter in Russia is the religious artist Ilya Glazunov, who is a staunch defender of the Russian Orthodox cultural tradition. Hundreds of thousands of people visit exhibitions of his work and he led the decoration of the Christ the Saviour Church.

Cinema

Russian – or rather Soviet – cinema first flourished shortly after the revolution. Sergey Eisenstein's *Battleship Potemkin* (1925) remains one of the landmarks of world cinema; Charlie Chaplin described it as 'the best film in the world'. It and scores of other films marked the output of Moscow's film studios, the most active in the country during the 20th century.

During the Communist era, the fate of any movie was decided by the vast bureaucracy of Moscow-based Goskino, which funded films and also distributed them. It was known for its aversion to risks, which during the Stalin era was undoubtedly smart.

It was during a 1986 congress of Soviet film-makers held in Moscow that glasnost touched the USSR's movie industry. By a large vote, the old and conservative directors were booted out of the leadership and renegades demanding more freedom put in their place. During the remaining years of communism, over 250 previously banned films were released. For the first time, films began to explore real, contemporary issues. Films such as *Little Vera* by Pichul and *Assa* by Soloviev provide a realistic glimpse of the drunken frustration that often pervaded Soviet households.

The 1990s were both good and bad for Russian film. The lack of state funds had an adverse effect on production. On the other hand, the West was opened up to Russian films as never before and many received recognition. Mikhalkov's celebrated *Burnt by the Sun*, the story of a loyal apparatchik who becomes a victim of Stalin's purges, won an Academy Award for best foreign film in 1994. But the open doors have also let in a flood of Hollywood films that have won a huge following at the expense of local productions.

Today, the Russian film industry – like most of the arts – suffers from a severe cash shortage. With financial assistance from wealthy patrons or Western sponsors, a few film-makers are continuing to probe the possibilities of this genre. *Prisoner of the Caucasus*, Bodrov's modern interpretation of a Tolstoy novella, is the story of Russian prisoners during the Chechen war. Other insightful films include Khotinenko's *The Muslim*, about a soldier who converts to Islam in Afghanistan and the trials he faces upon returning to his Russian village, and Rogozhkun's amusing *Pecularities of National Hunt*, in which the characters never get around to hunting because they are too busy drinking.

Circus

The Russian circus – complete with prancing horses with acrobats on their backs, snarling lions and tigers, heart-stopping high-wire artists and clowns that are hilarious in spite of the language barrier – launches spectators back to their childhood. It continues to be among the most popular of the performing arts in Moscow.

The Russian circus has its roots in the medieval travelling minstrels called *skomorokhi*. And circus performers today still have the lifestyle of such travelling minstrels. The Russian State Circus company, RosGosTsirk, assigns its members to a particular circus for a performance season, then rotates them around to other locations. What they give up in stability, however, they gain in job security. RosGosTsirk ensures them employment throughout their circus career.

Many circus performers find their calling not by chance, but by ancestry. It is not unusual for generations of one family to practice the same circus skill, be it tightrope walking or lion taming. As one acrobat explained quite matter-of-factly: 'We can't live without the circus. There are very few who leave.'

Moscow is home to several circuses, including the acclaimed Nikulin Circus on bulvar Tsvetnoi. Its namesake is the beloved clown Yuri Nikulin, who is described as 'the honour and conscience of the Russian circus' (see Circus in the Entertainment chapter).

SOCIETY & CONDUCT
Hospitality

If you visit a Muscovite at home, you can expect to be regaled with stories, to be drowned in vodka, to offer and receive many toasts and to eat loads of food off small plates.

In short, you can expect a bear hug of an embrace, both physically and mentally.

Should you be lucky enough to be invited to a Russian's home, bring a gift. Wine, confectionery and cake are all appropriate. Keep in mind that food items are a matter of national pride, so unless you bring something really exotic (eg, all the way from home), a Russian brand will be better appreciated. Flowers are also popular – make certain there's an odd number because even numbers are for funerals. Also, be prepared to remove your shoes once inside the door.

Once the festivities begin, you can't refuse any food or drink offered, unless you wish to cause grave offence (see the boxed text 'Just Say Nyet' in the Places to Eat chapter). When you are in any setting with other people, even strangers such as those in a train compartment, you should offer to share anything you have to eat, drink or smoke.

The world-famous Bolshoi Theatre on Teatralnaya ploshchad

One of Stalin's 'Seven Sisters'

The 1690s' Epiphany Cathedral, Kitai Gorod

A mixture of architectural styles on the banks of the Moscow River

Taxis – both private and official – play a major part in beating the hustle and bustle of getting around

Facts for the Visitor

WHEN TO GO

Moscow's climate really consists of two seasons: winter and summer. Russian winter, if you're prepared, can be an adventure: furs and vodka keep people warm, and snow-covered landscapes are picturesque. A solid snow pack covers the ground from November to March. The lowest recorded temperature is -42°C, although it's normally more like -10°C for weeks on end. Occasional southerly winds can raise the temperature briefly to a balmy 0°C. Days are very short.

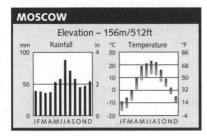

During the spring thaw – in late March and early April – everything turns to mud and slush.

Summer comes fast in May and temperatures are comfortable until well into September. The highest recorded temperature is 39°C, although on a humid August day you'll swear it's hotter than that. July and August are the warmest months and the main holiday season. Train tickets and accommodation can be difficult to come by during these months, and attractions around Moscow tend to be overrun with visitors. They are also the dampest months in Moscow, with as many as one rainy day in three. Rain showers are brief but thunderstorms can be violent. For these reasons, early summer, with its long days, and early autumn, with its colourful foliage, are many people's favourite seasons.

ORIENTATION

Picture Moscow as four ring roads that spread out from the centre:

Inner Ring Road About 500m north of the Kremlin; formed by the streets ulitsa Mokhovaya, Okhotny ryad, Teatralny proezd, Novaya ploshchad and Staraya ploshchad. Three other important squares – Manezhnaya ploshchad, Teatralnaya ploshchad and the Lubyanskaya ploshchad – punctuate this ring.

Boulevard Ring (Bulvarnoe Koltso) About 1km from the Kremlin. It's mostly dual carriageway, with a park strip down the middle. Each section has a different name, always ending in 'bulvar'. The Boulevard Ring ends as it approaches the Moscow River in the southwest and southeast.

Garden Ring (Sadovoe Koltso) About 2km out. Most of this ring's northern sections are called Sadovaya-something (Garden-something) ulitsa; several of its southern sections are called ulitsa-something-val, recalling its origins as a rampart *(val)*. And the difference between the Garden and Boulevard rings? The Garden Ring is the one *without* any gardens.

Outer Ring Road (Moskovskaya Koltsovaya Avtomobilnaya Doroga) Some 15km to 20km from the Kremlin. It forms the city limits.

Radial roads spoke out across the rings, and the Moscow River meanders across everything from northwest to southeast. The Kremlin, a north-pointing triangle with 750m sides, is at Moscow's heart in every way. Red Square lies along its eastern side while the Moscow River flows to the south.

The only elevation worth the name in the whole flat expanse is the Sparrow Hills, 6km southwest of the Kremlin, topped by the Moscow University skyscraper. The Sparrow Hills afford the most panoramic view the city has to offer. Moscow's most prominent buildings are Stalin's 'Seven Sisters' skyscrapers. See the boxed text 'Stalin's Seven Sisters' in the Facts about Moscow chapter.

MAPS

It is a challenge to find up-to-date, non-Cyrillic maps of Moscow reflecting all the street name changes of the early 1990s. Cartographia and Kummerly + Frey both have good versions which are sensibly called the *Moscow City Map*. Another good option is the 2nd edition of *The New Moscow City Map and Guide* published by Russia Information Services of Montpelier, Vermont, USA.

Accurate maps in Cyrillic are easily available in Moscow. Good sources include **Atlas** *(Map 2;* ☎ *928 61 09; ul Kuznetsky Most 9)* and **Torgovy Dom Biblio-Globus** *(Map 2;* ☎ *928 3567; ul Myasnitskaya 6).*

RESPONSIBLE TOURISM

Prostitution is widespread in Moscow as it is not illegal. Prostitutes make rounds of the hotels, nightclubs and streets. The Russian age of sexual consent is 16, and there are large numbers of teenage prostitutes.

As a rule, working churches are open to one and all, but as a visitor take care not to disturb any devotions or offend sensibilities. Hands in pockets attract frowns. Sitting with your legs crossed can bring the pious running with their fingers wagging. Men bare their heads and women usually cover theirs. Women visitors can often get away without covering their heads, but miniskirts are unwelcome and even trousers sometimes attract disapproval. Photography during services is generally not welcome, though it can't hurt to ask.

TOURIST OFFICES

Moscow still has no official tourist offices. Information can best be sought at travel agencies or at upmarket hotels. Keep in mind, however, that these firms are trying to sell their services and they may not be forthcoming with information if they do not believe you are buying.

Russia has no tourist offices abroad and most of its consulates and embassies do not have much practical country information. Foreign travel agencies specialising in Russian travel can be useful (see the Getting There & Away chapter).

TRAVEL AGENCIES

Infinity Travel *(Map 4;* ☎ *234 6555, fax 234 6556;* Ⓦ *www.infinity.ru; Komsomolsky pr 13)*, formerly IRO Travel, is affiliated with the Travellers Guest House. It offers rail and air tickets, visa support service, and

Trans-Siberian and Central Asia packages. This is a great source for cheap airline tickets.

Andrew's Consulting *(Map 4;* ☎ *916 9898, fax 916 9828;* Ⓔ *recept@88.ru; ul Volkhonka 18/2)* offers a full range of services aimed at business travellers.

G&R International *(*☎ *378 0001, fax 378 2866;* Ⓦ *www.hostels.ru; ul Zelendolskaya 3/2, 15th floor)* is located in the G&R Asia Hostel. This efficient and convenient organisation offers all the normal services.

DOCUMENTS
Visas

All foreigners visiting Russia need visas. To get one you must technically have confirmed accommodation for every night you'll be in the country, though in practice there are ways around this.

A Russian visa can be a passport-sized paper document that is separate from your passport, a sticker in your passport, or both. Both the separate form and the sticker visa list entry/exit dates, your passport number, any children travelling with you, and visa type. It's an exit permit too, so if you lose it (or overstay), leaving the country can be harder than getting in.

The six types of visa available to all foreign visitors are listed below, along with details of the scheme for 72-hour stay visas for citizens of Schengen-agreement countries,

New Visa Regulations

Late in 2002, new immigration regulations were implemented, affecting the way that visas are issued. These changes include (but may not be limited to) the following:

• Invitations for business visas must come from the Ministry of Foreign Affairs (MID) or its regional representatives, the Ministry of Internal Affairs (MVD) or its regional representatives, or other authorised agencies.

• The Department of Visas and Registration (OVIR) has changed its name to the Passport and Visa Service (Passport i Viza Upravlenie) or PVU. It is still commonly known by its old acronym.

HIV/AIDS Testing

At the time of writing, HIV/AIDS testing was required for foreigners staying in the Russian Federation longer than three months. By definition, this does not affect tourist visas, which are only issued for shorter stays. The medical certificate must be in English and in Russian. Consult the company sponsoring your business visa for the latest regulations.

and Britain, Switzerland and Japan. For all visas you'll need:

• A passport valid for at least a month beyond your return date. Usually only a photocopy of the data pages of your passport is required, but some consulates may want to see the original.
• Three passport-size (4cm by 4.5cm), full-face photos, not more than one year old. Vending-machine photos with white background are fine if they're identical.
• A completed application form, including entry/exit dates
• The handling fee, usually in the form of a company check or money order. The handling fee varies depending on your citizenship: US citizens pay the most, in retaliation for high fees for American visas.

You're also going to need a visa support letter of some kind (see Tourist Visas). This will either be arranged by your tourist operator or, if you're applying for a visa independently, can be gained from many organisations in Russia – see Travel Agencies earlier in this chapter for details.

Tourist Visas These are the most straightforward and inflexible visas available. In theory, you're supposed to have booked accommodation for every night in Russia, but in practice you can often get away with only booking a few, even just one. Once you've had your visa registered, you can move freely, to stay where you like.

Extending a tourist visa is a hassle and the extension, if granted, will usually be only for a short time. Tourist visas are best for trips when you know exactly what you're doing and when, where and for how

long you'll be doing it. To obtain a tourist visa, you will need, in addition to the above items:

• Confirmation of hotel reservations, which can be a faxed copy on hotel letterhead signed and stamped by the hotel; or
• Confirmation of bookings from a travel agent; or
• A visa-support letter from a youth hostel or guesthouse.

Business Visas Far more flexible and desirable for the independent traveller is a business (or commercial) visa supported by a Russian company. To obtain a business visa you must have a letter of invitation from a registered Russian company and a covering letter from your company (or you) stating the purpose of your trip. The invitation eliminates the need for pre-arranged hotel confirmations.

Any of the organisations listed under Travel Agencies earlier in this chapter can provide an invitation for a business visa for a fee – usually about US$50. **Intour Visa Consulting** (☎ 914-473 2333, fax 212-575 3434; ⓦ www.russian-site.com; 130 West 42 Street, Suite 412, New York, NY 10036) charges US$170 for the invitation and processing for a business visa (inclusive of consular fees). This eliminates the hassle of interacting with the Russian consulate. The catch is the registration, which is an additional US$50 in Moscow, so this service is only really useful if you are staying in a hotel in Moscow (in which case registration is free).

Student Visas Student visas are flexible, extendable and even entitle you to pay Russian prices for items affected under the country's dual-pricing system (see Costs later in this chapter). You'll need proof of enrolment at an accredited Russian school or university, which usually requires prepayment.

'Private' Visas This is the visa you get for a visit by personal invitation, and it's also referred to as an 'ordinary' visa by some authorities. The visa itself is as easy to get as a tourist visa, but getting the invitation is a complex matter.

The person who is inviting you must go to their local office of OVIR (Otdel Viz i Registratsii), the Department of Visas and Registrations, and fill out an invitation form for approval of the invitation. Approval, which takes several weeks, comes in the form of a notice of permission *(izveshchenie)*, good for one year, which the person inviting you must then send to you. You will need this invitation approval notice, together with the standard application form, to apply for the visa, which is valid for as many as 60 days in your host's town. On arrival in Russia you will also have to go to the local OVIR office to register your visa (see Registration later in this chapter).

'On-the-Spot' Visas These are fast-track business visas that don't require an advance invitation. Individuals arriving at Moscow's Sheremetevo-2 airport can get short-term visas at a special consular office before going through passport control. To get one of these visas, you'll have to have a copy of a Ministry of Foreign Affairs (MID) invitation and have a representative of your inviting company meet you at the airport. Note, however, that airlines may not necessarily let you board your flight to Russia, because if you're turned down for the fast-track visa the airline is responsible for bringing you out again – so make sure to check with the airlines in advance.

St Petersburg & Moscow 72-hour Stay Visas Since February 2002, Russia has been running a trial scheme whereby tourists from Schengen countries, as well as citizens of Britain, Switzerland and Japan, who wish to visit St Petersburg and Moscow for less than 72 hours, can receive their visas directly upon entry.

Travellers must apply at one of 29 authorised tour operators in their home country 48 hours before departure, where they fill in an application, pay a fee of US$35 and then collect the visa on arrival at one of six entry points, including Sheremetevo-2 airport (Terminal 2).

The aim is to increase Russia's tourist intake from non-CIS countries. For the time being, US citizens are not eligible for the new visas because the Tourism Ministry believes that few US tourists would travel to Russia for less than a week. The government hopes the scheme, scheduled initially to run for a year, will make Russia's major cities more attractive to Europeans seeking weekend getaways.

Transit Visas This is for 'passing through', which is loosely interpreted. For transit by air, it's usually good for 48 hours. For a nonstop Trans-Siberian Railway journey, it's valid for 10 days, giving westbound passengers a few days in Moscow without the obligatory hotel prebooking (those heading east can't linger in Moscow). Under certain circumstances, travellers transiting Russia and holding valid entry/exit visas to Armenia, Belarus, Kazakhstan, Kyrgyzstan, Tajikistan or Uzbekistan need not apply for a Russian transit visa. The requirements on this are sketchy, and while a Russian consulate may say it's unnecessary, the odds of being allowed into or out of Russia on the premise that you're holding a Tajik visa are slim. Many border guards are not familiar with the latest regulations handed down in Moscow, so it's always best to play it safe, especially when travelling to border crossings in remote areas.

How & When to Apply Apply as soon as you have all the documents you need (but not more than two months ahead). Business, tourist, private and student visas all take the same amount of time to process once you have the paperwork. Processing time ranges from 24 hours to two weeks, depending on how much you are willing to pay. Transit visas normally take seven working days, but may take as little as a few hours at the Russian embassy in Beijing.

It's possible to apply at your local Russian consulate by dropping off all the necessary documents with the appropriate payment, or by mailing it all (along with a self-addressed, postage-paid envelope). When you receive the visa, check it carefully – especially the expiry, entry and exit dates and any restrictions on entry or exit points.

The Great Moscow Police Tourist Rip-off

Red Square is a prime location for policemen to stop unsuspecting tourists to 'check' their documents. These diligent law enforcers will invariably find something wrong with their victims' visa or registration (even if they are really in perfect order). The fine for this imaginary crime is often as much as RR2000.

If the policeman is feeling magnanimous, he may present the option of appearing at the police station to pay the fine – only if he knows it is impossible for the tourist to do so. (One reader was booked on a train out of Moscow within two hours. Upon learning this, the officer informed him that he could pay his fine at the station, but only after four hours. Otherwise, he should pay on the spot.) This scam is big business for the MVD officers, who have found an entrepreneurial way to supplement their meagre salaries. They may even furnish you with a (totally meaningless) receipt for your troubles.

So, what should you do when a humourless cop demands to see your documents?

To avoid potential problems, get your visa registered in Moscow, even if it has already been registered in another city. Interpretation and enforcement of the policy is inconsistent, but as a rule, you can never have too many stamps and signatures.

Never volunteer your time or date of intended departure.

Before handing over your documents, ask to see the officer's identification and write down the seven-digit number. Make sure he knows that you know who he is.

Show the officer a photocopy of your passport and visa (made after you arrive in Moscow, so that your visa registration is visible). Do not give up your passport.

If you have a cell (mobile) phone, pull it out and tell the officer you would like to ring your embassy to have somebody meet you at the station. One reader writes: 'This exact situation has happened to me four times. Once it cost me RR1500; since the mobile it has cost nothing at all.'

Registration When you check in at a hotel, camping ground or hostel, you surrender your passport and visa so the hotel can register you with OVIR. You'll get your documents back the next morning, if not the same day. Alternatively, the tourist agency that issued your visa is responsible for your registration.

Otherwise, you can register yourself at the main branch of OVIR, also known as the **UVIR** (Upravlenia Viz i Registratsii; Map 3; ☎ 200 8497; ul Pokrovka 42; open 9am-1pm, 2pm-6pm Mon-Fri), the city's main visa and registration office. It also deals with visa extensions and replacing lost visas.

All Russian visas must be registered with OVIR within three business days of your arrival in Russia (see the boxed text 'The Great Moscow Police Tourist Rip-off'). No ifs or buts about it. Sometimes you may have to pay a registration fee, but it should not be more than US$5 to US$10.

The company or organisation that invites you to Russia is responsible for your initial registration – and no other company can support your visa. If you're not sure which organisation invited you (if the sponsorship line – on tourist visas this begins with the words В Учреждение – has a name you've never heard of), the simplest option is to spend a night at one of the major hotels, which will register your visa for you right at the front desk. There may be a fee involved, but usually the cost of the room will suffice.

Extending a visa that's not registered can be impossible, and getting out of the country with an unregistered visa could be a very expensive proposition.

Visa Extensions & Changes Extensions are time-consuming, if not downright difficult. Try to avoid the need for an extension by asking for a longer visa than you might need. You can always leave earlier, but leaving later than the visa allows will waste time and money. Many trains out of St Petersburg and Moscow to Eastern Europe cross the border after midnight, so make sure your visa is valid up to and including this day. Don't give border guards any excuses for making trouble.

Travel Insurance

Make sure that you have adequate health insurance. A travel insurance policy to cover theft, loss and medical problems is a wise idea. Make certain that your policy will cover medical evacuation back to your home country from any part of Russia (beyond Moscow) where you are likely to travel.

Copies

In order to replace your documents it is imperative that you make photocopies of them, especially your Russian visa. Your embassy in Moscow can replace a lost or stolen passport, but if you lose your visa you must go to the local visa office, OVIR. A Russian travel agent, your hotel service bureau, or the youth hostels can help with this, including reporting the loss to the police.

All important documents (passport data page and visa page, credit cards, travel insurance policy, air/bus/train tickets, driving licence etc) should be photocopied before you leave home. Leave a copy with someone at home and keep another with you, separate from the originals. Also take some spare passport photos. After you have entered Russia, try to get a photocopy of your customs declaration (deklaratsia). All these will be very useful if your documents go astray.

It's also a good idea to store the details of your vital travel documents in Lonely Planet's free online Travel Vault, in case you lose the photocopies or can't be bothered with them. Your password-protected Travel Vault is accessible online anywhere in the world – create it at w www.ekno.lonely planet.com.

EMBASSIES & CONSULATES

If you're going to be travelling in Russia for a long period of time (a month or more) – and particularly if you're heading to remote locations – it's wise to register with your embassy. This can be done over the telephone, or even by email.

Russian Embassies & Consulates

Check w www.russianembassy.net for any changes to these Russian embassies:

Australia
Embassy: (☎ 02-6295 9033/9474, fax 6295 1847; e rusemb@dynamite.com.au) 78 Canberra Ave, Griffith, ACT 2603
Consulate: (☎ 02-9326 1188, fax 9327 5065; e russcon@ozemail.com.au) 7 Fullerton St, Woollahra, NSW 2025

Canada
Embassy: (☎ 613-235 4341, fax 236 6342; e rusemb@intranet.ca) 285 Charlotte St, Ottawa, Ontario, Canada
Visa Department: (☎ 613-336 7220, fax 238 6158)
Consulate: (☎ 514-843 5901, 842 5343, fax 842 2012; e consulat@dsuper.net) 3685 Ave Du Musée, Montreal, Quebec, H3G 2EI

France
Embassy: (☎ 01 45 04 05 50, 01 45 03 40 20, fax 01 45 04 17 65; e rusembfr@clubinternet .fr) 40–50 Boulevard Lannes, 75116 Paris
Consulate: (☎ 04 91 77 15 15, fax 04 91 77 34 54; e consrus@aix.pacwan.net) 8 Ave Ambrois Pare, 13008 Marseilles
Also consulate in Strasbourg

Germany
Embassy: (☎ 030-220 2821, 226 6320, fax 229 9397; e russembassyg@trionet.de) Unter den Linden 63–65, 10117 Berlin
Consulate: (☎ 0228-312 085, fax 312 164; e bonn@russische-botschaft.de) Waldstrasse 42, 53177 Bonn
Also consulates in Hamburg, Leipzig, Munich and Rostok

Ireland
Embassy: (☎ 01-492 3492, ☎/fax 492 3525; e russiane@indigo.ie) 186 Orwell Rd, Rathgar, Dublin 14

UK
Embassy: (☎ 020-7229 3628, fax 7727 8625; w www.russialink.couk.com/embassy) 13 Kensington Palace Gardens, London W8 4QX
Consular Section: (☎ 020-7229 8027, visa information message ☎ 0891-171 271, fax 020-7229 3215) 5 Kensington Palace Gardens, London W8 4QS
Consulate: (☎ 0131-225 7121, fax 225 9587; e visa@edconsul.demon.co.uk) 58 Melville St, Edinburgh E13 7HL

USA
Embassy: (☎ 202-298 5700/01, fax 628 0252) 2641 Wisconsin Ave NW, Washington DC 20007

FACTS FOR THE VISITOR

Visa Department: (☎ 202-939 8907, fax 939 8909) 2641 Tunlaw Rd NW, Washington DC 20007
Consulate: (☎ 212-348 0926, fax 831 9162) 9 East 91 St, New York, NY 10128
Consulate: (☎ 415-928 6878, fax 929 0306) 2790 Green St, San Francisco, CA 94123
Consulate: (☎ 206-728 1910, fax 728 1871; W www.ruscon.com) 2323 Westin Building, 2001 Sixth Ave, Seattle, WA 98121-2617

Embassies in Moscow

The area code for the telephone numbers in the following list is ☎ 095. For a full list of embassies check W www.themoscowtimes .ru/travel/facts/embassies.html.

Australia (Map 4; ☎ 956 6070, fax 956 6170; W www.australianembassy.ru) Kropotkinsky per 2
Canada (Map 4; ☎ 956 6666, fax 232 9948) Starokonyushenny per 23
France (Map 4; ☎ 937 1500, fax 937 1577; W www.ambafrance.ru) ul Bolshaya Yakimanka 45
Germany (Outer South Moscow map; ☎ 937 9500, fax 936 2143; W www.germany.org.ru) Mosfilmovskaya ul 56
Consular Section: (☎ 936 2401) Leninsky pr 95A
Ireland (Map 3; ☎ 937 5911) Grokholsky per 5
Netherlands (Map 2; ☎ 797 2900) Kalashny per 6
UK (Map 2; ☎ 956 7200, fax 956 7201; W www.britemb.msk.ru) Smolenskaya nab 10
USA (Map 2; ☎ 728 5000, fax 728 5090; W www.usembassy.state.gov/moscow) Bol Devyatinsky per 8

CUSTOMS

You may be asked to fill in a declaration form *(deklaratsia)* upon arrival – keep this customs-stamped form until your departure from Russia. If you bring in currency and goods valued in excess of US$1500 you *must* fill out this form. It can't hurt to fill one out and have it stamped even if you have less than US$1500 cash on you.

If you are arriving by air, the airline will probably give you two declaration forms in English. Keep one to fill out when you leave. Border posts and airports rarely have forms in English. The first six lines ask your full name; citizenship; the country you are arriving from; your destination country; the purpose of your visit (the answers can be short: business, tourism, private etc); and how many pieces of luggage (including hand luggage) you're carrying.

The next five lines have Roman numerals. The first three ask if you are carrying (I) weapons and ammunition; (II) narcotics and appliances to use them – note that if you have prescribed syringes you mention them here; and (III) antiques and works of art. The next (IV) asks you to list any Russian roubles, state loan bonds or Russian lottery tickets you are carrying. Item five (V) is a table in which you list all currency you are bringing in. You write the type of currency then the amount in digits and words. The next item asks you to name any roubles, other currency or valuables you are bringing in that belong to another person. Finally, just above where you give the date and sign your name, you list how many pieces of luggage – if any – you've sent separately.

If the total value of what you've listed is US$1500 or more (or is even close to this amount) you must go through a red lane and have the form stamped by a customs official, who may also check your luggage. In practice this is a formality, but it is important that you respect it. If the total value of your declared items is comfortably below US$1500, you can use a green line, if one exists.

When you leave Russia you will have to fill out an identical form declaring what you are removing from the country. If you have a stamped customs form, your exit customs form cannot show you are leaving with more than you brought in. If you did not get your form stamped on the way in, your exit form cannot show you are taking out items with a total value of more than US$500.

Treat a stamped customs declaration as carefully as you treat your passport. If you should lose it then you will need a police report confirming the loss, which you present to customs when you leave Russia.

What You Can Bring In

You may bring in modest amounts of anything for personal use except, obviously, illegal drugs and weapons. Less obviously, visitors are banned from bringing in GPS devices. If you're travelling with hypodermic needles, bring in a prescription for them and declare them under the line 'Narcotics and appliances for use thereof'.

Up to 1000 cigarettes and 5L of alcohol are allowed (remember that prices for such items in Russia will almost certainly be cheaper than abroad), but large amounts of anything saleable are suspect. Food is allowed (except for some fresh fruit and vegetables).

What You Can Take Out

Anything bought from a legitimate shop or department store can go out, but save your receipts. Leaving with modest amounts of roubles isn't a problem, but change any large sums you may have beforehand.

Anything vaguely 'arty', such as manuscripts, instruments, coins, jewellery, antiques or antiquarian books (meaning those published before 1975) must be assessed by the **Committee for Culture** (Map 2; ☎ 921 3258; ul Neglinnaya 8/10, room 298). The bureaucrats there will issue a receipt for tax paid (bring your receipt to determine the amount of the tax owed), which you show to customs on your way out of the country. If you buy something large, a photograph will usually be fine for assessment purposes.

A painting bought at a tourist art market, in a department store, or from a commercial gallery should be declared and receipts should be kept. Generally speaking, customs in airports is much more strict and thorough than at any border crossing.

MONEY
Currency

Russian currency is the rouble, written as рубль or abbreviated as ру or р. There are 100 kopecks in the rouble, and these come in small coins that are worth one, 10 and 50 kopecks.

The rouble was revalued in 1998 by a factor of 1000 to one. Notes dating from prior to the revaluation are no longer valid, so if you see rouble notes with lots of zeros in them, treat them as souvenirs. Roubles are issued in coins in amounts of one, two and five roubles. Banknotes come in values

of 10, 50, 100 and 500 roubles. Small stores, kiosks and many other vendors have difficulty changing large notes, so save those scrappy little ones.

Exchange Rates

The exchange rate used throughout this book is US$1 = RR30. The exchange rates below were valid at the time of printing, but are likely to change (and note the change in the US$/rouble rate). For up-to-date exchange rate information, please see ⓦ www.oanda .com/convert/classic.

country	unit		rouble (RR)
Australia	A$1	=	17.88
Canada	C$1	=	20.36
China	Y10	=	38.54
euro zone	€1	=	31.67
Japan	¥100	=	26
New Zealand	NZ$1	=	15.89
UK	UK£1	=	49.64
Ukraine	10 hv	=	61.79
USA	US$1	=	31.86

Exchanging Money

Cash You'll get the best rates for US dollars, which can be exchanged anywhere; otherwise, the euro can be easily changed in Moscow, but outside the city you're likely to run into difficulties. Forget about any other forms of currency.

Money Changes Everything

Since the economic crash of 1998, the rouble has stabilised, with exchange rates hovering around RR30 to US$1. Most prices in this book are quoted in roubles.

Some hotels and restaurants continue to tie their prices to the US dollar, or to its equivalent 'standard unit' (uslovnye yedenitsy), abbreviated у.е. In these cases, this book also quotes prices in US dollars, abbreviated US$.

In any case, your final bill will be in roubles. If the price was quoted in dollars, the final bill will be calculated according to the exchange rate of the day. It is illegal to pay for services in any other currency except roubles.

Whatever currency you bring should be in pristine condition. Banks and exchanges do not accept old, tatty bills with rips or tears. For US dollars make certain that besides looking and smelling newly minted, they are of the new design, which has the large off-set portrait.

When you visit the exchange office, be prepared to fill out a lengthy form and show your passport. Your receipt is for your own records, as customs officials no longer require documentation of your currency transactions. As anywhere, rates can vary from one establishment to the next, so it's always worth shopping around.

Travellers Cheques Travellers cheques can be difficult to exchange outside Moscow. Also, the process can be lengthy, involving trips to numerous different cashiers in the bank, each responsible for a different part of the transaction. Expect to pay 1% to 2% commission.

Not all travellers cheques are treated as equal by Russian establishments willing to handle them.

In descending order of acceptance are American Express (AmEx), Thomas Cook and Visa. You'll have little or no luck with other brands.

ATMs Automatic teller machines (ATMs) linked to international networks such as AmEx, Cirrus, Eurocard, MasterCard and Visa are now common throughout Moscow. Look for signs that say **bankomat** (банк-омат). Using a credit card, or the same card you use in ATMs at home, you can obtain cash as you need it – usually in roubles, but sometimes in dollars, too. See Safety Concerns later in this chapter for warnings of ATM scams.

Banks Among the more established banks in Moscow is **Alfa Bank** (Map 2; ul Arbat 4/1 • Map 2; Kuznetsky Most 7 • Map 2; Marriott Grand Hotel, Tverskaya ul 26; all open 8.30am-8pm Mon-Sat) which has locations all over the city (the ATMs at the locations that are listed here dispense both roubles and dollars).

Credit Cards Credit cards, especially Visa and MasterCard, are becoming more widely accepted, not only at upmarket hotels, restaurants and stores. You can also use your credit card to get a cash advance at most major banks in Moscow.

American Express The most reliable place to cash AmEx travellers cheques is – you'll never guess – **American Express** (Map 4; ☎ 933 6636, fax 933 6635; ul Usacheva 33). It also offers ATM, mail holding and travel services for AmEx card holders.

Wire Transfers Contact **Western Union** (Map 5; ☎ 797 2194; ul Taganskaya 17-23) for wire transfers of money.

Black Market Because the rouble floats – some cynics will say sinks – freely on international exchange markets, there is no reason for the black market to exist. Should some shadowy character offer to exchange money for you at a tempting rate, remember that they can't give you a better rate than banks and profit. Thus they are either crooks or insane.

Security

Don't leave money – in any form – lying around your room. Preferably, keep it in several different places about your person and baggage. When you go out, carry what you'll need in your pockets (but avoid eye-catching wallet bulges), with any extra tucked away under your clothing – best in a money belt, shoulder wallet or ankle pouch. Wrapping cash carefully in plastic and tucking it under the insole of your shoe is another good idea.

Costs

Moscow is among the most expensive cities in the world, up there with London and Hong Kong. Expect to pay at least US$20 a head for a meal in a restaurant. If you self-cater or dine at cafeterias you can probably get by on US$15 a day for meals.

Lodgings prices are also very high, as the simple but cheap hotels found in Western Europe don't exist here. The cheapest accommodation is not going to be much under US$20 a day.

With some serious economising you could scrape by on US$30 a day in Moscow, but if you visit museums, take excursions and indulge in the nightlife you're heading towards the US$100 a day mark. The only bargain you'll share with the locals is riding the metro or attending the theatre (but not the Bolshoi).

Dual-Pricing System Although dual pricing for airplane and train tickets has now finished, as a foreigner in Russia you'll still often find yourself paying more than a Russian. Many hotels (except the most expensive Western-style ones) and museums have a two-tier pricing system with foreigners paying more. In hotels the difference can be as much as 50%. Note too that often the only rooms available to foreigners will be the better-appointed ones.

The highest mark-up, percentage wise, is made by museums (it's not unusual for it to be 10 times what the Russians pay). There's a certain fairness here, given the vast disparity between Western and Russian incomes. Take heart that the extra money you shell out is desperately needed to protect the very works of art and artefacts you've come to see.

Tipping & Bargaining

Tipping is standard in the better restaurants (count on leaving 10%), whereas elsewhere 5% to 10% of the total is fine. Tipping your guide, if you have one, is an accepted practice. Generally about US$5 to US$10 for a day would be a good tip. Small gifts, such as a bottle of skin cream, a box of chocolates, or a cassette or CD are appropriate if the service has been great.

Prices in stores are firm. In markets, food vendors will sometimes offer a deal that is their best offer. Take it or you will be quibbling over some tiny amount. For other goods in markets and souvenir stalls, you can make a counterbid that is somewhat lower than the price the merchant is asking, but Russia is not a place where you can expect protracted haggling.

Taxes

The value-added tax (VAT, in Russian NDS) is 20% and is usually included in the price listed for purchases, but ask just to make sure. Moscow also has a 5% sales tax that is usually only encountered in top hotels.

POST & COMMUNICATIONS
Post

Although service has improved dramatically in recent years, the usual warnings about delays and disappearances of incoming and outgoing mail apply to Moscow. Airmail letters take two to three weeks from Moscow to the UK, and three to four weeks to the USA or Australasia. For airmail letters under 20g the cost for regular/registered post is RR10/16 to practically all places abroad.

The convenient **Central Telegraph** (Tsentralny Telegraf; Map 2; Tverskaya ul 7; postal counters open 8am-10pm daily, telephone office open 24hr) offers telephone, fax and Internet services. Moscow's **main post office** (Moskovsky Glavpochtamt; Map 3; ul Myasnitskaya 26; open 8am-8pm Mon-Fri, 9am-7pm Sat & Sun) is on the corner of Chistoprudny bulvar.

Incoming mail is so unreliable that many companies, hotels and even individuals use private services that have addresses in either Germany or Finland. The mail completes its journey to its Russian destination with a private carrier. Unfortunately, other options do not really exist. Anything addressed to poste restante should be considered lost before it is sent, and embassies and consulates won't hold mail for transient visitors.

Should you decide to send mail to Moscow or try to receive it, note that addresses should be written in reverse order: Russia (Россия), postal code, city, street address, name.

Express Services The major air-courier services operating in Moscow include **DHL Worldwide Express** (☎ 956 1000), **Fedex** (☎ 234 3400), **TNT** (☎ 797 2777) and **UPS** (☎ 961 2211). They can advise on drop-off locations and arrange pick-ups.

Telephone

The Moscow city code is ☎ 095, which is the area code for phone numbers listed in this book, unless otherwise stated. If calling Moscow from abroad, do not drop the 0. The telephone country code for Russia is ☎ 7.

Private Telephones From a private phone in Russia, dialling outside the country is very simple, but the prices keep rising and are now even higher than prices for equivalent calls from the West to Russia. To call internationally, dial ☎ 8, wait for the second tone, then dial ☎ 10 plus the country and city codes, then the number. Omit any zeroes from the city code (eg, to call London the code would be ☎ 8 (tone) 10 44 20 and then the phone number).

At the time of writing, daytime (8am to 8pm weekdays) telephone prices from Moscow and St Petersburg per minute were RR15 to Europe, RR19.50 to the USA and Canada and RR35.40 to Australasia. Calls are cheaper from 8pm to 8am weekdays and all day on weekends.

Pay Phones Pay phones (Таксофон, *taksofon*) are located throughout most cities and are usually in working order. Most take prepaid phonecards, which are available from metro token booths and from kiosks. Cardphones can be used for local and domestic or international long-distance calls. Cards in a range of units are available; international calls will require at least 100 units. The only trick is to remember to press the button with the speaker symbol when your party answers the phone.

Some older phone booths accept metal tokens *(zhetony)* as payment. Place the token in the slot on top of the phone and dial the number; when the party answers, the token should drop. A series of beeps means you must place another token in the slot or risk disconnection.

Domestic long-distance calls (which means within Russia or to any former Soviet republic) may be made from pay phones marked Междугородный *(mezhdugorodnyy)*, using different, wrinkled-metal tokens available only in telephone offices. They work on a similar principle, but you need to push the Ответ *(otvet)* button on the phone's face when your party answers. Dial

☎ 8, wait for the second tone, then dial the city code (including zeroes) and the number.

Telephone Offices The convenient **Central Telegraph** *(Tsentralny Telegraf; Map 2; Tverskaya ul 7)* is open for phone calls 24 hours a day. You leave a deposit with an attendant and are assigned a private booth where you dial your number directly as outlined above.

In some other offices, you may have to give your number to an attendant who dials the number and then sends you to a booth to take the call. You can collect change from your deposit when you leave. Rates are similar to home services.

Country Direct Major Western telephone service companies have access-code telephone numbers for Moscow that allow you to put through collect or calling-card calls to numbers outside Russia. These include **MCI** *(☎ 747 3322, 960 2222)*, **AT&T** *(☎ 755 5042)*, and **Sprint** *(☎ 747 3324)*. Note that you pay for this reliability and convenience with high rates. The access numbers for these services change frequently, so check the number with the provider before you leave for Russia.

Hotel Phones At most traditional Russian hotels, local calls are free. Placing a long-distance call can be more difficult and you'll have to work the details out with the front desk. Calls from expensive Western hotels are, well, expensive. A direct-dialled call abroad from your room can cost over US$100 for 20 minutes of chatting. If you or your company don't want to pay this kind of rate, you'll either have to use a country-direct service (which, while expensive, will be cheaper than hotel phones) or go outside.

Most hotel-room telephones provide a direct-dial number for incoming calls, which saves you having to be connected through the switchboard. However, this can lead to unwanted disturbances. See Safety Concerns later in this chapter.

Cellular Service Mobile (or cellular) phones are becoming increasingly popular with Russians who want to bypass the anti-quated state system. In Moscow they're as common as in most major Western cities. There are several different systems and you may be able to use your regular cellphone while you are in Russia – check with your service provider for details.

Fax

Faxes can be sent from most post offices and better hotels. Rates at post offices are usually around RR60 a page to Europe, the USA and Canada and RR90 a page to Australia.

Email & Internet Access

If you are travelling with a laptop and you want to have Internet access while in Moscow, you can sign up for a temporary account with a local provider such as **Russia On-Line** (*Map 2; ☎ 787 1222; Gazetny per 9/2; open 10am-8pm Mon-Fri, noon-6pm Sat*). For about US$20, you can purchase a plan which allows you to spend 40 hours online over the course of 30 days. Other plans for lesser usage are also available. Otherwise, there is no shortage of Internet cafés in Moscow.

Time Online (*Map 6; ☎ 363 0060; RR30-60 per hr; open 24hr*), on the lower level of the Okhotny Ryad shopping mall near Red Square, claims to be the largest Internet café in Eastern Europe. No drinks are served, but its 200-plus zippy terminals get the job done. After hours, enter from the Kuznetsky Most underground station.

Drinks and competitive rates are also available at the equally central **Internet Club** (*Map 2; ☎ 924 2140; Kuznetsky Most 12; RR60 per hr; open 9am-midnight daily*).

Nearby, **NetLand** (*Map 2; ☎ 105 0021; Teatralny proezd 5*) is on the 4th floor of Detsky Mir children's store.

Netcity (*Map 5; ☎ 969 2125; Paveletskaya Ploshchad 2*) has fast terminals, and more of a café feel with drinks and music.

An easy option for sending mail is to open a free Web-based ekno account online at W www.ekno.lonelyplanet.com. You can then access your mail from anywhere in the world from any Net-connected machine running a standard Web browser.

DIGITAL RESOURCES

A good starting place for links about Moscow is W www.lonelyplanet.com, Lonely Planet's award-winning travel website. Here you'll find succinct summaries on travelling to most places on earth, postcards from other travellers and the Thorn Tree bulletin board, where you can ask questions before you go or dispense advice when you get back. You can also find travel news and updates to many of our most popular guidebooks, while the subwwway section links you to the most useful travel resources elsewhere on the Web.

Other suggestions include:

W **www.departments.bucknell.edu/russian** Bucknell University in the USA runs this huge award-winning site with links to just about any topic on Russia you can imagine

W **www.expat.ru** The self-dubbed 'Moscow Expat Site' publicises events targeting Moscow's English-speaking community

W **www.infoservices.com/moscow** The *Traveller's Yellow Pages* is a useful directory of local businesses

W **www.interknowledge.com/russia/moscow01.htm** This is another official-type page that has a photographic tour of the city

W **www.md.mos.ru/eng/index.htm** Sponsored by the United Nations Environment Programme (UNEP), the site has more information than you ever wanted to know about the state of the environment in Moscow and – on a brighter note – what is being done to clean it up

W **www.moscow-guide.ru** The official website run by the Moscow government is frequently updated with information on a range of topics, from transport to culture

W **www.moskva.ru** This site has extensive historical information, tourist tips and student networking, although most of it is in Russian only. Parts of the site are available in English.

W **www.russiatravel.com** The official website of the Russian National Tourist Office is useful for its calendar of events, as well as practical information

W **www.theatre.ru** This site, dedicated to the classical performing arts in Moscow, is primarily in Russian, but includes links to almost all of the local theatres

W **www.themoscowtimes.com** This excellent site for the local English-language newspaper includes a thorough guide to Russia, entertainment listings and news items

W www.waytorussia.net A local operation hosts this page, which offers restaurant and accommodation options and lots of information about local events, sights and transportation

BOOKS
Most books are published in different editions by different publishers in different countries. As a result, a book might be a hardcover rarity in one country while it's readily available in paperback in another. Fortunately, bookshops and libraries search by title or author, so your local bookshop or library is best placed to advise you on the availability of the following recommendations.

Because of Moscow's pre-eminent place in Russian life, most books on the nation include extensive coverage of the capital.

Lonely Planet
Lonely Planet's *Russia & Belarus* provides comprehensive coverage of both countries, while *Ukraine* is scheduled to come out in 2004. *St Petersburg* is a comprehensive and practical city guide to Russia's second city. *Trans-Siberian Railway* provides details on the most famous cross-continental journey.

Guidebooks
A Travel Guide to Jewish Russia & Ukraine, by Ben G Frank, was published in 1999 and is an impressive work documenting the Jewish culture and its effects on these lands. *Live & Work in Russia and Eastern Europe*, by Jonathan Packer, is a good reference for people hoping to find a job or start a business in Russia.

History & Politics
Pre-Soviet Era Sir Fitzroy Maclean is a Scot whose lifelong affair with Russia and other ex-Soviet republics goes back to days as a diplomat in Moscow in the 1930s. He has written several entertaining, intelligent books on the country, including *Holy Russia* (1978), a good short Russian history by a great storyteller, plus a walk through Moscow, St Petersburg and other history-rich cities. His *All the Russias: The End of an Empire* (1992) covers the entire former USSR.

Going even further back, *Letters From Russia*, by the Marquis de Custine, is a French aristocrat's jolly account of visiting St Petersburg and Moscow and hobnobbing with the tsar and high society in 1839. His description of St Basil's Cathedral is hard to beat: 'a sort of irregular fruit bristling with excrescences, a cantaloupe melon with embroidered edges…a crystallisation of a thousand colours…this confectionery box'.

One of the best books on any single strand of pre-Soviet history is *Peter the Great – His Life & World*, by Robert K Massie. It's a good read about one of Russia's most famous and influential rulers. *Nicholas and Alexandra*, by the same author, is an intriguing account of the last tsar and tsarina. *Catherine the Great: Life and Legend*, by John T Alexander, is a highly readable account of the empress that best of all makes a case for some of the more salacious tales of her life.

Soviet Era *The Rise & Fall of the Soviet Empire*, by Stephen Dalziel, describes its title in a lively style, covering the years 1917–92, with some good photos. *A History of the Soviet Union*, by Geoffrey Hosking, is a dense, analytical look at the Soviet era up to 1985. If you need to know why Kamenev fell out with Kalinin or why Left Social Revolutionaries loathed Kadets, Hosking's your man.

Ten Days That Shook the World is a melodramatic, enthusiastic, contemporary account of the Bolsheviks' 1917 power grab by US journalist John Reed, who himself ended up entombed on Red Square.

Recent History New books about recent events continue to hit the shelves, as so many foreign correspondents assigned to cover Russia mark the end of their assignment with a book.

Dominic Lieven's *Empire* is an astute, scholarly book written with great love and understanding of Russia. *Night of Stone: Death and Memory in Russia*, by Catherine Merridale, is equally enthralling, mixing the bleak recent history of the country with psychology and philosophy.

David Remnick's *Lenin's Tomb* and *Resurrection: The Struggle for a New Russia* are both notable volumes by the *Washington Post*'s famous, award-winning, former Moscow correspondent.

Eternal Russia, by Jonathan Steele, the *Guardian*'s Moscow correspondent from 1988, covers the Gorbachev years and continues up to the 1993 White House shoot-out and subsequent elections. *Martin Walker's Russia*, a collection of articles by Steele's *Guardian* predecessor in Moscow, is worth reading for the excitement it conveys of early *glasnost* (liberalisation) and for its snapshots of daily life.

Vladimir Putin has allowed some of his carefully chosen thoughts and biographical details to be put to paper in *First Person*, which sadly doesn't live up to its subtitle: *An Astonishingly Frank Self-Portrait*.

General

USSR: From an Original Idea by Karl Marx, by Marc Polonsky & Russell Taylor, is a 1980s street-wise look at the headaches of travel by authors experienced in organising 'real life' Soviet tours – funny enough to keep you up when the trip gets you down.

Women's Glasnost vs Naglost, by Tatyana Mamonova (1994), combines essays by this Russian women's movement leader with interviews of a cross-section of women in a country where wife-beating and abortion reach incredible levels.

A History of Russian Architecture, by William Craft Brumfield, is the definitive work on the topic, from wooden huts to the bombastic last gasps of the Soviet Union. *Russian Art of the Avant-Garde* is a collection of essays that shows that Soviet artists weren't painting in a vacuum and led the West in many trends.

Towards Another Shore, by Aileen M Kelly, is a brilliant examination of the development of Russian ideological thinking. *The Sexual Revolution in Russia*, by Igor S Kon, is considered the authoritative history of sexual mores and habits among the Russians throughout history. *Pushkin's Button*, by Serena Vitale, is a fascinating recounting of the duel in which the poet was killed.

Popular Fiction

Moscow has been an ideal setting for numerous works of popular fiction, some of which have turned up on the silver screen as well. None of the following books will appear on any self-respecting college's reading list, but they will entertain and evoke some good images of the city (see the Facts about Moscow chapter for some of the more notable literary works by Russian authors).

Martin Cruz Smith has written several thrillers set in Russia, featuring detective Arkady Renko. *Gorky Park* and *Red Square* are both set in Moscow. John le Carré draws on his background as real-life spy in *The Russia House*, which is set in early *perestroika* (literally, 'restructuring') Moscow.

British novelist and colourful politician Jeffrey Archer kills off Yeltsin and replaces him with a loony (really, this is fiction) in *The Eleventh Commandment*. Robert Harris captures the moods and atmosphere of late 1990s Moscow in the bittersweet and almost literary *Archangel*.

FILMS

In 2001, Alexander Zeldovich came out with *Moscow*, set in the hedonistic, Bohemian city of the 1990s. The storyline is a bit much, but it does capture the spirit of the city (see Cinema under Arts in the Facts about Moscow chapter for other Soviet and Russian films).

The Russian capital has been the setting for a few Western flicks as well, although the Soviet Union was not exactly welcoming to Western filmmakers. *Gorky Park*, for example, while set in Moscow, was actually filmed in Helsinki.

With the opening of borders, however, Hollywood has come to Moscow, and not just to show films.

The Russia House (1990), based on the book by John le Carré, was shot partly in Moscow. The spy thriller is worth a watch just to see Sean Connery do what he does best. The ludicrous *Police Academy 7: Mission to Moscow* (1995) mixes typical car chase and explosion nonsense with the Russian mafia; you can guess the outcome. Love and intrigue lead both Val Kilmer and

Elizabeth Shue through Moscow's streets and sewers in *The Saint* (1997), yet another action–adventure flick.

NEWSPAPERS & MAGAZINES
Russian-Language
Though a far cry from the one-note news days of the Soviet era, most of Russia's biggest papers today are, to some degree, mouthpieces for the various powerful bodies that own them, be they political parties or rich businessmen.

The most popular Russian dailies are *Izvestia*, *Kommersant* and *Komsomolskaya Pravda*. The government's official newspaper is the *Rossiyskaya Gazeta*. The tabloid category is covered by *Moskovsky Komsomolets Versiya*, *Sovershenno Sekretno* and the anti-Putin *Novaya Gazeta*.

The weekly *Argumenty I Fakty* is one of the most popular papers in the country, selling over 30 million copies a week. Reputed to be relatively free from outside influences, it covers politics, economics and the social scene.

As for magazines, the market is similarly flooded with local titles as well as Russian-language versions of popular Western ones such as *Cosmopolitan* and *GQ*. In Moscow, *Afisha* is a trendy monthly that's worth a look.

English-Language
Top hotels in Moscow usually have day-old copies of the main dailies such as the *International Herald-Tribune* and the *Financial Times* as well as top news weeklies, such as the *Economist*, *Time* and *Newsweek*.

The undisputed king of the hill in locally published English-language news is the *Moscow Times* (W *www.moscowtimes.ru*), a first-rate daily staffed by top-notch journalists and editors covering Russian and international issues. It's available free at hotels, business centres and restaurants, and also by subscription. The Thursday edition is a great source for what's happening at the weekend.

Another Moscow daily, the *Moscow Tribune*, always seems to be on the verge of closing.

The weekly *Moscow News* is the oldest English-language publication; it made a name for itself as a progressive, independent newspaper during the glasnost years. The irreverent *Exile* (W *www.exile.ru*), a free weekly, has extensive entertainment listings.

Numerous other English-language weeklies and monthlies seem to appear at random, last a few issues and then vanish. One very useful established monthly is the *Moscow Business Telephone Guide*, a free, invaluable, bilingual phone book. The *Capital Perspective* is a glossy bi-monthly with great photos and in-depth articles about cultural events and places around Moscow. Both can be found in the same places as the aforementioned publications.

RADIO
Russian-Language
Radio in Russia is broken into three bands: AM, UKV (the lower band of FM, 66–77MHz) and FM (100–107MHz).

A Western-made FM radio usually won't go lower than 85MHz. Some of the more popular radio stations include:

Ekho Moskvy, FM 91.2 Interviews, news, jazz and some Western and local pop music
Radio Rossii Nostalgie, FM 100.5 Western retro rock from the USA, Britain and France (!)
Radio-7, FM 104.7 Mainly Western pop and rock plus some Russian rock from bands like Aquarium and DDT
Radio Maximum, FM 103.7 European rock and pop, Russian...intellectual pop, if this is not a contradiction in terms
Ultra, FM 100.5 Alternative Western music
Silver Rain, FM 100.1 Mellow Western pop music, sometimes retro
Love radio, FM 106.6 Russian and Western pop featuring, you guessed it, love songs

English-Language
The clearest BBC World Service shortwave (SW) frequencies in the morning, late evening and at night are near 9410kHz, 12,095kHz (the best) and 15,070kHz – though the exact setting varies with location in Russia. The BBC broadcasts at the following times and frequencies:

time	frequency (kHz)
2am to 5am	9410
3pm to 9pm	9410
2am to 5am	6195
6pm to 8pm	6195
5am to 9pm	12,095
6am to 3pm	15,565
7am to 3pm	17,640
8pm to midnight	5930
	6180
	7325

TV
Russian-Language
In recent years Russian TV has caused a clash of interests between the state and the bankrolling tycoons who own some stations and journalists.

In 2001, the controversial takeover of NTV, Russia's first truly professional (and, crucially, critical of government) station, by the state-controlled natural gas monopoly Gazprom, led to demonstrations on Moscow streets and a walkout by the station's top journalists. Many went to work for another independent station, TV6, but in January 2002 it also was shut down.

In an interesting turn of events, the ex-NTV journalists, led by Yevgeny Kiselyov, who also spent time at TV6, were awarded the licence to broadcast on the successor to TV6, TVS, but only because they agreed to work in alliance with various Putin and government supporters. Kiselyov and his team are back on air, doing pretty much what they did before, undermining the prevailing Western view that Putin is out to control the media at all costs.

Media insiders tell us that what Russia is left with, after all these shenanigans, is effectively three clones of the old NTV – RTR (Channel 2), the new NTV and TVS. ORT (Channel 1, the state channel) is also working hard to match NTV's standards, and RenTV (effectively a mouthpiece for right-wing politicians) is moving in the same direction.

Amid all the badly dubbed films, soap operas and cheesy game shows, you will find some interesting programming. Channel 5, Kultura, remains outside all these politics, showing a mix of new and old films from many countries, plays, concerts, as well as historical and educational programmes. The first half of the day on Channel 5 is occupied by the Russian version of Euronews. Russia's own MTV dishes up a hi-energy mix of local and international pop videos.

English-Language
In major hotels you will have access to those modern-day staples of international travel, CNN and BBC World, plus most likely a broad range of other satellite channels which broadcast in English and other languages.

VIDEO SYSTEMS
The predominant video format in Russia is Secam, a system incompatible with that used in most of Europe (France and Greece are among the exceptions), Australia, and the USA.

Hi8 and SVHS cassettes are easy to find in most big cities. If your camera records in NTSC (ie, the North American standard), these cassettes will be fine, even if they are labelled PAL. You might have a hard time, though, connecting your camera to a TV or transferring your film onto a VHS, depending on whether or not the TV reads or the VCR records NTSC.

PHOTOGRAPHY & VIDEO
Major brands of print film are widely available in Moscow at prices typical for Western Europe. As anywhere else, slide film is not widely sold. Whatever film you purchase, check the expiry date carefully. For developing, photographic equipment, slide film, camcorder tapes and other items to help you record your Russian visit, try **Focus Photoshop** (Map 2; Tverskaya ul 4; open 8am-8pm daily) which is conveniently located.

Some museums and galleries forbid flash pictures, some ban all photos and most will charge you extra if you want to take photos anyway. Caretakers in a few churches and other historical buildings charge mercilessly for the privilege of using a still or video camera.

Photographing People

As anywhere, use good judgement and discretion when taking photos of people. It's always better to ask first; if people don't want to be photographed, respect their privacy.

A lifetime with the KGB may make older people uneasy about having their picture taken. A (genuine) offer to send a copy can loosen a subject up. Many people are touchy about your photographing embarrassing things like drunks, run-down housing or other signs of social decay.

The Russian for 'may I take a photograph of you?' is *Mozhno vas sfotografirovat?* (**mozh**-na vas sfa-ta-gruh-**fee**-ra-vut?).

TIME

From the end of September to the end of March, Moscow time is GMT/UTC plus three hours. From the last Sunday in March to the last Sunday in September, 'summer time' is in force and it's GMT/UTC plus four hours. Most of European Russia is in the same time zone as Moscow.

ELECTRICITY

Standard voltage is 220V, 50Hz AC, though some places still have an old 127V system. Sockets require a continental or European plug with two round pins. Look for voltage (V) and frequency (Hz) labels on your appliances. Some trains and hotel bathrooms have 110V and 220V shaver plugs.

WEIGHTS & MEASURES

Russia operates on the metric system (see the back of the book for conversions from other units). Restaurant menus often list the weight of food and drink servings in grams. Drinks, in particular, are ordered by weight: a teacup is about 200g, a shot-glass about 50g. Other items, such as eggs, are sold by the piece, or *shtuka*.

LAUNDRY

Still a rarity in Moscow, there is a **self-serve laundry** (*Outer South Moscow map; ul Vavilova 11; RR60 per load; open 7am-10pm Mon-Sat*). Take tram 39 from Leninsky Prospekt or Universitetskaya, head up the short flight of stairs and enter through the unmarked white door. You will also find that many places to stay offer laundry services for a reasonable price.

TOILETS

Pay toilets are identified by the words Платный Туалет (*platny tualet*). In any toilet Ж stands for women's (*zhenskiy*), while M stands for men's (*muzhskoy*).

Plastic-cabin portable loos are scattered around Moscow in public places, but other public toilets are rare. Where they do exist, they are often dingy and uninviting. If you can hold on, use the loos in major hotels or in modern food outlets. In public toilets, the babushka to whom you pay your RR5 will have toilet paper, but it's always a good idea to carry your own. It's easy to buy, but maybe not when you need it most.

LEFT LUGGAGE

You can check your bags in at most of the major hotels.

The major train stations have either a left-luggage room (камера хранения, *kamera khranenia*) or left-luggage lockers (автоматические камеры хранения, *avtomaticheskie kamery khranenia*). These are generally secure, but make sure you note the opening and closing hours. To utilise the left-luggage lockers:

1. Buy two tokens (*zhetony*) from the attendant
2. Find an empty locker and put your stuff in
3. Decide on a combination of one Russian letter and three numbers and write it down
4. Set the combination on the inside of the locker door
5. Put one token in the slot
6. Close the locker

To open the locker, set your combination on the outside of the door. It seems as if the knobs on the outside of the door should correspond directly with those on the inside, but the letter is always the left-most knob, followed by three numbers, on both the inside and the outside. After you've set your combination, put a token in the slot, wait a second or two for the electrical humming sound, and pull open the locker.

HEALTH

Although Moscow's tap water is considered safe to drink, locals regard it with deep suspicion and usually boil it first. Air pollution is another common health concern, as a result of industrial pollution, automobile emissions and wind-blown dust.

Cheap vodka bought from shops or kiosks can make you ill. Try to purchase name-brand vodka from respectable establishments such as the food stores listed in the Places to Eat chapter. Make sure that bottles are unopened when you purchase them. The same goes for bottled water.

Predeparture Planning

Most visitors to Moscow don't experience any serious health problems, but decent travel insurance is essential.

If you are visiting in winter, be prepared for cold conditions. Make sure childhood vaccinations, including polio, diphtheria and tetanus, are up to date. It's a good idea to travel with a basic medical kit (including aspirin or paracetamol, antiseptic, Band-aids etc) even though most medical supplies should be available in large pharmacies. Don't forget medication you're already on.

Under a 1995 Russian law, anyone applying for a visa for a stay of more than three months must have a certificate showing HIV-negative status. This certificate needs to be in English and Russian (see boxed text 'HIV/Aids Testing' earlier in this chapter).

Health Risks

Diarrhoea Simple things such as a change of water, food, or climate can all cause a mild bout of diarrhoea, but a few rushed toilet trips with no other symptoms is not indicative of a major problem.

Dehydration is the main danger with any diarrhoea, particularly in children or the elderly as dehydration can occur quickly. Under all circumstances, *fluid replacement* (at least equal to the volume being lost) is the most important thing to remember. Weak black tea with a little sugar, soda water, or soft drinks allowed to go flat and diluted 50% with clean water are all good. With severe diarrhoea, a rehydrating solution is preferable to replace minerals and salts lost. Commercially available oral rehydration salts (ORS) are very useful; add them to boiled or bottled water. In an emergency you can make up a solution of six teaspoons of sugar and a half-teaspoon of salt to a litre of boiled or bottled water. You need to drink at least the same volume of fluid that you are losing in bowel movements and vomiting. Urine is the best guide to the adequacy of replacement – if you have small amounts of concentrated urine, you need to drink more. Keep drinking small amounts often. Stick to a bland diet as you recover.

Gut-paralysing drugs, such as loperamide or diphenoxylate, can be used to bring relief from the symptoms, although they do not actually cure the problem. Only use these drugs if you do not have access to toilets (ie, if you *must* travel). Note that these drugs are not recommended for children under 12 years.

HIV/AIDS & Sexually Transmitted Infections HIV/AIDS can be transmitted through sexual contact. Infection with the human immunodeficiency virus (HIV) may lead to acquired immune deficiency syndrome (AIDS), which is a fatal disease. Any exposure to blood, blood products or body fluids may put the individual at risk. The disease is often transmitted through sexual contact or dirty needles – vaccinations, acupuncture, tattooing and body piercing can be potentially as dangerous as intravenous drug use.

Other STIs include gonorrhoea, herpes and syphilis; sores, blisters or rashes around the genitals and discharges or pain when urinating are common symptoms. In some STIs, such as wart virus or chlamydia, symptoms may be less marked or not observed at all, especially in women. Chlamydia infection can cause infertility in men and women before any symptoms have been noticed. Syphilis symptoms eventually disappear completely, but the disease continues and can cause severe problems in later years. While abstinence from sexual contact is the only 100% effective prevention, using condoms is also effective. The treatment of gonorrhoea and syphilis is with antibiotics. Different sexually transmitted diseases each require specific antibiotics.

Ticks Travellers should be aware of this possibility in any forested areas, especially places such as the forests around Lake Seliger, Valdai National Park or Zavidovo. Many dachas are in undeveloped areas that might have ticks. You should always check all over your body if you have been walking through a potentially tick-infested area, as ticks can cause skin infections and other more serious diseases. If a tick is found attached, press down around the tick's head with tweezers, grab the head and gently pull upwards. Avoid pulling the rear of the body, as this may squeeze the tick's gut contents through the attached mouth parts into the skin, increasing the risk of infection and disease. Smearing chemicals on the tick will not make it let go and is not recommended.

Medical Services

Several foreign-run health services are available in Moscow. They offer Western standards of treatment, are very expensive and can be fiscally ruinous without valid insurance coverage.

American Medical Center *(Map 3; ☎ 933 7700, fax 933 7701; Grokholsky per 1)* offers 24-hour emergency service, consultations (from US$175), a full range of specialists, including paediatricians and dentists, and an English-speaking pharmacy (open 8am to 8pm weekdays, 9am to 5pm weekends).

Apart from the American Medical Center, **Pharmacy Kutuzovskaya** *(Map 4; ☎ 243 1601; Kutuzovsky pr 19-21)* is open 24 hours and stocks Russian and Western medicines.

European Medical Center *(Map 2; ☎ 787 7000; Spirodonovsky per 5)* is similar in terms of both service and cost.

The best Russian facility is **Botkin Hospital** *(Map 2; ☎ 945 0045; 2-y Botkinsky proezd 5)*.

Embassies usually have lists of local doctors who speak the language of their citizens.

WOMEN TRAVELLERS

Although sexual harassment on the streets is rare, it is common in the workplace, in the home and in personal relations (see the boxed text 'A Woman's Work is Never Done'). Discrimination and domestic violence are hard facts of life for many Russian women. Some estimates have as many as 12,000 to 16,000 women a year dying at the hands of their partners. (Alcoholism, unemployment and feelings of passivity and impotence in men are related problems.)

Activists ridicule as hypocritical the 8 March Women's Day celebrations in Russia. It is one of the year's major celebrations, a national holiday where businesses shut down for as many as three days, and when women are traditionally presented with flowers.

Foreign women are likely to be propositioned on the streets, although this interest is rarely dangerous. An interested stranger may approach you out of the blue and ask: *'Mozhno poznokomitsa?'* (May we become acquainted?). The easiest answer is a gentle, but firm, *'Nyet'*. The conversation usually goes no further, although drunken men may be more persistent. The most efficient way to lose an unwelcome suitor is to enter an upmarket hotel or restaurant, where ample security will come to your aid. Women should certainly avoid taking private taxis alone at night.

Russian women dress up and wear lots of make-up on nights out. If you are wearing casual gear, you might feel uncomfortable at dinner in a restaurant, or at a theatre or the ballet.

The following websites provide useful information about women's organisations in Moscow:

W **www.members.tripod.com/IWC_Moscow/**
The International Women's Club is an active group of expat women. They are involved in organising social and charity events.
W **www.womnet.ru** The Women Information Network (WIN) site, in Russian only, is updated regularly. It has news items, local events, book reviews and grant information for women's organisations.
W **www.womnet.ru/db/english/english.html**
WIN maintains this extensive database of women's organisations throughout Russia. Search by name, location or area of interest.

FACTS FOR THE VISITOR

A Woman's Work is Never Done

In her difficult procession to the bright future the woman proletarian learns to throw off all the virtues imposed on her by slavery; step by step she becomes an autonomous worker, an independent personality, a free lover.

Alexandra Kollontai, feminist and communist heroine

In the Soviet past, women were primarily responsible for household concerns, from serving vodka to their husbands to teaching Pushkin to their children. Women also held full-time jobs outside the home. Soviet propaganda boasted that the high percentage of women in the labour force demonstrated equality of the sexes.

These figures, however, belied the real disparity between sexes in the Soviet workplace. Women worked out of economic necessity. They were relegated to nontechnical factory work, meagre wage service positions and low-status professions. The job sectors dominated by women included textiles, food processing and healthcare.

The past 10 years have dramatically transformed the labour market as moribund socialist industries have given way to a dynamic consumer revolution. The burgeoning service sector is now a respectable option for young people and students to earn cash. New private and foreign firms offer career advancement and higher salaries to individuals who can market their products and manage their offices. These opportunities are available to women like never before.

Russia's new economy has particularly benefited young, university-educated women. They are gaining valued skills, professional experience and access to information, yielding greater economic independence and self-confidence. For example, 26-year-old Victoria claims that she learned the importance of sales – not only selling products and services to clients, but also selling her own work and ideas to her superiors. Alyona, also 26, explains that she used to be intimidated by a closed door in an office building or an uncooperative face at the checkout counter. Her job improved her communication skills, and she now commands the respect she deserves from people in day-to-day life, as well as on the job.

As women succeed in the workplace, it leads inevitably to changes at home. Ten years ago, Tanya was married at the age of 19; one year later she was home with a child, and two years later she was divorced.

Tanya's situation was not unusual for young women in the Soviet Union: in 1985, the average female age at marriage was 22.

Today, 22-year-old Vera is single, newly graduated from university, and gainfully employed in a promising job. On her 22nd birthday, a friend teased her with: 'According to Russian custom you should be getting married now.' Her retort was: 'According to Russian custom I should be getting divorced now!' Women Vera's age are rejecting the traditional ideas about marriage that Tanya once embraced.

Meanwhile, many women who are in Tanya's position have also had a change of heart: they are going back to school, concentrating on their careers and supporting families on their own.

Unfortunately, not all women are able to take advantage of these changes. The transition has been especially severe for pensioners, some of whom have taken to begging. Career shifts have not come easily for middle-aged or unskilled women; women represent two-thirds of the unemployed. Some women have survived by finding work in Russia's seamy sex trade. Others have sought to leave the country, and marriage agencies – which hook up Russian women with foreign men – do a bustling business.

Madame Kollontai's hopes for women were left unfulfilled by communist Russia. Whether they will be realised in the new Russia remains to be seen.

GAY & LESBIAN TRAVELLERS
While girls walking hand in hand and drunken men being affectionate are common sights throughout Russia, open displays of same-sex love are not condoned. In general, the idea of homosexual acts is well tolerated by the younger generation, though overt gay behaviour is frowned upon. Indeed, in 2002 a group of publicity-seeking MPs in the State Duma attempted (and failed) to recriminalise homosexuality.

There is an active gay and lesbian scene in Moscow, and newspapers such as the *Moscow Times* feature articles about gay and lesbian issues, and listings of gay and lesbian clubs, bars and events. However, don't expect anything near as organised as you might find in other major world cities. Even in Moscow – probably the most open city in Russia – the founder of the Gay & Lesbian Archive, a centre for gay literature and writing, prefers to remain anonymous for fear of being sacked from her regular job. Some useful sites for contacts and information on the gay community in Moscow include:

W www.gay.ru/english/ The English version of this site includes updated club listings, plus information on gay history and culture in Russia

W www.gayrussia.msk.ru The first commercial Russian website, sponsored by the Gay Business Association of Russia, has lots of information (Russian only), on the legal situation, bars, restaurants, saunas, publications and escort services

W www.vmt.com/gayrussia The information on events is outdated, but many of the links still work and there are some interesting articles in English

Cracks in the Iron Closet: Travels in Gay & Lesbian Russia, by David Tuller & Frank Browning, is a fascinating account of the gay and lesbian scene in modern Russia. A combination of travel memoir and social commentary, it reveals an emerging homosexual culture that is surprisingly different from its US counterpart.

Queer Sites, by Dan Healy, traces the history of seven world cities, including Moscow, focusing on sexual mores, the homosexual experience, and how they have changed over time.

DISABLED TRAVELLERS
Inaccessible transport, lack of ramps and lifts, and no centralised policy for people with physical limitations make Russia a challenging destination for wheelchair-bound visitors. More mobile travellers will have a relatively easier time, but keep in mind that there are obstacles along the way. Toilets are frequently accessed from stairs in restaurants and museums; distances are great; public transport is extremely crowded; and many footpaths are in a poor condition and hazardous even for the mobile.

Readers who use wheelchairs report that Russians are anxious to help, but don't know how, thus either speaking Russian or having a translator is essential. In museums, staff may say that most floors are inaccessible because they don't want to suggest the freight elevator for fear of offending.

In Moscow, the **All-Union Association for the Rehabilitation of the Disabled** (☎ 298 8737, fax 230 2407; Birzhovaya pl 1) does not offer any services to travellers, but may provide publications (in Russian) on legal issues or local resources.

Before setting off, get in touch with your national support organisation (preferably with the travel officer, if there is one). In the UK contact **Radar** (☎ 020-7250 3222; W www.radar.org.uk; 250 City Rd, London EC1V 8AF) or the **Holiday Care Service** (☎ 01293-774 535). In the USA, contact **Mobility International USA** (☎ 541-343 1284; W www.miusa.org; PO Box 10767, Eugene, Oregon, 974400).

Disabled Peoples International (W www.dpi.org) is a nonprofit organisation that hosts a website with tons of listings and great links; those behind it are based in Canada and seem to think truly globally.

SENIOR TRAVELLERS
Travellers over the age of 60 can expect senior citizen discounts and good treatment from Moscow ticket agents. Respect for the elderly is far more ingrained in Russia than in some countries. Organisations in your

home country, such as the **American Association of Retired Persons** (w *www.aarp.org*), which you can join even if you're not retired or a senior, can assist with any age-specific information before you leave.

MOSCOW FOR CHILDREN

Kids in Moscow? Take them to **Gorky Park** (☎ 237 1266; *ul Krymsky Val*). Thrill rides in summer and ice skating in winter make it the ultimate kids' venue in Russia. For a more post-Soviet experience (or in case of bad weather), **VDNKh** has a pavilion devoted to video games. (See the Things to See & Do chapter for detailed information on these venues.)

If there is one arena in which Russia excels, it is the circus. Crazy clowns and daring acrobatics are all the rage at two locales: the huge **New Circus** (Nikulin) or the more atmospheric **Old Circus**. Another Russian favourite is the puppet theatre. **Obraztsov Puppet Theatre & Museum** runs colourful Russian folk tales and adapted classical plays. Kids can get up-close and personal with the incredible puppets at the museum. (See the Entertainment chapter for detailed information on these venues.)

What better entertainment for kiddies than performing kitties? At the **Cat Theatre**, Yuri Kuklachev's acrobatic cats do all kinds of stunts to the audience's delight. See the Entertainment chapter.

Bigger cats are the highlight of the **Moscow Zoo** (see Barrikadnaya in the Things to See & Do chapter), which is an obvious destination for children. For a trip out of the city, take the young ones to the **Prioksko-Terrasny Biosphere Reserve** (see the Excursions chapter), where highly informative educational programmes are especially designed for children.

Russians love children, and yours will probably elicit nods of approval and playful interactions from most people on the street. Moscow does not present any particular hazards to your kids, save the ornery babushkas. Lonely Planet's *Travel with Children* contains useful advice on how to cope with kids on the road and what to bring to make things go more smoothly.

SAFETY CONCERNS
Crime

The Russian 'Mafia' – a broad term encompassing the many thousands of corrupt officials, businesspeople, financiers, police, small- and big-time gangsters – will be the least of your problems while travelling in the country. Despite occasional beat-ups in the Western media, the lawless situation that existed in the early 1990s has now largely disappeared and big-time crime's impact on tourists is pretty much nonexistent these days.

Moscow's streets are about as safe, or as dangerous, as those of New York or London. There's petty theft, pocket-picking, purse-snatching and all the other crimes that are endemic in big cities anywhere in the world. Don't leave valuables in a car or hotel room. Travellers have reported problems with groups of children who surround foreigners, ostensibly to beg, and end up closing in, with dozens of hands probing Westerners' pockets or worse. The most common hazard is violent and xenophobic (or even worse, over-friendly) drunks.

Unfortunately, police officers in Moscow are not always your friends. Officials asking to see your papers may be on the lookout for a bribe (see the boxed text 'The Great Moscow Police Tourist Rip-off' earlier in this chapter). Members of the police force will likely harass anybody who looks African, Asian or Caucasian. The latest word from a Moscow synagogue is 'cover your kippa'.

One reported scam involves the use of devices in ATMs that read credit card and PIN details when you withdraw money from the machines, enabling accounts to be accessed and additional funds withdrawn. In general, it's safest to use ATMs at well-established banks (see Banks under Exchanging Money earlier in this chapter).

Racism & Discrimination

Despite many decades of 'let's-all-love-our-comrades' communism in Russia, the populace maintains a disturbingly high level of entrenched racism. In recent years, some embassies have issued warnings to foreigners to stay off the streets around Hitler's birthday, 20 April, when bands of right-wing thugs have been known to roam about spoiling for a fight with anyone who doesn't look Russian. Frightening reports of racial violence appear from time to time in the media and it's a sure thing that if you look Caucasian or have dark skin then you will be treated with suspicion by many people (particularly by the police).

What is most surprising is that racist attitudes or statements can come from otherwise highly educated Russians. Jews, targets of state-sponsored anti-Semitism during the Communist reign, are more distrusted than hated. Gypsies, also known as Roma or Travellers, are openly reviled.

Annoyances

Russians have very specific rules for queuing, eg, holding someone's place in the line while they go off shopping for several hours is permissible, as is pushing in at the last minute if, say, you're at the train station and the train is about to go. In most cases, neither being polite nor getting angry when someone shoves in front of you will help. If you have the head for it, sharpen your elbows, learn a few scowling phrases, and plough head first through the throng. Good luck.

Prostitution is common, with unsolicited prostitutes still sometimes visiting or telephoning your hotel room offering sex. Also be prepared for strip shows, both male and female, at many of the nightclubs and some restaurants.

BUSINESS HOURS

Government offices open from 9am or 10am to 5pm or 6pm weekdays. Banks usually open from 9am to noon and 1pm to 6pm weekdays. Currency-exchange booths

Emergency Numbers

Emergency telephone numbers (with Russian-speaking operators) are ☎ 01 for fire, ☎ 02 for police and ☎ 03 for ambulance. For English-language emergency assistance, call ☎ 257 4503.

open long hours on weekdays, and on Saturday and sometimes Sunday too.

Most shops are open Monday to Saturday. Food shops tend to open from 8am to 8pm except for a break *(pereryv)* from 1pm to 2pm or 2pm to 3pm; some close later while some open Sunday until 5pm. Other shops mostly operate from 10am or 11am to 7pm or 8pm with a 2pm to 3pm break. Department stores may run from 8am to 8pm or 9pm without a break. A few shops stay open through the weekend and close on Monday.

Moscow has more and more 24-hour kiosks selling food and drink. Restaurants typically open from noon to midnight, except for a break between afternoon and evening meals.

Museum hours change often, as do their weekly days off. Most shut entrance doors 30 minutes or an hour before closing time and may have shorter hours on the day before their day off. Many museums close for a 'sanitary day' during the last week of every month.

PUBLIC HOLIDAYS

The main public holidays are:

New Year's Day 1 January
Russian Orthodox Christmas Day 7 January
International Women's Day 8 March
International Labour Day/Spring Festival 1 and 2 May
Victory (1945) Day 9 May
Russian Independence Day 12 June (when the Russian republic inside the USSR proclaimed its sovereignty in June 1991)
Day of Reconciliation and Accord 7 November (the rebranded Revolution Day)

Other days that are widely celebrated are 23 February (Defenders of the Motherland Day), Easter Monday and 12 December (Constitution Day). The old Great October Socialist Revolution Anniversary (7 November) is still a big day for marches by the Communist Party. Much of Russia shuts down for the first half of May and its wealth of holidays.

Easter (Paskha) is the main festival of the Orthodox Church's year. It is held in March/April. Easter Day kicks off with celebratory midnight services, after which people eat special dome-shaped cakes known as *kulichy* and curd-cakes called *paskha*, and may exchange painted wooden Easter eggs. The devout deny themselves meat, milk, alcohol and sex in the 40-day pre-Easter fasting period of Lent.

SPECIAL EVENTS

The Contemporary Music Festival is held at venues all over the city for a few weeks in early summer. Top Russian and international acts perform. Check the *Moscow Times* and other local publications for details.

December Nights Festival is held at the main performance halls, theatres and museums from mid-December to early January. Classical music at its best is performed in classy surroundings by the best Russian and foreign talent.

The Winter Festival is an outdoor funfest for those with antifreeze in their veins (and you can bet plenty of people use vodka for this purpose) during early January. Teams compete to build elaborate ice sculptures in front of the Pushkin Museum and on Red Square. But the real nutters (or those who have *far* too much antifreeze in their veins) can be found punching holes in the ice on the Moscow River and plunging in for a dip. Do this and you're a member of the 'Walrus Club'.

For details on the famed International Tchaikovsky Competition, see Classical Music in the Entertainment chapter.

WORK

Working in Russia can be an exciting, rewarding, enlightening, frustrating, insanity-inducing experience. Opportunities for employment have lessened since the economic crash of August 1998, but there are still loads of Westerners employed by multinational and local companies, as well as foreigners who have formed partnerships with Russians to set up their own businesses.

If you are interested in working in Russia, Jonathan Packer's book *Live & Work in Russia and Eastern Europe* is a good reference. English-language publications such as the *Moscow Times* also have job listings.

The groups listed here can provide a wealth of information and important contacts for doing business in Moscow: **American Chamber of Commerce** (☎ 961 2141, fax 961 2142; ⓦ www.amcham.ru), **European Business Club** (☎ 721 1760, fax 721 1761; ⓦ www.ebc.ru), and the **Russian-British Chamber of Commerce** (☎ 937 8249, fax 937 8278; ⓦ www.rbcc.co.uk).

Getting There & Away

AIR
Airports

Moscow's five airports serve a range of destinations. For information on flights in and out of all airports, call ☎ 941 9999.

Sheremetevo-2 This airport, 30km northwest of the city centre, handles flights to/from places outside the former Soviet Union. This is a major international airport and offers all of the services that one would expect. For detailed flight information, call ☎ 956 4666.

Arriving at Sheremetevo-2, you'll find that passing through passport control can be time-consuming, sometimes taking more than an hour. Checked luggage is also slow, although reports of theft have declined.

The only problem with departing from Sheremetevo-2 is the customs checks you must endure before departure – waiting in disorganised queues can last more than an hour on a busy day.

For this reason you should plan to be at Sheremetevo-2 about two hours before your flight departs. Fill out a customs form before

inspection (see Customs in the Facts for the Visitor chapter).

International flights from Moscow's airports incur a departure tax, which is sometimes split between arrival and departure. In any case, the taxes are included in the price of the airline ticket.

Domodedovo This airport, 40km south of the city centre, has undergone extensive upgrades in recent years. Most notably, the express train from Paveletsky Station facilitates access to this airport. As a result, more flights are going in and out of Domodedovo, including some international flights. At the time of writing, Domodedovo serviced Transaero, Swiss and Sabena. For flight information, call ☎ 933 6666.

Other Airports Moscow has three other airports handling flights in Russia and the CIS:

Bykovo (☎ 558 4738) About 30km southeast of Moscow
Sheremetevo-1 (☎ 232 6565) Across the runways from Sheremetevo-2
Vnukovo (☎ 941 9999) About 30km southwest of Moscow

For details on how to get to/from the airports from the city centre, see the Getting Around chapter. Plan to arrive at least 90 minutes before your flight in order to navigate the formalities of check-in and security. Services at the airports are very basic.

Within Russia

The former Soviet state airline, Aeroflot, has been decentralised into hundreds of smaller airlines ('baby-flots'). These come and go with such a rapidity that not even the Russian Department of Air Transport (RDAT) can say how many exist.

The upshot of this orgy of aerobatic entrepreneurship is virtually unregulated skies and a bad safety record. Tales of Russian airline safety lapses are commonplace. Getting reliable statistics is difficult, but people familiar with the Russian aviation scene say that the safety of domestic airlines differs widely.

Generally speaking, **Aeroflot Russian International Airlines** (w *www.aeroflot.com*) is thought to have the highest standards. This airline took over the old international routes of the Soviet-era Aeroflot and today offers Western-style services on mostly Western-made aircraft such as the Boeing 777. The airline also offers domestic services on many routes. The relationship between Aeroflot and the 'baby-flots' is confusing, but you may wish to investigate exactly which company is operating the domestic flight you are thinking of taking. Check out the website for further information.

In some cases, you may not have a choice of airlines. Information on the various airlines is limited, which makes it difficult to determine how safe the air journey is. When making a decision on whether or not to fly, keep in mind that travelling by road presents its own hazards. Trains are generally safe and reliable, but, depending on distances, the time factor may be a hindrance.

Timetables & Tickets Domestic timetables are confusing, especially since all of the airlines are listed together, and distinguished only by their flight codes.

You can buy domestic airline tickets at most travel agents and Aeroflot offices all over town. The convenient **Aeroflot office** (*Map 2; ☎ 753 5555; open 9am-7pm Mon-Sat, 9am-3.30pm Sun*) at ulitsa Petrovka 20/1 has friendly and helpful staff. **Transaero airlines** also has several ticket offices, including a very convenient one in the corner of Hotel Moskva (*Map 6; ☎ 241 4800; Okhotny ryad 2; open 9am-9pm daily*). You'll need your passport and visa to book tickets.

Costs Airline fares can be remarkably reasonable – sometimes little more than a berth on a train. Return fares are usually just double the one-way fares. The following approximate one-way foreigner fares and flying times from Moscow to other Russian cities are representative of those throughout the country:

destination (hours)	fare (RR)	duration
Arkhangelsk	2800	3
Astrakhan	3300	2½
Irkutsk	3300	7½
Murmansk	2460	3
Novgorod	1540	1½
Novosibirsk	4650	4
St Petersburg (Transaero)	2100	1½
Sochi	2900	2½
Vladivostok	7550	9
Volgograd	2320	2
Yekaterinburg	3580	2½

Check-In This should take place 40 minutes to 1½ hours before departure and airlines are entitled to bump you if you arrive later than that. Have your passport and ticket handy throughout the various security and ticket checks, which can last right up until you find a seat. Some flights have assigned seats; sometimes, seating is a free-for-all. Note that you put your carry-on luggage under your own seat, not the one in front of you.

Service and food quality vary widely on domestic flights. Aeroflot Russian International Airlines and Transaero are reliable and conscientious, providing Western standards of service.

Ticket Offices

See Travel Agencies in the Facts for the Visitor chapter for agents who sell international flight tickets – or you can deal directly with the airlines themselves. International airline offices in Moscow include:

Air China (Map 2; ☎ 292 3387) ul Kuznetsky Most 1/8/5
Air France (Map 4; ☎ 937 3839) ul Korovy Val 7
Alitalia (Map 2; ☎ 258 3601) Renaissance Moscow Hotel at Olimpiysky pr 18
Austrian Airlines (Map 4; ☎ 995 0995) Golden Ring Swiss Diamond Hotel, Smolenskaya ul 5
British Airways (Map 2; ☎ 363 2525) Business Centre Parus, ul Tverskaya-Yamskayya 1-ya 23
Czech Airlines (Map 2; ☎ 973 1847) ul 2-ya Tverskaya-Yamskaya 31/35

Delta Air Lines (Map 4; ☎ 937 9090)
Gogolevsky bul 11
Finnair (Map 4; ☎ 933 0056) Kropotinsky per 7
Japan Airlines (Map 2; ☎ 921 6448) ul Kuznet-
sky Most 3
KLM (Map 4; ☎ 258 3600) ul Usacheva 33/2
LOT Polish Airlines (Map 2; ☎ 229 8525)
Tverskoy bul 26
Lufthansa (Map 2; ☎ 737 6400) Renaissance
Moscow Hotel at Olimpiysky pr 18
Sabena/Swiss (Map 4; ☎ 937 7767) Gogolevsky
bul 11
SAS (Map 2; ☎ 925 4747) ul Kuznetsky Most 3
Turkish Airlines (Map 2; ☎ 292 4345) ul
Kuznetsky Most 8/1

Former Soviet Republics

There are frequent flights to/from the capitals of the countries of the former Soviet
Union, operated both by Aeroflot and by
their local successor airlines, such as Air
Ukraine. Sample one-way fares include:

destination	fare (RR)	frequency
Baku	3400	5
Kyiv (Kiev)	2450	2
Minsk	2900	1
Yerevan	4000	4

USA & Canada

Discount travel agents in the USA are
known as consolidators; they can be found
through the *Yellow Pages* or the travel sections of major daily newspapers such as the
New York Times and the *Los Angeles Times*.
Canadian consolidators advertise their specials in major daily newspapers such as the
Toronto Star and the *Vancouver Sun*.

A good place to start your search for
cheap tickets is **STA Travel** *(☎ 800-781 4040;
W www.statravel.com)*, which has a wide
network of offices. **Council Travel** is the
USA's largest student travel organisation
and has around 60 offices throughout that
country, including its **head office** *(toll-free
☎ 800- 226 8624; W www.counciltravel.com;
205 E 42nd St, New York, NY 10017)*.

The main airlines flying direct between
major US cities and Moscow are Delta and
Aeroflot. Economy-class air fares from New
York to Moscow can go as low as US$450/

550 one-way/return with Aeroflot. From Los
Angeles you're looking at fares to Moscow
of US$550/960.

The Canadian student travel agency is
Travel CUTS *(☎ 866-246 9762; W www
.travelcuts.com)*. In general, the fares from
Canada to Russia cost 10% more than from
the USA. Air Canada and Aeroflot jointly
operate a direct flight between Vancouver
and Moscow, but most Canadian cities will
require a connection in New York or Europe. For a flight from Vancouver to Moscow the cost is US$720/1150, and from
Montreal it's US$770/940.

Australia & New Zealand

Cheap flights from Australia to Europe generally go via Southeast Asian capitals, which
involves stopovers at Kuala Lumpur, Bangkok or Singapore. If a long stopover between connections is necessary then transit
accommodation is sometimes included in
the price of the ticket. If the fare requires
you to pay for transit accommodation yourself, it may be worth considering a more expensive ticket.

Quite a few travel offices specialise in
discount air tickets. Some travel agents,
particularly smaller ones, advertise cheap
air fares in the travel sections of weekend
newspapers, such as the *Age* in Melbourne
and the *Sydney Morning Herald*. The *New
Zealand Herald* has a travel section in
which travel agents advertise fares.

Well-known agents for cheap fares, with
offices throughout Australia and New
Zealand, are **Flight Centre** *(☎ 133 133 in
Australia;* W *www.flightcentre.com.au • ☎ 09-309
6171 in New Zealand)* and **STA Travel** *(☎ 131
776 in Australia;* W *www.statravel .com.au
• ☎ 09-309 0458 in New Zealand; 10 High St,
Auckland)*.

The most direct flight you'll get would be
something like Sydney–Bangkok–Moscow;
a Qantas/Aeroflot codeshare deal starts at
AUD$1100/1450 one-way/return.

UK

Newspapers and magazines such as *Time
Out* and *TNT Magazine* in London regularly
advertise very low fares to places such as

Moscow and Beijing. A good place to start shopping for fares is with the major student- or backpacker-oriented travel agencies. Reputable agencies in London include:

Bridge the World (☎ 0870-444 7474, 020-7813 3350; W www.b-t-w.co.uk) 4 Regent Place, London W1R 5FB

Flightbookers (☎ 0870-010 7000; W www.ebookers.co.uk) 34-42 Woburn Place, London WC1H 0TA

STA Travel (☎ 0870-1600 599; W www.statravel.co.uk) 40 Bernard Street, London WC1N 1LJ

Trailfinders (☎ 020-7938 3939; W www.trailfinders.co.uk) 194 Kensington High St, London W8 7RG

Shop around and you might discover a low-season one-way/return fare to Moscow for £150/200. British Airways, Aeroflot and Transaero all have direct flights to Moscow; Aeroflot generally offers the cheapest deals.

Continental Europe

Though London is the travel discount capital of Europe, there are several other European cities where you will find a range of good deals. Generally, air fares do not vary much between the main European cities. All the major airlines usually offer some sort of deal, as do travel agents, so shop around. Aeroflot has daily flights between most of the major cities in Europe and Moscow. National airlines generally offer direct flights from their major cities to Moscow.

French travel agencies specialising in youth and student fares include **OTU Voyages** (☎ 01 40 29 12 12; W www.otu.fr; 39 Ave Georges Bernanos, 75005 Paris). Another general travel agency offering good services and deals is **Nouvelles Frontières** (☎ 01 45 68 70 00; W www.nouvelles-frontieres.fr; 87 Blvd de Grenelle, 75015 Paris), with many other branches around France.

Agencies in Germany include **STA Travel** (☎ 01805-456 422; W www.statravel.de) and **Travel Overland** (☎ 089-27 27 63 00; W www.travel-overland.de), both with many offices around the country.

A Netherlands agency specialising in discount tickets is **Air Fair** (☎ 020-620 5121, fax 620 5306; W www.airfair.nl; Rokin 52, 1012 KV Amsterdam). Owner Ed Latjes has moved the head office of his discount travel agency (formerly known as Malibu) to the Costa Rican jungles; however, in its new digs, the **European Travel Network** (☎ 20-524 1380; W www.etn.nl/malibu) is still virtually accessible to independent travellers looking for cheap fares.

In Belgium, try the Web-based **Travel Price** (☎ 070-224 000, fax 02-640 3349; W www.travelprice.be; 510 Kroonlaan, 1050 Brussels) or **Wats NV** (☎ 03-233 7020, fax 03-232 1764; De Keyserlei 44, 2018 Antwerp).

Airlines The following European airlines offer services to Moscow:

Aeroflot Daily flights to/from most of the major cities in Europe
Air France Daily flights to/from Paris
Alitalia Daily flights to/from Milan
Austrian Airlines Daily flights to/from Vienna
Czech Airlines Daily flights to/from Prague
Finnair Daily flights to/from Helsinki
KLM Daily service to/from Amsterdam
LOT Polish Airlines Daily flights to/from Warsaw
Lufthansa An extensive schedule of flights to/from Frankfurt, Munich, Berlin and Düsseldorf
Malev-Hungarian Airlines Daily flights to/from Budapest
Sabena Daily flights to/from Brussels
Scandinavian Airlines Daily flights to/from Copenhagen and Stockholm
Swiss Daily flights to/from Geneva and Zurich
Transaero Airlines Daily flights to/from Frankfurt
Turkish Airlines Daily flights to/from Istanbul

Asia

Although most Asian countries are now offering fairly competitive deals, Bangkok and Singapore are still the best places to shop around for discount tickets.

Khao San Rd in Bangkok is the budget travellers' headquarters. Bangkok has a number of excellent travel agents, but there are also some suspect ones; ask the advice of other travellers before handing over your cash. **STA Travel** (☎ 02-236 0262; 33/70 Surawong Rd) is a reliable place to start. Aeroflot has direct flights to Moscow from Bangkok.

STA has a **Singapore branch** (☎ 737 7188; 33A Cuppage Rd, Cuppage Terrace) offering competitive discount fares for Asian destinations and beyond. Singapore, like Bangkok, has hundreds of travel agents, so you can compare prices on flights.

In Japan, STA has a **Tokyo branch** (☎ 03-5485 8380, fax 5485 8373; ⓦ www.sta travel.co.jp; 1st Floor, Star Plaza Aoyama Building, 1-10-3 Shibuya) and an **Osaka branch** (☎ 06-6262 7066; 6th Floor, Honmachi Meidai Building, 2-5-5 Azuchi-Machi). Other reliable discount agencies include **No 1 Travel** (☎ 03-3200 8871; ⓦ www.no1 -travel.com) and **A'cross Travellers Bureau** (☎ 03-3373 9040; ⓦ www.across-travel.com).

One-way/return flights from Tokyo to Moscow are generally around ¥130,000/ 221,000, although at certain times of the year 60-day excursion fares on Aeroflot can go as low as ¥60,000 return.

TRAIN

Moscow has rail links to most parts of Russia, most former Soviet states, numerous countries in Eastern and Western Europe, and China and Mongolia.

The whole Russian rail network runs on Moscow time. You'll usually find timetables and station clocks on Moscow time, but if in doubt confirm these details carefully. The only general exception is suburban rail services, which stick to local time.

Stations

Moscow's nine main stations, all with accompanying metro stations, are:

Belorussia Station (Belorussky vokzal; Map 2; Tverskaya Zastava ploshchad; metro: Belorussky) For trains heading west, including trains to/from Belarus, Lithuania, Poland and Germany, and some trains to/from the Czech Republic

Kazan Station (Kazansky vokzal; Map 3; Komsomolskaya ploshchad; metro: Komsomolskaya) The starting and ending point for trains to/from the southeast, including Central Asia

Kursk Station (Kursky vokzal; Map 3; ploshchad Kurskogo Vokzala; metro: Kurskaya) Serves points southeast, including the Caucasus, eastern Ukraine, Crimea, Georgia, Azerbaijan

Kiev Station (Kievsky vokzal; Map 4; ploshchad Kievskogo vokzala; metro: Kievskaya) Serves points southwest, including Kiev, western Ukraine, Moldova, Slovakia, Hungary, Austria, Romania, Bulgaria and Venice, as well as some trains to/from the Czech Republic

Leningrad Station (Leningradsky vokzal; Map 3; Komsomolskaya ploshchad; metro: Komsomolskaya) For trains heading to/from the northeast, including St Petersburg, Vyborg, Murmansk, Estonia, Helsinki

Pavelets Station (Paveletsky vokzal; Map 5; Paveletskaya ploshchad; metro: Paveletskaya) For trains to/from points south, including the express train to Domodedovo airport

Riga Station (Rizhsky vokzal; Outer North Moscow map; Rizhskaya ploshchad; metro: Rizhskaya) Serves Latvia

Savyolov Station (Savyolovsky vokzal; Outer North Moscow map; ploshchad Savyolovskogo vokzala; metro: Savyolovskaya) For trains to/from the northeast

Yaroslavl Station (Yaroslavsky vokzal; Map 3; Komsomolskaya ploshchad; metro: Komsomolskaya) Serves the longest-distance trains, including those to Mongolia, China, Russian Far East and anything east of the Urals

Tickets

For long-distance trains it's best to buy your tickets in advance. Tickets on some trains may be available on the day of departure, but this is less likely in summer. Always take your passport along when you are buying a train ticket.

Besides the train station proper, tickets are sold throughout the city at any **Central Railway Agency ticket office** (Tsentralnoe Zheleznodorozhnoe Agentstvo; Map 3; ☎ 262 2566; Maly Kharitonevsky per 6; open 8am-1pm & 2pm-7pm daily). Alternatively, travel agents and other ticket offices (kassa zheleznoy dorogi) also sell tickets, sometimes for a small commission, but frankly, it's worth it.

Types of Train

The regular long-distance service is a fast train (skoryy poezd).

It stops more often than the typical intercity train in the West and rarely gets up enough speed to merit the 'fast' label. Foreigners booking rail tickets through agencies are usually put on a skoryy train.

Generally, the best skoryy trains *(firmennye poezdy)* have cleaner cars, more polite attendants and much more convenient arrival/ departure hours; they sometimes also have fewer stops, more 1st-class accommodation or functioning restaurants.

A passenger train *(passazhirskiy poezd)* is an intercity-stopping train, found mostly on routes of 1000km or less. These can take an awfully long time, as they clank and lurch from one small town to the next.

For details of suburban trains *(prigorodnye poezdy* or *elektrichky)*, see under Train in the Getting Around chapter.

Classes

With a reservation, your ticket will normally give the numbers of your carriage *(vagon)* and seat *(mesto)*.

Compartments in a 1st-class carriage, also called soft class *(myagkiy)* or sleeping car *(spalnyy vagon, SV* or *lyux)*, have upholstered seats and also convert to comfortable sleeping compartments for two people. Not all trains have a 1st-class carriage.

Compartments in a 2nd-class carriage, also called hard class *(zhyostkiy)* or compartmentalised *(kupeynyy* or *kupe)*, are four-person (occasionally three-person) couchettes.

Reserved-place *(platskartnyy)*, sometimes also called hard class or 3rd-class, has open bunk accommodation. Groups of hard bunks are partitioned, but not closed off, from each other. This class is low on comfort, privacy and security. For a detailed look at travelling on Russian trains, see Lonely Planet's *Russia & Belarus* or *Trans-Siberian Railway*.

Within Russia

European Russia is crisscrossed with an extensive rail network that makes rail a viable means of getting to practically anywhere from Moscow, since it is the main hub for service. Train journeys are cheap, comfortable and slow. If you like trains, and if you speak Russian, they're an excellent way to get around, see the countryside and meet Russians from all walks of life. Depending on the train, a 1st- or 2nd-class berth on a Russian sleeper train is often more civilised than its Western European counterpart.

Neighbouring Countries

Train fares for trips to/from Russia listed under individual countries in this section are for a berth in a four-berth compartment.

Trains to/from the Baltic countries include trains that run daily between Moscow and Tallinn (US$42, 16 hours), daily between Riga and Moscow (US$97, 15 hours), and three times weekly between Vilnius and Moscow (US$103, 15 hours). Moscow is also connected with Helsinki by a daily night train (US$105, 16 hours).

There are trains every other day running between Moscow and Baku via Rostov-on-Don (US$96, 57 hours), as well as between Moscow and Tbilisi (US$112, 72 hours). Trains run every two days between Moscow and Almaty (50 hours).

A daily service links Warsaw with Moscow (US$94, 21 hours) via Minsk. A transit visa is required for Belarus. From Moscow there are also regular international services to Belgrade, Berlin, Bratislava, Budapest, Prague, Sofia, Vienna, Venice and Warsaw.

Most major Ukrainian cities have daily services to Moscow, with two border crossings: one used by trains heading to Kyiv (Kiev), the other by trains passing through Kharkiv. Trains between Kyiv and Moscow (US$23, 14 hours, 10 services daily) go via Bryansk (Russia) and Konotop (Ukraine), crossing at the Ukrainian border town of Seredyna-Buda. The best trains to take (numbers are southbound/northbound) between Moscow and Kyiv are No 1/2, the *Ukrainia*, or No 3/4, the *Kyiv*; both travel overnight.

Daily international trains passing through Ukraine to/from Moscow's Kyivsky Vokzal include the *Slovakia Express*, Kyiv–Lviv–Chop–Bratislava–Vienna; No 15/16 Kyiv–Lviv–Chop–Budapest, with a carriage to Ve-nice twice weekly; and No 7/8, *Dukla Express*, Kyiv–Lviv–Chop–Uzhhorod–Prague.

Trains depart from Yaroslavl station every two days for the 6½-day journey to Vladivostok. The two other routes frequently called 'trans-Siberian' go to Beijing, via Mongolia and Manchuria respectively. For details, see Lonely Planet's *Trans-Siberian Railway*.

BUS

Buses run to a number of towns and cities within about 700km of Moscow. Fares are similar to the Russian fares for kupeynyy class on trains. Buses tend to be crowded, however, they are usually faster than the prigorodny trains, and are convenient to some destinations.

To book a seat you have to go out to the long-distance bus terminal, the Shchyolkovsky Avtovokzal (Шёлковский автовокзал), beside the Shchyolkovskaya metro station in the east of the city. Queues can be bad; it is generally advisable to book ahead, especially for travel on Friday, Saturday or Sunday.

Places to which it's well worth considering bus travel are those with poor train services, such as Pereslavl-Zalessky (which is not on a train line) and Vladimir (which has few afternoon trains from Moscow).

From May to October, there's a weekly direct bus service to Moscow from London's Victoria Station, Leicester and Manchester via Berlin and Minsk.

The journey, which takes just under 48 hours, costs £110/160 one-way/return from London, and £130/180 from Leicester and Manchester. Contact **Eastern European Travel Ltd** (☎ 01706-868 765, ⓔ eetravel@breathe .co.uk) for details.

From Berlin, Cologne, Hamburg, Munich and Stuttgart, it's also possible to take a coach to Riga or Tallinn, where there are direct bus connections to Moscow. For details contact **Eurolines** (ⓦ www.eurolines.com).

BOAT

In summer, passenger boats from Moscow ply the rivers and canals throughout Russia all the way north to St Petersburg, and south to Astrakhan on the Volga Delta, near the Caspian Sea.

The St Petersburg route follows the Moscow Canal and then the Volga River to the Rybinsk Reservoir; then the Volga-Baltic Canal to Lake Onega; the Svir River to Lake Ladoga; and the Neva River to St Petersburg.

The main southbound route takes the Moscow Canal north to the Volga; it then follows the Volga east before heading south all the way downstream to Astrakhan (which is nine days from Moscow), via Uglich, Yaroslavl, Kostroma, Nizhny Novgorod, Kazan, Ulyanovsk, Samara, Saratov and Volgograd.

The Moscow terminus for these sailings is the **Northern River Station** (Severny Rechnoy Vokzal; Outer North Moscow map; ☎ 459 7476; Leningradskoe sh 51). To get there, take the metro to Rechnoy Vokzal, then walk 15 minutes due west, passing under Leningradskoe shosse and through a nice park.

Capital Shipping Company (☎/fax 458 9163), as well as other boat and tour companies, operates ships between Moscow and St Petersburg that stop at some of the Golden Ring towns.

Some travel agencies specialising in cruises include:

Cruise Marketing International (toll-free ☎ 800-578 7742; ⓦ www.cruiserussia.com; 3401 Investment Blvd, Ste 3, Hayward, CA 94545-3819 USA)
Page & Moy Holidays (☎ 0116-250 7979; 136-140 London Rd, Leicester LE2 1ED UK)

ORGANISED TOURS

If you have time, and a certain degree of determination, organising your own trip to Russia is feasible. But many will appreciate the assistance of an agent in drawing up an itinerary or booking accommodation, not to mention helping with the visa paperwork. Note that arranging any extended outdoor activity such as trekking usually requires the assistance of an expert agent.

The following agencies and tour companies provide a range of travel services. Many more locally based agencies can provide tours once you're in Moscow (see the boxed text 'Want a Guide for a Day?' in the Things to See & Do chapter).

Note that Intourist is no longer the monolithic monopoly it once was (although a few bureaus may still act like it). We list some companies related to the surviving Intourist structure to some extent. They usually have an extensive selection of tours and other services available.

Australia

Eastern Europe Travel Bureau (☎ 02-9262 1144, fax 9262 4479; ⓔ eetb@optusnet.com.au) Level 5, 75 King St, Sydney, NSW 2000. Can arrange train tickets, homestays and visas and put together individual itineraries throughout Russia

Passport Travel (☎ 03-9867 3888, fax 9867 1055; Ⓦ www.travelcentre.com.au) Suite 11A, 401 St Kilda Rd, Melbourne, VIC 3004. Respected agency that can arrange visa invitations, independent itineraries, language courses and more

Russian Gateway Tours (☎ 02-9745 3333, fax 9745 3237; Ⓦ www.russian-gateway.com.au) 48 The Boulevarde, Strathfield, NSW 2135. Experienced Russia specialist with its own range of trans-Siberian tours as well as a host of accommodation packages for the major cities. It also arranges visas and individual tickets.

Canada

The Adventure Centre (☎ 416-922 7584, fax 922 8136; Ⓦ www.theadventurecentre.com) 25 Bellair St, Toronto, Ontario M5R 3L3. Canada's top adventure-tour agency also has branches in Vancouver, Edmonton and Calgary

UK

Intourist Travel (☎ 020-7538 8600, 7727 4100, fax 7727 8090; Ⓦ www.intourist.co.uk) 7 Wellington Terrace, Notting Hill, London W2 4LW. The old monopolistic Russian bureau is no longer the only kid on the Russian tourism block, but it still knows the scene well and offers all manner of packages and services

Regent Holidays (☎ 0117-921 1711, fax 925 4866; Ⓦ www.regent-holidays.co.uk) 15 John St, Bristol BS1 2HR. Often-recommended agent

with lots of experience in arranging tours and individual trips in this part of the world

Steppes East (☎ 01285-65 1010, fax 88 5888; Ⓦ www.steppeseast.co.uk) The Travel House, 51 Castle St, Cirencester, Gloscester GL7 1QD. Specialises in catering to off-beat requirements and has plenty of experience in the region, including running tours of the Golden Ring

Travel For The Arts (☎ 020-8799 8350, fax 8998 7965; Ⓦ www.travelforthearts.co.uk) 12-15 Hangar Green, London W5 3EL. Organises luxury culture-based tours to Russia and other European destinations for people with a specific interest in opera and ballet

Wallace Arnold Tours (☎ 0113-231 0739, fax 231 0563; Ⓦ www.wallacearnold.com.uk) Gelderd Rd, Leeds LS12 6DH. Operates bus tours between the UK and Russia aimed at older travellers

USA

Mir Corporation (☎ 206-624 7289, fax 624 7360; Ⓦ www.mircorp.com) 85 South Washington Street, Suite 210, Seattle, WA 98104. This agency specialises in designing special-interest trips, which focus on anything from the art of clowning to the history of brewing

Russiatours (☎ 800-633 1008, fax 251 6685; Ⓦ www.russiatours.com) 13312 N 56th St, Suite 102, Tampa, FL 33617. This agency specialises in luxurious group tours to Moscow and St Petersburg

White Nights (☎/fax 916-979 9381; Ⓦ www.concourse.net/bus/wnights) 610 La Sierra Drive, Sacramento CA 95864. Assists with purchasing tickets or obtaining visas without requiring clients to book an entire tour. It also has offices in the Netherlands, Germany and Switzerland.

Moscow Walks

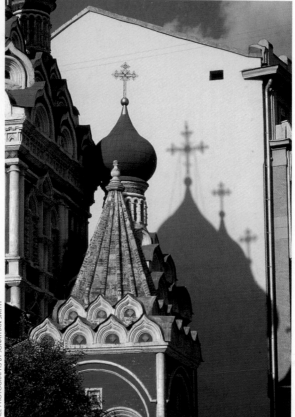

Title page: Colourful St George's Church dates from 1658

Top: Dome of the Monastery of the Epiphany and new restaurant signs on Teatralnaya ploshchad

Bottom: The Russian baroque Church of the Trinity in Nikitniki

Kitai Gorod Tour

This walking tour winds its way through Kitai Gorod, which – settled in the 13th century – is among the oldest parts of Moscow. Kitai Gorod translates as 'Chinatown', but the name actually derives from *kita*, meaning 'wattle'. It refers to the palisades that reinforced the earthen ramp erected around this early Kremlin suburb. Kitai Gorod was an active trade and financial centre. Records from the 17th century show that this area contained 72 rows of trading arcades. Present-day street names such as Khrustalny pereulok (Crystal lane) and Vetoshny pereulok (Carpet lane) remain from that era. Even more intriguing are the old city wall and the tiny, colourful churches – remains of which pepper the narrow streets of Kitai Gorod.

KITAI GOROD TOUR

1 Starye Polya
2 No 17 ulitsa Nikolskaya, Slavyansky Bazaar
3 No 15 ulitsa Nikolskaya, Synod Printing House
4 Nos 7-9 ulitsa Nikolskaya, Zaikonospassky Monastery
5 No 2 Bogoyavlensky pereulok, Monastrey of the Epiphany
6 Arshinov Trading House
7 No 4 Staropasny pereulok, Cathedral of Sts Kostya & Damian in the Old Pan
8 No 6 ulitsa Ilyinka, Old Stock Exchange
9 No 3 ulitsa Ilyinka, Cathedral of the Holy Prophet Ilyn
10 Old Merchants' Court
11 St Barbara's Church
12 English House
13 No 4 ulitsa Varvarka, Church of St Maxim the Blessed
14 No 8 ulitsa Varvarka, Monastery of the Sign
15 Hotel Rossiya
16 No 10 ulitsa Varvarka, Chambers in Zaryadie Museum
17 Cathedral of St Nicholas 'Beautiful Sound'
18 Church of the Trinity in Nikitniki
19 No 12 ulitsa Varvarka, St George's Church
20 All Saints Cathedral on the Kulishka

Start at the Hotel Metropol and walk east down Teatralny proezd to the stately gate which leads down Tretyakovsky proezd.

This historical and architectural complex is *Starye Polya* (Old Fields), probably because it was a gateway out of the city, so the area outside the wall was largely undeveloped. In 1999, archaeologists uncovered the 16th-century **fortified wall** which used to surround Kitai-Gorod, and the foundations of the 1493 **Trinity Church**, destroyed in 1934. Coins, jewellery and tombstones were excavated from the site. Besides the remains of the wall and the church, you can now see the memorial statue of Ivan Fedorov, the 16th-century printer who is responsible for Russia's first book. The gated walkway **Tretyakovsky Proezd** leads into Kitai Gorod.

Walk down Tretyakovsky proezd to ulitsa Nikolskaya, Kitai Gorod's busiest street. Turn right to head west on Nikolskaya.

Ulitsa Nikolskaya used to be the main road to Vladimir. Home to three monasteries, it was also the centre of a busy trade in icons.

The ornate building at **No 17** was formerly a hotel known as the Slavyansky Bazaar. Here, in 1897, directors Stanislavsky and Nemirovich held their celebrated and extended meeting, during which they founded the MKhAT theatre (see the boxed text 'Stanislavsky's Methods' in the Entertainment chapter). The famous hotel is also featured in the Chekhov short story, *The Lady with a Lapdog*, as the hotel where Gurov's lover stays when she comes to Moscow.

The green and white building, with the lion and unicorn above its entrance at **No 15**, is the Synod Printing House. This is where Ivan Fyodorov reputedly produced Russia's first printed book, *The Apostle*, in 1563. Over a century later, in 1703, the first Russian newspaper *Vedomosti* was also printed here. Up until the early 19th century, Kitai Gorod was something of a printing centre, home to 26 out of Moscow's 31 bookshops at the time.

The Zaikonospassky Monastery at **Nos 7–9** was founded by Boris Godunov in 1600, although the church was built in 1660. The name means 'behind the icon stall', a reference to the busy icon trade which took place here. On the orders of Tsar Alexei, the Likhud brothers, scholars of Greek, opened the Slavonic Greek and Latin Academy on the monastery premises in 1866. Mikhail Lomonosov was a student here. The school later became a divinity school, and was transferred to the Trinity Monastery of St Sergius (Sergiev Posad) in 1814.

Turn left on Bogoyavlensky pereulok and head south.

The Monastery of the Epiphany at **No 2**, the second oldest in Moscow, was founded in 1296 by Prince Daniil, son of Alexander Nevsky. One of the first abbots of the monastery was Stefan, the brother of Sergei Radonezhsky (patron saint of Russia and founder of the Trinity Monastery of St Sergius). The present Epiphany Cathedral was constructed in the 1690s in the Moscow baroque style. If you are lucky, you might catch a concert (or rehearsal) performed in the bell tower.

Turn left and walk east on Staropasny pereulok.

This tiny street holds a few hidden gems. The Cathedral of Saints Kostya and Damian in the Old Pan at **No 4** takes its name from the old word 'pan', or Polish landowner, referring to this property's 16th-century status. The wooden section of the church dates to 1468. The entire thing was hidden by scaffolding at the time of research, but it promises to be a treat when renovations are complete. Across the street, the old **Arshinov Trading House** (Torgovy Dom Arshinova) was designed by Art Nouveau architect Fyodor Shekhtel, who designed the Gorky House-Museum.

Turn right on Bolshoy Cherkassky pereulok and head south. Take an immediate right on ulitsa Ilyinka.

As you walk back down towards Red Square, notice the exquisite details on the buildings on the south side of the street. Ulitsa Ilyinka was Moscow's financial heart in the 18th and 19th centuries. At **No 6,** at the corner of Rybny pereulok, is the old Stock Exchange, built in the 1870s; it now houses the Chamber of Commerce and Industry.

At **No 3**, the tiny Cathedral of St Ilyn the Prophet of God is another one that is undergoing renovation, but the interior is open. The exposed brick and eroding walls give an air of authenticity to this 1519 church, among the oldest in Moscow.

Turn left and walk down Khrustalny pereulok.

The **Old Merchants' Court** (Stary Gostinny Dvor), which occupies the block between ulitsas Ilyinka and Varvarka, has been renovated for shops and restaurants.

Take another left and head east on ulitsa Varvarka, which is crowded with tiny churches, old homes and the giant Hotel Rossiya.

The pink and white **St Barbara's Church** (Tserkov Varvary; Map 2), now government offices, dates from the years 1795 to 1804. Like its predecessor on this site, it was a merchants' church, built with funds donated by the rich traders who lived in the nearby Zaryadie region.

The reconstructed 16th-century **English House** (Palaty starogo angliyskogo dvora; Map 2; ☎ 298 3952; admission RR20; open 11am-6pm Tues-Sun), white with peaked wooden roofs, was the residence of England's first emissaries to Russia (sent by Elizabeth I to Ivan the Terrible). It also served as the base for English merchants who were allowed to trade duty free, in exchange for providing military supplies to Ivan.

Built in 1698, the **Church of St Maxim the Blessed** (Tserkov Maxima Blazhennogo; Map 2; ul Varvarka 4) is now a folk-art exhibition hall. Next along is the pointed bell tower of the 17th-century **Monastery of the Sign** (Znamensky monastyr; Map 2; ul Varvarka 8). Between the street and the western half of Hotel Rossiya's access ramp are the monastery's monks' building and a **golden-domed cathedral**.

Between the street and the eastern half of the ramp is the small but interesting **Chambers in Zaryadie Museum** (Muzey Palaty v Zaryadie; Map 2; ul Varvarka 10; admission RR100; open 10am-5pm Thur-Mon, 11am-6pm Wed), devoted to the lives of the Romanov family before they became tsars and were mere *boyars* (high-ranking nobles). The house was built by Nikita Romanov, whose grandson Mikhail later became the first of the 300-year Romanov dynasty. The entrance is on the Hotel Rossiya side. It is closed on the first Monday of the month.

The colourful **St George's Church** (Tserkov Georgiya; Map 2; ul Varvarka 12), another crafts gallery, dates from 1658.

Walk around to the southeastern corner of the Hotel Rossiya, where the back drive overlooks the Moscow River.

Look down on the pretty little 15th- and 16th-century, Pskov-style **Church of St Anne's Conception** (Tserkov Zachatiya Anny; Map 4). From here there are incredible views of the Kremlin, Moscow River and the Kotelnicheskaya apartment complex, one of Stalin's 'Seven Sisters'.

Back on ulitsa Varvarka, cross the street and walk up Nikolsky pereulok.

The 1561 **Cathedral of St Nicholas 'Beautiful Sound'** (Khram Svyatitelya Nikolaya 'Krasny Zvon') at No 7 earned its name after the installation of its sweet-sounding bells in 1573.

Back on ulitsa Varvarka, walk up Ipatyevsky pereulok which is across from St George's Church.

The 1630s **Church of the Trinity in Nikitniki** (Tserkov Troitsy v Nikitnikakh; Map 2) is a fine example of Russian baroque. Its onion domes and lovely tiers of red and white spade gables rise from a square tower. Closed for renovation at the time of research, the interior is covered with 1650s' gospel frescoes by Simon Ushakov and others. A carved doorway leads into St Nikita the Martyr's chapel, above the vault of the Nikitnikov merchant family, one of whom built the church.

Head east on Ipatevsky pereulok out to Staraya ploshchad.

At the southern end of Staraya Ploshchad, **All Saints Cathedral on the Kulishka** (Khram vsekh svyatikh na Kulishkakh) was built in 1687. In 1380, Dmitry Donskoy built the original wooden church on this site to commemorate those who died in the battle of Kulikovo.

Some remains of the old city wall can be seen in the underground passage at the corner of ulitsa Varvarka and Staraya ploshchad. This *perekhod* (cross walk) is also the entrance to the Kitai Gorod metro stop.

Literary Tour

This walk provides a chance to see some original settings from Russian literature, as well as the environs where various authors and poets lived and worked. At the same time, the walk passes through several neighbourhoods with prime examples from over 300 years of Russian architecture. The tour covers the area to the northwest of the Kremlin, between the Boulevard Ring and the Garden Ring, known from the 17th century as Zemlyanoy Gorod.

Start from Pushkinskaya Square at the west side of Tverskaya Street. Take the promenade in the middle of the park between two lanes of traffic, Tverskoy bulvar, and walk west.

Tverskoy bulvar was the most popular walking street from the 18th century; even the Shcherbitskiye sisters in Leo Tolstoy's *Anna Karenina* promenaded here. On the south side, the 19th-century, salmon-coloured **No 26A** now houses the exquisite *haute russe* cuisine Café Pushkin. Yellow **Nos 26** and **24** date from 18th-century Moscow and belonged to a noble family close to Catherine II.

No 23 on the north side, a classical Russian Empire-style mansion, houses the Pushkin Drama Theatre. The huge brown block at **No 22** is

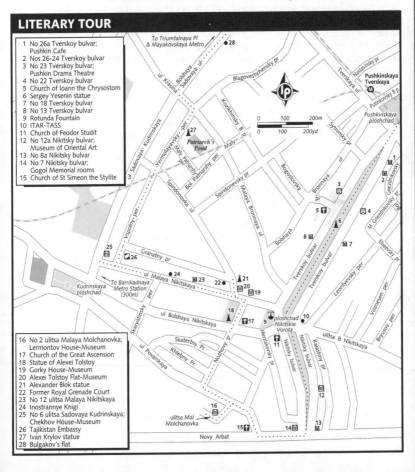

LITERARY TOUR

1 No 26a Tverskoy bulvar;
   Pushkin Cafe
2 Nos 26-24 Tverskoy bulvar
3 No 23 Tverskoy bulvar;
   Pushkin Drama Theatre
4 No 22 Tverskoy bulvar
5 Church of Ioann the Chrysostom
6 Sergey Yesenin statue
7 No 18 Tverskoy bulvar
8 No 13 Tverskoy bulvar
9 Rotunda Fountain
10 ITAR-TASS
11 Church of Feodor Studit
12 No 12a Nikitsky bulvar;
   Museum of Oriental Art
13 No 8a Nikitsky bulvar
14 No 7 Nikitsky bulvar;
   Gogol Memorial rooms
15 Church of St Simeon the Stylite

16 No 2 ulitsa Malaya Molchanovka;
   Lermontov House-Museum
17 Church of the Great Ascension
18 Statue of Alexei Tolstoy
19 Gorky House-Museum
20 Alexei Tolstoy Flat-Museum
21 Alexander Blok statue
22 Former Royal Grenade Court
23 No 12 ulitsa Malaya Nikitskaya
24 Inostrannye Knigi
25 No 6 ulitsa Sadovaya Kudrinskaya;
   Chekhov House-Museum
26 Tajikistan Embassy
27 Ivan Krylov statue
28 Bulgakov's flat

the new building of the MKhAT (Moscow Art Theatre) named after Maxim Gorky (see the Entertainment chapter for details on these theatres). Previously on this site stood the house of Praskova Yurevna, a socialite who was very fond of hosting extravagant balls and opera performances. One of these infamous events is supposedly where Alexander Pushkin first met his future wife Natalya Goncharova.

Hidden behind other buildings on the north side is the 17th-century **Church of Ioann Chrysostom** (Tserkov Ioanna Bogoslova), which was commissioned by Mikhail Romanov to house the *Icon of Ioanna Bogoslova*. The church was taken over by the Pushkin Drama Theatre during the Soviet period, and the fate of the icon is unknown.

In the middle of the boulevard is a **statue of Sergei Yesenin**, an early-20th-century poet who was in and out of favour throughout the Soviet era. Writing about love and landscapes earned him the nickname 'the peasant poet'.

His short, stormy life was torn apart by no less than five marriages and violent bouts with alcoholism. He finally ended his own life in 1925 at the age of 30.

Further down, note the Art Nouveau style of **No 18**; the formidable edifice and Russian Empire features of Promstroybank at **No 13**; and the elegant apartment buildings from the early 1900s. At the foot of the street, the grey cube on the east side of the intersection is the famous TASS news agency that's now known as ITAR-TASS. Its windows usually feature fantastic photographs of the week's headline stories.

On the west side of the intersection is one of the most beautiful squares in Moscow. **Nikitskie Vorota** (Nikitskie Gates) takes its name from the gates of a wall that stood here from the 15th to the 18th centuries. At the corner of the square, the **Rotunda Fountain**, by the tireless Zurab Tsereteli, hides a statue of Pushkin and Goncharova, erected in 1999 to celebrate the poet's birthday.

South of the square, the beautiful **Church of Feodor Studit** (Tserkov Feodora Studita) is all that remains of a 17th-century monastery that was founded by the Patriarch Filaret. The enchanting white bell tower is a 1990s' replica of the original.

Continue south on the Boulevard ring, now called Nikitsky bulvar.

The classical building at **No 12A** now houses the Museum of Oriental Art, but it was built for the musical Lunin family. The moulded lyre on the front of the elegant house is a symbol of the many musical evenings which took place here.

The quiet courtyard at **No 7** contains a statue of an emaciated, gloomy Nikolai Gogol, surrounded by some of his better-known characters in bas-relief around the base. The building on the right houses the **Gogol Memorial Rooms**, where the writer spent his final, tortured months.

The rooms – now a small but captivating museum – are arranged as they were when Gogol lived here. You can even see the fireplace where he infamously threw his manuscript of *Dead Souls*. For details, see Arbat Region in the Things to See & Do chapter.

Across the street at **No 8A** is an 18th-century mansion which was formerly home to Colonel Kiselyov, a fanatic of literature and a friend of Pushkin. Apparently, Pushkin and Goncharova attended a ball at the colonel's home on the day after their wedding in 1831. During the Soviet period, this building became the House of the Press, and writers such as Yesinin, Blok and Mayakovsky all presented their work here. In 1925, just two months after Yesinin recited his poem *Flowers* here, his fans returned to pay him their last respects.

Proceed down to ulitsa Novy Arbat and turn right. Head west for one block.

The 17th-century **Church of St Simeon the Stylite** (tserkov Simeona Stolpnika) was Gogol's regular parish church. It was also the scene of the wedding of 19th-century writer Ivan Aksakov to Olga Zaplatina.

Head north on ulitsa Povarskaya and take the first left on ulitsa Malaya Molchanovka.

The pink house at **No 2** was home to Mikhail Lermontov, author of *A Hero of Our Time*. For details on the house-museum, see Arbat Region in the Things to See & Do chapter.

Return to ulitsa Povarskaya and turn left, heading northwest.

Ulitsa Povarskaya (Cooks' street) was once inhabited by the royal court's cooks. The names of the lanes in this area still evoke the Tsar's kitchen: Stolovy (dining room), Skatertny (table cloth), Khlebny (bread) and Nozhovy (cutlery). During the reign of Peter the Great, the cooks' settlement was abolished. The area was taken over completely by nobility, whose fancy homes still line the streets. Many of the buildings now house foreign embassies.

Turn right on Nozhovy pereulok and head north. Cross ulitsa Bolshaya Nikitskaya.

The graceful **Church of the Great Ascension** was built between 1798 and 1816 by Vasily Bazhenov and Matvei Kazakov. Here Pushkin married Goncharova in 1831.

A lesser-known Tolstoy (and distant relative of Leo), Alexei Tolstoy stands in the small park across the lane. Also a writer, Alexei Tolstoy is known primarily for his 20th-century novels about the Civil War and the revolution, the most famous being the trilogy *The Ordeal*.

Continue north on Nozhovy pereulok until it ends at ulitsa Malaya Nikitskaya.

Across ulitsa Malaya Nikitskaya, from the Church of the Great Ascension, is an Art Nouveau masterpiece at **No 6/2** that once was the house of a wealthy merchant, Stepan Ryabushinksy. Designed by Fyodor Shekhtel, with mosaics by Mikhail Vrubel, the house was later gifted to writer Maxim Gorky, who often complained about the decor's extravagance. The building still houses his museum, but is worth visiting for its fantastical interior (see Tverskoy Region in the Things to See & Do chapter).

From ulitsa Malaya Nikitskaya, take an immediate right and head north on ulitsa Spiridonovka.

Behind the Ryabushinsky mansion is the flat where Alexei Tolstoy lived. Across the street is a group of whitewashed houses dating from the 17th century. They used to be the charmingly named 'Palaty Granatnogo Dvora' (Chambers of the Grenade Court), where grenades and other explosives for the Russian royal army were made.

The statue of another early-20th-century poet, Alexander Blok, stands a bit further up ulitsa Spiridonovka. The revolutionary Blok believed that individualism had caused a decline in society's ethics, a situation which would only be rectified by a communist revolution.

Head back to ulitsa Malaya Nikitskaya and turn right.

This quiet, shady area is lined with some lovely examples of Russia's prerevolutionary architecture. The 18th-century classical estate at **No 12** once belonged to the Bobrinsky family. It was also depicted by Alexander Pushkin as the Larins' house in *Yevgeny Onegin*. **No 16** houses the Inostrannye Knigi shop. The name means 'foreign books', but don't be misled; it's more like an antique shop full of treasures. See the Shopping chapter for details.

At the end of ulitsa Malaya Nikitskaya, turn right onto the Garden Ring.

The 19th-century writer Anton Chekhov lived and worked at **No 6** ulitsa Sadovya Kudrinskaya. Now a museum dedicated to the writer (see Barrikadnaya in the Things to See & Do chapter), this house is where he composed such masterpieces as *Three Sisters* and *The Seagull*. Chekhov himself described his style: 'All I wanted was to say honestly to people: Have a look at yourselves and see how bad and dreary your lives are! The important thing is that people should realize that, for when they do, they will most certainly create another and better life for themselves.'

Head back on ulitsa Malaya Nikitskaya. Take the first left and walk north on Vspolny pereulok.

The lovely early-20th-century house at the corner of Granatny pereulok, **No 13**, now houses the Tajikistan Embassy.

At the intersection with ulitsa Spiridonovka, the name changes to Yermolayevsky. Proceed another 200m to reach the Patriarch's Ponds.

The small park to the west of the pond has a huge statue of 19th-century Russian writer Ivan Krylov, known to every Russian child for his didactic tales. Scenes from his stories surround the statue of the writer.

Once this area contained several ponds which kept fish for the Patriarch's court (thus the name). This peaceful fishpond (Patriarshy prudy) was immortalised by writer Mikhail Bulgakov, who had the devil appear here in *The Master and Margarita*, one of the most loved 20th-century Russian novels.

The area to the north of the pond is described in the initial paragraph of the novel, when the devil enters the scene and predicts the rapid death of Berlioz.

Turn left on ulitsa Malaya Krasina and head out to the Garden Ring. Turn right and walk one block north.

The otherwise nondescript building at **No 10** is Bulgakov's flat where he wrote the novel and lived up until his death. Although the empty flat used to be a hang-out for dissidents and hooligans, now the building has tight security appropriate for this high-rent district.

Up ahead is Triumfalnaya ploshchad, previously named for the poet and playwright Vladimir Mayakovsky, whose statue stands in its centre. A favourite of the Bolshevik regime, Mayakovsky sought to demystify poetry, adopting crude language and ignoring traditional poetic techniques.

Grand Houses Tour

Hordes of tourists, both domestic and foreign, dutifully tread the cobblestones of the Arbat. Packed with souvenir stalls and overpriced cafés, ulitsa Arbat is unlike anywhere else in Moscow. But while the idea of a walking street was an exciting concept in the 1980s, the entire street is fading a bit as entertainment options throughout the city have proliferated.

However, just off the well-worn cobblestones lie the quiet lanes of old Arbat where you can still get a feel for 19th-century Moscow, a city inhabited by writers and their heroes, old nobles and the nouveau riche. The era and its people are long gone, but you can still sense them in the grand houses they left behind.

The tour starts at the east end of the Arbat (metro: Arbatskaya).

Walk westwards along ulitsa Arbat and turn south into Starokonyushenny pereulok.

The green, wooden house at **No 38** – covered in scaffolding at the time of research – should be exquisite when the renovation is complete.

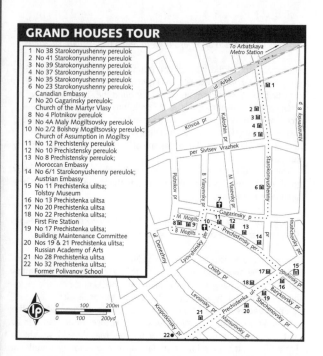

GRAND HOUSES TOUR

1 No 38 Starokonyushenny pereulok
2 No 41 Starokonyushenny pereulok
3 No 39 Starokonyushenny pereulok
4 No 37 Starokonyushenny pereulok
5 No 35 Starokonyushenny pereulok
6 No 23 Starokonyushenny pereulok;
   Canadian Embassy
7 No 20 Gagarinsky pereulok;
   Church of the Martyr Vlasy
8 No 4 Plotnikov pereulok
9 No 4A Maly Mogiltsovsky pereulok
10 No 2/2 Bolshoy Mogiltsovsky pereulok;
   Church of Assumption in Mogiltsy
11 No 12 Prechistenky pereulok
12 No 10 Prechistenky pereulok
13 No 8 Prechistensky pereulok;
   Moroccan Embassy
14 No 6/1 Starokonyushenny pereulok;
   Austrian Embassy
15 No 11 Prechistenka ulitsa;
   Tolstoy Museum
16 No 13 Prechistenka ulitsa
17 No 20 Prechistenka ulitsa
18 No 22 Prechistenka ulitsa;
   First Fire Station
19 No 17 Prechistenka ulitsa;
   Building Maintenance Committee
20 Nos 19 & 21 Prechistenka ulitsa;
   Russian Academy of Arts
21 No 28 Prechistenka ulitsa
22 No 32 Prechistenka ulitsa;
   Former Polivanov School

Otherwise, you can ignore the east side of the street. The west side has much more to offer: the tile work of **No 41**, the somewhat disproportionate sculptures supporting the balconies of **No 39**, the imitation rough stone of **No 37** and the neo-Empire style of **No 35** that all read like a textbook of Art Nouveau. These are the so-called *dokhodnye doma*, the flats built for rich professionals who couldn't afford their own house, but were wealthy enough to afford the luxury of a spacious and stylish apartment. In the next block, on the right, and dating from the late 19th century, **No 23** is now the Canadian Embassy.

Turn right and head west on Gagarinsky pereulok.
Hidden in the yard at **No 20** is the Church of the Martyr Vlasy (Tserkov Velikomuchenika Vlasiya). The church itself dates from the 17th century, and the refectory and bell tower are from the 19th century.

Turn south into Bolshoy Vlasyevsky pereulok making another turn west and proceeding along Maly Mogiltsovsky pereulok.

Notice the subdued shade of green stucco decorations of **No 4A**.

Turn south on Plotnikov pereulok once you reach the end of the lane.

The frieze at **No 4** has frivolous full-sized reliefs of Tolstoy, Pushkin, Gogol and others, all enjoying the company of Greek gods. The building, erected in 1907 by the architect Zherikhov, is said to have housed a brothel popular with Moscow's political and intellectual elite.

Turn left and walk east along Bolshoy Mogiltsovsky pereulok.

At **No 2/2** you'll find the run-down 18th-century Church of Assumption in Mogiltsy. According to Leo Tolstoy, this is the church Natasha Rostova attended.

Walk around the church in a counterclockwise direction till you reach Prechistenky pereulok. Turn right and proceed westward along the lane.

In 1930–32, the Moscow writer Ostrovsky lived in **No 12**, where he wrote *How the Steel was Tempered*. At the time of research, the dilapidated, but still elegant, Art Nouveau mansion at **No 10** was being renovated for a private residence. Nearby, **No 8**, now housing the Moroccan Embassy, was built by the architect Valcott, who also designed Hotel Metropol. The affluent mansion at **No 6/1** is the **Austrian Embassy**.

As the lane slightly bends south, proceed along it till you reach the crossroads. Now you are at your ultimate destination, Prechistenka ulitsa, running from the northeast to the southwest and connecting the Boulevard and Garden Rings. Catch your breath as you prepare to see a dozen of the loveliest buildings from the 17th to the early 20th centuries clustered along one street. Turn southwest on Prechistenka ulitsa.

On the west side at **No 11** the former Lopukhin mansion now houses the Tolstoy Museum (see Arbat Region in the Things to See & Do chapter). A member of the Fabergé family lived in one of the luxurious apartments at **No 13**.

In 1917, he fled Russia in a hurry, leaving all his belongings behind, which gave rise to rumours that there were treasures hidden in the walls of the apartment. And, in fact, there were. In the late 1970s a cache of silver was found during planned repairs.

Opulent **No 20** once belonged to the 1812 Napoleon war hero General Yermolov. Later, the millionaire Ushkov purchased the house and completely rebuilt it according to the tastes of his wife, the finicky prima ballerina Alexandra Balashovaya. **No 22** dates back to the 18th century, but is best known as the first Moscow fire station, which was founded here in 1835.

No 17, on the east side, once belonged to Denis Davydov, another hero of the Napoleonic Wars. It now houses the city's Building Maintenance Committee. Appropriately enough, the building was undergoing maintenance at the time of research.

No 19, the home of the Russian Academy of Arts, is a masterpiece by Lev Kekushev. The last owner, before the revolution, of the red, neo-Russian building next door at **No 21** was the industrialist Morozov. This great lover of impressionist art rebuilt this mansion to house his famous art collection. The collection now belongs to the Academy, as does this building.

The luxurious, early-20th-century *dokhodny dom* at **No 28**, again by Kekushev, is generously decorated with sculptures, stucco, iron grilles and other details. The building at **No 32** used to house the private men's school Polivanov. The famed school's students included the poet Bryusov, the artist Golovin, and the first Russian world champion chess master, Alexin.

Farther south is the noisy Garden Ring, from where Park Kultury metro is a short walk east.

Getting Around

The central area around the Kremlin, the Kitai Gorod and the Bolshoi Theatre are best seen on foot. To almost anywhere else, the fastest, cheapest and easiest way to get around is on the metro and on foot, though buses, trolleybuses and trams come in handy sometimes.

TO/FROM THE AIRPORTS

For information about the airports and flights to/from Moscow, see the Getting There & Away chapter.

You can get between all five airports and the city centre cheaply by a combination of bus and metro or suburban train. If you're in a hurry, going early in the morning or late at night, or have a lot of baggage, you'll probably need a taxi.

The easiest and surest way to get from any airport into the city is to book your transfer in advance through a travel agent. The driver will meet your flight with a sign and drive you straight from the airport to your destination in the city. You may not have to pay any more than a normal taxi fare (eg, G&R International charges US$25 for transfers to/from Sheremetevo-2). Some travel firms have airport desks where you can book transfers on the spot.

When you're leaving Moscow, your hotel or accommodation will always be able to arrange a taxi for you, but you may be able to get one cheaper yourself. See Taxi later in this chapter for information on ordering one.

You can avoid the hassle of a taxi by using the metro or suburban trains, in conjunction with minivan services, for all five airports. Not only do you save money, but during times of heavy traffic you save time as well. The only disadvantage is that the minivans only leave when full, and don't have much room for luggage.

The **City Air Terminal** *(Gorodskoy aerovokzal; Outer North Moscow map; Leningradsky pr 37)* has bus services to/from all the airports. However, the terminal itself is hard to reach, as it is almost 1km from Dinamo,

the nearest metro. Also, bus services from the terminal are infrequent and confusing.

Sheremetevo

At Sheremetevo-2, the minibuses leave from a special area 200m in front of the terminal. Walk straight out of the arrivals area and to the right around the car park, staying inside the auto ramp. The bus stop has a small shelter and lies between the auto ramps leading to/from the upper departures level.

Minibuses go between Rechnoy Vokzal and Sheremetevo-1, with Sheremetevo-2 the middle stop in either direction (so make certain you get a minibus going in the right direction from Sheremetevo-2). They make the journey as soon as they are full, which is about every 30 minutes or less.

At Rechnoy Vokzal, leave the metro platform by the exit at the front end of your train. Walk 100m straight ahead, out of the metro station to the road, where the minivans are waiting. The combined metro/minivan trip, to or from Sheremetevo-2, takes about one hour; Sheremetevo-1 takes 70 minutes.

Large, blue Aeroflot buses follow the same route and charge about the same amount, but they run less frequently. City bus No 551 also follows this route, but it makes many stops and takes much longer.

A taxi arranged on the spot, between Sheremetevo airports and the city centre, takes about 45 minutes. You should pay around RR1000, though absurd prices may be asked of tourists. If you speak Russian and you can haggle, you may negotiate the price down to RR500 or so. A better bet is to arrange one in advance from **Logus 88** *(☎ 911 9747)*, which charges RR500/800 for a prebooked car to/from the Sheremetevo airports. **Taxi Bistro** *(☎ 324 9974, 324 5144)* is even cheaper, charging RR450 to the airport, or RR120 per hour otherwise.

Domodedovo

As of 2002, a brand new express train leaves Pavelets Station every two hours for

GETTING AROUND

Domodedovo airport. A one-way trip costs RR30 and takes about 45 minutes. This route is particularly convenient, as you can check in for your flight at the train station.

The airport is linked to Domodedovskaya metro by minibuses, from about 7am to 9pm. The trip takes 30 to 40 minutes. Going out to the airport, you should allow 90 minutes for the combined metro/minibus trip.

A taxi to/from the city centre should cost about RR1000. The trip takes one to 1½ hours, depending on traffic.

Bykovo

Suburban (prigorodnye) trains run between Bykovo train station, 400m from the airport, and Kazan Station in the city. One of their stops en route is Vykhino, by Vykhino metro.

Going out to the airport, most trains heading for Vinogradovo, Shifernaya or Golutvin, stop at Bykovo (as well as those marked 'Bykovo'), but just a few go straight through, so always check. The trains, which take about one hour, go about every 20 minutes from 5am to 10pm.

A taxi to/from the city centre is about RR1000 and can take 1½ hours.

Vnukovo

Minibuses link the airport with the Yugo-Zapadnaya metro, from about 7am to 9pm. The trip takes 30 minutes and costs RR15. A taxi to/from the city centre costs about RR1000 and can take over an hour.

TRAIN

One important distinction to grasp when taking trains from Moscow is the difference between long-distance and 'suburban' trains.

Long-distance trains run to places at least three or four hours out of Moscow, with limited stops and a range of accommodation classes (see Train in the Getting There & Away chapter).

Suburban trains, known as *prigorodnye poezdy* or *elektrichky*, run to within just 100km or 200km of Moscow, stop almost everywhere, and have a single class of hard bench seats. You simply buy your ticket before the train leaves, and there's no limit on

capacity – so you may have to stand for part of the way. Most Moscow stations have a separate ticket hall for suburban trains, usually called the *prigorodny zal* and often tucked away at the side or back of the station building. Suburban trains are also usually listed on separate timetables, and may go from a separate group of platforms.

Suburban train services from Moscow's nine main stations (with their accompanying metro stations given) are:

Belorussia Station (Belorussky vokzal; Map 2; Tverskaya Zastava ploshchad; metro: Belorusskaya) To/from the west including Mozhaysk, Borodino, Zvenigorod

Kazan Station (Kazansky vokzal; Map 3; Komsomolskaya ploshchad; metro: Komsomolskaya) To/from the southeast including Bykovo airport, Kolomna, Gzhel, Ryazan

Kursk Station (Kursky vokzal; Map 3; ploshchad Kurskogo Vokzala; metro: Kurskaya) To/from the east and south including Petushki, Vladimir, Podolsk, Chekhov, Serpukhov, Tula

Kiev Station (Kievsky vokzal; Map 4; ploshchad Kievskogo vokzala; metro: Kievskaya) To/from the southwest including Peredelkino, Kaluga

Leningrad Station (Leningradsky vokzal; Map 3; Komsomolskaya ploshchad; metro: Komsomolskaya) To/from the northwest including Klin, Tver

Pavelets Station (Paveletsky vokzal; Map 5; Paveletskaya ploshchad; metro: Paveletskaya) To/from the southeast including Domodedovo airport

Riga Station (Rizhsky vokzal; Outer North Moscow map; Rizhskaya ploshchad; metro: Rizhskaya) To/from the northwest including Istra, Novoierusalimskaya

Savyolov Station (Savyolovsky vokzal; Outer North Moscow map; ploshchad Savyolovskogo vokzala; metro: Savyolovskaya) To/from the north

Yaroslavl Station (Yaroslavsky vokzal; Map 3; Komsomolskaya ploshchad; metro: Komsomolskaya) To/from the northeast including Abramtsevo, Khotkovo, Sergiev Posad, Alexandrov

METRO

The metro is the easiest, quickest and cheapest way of getting around Moscow. With elegant, graffiti-free stations – many of them marble-faced, frescoed, gilded works of art – this is one Stalinist project

Reading a Train Timetable

Russian train timetables usually list destination, train number, category of train, frequency of service, and time of departure and arrival.

Trains in smaller city stations generally begin somewhere else, so you'll see a starting point and a destination on the timetable. For example, when catching a train from Klin to Tver, the timetable may list Moscow as an origination point and Tver as the destination. The following are a few key points to look out for.

Number
The higher the number, Номер (*Nomer*), of a train, the slower it is; anything over 900 is likely to be a mail train.

Category
Скорый (*Skory*, fast), Пассажирский (*Passazhirsky*, passenger), Почтовый-багажный (*Pochtovy-bagazhny*, post-cargo), Пригородный (*Prigorodny*, suburban) and various abbreviations thereof, are train categories. There may also be the name of the train, usually in Russian quotation marks, eg, "Нижегородец" (*'Nizhegorodets'*).

Frequency
Ежедневно (*yezhednevno*, daily), чётные (*chyotnye*, even dates), нечётные (*nechyotnye*, odd dates), and отменён (*otmenyon*, cancelled) may also appear in various abbreviations. Days of the week are listed usually as numbers (where 1 is Monday and 7 Sunday) or as abbreviations of the name of the day (Пон, Вт, Ср, Чт, Пт, С, and Вск are, respectively, Monday to Sunday).

On some trains, frequency depends on the time of year, in which case details are usually given in hard-to-decipher, abbreviated, small print, eg, '27/VI – 31/VIII X; 1/IX – 25/VI 2,5' means that from 27 June to 31 August the train runs on even dates, while from 1 September to 25 June it runs on Tuesday and Friday.

Arrival & Departure Times
Most train times are given in a 24-hour time format, and almost always in Moscow time (Московское время, *Moskovskoe vremya*). But suburban trains are usually marked in local time (местное время, *mestnoe vremya*). From here in it gets tricky (as though the rest wasn't), so don't confuse the following:

время отправления (*vremya otpravlenia*), which means time of departure
время отправления с началного пункта (*vremya otpravlenia s nachalnogo punkta*), the time of departure from the train's starting point
время прибытия (*vremya pribytia*), the time of arrival at the station you're in
время прибытия на конечный пункт (*vremya pribytia na konechny punkt*), the time of arrival at the destination
время в пути (*vremya v puti*), the duration of the journey

Corresponding trains running in opposite directions on the same route, may appear on the same line of the timetable. If so, you may find route entries such as время отправления с конечного пункта (*vremya otpravlenia s konechnogo punkta*), or the time the return train leaves its station of origin.

Distance
You may sometimes see the растояние (*rastoyanie*) – distance in kilometres – on the timetable as well, but it's usually wrong.

Muscovites are proud of, and nine million of them use it every day. The stations were meant to double as air-raid shelters, which is why escalators seem to plunge halfway to the centre of the earth.

The 150-plus stations are marked outside with big 'M' signs. Magnetic tickets are sold at ticket booths for one, two, or more rides. Each ride costs RR5, unless you buy in bulk (10 rides for RR35, 20 for RR70, 60 for RR150). Insert your ticket into the gate and when the green light illuminates, take your ticket and walk on. If you go too soon, bars will pop across your path.

Underground Art

The Moscow metro is justly famous for the art and design of many of its stations. The circular line is a tourist attraction in its own right. All the stations are done in marble and decorated in bas-reliefs, stucco, mosaics and chandeliers. Diversity of theme is not the strong point here: it's history, war, the happy life of Soviet people, or a mix of all. The highlights of the circular line stations are as follows:

Taganskaya Features a war theme with the heads of unknown war heroes set in luscious floral stucco frames made of white and blue porcelain with gold linings

Prospekt Mira Also decorated in elegant gold-trimmed white porcelain, but the bas-reliefs receive some development and action. It's no longer just some motionless heads, but happy farmers picking fruit, children reading books etc.

Novoslobodskaya Has brightly illuminated stained-glass panels with happy workers, farmers and even more flowers. There is also a pianist, an artist, and someone sitting at the desk by the globe. Who might that be?

Belorusskaya Has mosaics on the ceiling with the same happy workers and farmers, and more action. They are milking cows, dancing, taking oaths and more. All of them are undoubtedly Belarusians, as they all happen to wear national Belarusian shirts for the occasion.

Komsomolskaya Has a huge stuccoed hall, the ceiling featuring the mosaics of past Russian military heroes including Peter the Great, Dmitry Donskoy, and Alexander Suvorov

Barrikadnaya Done in dramatic red and white marble and has bas-reliefs depicting the fateful events of 1905 and 1917

Kievskaya This is good, as you don't have to break your neck looking at the ceiling. The hall is decorated in mosaics that are all labelled. Among them are: *Friendship of Russian and Ukrainian Farmers*, *Pushkin in Ukraine* featuring Pushkin among Ukrainian folk singers, and *Chernyshevsky, Dobrolyubov, Nekrasov and Shevtchenko in St Petersburg* (the first three are Russian writers, the last one is a Ukrainian). Other mosaics show dates such as *1905 in Donbass* or *The Battle of Poltava, 1709*.

The most decorated of the radial line stations, most near the centre, include:

Mayakovskaya Grand-prize winner at the 1938 World's Fair in New York, has a central hall that's all stainless steel and marble

Novokuznetskaya Has military bas-reliefs done in sober khaki colour and colourful ceiling mosaics with pictures of the happy life. The elegant marble benches came from the first Church of Christ the Saviour.

Ploshchad Revolyutsii The life-size bronze statues in the main hall and beside the escalators illustrate the idealised roles of common men and women. Heading up the escalators, the themes are, from the bottom: force to carry out and protect the revolution, industry, agriculture, hunting, education, sport and child-rearing.

Izmailovsky Park Has floral bas-reliefs that are decorated with AK-47 machine guns

Stations have maps of the system, and signs on each platform show the stations each train goes to. Interchange stations are linked by underground passages, indicated by *'perekhod'* (crossover) signs which are usually blue with a stick figure running up the stairs. Once you've figured out which train you need, you'll rarely wait more than two minutes for it. With elementary Cyrillic and by counting stops, you can manage very well. If you get lost, the kindly women who supervise the escalators can point you in the right direction.

These days, the Moscow metro has implemented a sort of public-relations campaign. You will notice posters decorated by pretty, smiling, young ladies in uniform promising 'Good Weather, Any time of year.' These *devushki* (young women) bear little resemblance to the babushkas sitting at the bottom of the escalators, but let's not mull over a technicality.

The carriages have maps inside that show the stops for that line, in both Roman and Cyrillic letters. The biggest confusion you may find is that often when two or more lines meet, each line's interchange station has a different name.

A few other metro facts:
• The first station opened in 1935; early work was driven by project manager Nikita Khrushchev (and we mean driven as thousands toiled around the clock under dire conditions).
• Up to nine million people a day ride the system, more than in London and New York City combined.
• The first stations are so deep because they really were designed to double as bomb shelters (you'll notice that newer stations aren't as deep after it was realised that you just couldn't dig deep enough to escape a hail of American nuclear bombs).

BUS, TROLLEYBUS & TRAM

Buses, trolleybuses and trams run almost everywhere the metro doesn't go. They can be useful along a few radial or cross-town routes that the metro misses, and are necessary for reaching sights away from the city centre.

To ride a bus, trolleybus or tram, you need a ticket to stick in one of the ticket-punchers inside the vehicle. *Talony*, which cost RR5, can be bought from drivers, from street kiosks, and sometimes in metro stations. The same talony are used for all three types of vehicle. Some vehicles have their very own *provodnitsa* (conductor), who sells tickets, so you don't have to punch them. Riding without a ticket is punishable by a fine of about US$5.

Bus stops are marked by the letter A for *avtobus*, and trolleybuses have the letter T. Tram stops are also marked by T, with the added clue of rails. Almost all the tram lines have been removed from the city centre as they were impeding traffic.

Some of the trolleybus routes are good for sightseeing, passing some interesting sights and – as a bonus – allowing passengers to disembark at any stop along the way. The best time for such a trip is Saturday or Sunday morning when there is not much traffic. These are the most scenic routes within the Garden Ring area:

No 1 Board at the Dobryninskaya metro. The route goes along Bolshaya Polayanka and across Bolshoy Kamenny bridge, which has a good Kremlin view. Succeeding sights include: Pashkov House, the old Moscow University, Hotel National, and north along scenic Tverskaya ulitsa to the Belorusskaya train station.

No 2 Makes a big circle around the Kremlin and Kitai Gorod, offering great views of the Kremlin, Hotel Rossiya, Kitai Gorod wall, Polytechnical Museum, Lubyanka ploshchad, Bolshoy Theatre, Hotel Metropol, Hotel National, Manezh ploshchad and old Moscow University. The route then turns on to ulitsa Vozdvishenka where you can enjoy the view of Arbat ploshchad, Novy Arbat ulitsa, Stalinesque Kutuzovsky prospekt, the Triumphal Arch, and Victory Park.

No 5 From the 1905 metro station goes along ulitsa Krasnaya Presnya and then passes the Moscow Zoo and one of Stalin's 'Seven Sisters' (the apartment block at Kudrinskaya) before crossing the Garden Ring. It next proceeds to Malaya Nikitskaya with the Gorky House Museum and the Church of the Great Ascension. Continuing along Nikitsky Boulevard, it passes the Museum of Oriental Arts, Arbat ploshchad,

Gogolevsky bulvar, Prechistenka ulitsa, Bolshaya Pirogovskaya and then on to the Novodevichy Monastery.

No 8 Offers great views of Zamoskorechie and its numerous churches. From the Dobryninskaya metro station, catch one north along ulitsa Pyatnitskaya. You can return back to the metro along Bolshaya Ordynka.

No 15 Offers the best tour of the Boulevard Ring. It passes Olimpiysky prospekt, Olympic Penta Hotel, Tsvetnoy bulvar and the Old Circus, Petrovsky and Strastnoy bulvars, Pushkinskaya ploshchad, Tverskoy bulvar with the Pushkin Drama Theatre, the ITAR-TASS building on Nikitsky bulvar and Gogolevsky bulvar. It turns onto Prechistenka ulitsa, with the Pushkin and Tolstoy literary museums and many beautiful buildings, then crosses the Garden Ring near the Park Kultury metro station and on to the Novodevichy monastery.

CAR & MOTORCYCLE

There's little reason for travellers to rent a car for getting around Moscow, as public transport is quite adequate, but you might want to consider it for trips out of the city.

Foreigners can legally drive on almost all of Russia's highways and can even ride motorcycles. On the down side, driving in Russia is truly an unfiltered Russian experience. Poor roads, maddeningly inadequate signposting, low-quality petrol and keen highway patrolmen, can lead to frustration and dismay.

Documents

To be allowed to drive your own or a rented car/motorcycle in Russia, you'll need to be 18 years old and have a full driving licence. In addition, you'll need an International Driving Permit with a Russian translation of your licence, or a certified Russian translation of your full licence (you can certify translations at a Russian embassy or consulate).

For your own vehicle, you will also need registration papers and proof of insurance. Be sure your insurance covers you in Russia. Finally, a customs declaration, promising that you will take your vehicle with you when you leave, is also required.

Car Rental There are lots of car-rental firms in Moscow, and most upmarket tourist hotels

have a rental desk of some kind. Many companies have a few car-rental caveats, such as prohibiting cars to leave the city, or renting only cars with drivers. Companies' policies change frequently, so it pays to ring around and compare prices and policies. Cars with drivers don't always prove to be more expensive, and they save you the trouble of coping with Russian roads.

The major international rental firms have outlets in Moscow. Generally, it is best to reserve your car before you arrive, as advance reservations and special offers can reduce the price by 50% or more. Prices quoted are for on-the-spot rental of the cheapest car available.

The following companies have desks at Sheremetevo-2 airport and will usually pick up or drop off the car at your hotel:

Avis (☎ 578 7179) US$62 per day
Budget (☎ 737 0407) US$68 per day
Hertz (☎ 937 3274) US$90 per day

Road Rules

Russians drive on the right and traffic coming from the right has the right of way. Speed limits are generally 60km/h in towns and between 80km/h and 110km/h on highways. There may be a 90km/h zone, enforced by speed traps, as you leave a city. Traffic lights that flicker green are about to change to yellow, then red. Children under 12 may not travel in the front seat, and safety-belt use is mandatory. Motorcyclists (and passengers) must wear crash helmets.

The maximum legal blood-alcohol content is 0.04%, but in practice it is illegal to drive after consuming *any* alcohol at all. This is a rule that is strictly enforced. The normal way of establishing alcohol in the blood is by a blood test, but apparently you can be deemed under its influence even without any test.

Officers of the State Automobile Inspectorate (Gosudarstvennaya Avtomobilnaya Inspektsia), better known as GAI, skulk about on the roadsides all around Moscow waiting for miscreant drivers. They are authorised to stop you (by pointing their striped stick at you and waving you towards the side), to issue on-the-spot fines and, worst of all, to shoot at your car if you refuse to pull over. The GAI also hosts the occasional speed trap – the road to Sheremetevo airport is infamous for this. If you are required to pay a fine, pay in roubles only – and make sure you get a receipt.

Fuel

Moscow has no shortage of gas stations that sell all grades of petrol. Most are open 24 hours, are affiliated with Western oil companies and can be found on the major roads in and out of town. There are parts, service and repair specialists for many Western makes of car in Moscow. See the *Moscow Business Telephone Guide* for listings.

TAXI

Almost any car in Moscow could be a taxi if the price is right. The simple way to get a taxi is to stand on the street and stick your arm out. Before too long a car will stop and, if the driver fancies going to your destination, you're on your way. Many private car drivers cruise around as unofficial taxis (gypsy cabs), and other drivers will often take you if they're going in roughly the same direction.

The price for such services varies, according to time of day and traffic conditions and, of course, how far you go. Pay anywhere from RR50 to RR150.

You may want to fix the fare before you get in to avoid any disagreements with your driver at the end of the ride.

Official taxis, which carry a little chequerboard logo on the side and/or a small green light in the windscreen, charge about the same. No driver uses a meter, even if the cab has one, and few drivers ever admit to having any change. You'll have to pay more if you catch a taxi right in front of a hotel.

Don't hesitate to wave on a car if you don't like the look of its occupant(s). You may not want to ride in cars that have more than one person in them when they pull over. Problems may be more likely to crop up if you take a street cab waiting outside a nightclub, or perhaps a tourist hotel or restaurant at night.

To book a taxi in advance, you can call the **Central Taxi Reservation Office** *(Tsentralnoe Byuro Zakazov Taxi;* ☎ *927 0000)* 24 hours daily. You should give it at least one, and preferably two or more, hours notice. Usually the dispatcher on the phone will speak a bit of English, though it may help if you can speak some Russian too. They'll want to ring you back a few minutes before pick-up, to confirm that you still want the booking and give you the car's registration number. You should be charged about RR50 for the booking, then around RR10 per kilometre. The car services mentioned earlier in this chapter are also reliable.

Things to See & Do

CITY CENTRE

The heart of the city lies in the arc round the Kremlin bound by Mokhovaya ulitsa, Okhotny ryad, Teatralny proezd and Lubyansky proezd.

Red Square (Moscow Kremlin Map)

Red Square (Krasnaya ploshchad) lies immediately outside the Kremlin's northeastern wall. Commanding the square from the southern end is the building that, more than any other, epitomises 'Russia' – St Basil's Cathedral.

Red Square used to be a market square that adjoined the merchants' area in Kitai Gorod. It has always been a place where the Kremlin's occupants chose to congregate, celebrate and castigate for all their people to see. Ivan the Terrible publicly confessed his misdeeds here in 1547, built St Basil's to commemorate his victories in the 1550s, and later had numerous perceived enemies executed here. The Cossack rebel Stepan Razin was dismembered here in 1671, and 2000 members of Peter the Great's mutinous palace guard, the Streltsy, were executed en masse here in 1698.

Soviet rulers chose Red Square for their military parades: perhaps most poignantly on 7 November 1941, when tanks rolled straight off to the front line outside Moscow; and during the Cold War, when lines of ICBMs (intercontinental ballistic missiles) rumbled across the square to remind the West of Soviet military might.

The name Krasnaya ploshchad has nothing to do either with communism or with the blood that flowed here. *Krasnyy* in old Russian meant 'beautiful': only in the 20th century did it come to mean 'red' too.

Red Square is closed to traffic, except for the limousines that whiz in and out of the Kremlin's Saviour Gate from time to time. Most people here are sightseers (see the boxed text 'The Great Moscow Police Tourist Rip-off' in the Facts for the Visitor

Highlights

- Discovering medieval Muscovy in the frescoes and iconography of the Kremlin
- Catching the sunset from a boat on the Moscow River
- Paying your respects to Vladimir Ilich in Red Square
- Getting close up and personal with fallen Soviet heroes at Sculpture Park
- Catching rays and watching people along Tverskoy bulvar
- Hearing them hit the high notes at a Tchaikovsky opera
- Sweating off your city smut at the Sandunovskiye Baths
- Gawking at the remains of Soviet economic achievement at VDNKh
- Discovering Moscow's Art Nouveau treasures such as Hotel Metropol and the Gorky House-Museum
- Packing a picnic and escaping to the tranquil grounds of Kolomenskoe

chapter), but that doesn't reduce the thrill of walking on these 400m by 150m of cobbles so central to Russian history. It's particularly atmospheric when floodlit at night.

The best way to enter Red Square is through the **Resurrection Gate** (Voskresenskiye Vorota). Rebuilt in 1995 with its twin red towers topped by green tent spires, it's an exact copy of the original completed on this site in 1680. The first gateway was destroyed in 1931, because Stalin considered it an impediment to the parades and demonstrations held in Red Square.

Within the gateway is a bright **Chapel of the Iverian Virgin** (Chasovnya Iverskoy Boromateri), originally built in the late 18th century to house the icon.

Lenin's Tomb The granite tomb of Lenin *(Mavzoley V I Lenina; ☎ 923 5527; admission*

free; open 10am-1pm Tues-Thur, Sat & Sun),
standing at the foot of the Kremlin wall, is
another of Red Square's must-sees, especially since (if some people get their way)
the former leader may eventually end up
beside his mum in St Petersburg. For now,
the embalmed leader remains as he has been
since 1924 (apart from a retreat to Siberia
during WWII).

From 1953 to 1961, Lenin shared the
tomb with Stalin. In 1961, during the 22nd
Party Congress, the esteemed and by then
ancient Bolshevik, Madame Spiridonova,
announced that Vladimir Ilich had appeared
to her in a dream, insisting that he did not
like spending eternity with his successor.
With that, Stalin was removed, and given a
place of honour immediately behind the
mausoleum.

Before joining the queue at the northwestern corner of Red Square, drop your
camera at the left-luggage office beneath
Kutufya Tower, as you will not be allowed
to take it with you. Humourless guards ensure that visitors remain respectful.

After trouping past the embalmed, oddly
waxy figure, emerge from the mausoleum
and inspect where Stalin, Brezhnev and
other Communist heavy-hitters are buried
along the Kremlin wall. See the boxed text
'Kremlin Wall' for details.

St Basil's Cathedral No picture can prepare you for the crazy confusion of colours
and shapes that is St Basil's Cathedral
*(Sobor Vasilia Blazhennogo; ☎ 298 3304; ad-
mission RR100; open 11am-5pm Wed-Mon).*
This ultimate symbol of Russia was created
between 1555 and 1561, replacing an existing church on the site, to celebrate Ivan the
Terrible's capture of the Tatar stronghold,
Kazan. The capture took place on 1 October

Lenin under Glass

Red Square is home to the world's most famous mummy. Vladimir Ilich (Lenin) died of a massive
stroke on 22 January 1924; he was 53 years old. For weeks a long line of mourners gathered pa-
tiently, in winter's harshness, to glimpse the body as it lay in state. Inspired by the spectacle, Stalin
proposed that the father of Soviet communism could continue to serve the cause as a holy relic. So
the decision was made to preserve Lenin's corpse for perpetuity, against the vehement protests of
his widow, as well as his own expressed desire to be buried next to his mother in St Petersburg.

Boris Zbarsky, a biochemist, and Vladimir Voribov, an anatomist, were issued a political order to
put a stop to the natural decomposition of the body. The pair worked frantically in a secret laboratory in search of a long-term chemical solution. In the meantime, the body's dark spots were
bleached, lips and eyes were sewn tight, and the brain was removed. Lenin's brain was taken to another secret laboratory where, for the next 40 years, scientists sliced and diced in the hope of un-
covering its hidden genius.

In July 1924, the scientists hit upon a formula, which successfully arrested the decaying process.
The technique was a closely guarded state secret. This necrotic craft was passed on to Zbarsky's son,
who ran the Kremlin's covert embalming lab for decades. After the fall of communism, Zbarsky came
clean on the details of the treatment. The body is wiped down every few days and every 18 months
is thoroughly examined and then submerged in a tub of chemicals, which include paraffin wax. The
institute of late has gone commercial, offering its services and secrets to wannabe immortals for a
mere US$1 million.

In the early 1990s, Boris Yeltsin expressed his intention to heed Lenin's request and bury him in
St Petersburg. The remarks set off a furore from the political left, as well as more muted objections
from Moscow tour operators. It now seems that the mausoleum, the most sacred shrine of Soviet
communism, and the mummy, the literal embodiment of the Russian Revolution, will remain in place
for at least several more years.

Kremlin Wall

Some of the worthies given the honour of burial beneath the Kremlin Wall include:

Felix Dzerzhinsky The founder of the Cheka (forerunner of the KGB)

Yakov Sverdlov A key organiser of the revolution and the first official head of the Soviet State

Andrey Zhdanov Stalin's cultural chief and the second most powerful man in the USSR immediately after WWII

Mikhail Frunze The Red Army leader who secured Central Asia for the Soviet Union in the 1920s

Inessa Armand Lenin's rumoured lover

John Reed (Dzhon Rid) The American author of *Ten Days that Shook the World*, a first-hand account of the revolution

Plaques in the wall mark the spots where the ashes of many more heroes lie, including:

Yury Gagarin The first astronaut

Marshal Georgy Zhukov The commander who defeated Hitler

Alexey Kosygin Brezhnev's initial partner in power in the 1960s

Igor Kurchatov The leader of the team that developed the Soviet hydrogen bomb

1552, the feast of the Intercession which gives the cathedral its official name (Intercession Cathedral by the Moat). Its design is the culmination of a wholly Russian style that had been developed building wooden churches. Legend has it that Ivan had its architect blinded so that he could never build anything comparable.

The cathedral owes its name to the barefoot holy fool Vasily (Basil) the Blessed, who predicted Ivan's damnation and added (correctly), as the army left for Kazan, that Ivan would murder a son. Vasily died while Kazan was under siege and was buried beside the church which St Basil's soon replaced. He was later canonised.

St Basil's apparent anarchy of shapes in fact hides a comprehensible plan of nine main chapels: the tall, tent-roofed one in the centre; four big, octagonal-towered ones, topped with the four biggest domes; and four smaller ones in between. An extra northeastern chapel over Vasily the Blessed's grave and a tent-roofed southeastern bell tower were added later. Only in the 1670s were the domes patterned, giving St Basil's its multicoloured appearance. In 1772–84 the cathedral received a metal roof and a whitewashing; its domes were gold-leafed in keeping with the fashion of the time. Although Napoleon ordered it destroyed in 1812, his troops did not have enough time to complete the task. In 1817 the cathedral returned to its present colourful appearance, the cemetery was closed and the houses and moat surrounding the cathedral were removed.

Today, the interior is open to visitors. The ground level holds a small exhibition on St Basil's itself, and there are some lovely frescoes of flower patterns and saints.

In front of St Basil's stands a statue of the butcher **Kuzma Minin and Prince Dmitry Pozharsky** (pamyatnik Mininu i Pozharskomu), who together raised and led the army that ejected the occupying Poles from the Kremlin in 1612. Just up the slope there's the round, walled **Place of Skulls** (Lobnoe Mesto), the spot where Ivan the Terrible made his public confession and Peter the Great executed the Streltsy.

GUM The **Gosudarstvenny Universalny Magazin** (State Department Store), which lines the northeastern side of Red Square, was built in the 19th century to house over 1000 shops. GUM once symbolised all that was bad about Soviet shopping – long queues and shelves empty of all but a few drab goods.

A remarkable transformation has taken place since *perestroika* (literally, 'restructuring'), and today, GUM is a bright and bustling place full of attractive shops stocked with imported and Russian goods of all kinds.

Benetton, Yves Rocher, Galeries Lafayette and many other big foreign names are represented here. There are a few snack places, and pay toilets at the southern end of ground level.

Kazan Cathedral The tiny Kazan Cathedral (*Kazansky sobor; Nikolskaya ul 3; admission free; open 8am-7pm, evening service 8pm Mon*) opposite the northern end of GUM, is a 1993 replica of the original. Founded in 1636 in thanks for the 1612 expulsion of Polish invaders, for two centuries it housed the *Virgin of Kazan* icon, which had supposedly helped to rout the Poles.

Three hundred years after its founding, the cathedral was completely demolished, allegedly because it impeded the flow of celebrating workers in May Day and Revolution Day parades.

State History Museum The State History Museum (*Gosudarstvenny Istorichesky Muzey;* ☎ 292 4019; *Red Square; adults/students RR150/75; open 11am-7pm Wed-Mon*) at the northern end of the square has an enormous collection covering the whole Russian empire from the Stone Age on. The building, which dates from the late 19th century, is itself an attraction. Each room is in the style of a different period or region, some with highly decorated walls which echo old Russian churches. Reopened in 1997, each year sees the addition of a few more galleries.

On the north side of the building, the **Marshall Zhukov statue** shows the most successful WWII commander, mounted on a horse, almost as he appeared at the Victory Day Parade in Red Square on 24 June 1945.

The former **Central Lenin Museum** (*pl Revolyutsii 2*) across the street, once the big daddy of all Lenin museums, was closed in 1993 after the White House shoot-out. Communist rabblerousers still congregate here.

Around Manezhnaya Ploshchad (Moscow Kremlin Map)

Wide Manezhnaya ploshchad, at the northern end of Red Square, has been transformed into the vast underground **Okhotny Ryad Shopping Mall** (☎ 737 8409), which makes its presence known in the square with a series of half-domes and balustrades, and a network of fountains and sculptures.

The long, low building on the southwestern side of the square is the **Manezh Central**

Exhibition Hall (☎ 202 8976; *open 11am-8pm daily*), home to some of Moscow's most popular art exhibitions. Prices vary depending on what is on show. On the northwestern side of the square are the fine old edifices of **Moscow State University**, built in 1793, and Hotel National, built in 1903.

The 1930s **Hotel Moskva** fronts the northeastern side of the square and it is half-constructivist, half-Stalinist. The story goes that Stalin was shown two designs for the hotel. Not realising they were alternatives, he approved both of them. Not daring to point out his error, the builders built half in each style, with predictably incongruous results.

The entrance to the new **Archaeological Museum** (☎ 292 4171; *Manezhnaya pl 1; admission RR30; open 10am-6pm Tues-Sun*) is at the base of the hotel facing the square. An excavation of the Voskresensky Bridge, which used to cross the Neglinnaya River and commence the road to Tver, uncovered coins, clothing and other artefacts. The museum displaying these treasures is situated in an underground pavilion which remains from the excavation itself.

The **Russian State Library** (*Rossiyskaya Gosudarstvennaya Biblioteka; cnr Mokhovaya & Vozdvizhenka uls; open 9am-9pm daily*) is one of the world's biggest, with over 20 million volumes. It incorporates one of Moscow's finest classical buildings, the 1784–87 **Pashkov House** (Dom Pashkova). If you are interested in visiting this grand, albeit financially troubled, institution, take along your passport and one passport photo. You will have to fill out some forms to get a free reader's card (*chitatelsky billet*).

Northeast of Manezhnaya ploshchad, Okhotny ryad passes between Hotel Moskva and the glowering **State Duma** (Gosudarstvennaya duma), where Russia's parliament now sits. This building was erected in the 1930s for Gosplan (the Soviet State Planning Department), and was the source of the USSR's Five-Year Plans. Next door is the green-columned **House of Unions** (Dom Soyuzov), which dates from the 1780s and used to be the Nobles' Club. Its Hall of Columns (originally a ballroom, now a concert hall) was, in 1938, the scene of one of

Stalin's most grotesque show trials, that of Nikolai Bukharin, a leading Communist Party theorist who had been a close associate of Lenin.

Teatralnaya Ploshchad (Map 2)

Teatralnaya ploshchad opens out on both sides of Okhotny ryad, 200m from Manezhnaya ploshchad. In the early 18th century, the Neglinka River ran through here and powered water mills where the Hotel Metropol is now. Only in the early 19th century did the square receive its grand appearance.

The northern half of the square is dominated by the famous **Bolshoi Theatre**, where Tchaikovsky's *Swan Lake* was premiered (unsuccessfully) in 1877. Initially overshadowed by St Petersburg's Mariinsky Theatre,

the Bolshoi didn't really hit the high notes until the 1950s, when foreign tours won great acclaim for its ballet and opera companies. The busy streets behind the Bolshoi constitute Moscow's main shopping centre (see Tverskoy Region later in this chapter). Across ulitsa Petrovka from the 'Big' Bolshoi is the 'Small' **Maly Theatre**, a drama theatre.

On the southern half of Teatralnaya ploshchad is the tiled, sculpted facade of the luxury **Hotel Metropol**, one of the finest examples of Art Nouveau architecture throughout Moscow. The mosaic *Printsessa Gryoza* (Princess of Dreams) at the western facade is the work of Mikhail Vrubel. The 1835 fountain by Vitali – partially blocked by the statue of Karl Marx – marks the centre of the square.

Judaism in Moscow

Moscow's Jewish population has experienced long periods of repression, punctuated by short intervals of opportunity. In the Middle Ages, Muscovite princes considered Jews as enemies of Christianity and forbade them from entering the realm. The Jewish population only became statistically notable in the late 18th century, when Imperial Russia annexed the eastern part of the Polish Kingdom. Several centuries earlier, Europe's Jews had been welcomed in the Poland-Lithuanian Republic after their expulsion from Western European states. In this community – known as the Jewish Pale – were the roots of the Jewish population in the Russian Empire.

Jewish trades and traditions were regarded as a threat to the social order of the empire. Official policy fluctuated from forced assimilation to social isolation. A brief respite occurred under Alexander II, the Tsar Reformer, who lifted residential restrictions on Jews with 'useful' talents, such as merchants, doctors and artisans.

Jews were allowed to enter new professions, such as banking and industry, and Moscow's small Jewish community flourished during these years.

But a wave of anti-Semitism accompanied the political reaction that came in the wake of Alexander's assassination. Authorities looked the other way when Jewish communities were overrun by pogroms of looting and violence. Tens of thousands of Moscow Jews were rounded up and expelled back to the Pale. Less than 1% of the empire's five million Jews lived in Moscow at the outset of the 20th century.

Lenin once said 'scratch a Bolshevik and you'll find a Russian chauvinist'. While the revolution provided another period of opportunity for individual Jews, the socialist regime was not tolerant toward Jewish language and customs. In the mid-1920s, Jews were the second largest ethnic group in the capital, comprising 6.5% of the city population. In 1930, Lazar Kaganovich, an ethnic Jew and Stalin crony, was made mayor of Moscow. He pleaded against the destruction of the Christ the Saviour Cathedral out of fear that he would be personally blamed and it would provoke popular anti-Semitism (both of which happened).

Anti-Semitism became official policy again in the late Stalinist period. The Jewish quarter in the Dorogomilova neighbourhood was levelled for new building projects. Two huge apartment houses

Around Lubyanskaya Ploshchad (Map 2)

For several decades the broad square at the top of Teatralny proezd was a chilling symbol of the KGB, or Komitet Gosudarstvennoy Bezopasnosti (Committee for State Security). In the 1930s, **Lubyanka Prison** was the feared destination of thousands of innocent victims of Stalin's purges.

Today the grey building, no longer a prison, looming on the northeastern side of the square is the headquarters of the KGB's successor, the FSB (Federal Security Service). The FSB doesn't operate foreign spies (that's now done by a separate External Intelligence Service, the SVR), but still keeps a pretty good eye on domestic goings-on. The building is not open to the public.

Behind Lubyanka is a four-room **KGB Museum** (*ul Bolshaya Lubyanka 12/1*) devoted to the history, propaganda and paraphernalia of the Soviet intelligence services. The museum is not open to casual callers but Dom Patriarshy (see the boxed text 'Want a Guide for a Day?' later in this chapter) occasionally takes groups there.

From 1926 to 1990, Lubyanskaya ploshchad was called ploshchad Dzerzhinskogo, after Felix Dzerzhinsky, who founded the Cheka, the KGB's forerunner.

A tall statue of Dzerzhinsky, which dominated the square, was memorably removed by angry crowds, with the assistance of a couple of cranes, when the 1991 coup collapsed. Now you can see the statue in all its (somewhat reduced) glory in the Sculptures

Judaism in Moscow

were constructed for the communist elite, at 24 and 26 Kutuzov prospekt, on top of the city's old Jewish cemetery. Systematic discrimination finally prompted the rise of a dissident movement, which battled Soviet officialdom for the right to leave the country.

In 1986, Mikhail Gorbachev announced that refusenik Anatoly Scharansky was permitted to emigrate, signalling a more relaxed official stance. Between 1987 and 1991, half a million Soviet Jews emigrated to Israel, and another 150,000 to the USA. Moscow's Jewish community declined as a result. In 1970, Jews accounted for 3.6% of the city's population (second after ethnic Russians), but by 1989, their number made up only 2% (Ukrainians were now the second largest ethnic group in the capital).

Today, Judaism in Moscow is enjoying a modest revival, as believers reconnect with their ancestry and traditions. As in earlier times, the new opportunities for Jews that have arisen in post-communist Russia have also stirred anti-Semitic incidents and rhetoric. For more information, contact the **Committee on Soviet Jewry** (**e** *mucsj@rambler.ru*).

The **Moscow Choral Synagogue** (*Choralnaya Synagoga; Map 3; Bolshoy Spasoglinishchevsky per 10*) was built in 1891 by the businessman Polyakov, who made his fortune in the sugar industry. The interior is exquisite. It was the only synagogue which continued to operate throughout the Soviet period, in spite of Bolshevik demands to convert it to a workers' club. Recently, a **Weeping Wall** (Stena Placha) has been built nearby.

Lyubavicheskaya Synagogue (*Map 2; Bolshaya Bronnaya ul 6*) was built in 1902, but was converted to a theatre in the 1930s. However, the building was still used for gatherings by the Jewish community. The rug on the altar hides a trapdoor leading to a small cell where Jews used to hide – from the communists or the Nazis or both. The building has since been returned to the Jewish community and has operated as a synagogue since 1991.

The **Memorial Synagogue at Poklyonnaya Mountain** houses the **Museum of Jewish Legacy History and Holocaust** (**☎** 148 1907; ul Minskaya; admission free; open 10am-6pm Tues-Thur, noon-7pm Sun). Admission is with a guide only, so you must make arrangements in advance, especially if you want a tour in English. Otherwise, you can join an existing group – usually children – at noon, 2pm or 4pm. Take bus No 130 from Universitetskaya.

THINGS TO SEE & DO

Park, where it stands among the others fallen from grace. There is a movement – backed by Mayor Luzhkov, strangely enough – to resurrect 'Iron Felix' and return him to his place of honour.

The much humbler **Memorial to the Victims of Totalitarianism** stands in the little garden on the southeastern side of the square. This single stone slab comes from the territory of an infamous 1930s labour camp situated on the Solovetsky Islands in the White Sea.

Vladimir Mayakovsky Museum (☎ 921 9387; Lubyansky proezd 3/6; admission RR50; open 1pm-9pm Thur, 10am-5pm Fri-Tues) is in a large prerevolutionary mansion where the poet lived in a communal apartment during the last years of his life. The room where he worked – and shot himself in 1930 – is preserved. Run by the poet's granddaughter, the museum also has an eclectic collection of his manuscripts and sketches.

The little **Moscow City History Museum** (☎ 924 8490; Novaya pl 12; admission RR15; open 10am-6pm Tues-Sun) is in the former Ioann the Chrysostom Church that was built in 1825 in Russian Empire style. The museum shows how the city has spread from its starting point at the Kremlin.

Across the street, the huge **Polytechnical Museum** (☎ 923 0756; Novaya pl 3/4; admission RR100; open 10am-5pm Tues-Sun) occupies a whole block. Its central section (1877) was built in the Russian Byzantium style. The eastern section (1896) is inspired by 17th-century Russian styles while the western section (1907) is Art Nouveau. The museum is closed on the last Thursday of the month.

KITAI GOROD (MAP 2)

The narrow old streets east of Red Square are known as Kitai Gorod, which literally means 'Chinatown', but actually has nothing to do with China. The name derives from 'kita' which means wattle, after the palisades that reinforced the earthen ramp erected around this early Kremlin suburb. This is one of the oldest parts of Moscow, settled in the 13th century as an early trade and financial centre.

Along Teatralny proezd, archaeologists uncovered the 16th-century fortified wall which used to surround Kitai Gorod, as well as the foundations of the 1493 Trinity Church. Coins, jewellery and tombstones were also excavated from the site, which is called **Starye Polya** (Old Fields; Map 2). The gated walkway **Tretyakovsky Proezd** (Map 6) leads into Kitai Gorod.

This area's ancient, bustling streets and exquisite, tiny churches make it an ideal place for a stroll. See Kitai Gorod Tour in the Moscow Walks special section for details.

TVERSKOY REGION (MAP 2)

In spite of soulless reconstruction in the 1930s, it's hard to imagine Moscow without Tverskaya ulitsa, the beginning of the road to Tver, and therefore to St Petersburg. The bottom end of the street, by Hotel National, is the city's hub: numerous places to eat and some of Moscow's classier shops dot the slope up to Pushkinskaya ploshchad. Trolleybus Nos 12 and 20 run up and down Tverskaya ulitsa as far as Belorus Station.

The streets around Tverskaya ulitsa comprise the vibrant Tverskoy Region of the city, characterised by old architecture and new commerce.

Inner Tverskaya Ulitsa

Through the arch across Bryusov pereulok is the unexpected little gold-domed **Church of the Resurrection** (Tserkov Voskresenia). The main building, built in 1629, is full of fine icons saved from churches torn down during the Soviet era. The refectory and bell tower date from 1820.

Tverskaya ploshchad is recognisable by its **statue of Yury Dolgoruky**, traditionally considered Moscow's founder. The buffed-up, five-storey building that faces it is the **Moscow Mayor's Office**. Behind the statue to the right is the 17th-century **Church of SS Cosma and Damian**.

On the eastern side of Tverskaya ulitsa, shortly before Pushkinskaya ploshchad, is the ornate **Yeliseev's Grocery Store** (☎ 229 5562; 14 Tverskaya ul), named after its founding owner, Pyotr Yeliseev, whose bust can be seen in the central hall. Originally a mansion, it has been restored to its former splendour with chandeliers, stained glass and marble columns.

Around Pushkinskaya Ploshchad

The parks that open out on either side of Tverskaya ulitsa, at the intersection with the Boulevard Ring, constitute Pushkinskaya ploshchad. From the square that bears his name, a **Pushkin statue** surveys his domain. Behind the statue the recently renamed **Pushkinsky Cinema** – the former Rossiya – is the main venue of Russian film-makers and celebrities. Pushkinskaya metro station is underneath. It seems Pushkin has been chosen to take the place of Lenin in the New Russian ideology.

The square is also famous as the site of Russia's first **McDonald's**, still popular for its predictable food and predictably clean toilets.

Pushkinskaya ploshchad is the nearest thing to a Russian Fleet St. On the northern side, east of Tverskaya ulitsa, squat the offices of *Izvestia*, formerly the newspaper of the USSR Supreme Soviet, now a bland daily. Opposite *Izvestia* (physically and politically) is the *Moskovskie Novosti* (Moscow News), a weekly published in several languages and a standard-bearer of reform.

Just off Pushkinskaya ploshchad stand the multiple tent roofs of the **Church of the Nativity of the Virgin in Putinki** (*Malaya Dmitrovka ul 4*). Curiously, these contributed to a ban on tent roofs on churches by Patriarch Nikon in 1652, the year this church was completed. Nikon thought them too Russian and secular, too far from the Church's Byzantine roots. Next to the Church of the Nativity, the **Lenkom Theatre** (*Teatr Lenkom; Malaya Dmitrovka ul*) occupies the former Merchants' Club, built in 1909.

Boulevard Ring

Pushkinskaya ploshchad forms part of Moscow's oddest-shaped park, 8km long and 20m wide, between the two carriageways of the Boulevard Ring (Bulvarnoe Koltso). Though hemmed in by traffic, the shady path down the middle of the road makes for a pleasant stroll, with statues to Russian cultural greats. Present-day Russian culture is also represented by street performers and cellphone (mobile phone) users enjoying the park.

The Boulevard Ring was created in the late 18th and early 19th centuries, replacing Moscow's old defensive walls with boulevards and terraces of handsome buildings, and some of that era's elegance lingers in the neighbourhoods southwest of Pushkinskaya ploshchad, off Tverskoy bulvar and Nikitsky bulvar.

Trolleybus Nos 15 and 31 run both ways along the ring between Trubnaya ploshchad and Kropotkinskaya metro.

Ulitsa Petrovka

Now restored to its prerevolutionary fashionable status, ulitsa Petrovka constitutes Moscow's glossiest central shopping area. The big department store **TsUM** (*ul Petrovka 2*), which stands for Tsentralny Universalny Magazin (Central Department Store), is a bright, busy place now given over to multitudes of separate shops. It was built in 1909 as the Scottish-owned Muir & Merrilees and was the first department store aimed at the middle-class shoppers. **Petrovsky Passazh** (*ul Petrovka 10*) has become the city's sleekest shopping arcade. A smaller, glitzier version of GUM, it too is dominated by foreign names, and dates from the 1900s.

The grand 19th-century **Sandunovskiye Baths** (*Sandunovskie bany, Sanduny for short; Zvonarsky per*), just off ulitsa Petrovka, is Moscow's most famous public bathhouse. See the boxed text 'Steaming – the Joys of Banya' later in this chapter for details.

The **Upper St Peter Monastery** (*cnr ul Petrovka & Petrovsky bul; admission free; open 9am-7pm daily*) was founded in the 1380s as part of an early defensive ring around Moscow. The grounds are pleasant, in a peaceful, near-deserted sort of way, and the churches are only open for services.

The main onion-domed **Virgin of Bogolyubovo Church** dates from the late 17th century. The loveliest structure is the brick **Cathedral of Metropolitan Pyotr** in the middle of the grounds, restored with a shingle roof. When Peter the Great ousted the Regent

Steaming – the Joys of Banya

Travellers to Russia have for centuries commented on the particular (in many people's eyes, peculiar) traditions of the *banya*. The closest English equivalents to this word, 'bathhouse' and 'sauna', don't quite sum it up. To this day, Russians (though more men than women seem to go to city public banyas) make it an important part of their week. You can't say you've really been to Russia unless you've visited one.

The banya's main element is the *parilka* (steam room) which can get so hot it makes the Finnish sauna look wussy in comparison. In the parilka a furnace heats rocks, onto which water is poured using a long-handled ladle. Often, a few drops of eucalyptus or pine oil (sometimes even beer) is added to the water to create a scent in the burst of scalding steam released into the room. After this, some people will stand up, grab hold of a tied bundle of birch branches *(venik)* and, well, beat themselves or each other with it.

Though it may sound sadomasochistic (and there are theories tying this practice with other elements of masochism in Russian culture) or at the very least painful, the effect is pleasant and, er, cleansing. Apparently, the birch leaves (sometimes oak or, agonisingly, juniper branches are used) and their secretions help rid the skin of toxins.

The tradition of the banya is deeply ingrained in Russian culture, emerging from ancient Novgorod; the Kievan Slavs would make fun of their northern brothers for all that steamy whipping. In folk traditions, it has been customary for bride and groom to take separate banyas the night before their wedding with their friends; the banya itself became the bridge to marriage (a modern version of this custom is depicted humorously in every Russian's favourite film, *Ironic Fate* (Ironia Sudba). Husband and wife would also customarily bathe together after the ceremony. Midwives used to administer a steam bath to women during delivery, and it was not uncommon to give a hot birch mini-massage to the newborn. The banya, in short, is a place for physical and moral purification.

This said, a few classy exceptions aside (we're thinking of the likes of Moscow's splendid Sandunovskiye banya here), many city banya these days are rundown and unappealing; grab any chance you get to try a traditional one in a log cabin in the countryside.

Wherever you find yourself bathing, the modern tradition goes something like this: usually at the same time every week, people head out to their favourite banya where they meet up with the same people they see each week (the Western equivalent would be meeting your work-out buddies at the gym). Many bring along a thermos filled with tea mixed with jams, spices and heaps of sugar (failing this, a few bottles of beer and some dried fish will do nicely).

After stripping down completely in the sex-segregated changing room and wishing *'Lyokogo para'* (something of the order of 'May your steam be easy'!) to your mates, you head off into a dry sauna first – just to get the skin nice and hot – then it's into the parilka. After the birch-branch bit (best experienced lying down on a bench while someone administers the 'beating'), you run outside and, depending on your nerve, plunge into an ice-cold pool, the *basseyn*. With your eyelids now draped back over your scull, you stammer back into the changing room to hear your mates say *'S lyogkim parom'* ('Hope your steam was easy!'). Then you drape yourself in sheets and discuss world issues before repeating the process (most banya experts go through these motions five to 10 times over a two-hour period).

Steve Kokker

Sofia in 1690, his mother was so pleased she built him a church.

The **Moscow Museum of Contemporary Art** (☎ 231 4405; ul Petrovka 25; adults/ students RR90/45; open noon-8pm Wed-Fri, noon-7pm Sat-Mon), housed in a classical 18th-century merchant's home, contains all kinds of 20th-century paintings, sculptures and graphics, including a lovely sculpture garden in the courtyard.

Just beyond the Garden Ring, the **Museum of Decorative and Folk Art** (☎ 923 7725; ul

Delegatskaya 3 & 5; admission RR30; open 10am-5pm Sat-Thur) has a good, two-room Palekh collection, as well as lots of regional folk art.

The **Glinka Museum of Musical Culture** *(☎ 972 3237; ul Fadeeva 4; admission RR20; open 11am-6pm Tues-Sun)*, named for one of Russia's greatest nationalist composers, has over 3000 musical instruments, including 13th-century Novgorod lutes and beautiful old balalaikas.

Outer Tverskaya Ulitsa

North of Pushkinskaya ploshchad, stone lions guard the fence of the **Contemporary History Museum** *(Muzey sovremennoy istorii; ☎ 299 6724; Tverskaya ul 21; admission RR25; open 10am-6pm Tues-Sun)*, which provides a pretty honest account of Soviet history from the 1905 and 1917 revolutions up to the 1980s. The highlight is the extensive collection of propaganda posters, in addition to all the Bolshevik paraphernalia. Look for the picture of the giant Palace of Soviets (Dvorets Sovietov) that Stalin was going to build on the site of the blown-up – and now rebuilt – Cathedral of Christ the Saviour. English-language tours are available for RR700 with advance notice.

Tverskaya ulitsa crosses the Garden Ring at Triumfalnaya ploshchad, where **Tchaikovsky Concert Hall** and a few other theatres are clustered. Though revolutionary bard Vladimir Mayakovsky no longer lends his name to the square, his statue still surveys it and the metro station beneath is still called Mayakovskaya.

Patriarch's Ponds

In the 17th century, three fishponds were used to keep fish for the Patriarch's residence and the area was inhabited by the Patriarch's household servants; today, only one pond remains. This peaceful fishpond (Patriarshy prudy) was immortalised by writer Mikhail Bulgakov, who had the devil appear here in *The Master and Margarita*, one of the most loved of 20th-century Russian novels. **Bulgakov's flat** *(Bolshaya Sadovaya ul 10)*, where he wrote the novel and lived up until his death, is around the corner on the Garden Ring. Although the empty flat used to be a hang-out for dissidents and hooligans, the building now has tight security appropriate to this high-rent district.

Bolshaya Nikitskaya Ulitsa

Bolshaya Nikitskaya ulitsa runs from the Moscow State University building on ulitsa Mokhovaya out to the Garden Ring. In the back streets off Bolshaya Nikitskaya ulitsa many old mansions have survived, some renovated, some dilapidated. Most of those inside the Boulevard Ring were built by 18th-century aristocracy; outside the ring, by rising 19th-century industrialists. With little traffic, this is an excellent area for a quiet ramble. See the Literary Tour in the Moscow Walks special section for details.

The white and festive **Church of the Small Ascension** *(Tserkov Vozneseniya; Map 2; cnr Voznesensky per & Bolshaya Nikitskaya ul)* was built in the early 17th century.

The **Museum of Folk Art** *(☎ 202 7316; Leontevsky per 7; admission free; open 11am-5pm Mon-Sat)* is a one-room sampler of traditional and contemporary Russian handicrafts. Across the street, the **Stanislavsky House-Museum** *(☎ 229 2855; Leontevsky per 6; admission RR50; open 2pm-6pm Wed-Sun)* has longer hours which vary from day to day. See the boxed text 'Stanislavsky's Methods' in the Entertainment chapter.

Ploshchad Nikitskie Vorota, where Bolshaya Nikitskaya ulitsa crosses the Boulevard Ring, is named after the Nikitsky Gates in the city walls, which the ring has replaced. On its eastern side is the headquarters of the Russian news agency **ITAR-TASS**, with its windows full of news photos.

South down the Boulevard Ring is the **Museum of Oriental Art** *(☎ 202 4555; Nikitsky bul 12A; admission RR60; open noon-8pm Tues-Sun)*, which mounts professional exhibitions from a large collection of art and religious artefacts from Asia and Africa.

Farther along towards Arbatskaya ploshchad are the **Gogol Memorial Rooms** *(☎ 291 1550; Nikitsky bul 7; open noon-7pm Mon-Fri, noon-5pm Sat-Sun)*. The 19th-century writer Nikolai Gogol spent his last, tortured months here. In the courtyard the gloomy statue has some of his best-known characters featured in bas-relief around the base.

In 1831 the poet Alexander Pushkin married Natalia Goncharova in the **Church of the Grand Ascension** (Tserkov Bolshogo Voznesenia) on the western side of ploshchad Nikitskie Vorota. Six years later he died in St Petersburg, defending her honour in a duel.

The couple is now featured in the **Rotunda Fountain**, erected in 1999 to commemorate the poet's 100th birthday.

Immediately north is the fascinating 1906 Art Nouveau **Gorky House-Museum** (☎ 290 5113; Malaya Nikitskaya ul 6/2; admission free; open 10am-5pm Thur, Sat & Sun, noon-7pm Wed & Fri). Designed by Fyodor Shekhtel and given to Gorky in 1931, the house is a visual fantasy – from the sculpted doorways, ceiling murals, stained glass and carved stone staircase to the exterior tile work. There's a tale that Stalin hastened Gorky's death (in 1936) by having the walls of the small, ground-level bedroom covered with toxic paint. Enter the museum at the back.

BARRIKADNAYA (MAP 2)

Bolshaya Nikitskaya ulitsa intersects the Garden Ring at Kudrinskaya ploshchad, and the surrounding neighbourhood is known as Barrikadnaya. It is so called because it saw heavy street fighting during the 1905 and 1917 uprisings.

Just north, on the inner side of the Garden Ring, is the **Chekhov House-Museum** (☎ 291 6154; Sadovaya-Kudrinskaya ul 6), which was closed for renovations at the time of research.

Behind Kudrinskaya ploshchad there's the main entrance to the big **Moscow Zoo** (☎ 255 5375; cnr Barrikadnaya & Bolshaya Gruzinskaya uls; admission RR60; open 9am-8pm daily in summer, earlier in the off season). Popular with families, the highlight is the big cats' exhibit, although the domestic animals and the kids are fun to watch too.

The **skyscraper** at the intersection of Bolshaya Nikitskaya ulitsa with the Garden Ring, is one of the Stalinist neo-Gothic monstrosities often called the 'Seven Sisters'.

See the boxed text 'Stalin's Seven Sisters' in the Facts about Moscow chapter.

A block south, next door to the US Embassy, there's the **Fyodor Shalyapin House-Museum** (☎ 205 6326; Novinsky bul 25; admission RR20; open 11.30am-4pm Tues-Thur, Sat & Sun). The world-famous operatic singer lived here from 1910 to 1918 and the museum has some original stage costumes. There are occasional concerts in the museum's white room.

The Garden Ring was created as a tree-lined boulevard in place of Moscow's old outer rampart. Today, this wide and noisy stretch of the Garden Ring makes it easy to believe the story that the ring's widening and tree felling in the 1930s were done to enable warplanes to land. If you fancy a trip round the entire 16km of the Garden Ring, hop on trolleybus No Б in either direction. It'll eventually bring you back to where you started (though you may have to change to another No Б at Kursk Station).

White House

Moscow's White House (Bely dom; Krasnopresnenskaya nab 2), scene of two crucial episodes in recent Russian history, stands just north of Kalininsky Most, a short walk west of the US embassy (Krasnopresnenskaya and Barrikadnaya are the nearest metro stations).

It was here that Boris Yeltsin rallied the opposition that confounded the 1991 hardline coup, then two years later sent in tanks and troops to blast out conservative rivals – some of them the same people who backed him in 1991.

The images of Yeltsin climbing on a tank in front of the White House in 1991, and of the same building ablaze after the 1993 assault, are among the most unforgettable from those tumultuous years.

The White House – now back to its original colour and officially called the House of Government of the Russian Federation (Dom pravitelstva Rossiyskoy federatsii) – fronts a stately bend in the Moscow River, with the Stalinist Hotel Ukraina rising on the far bank. This corner of Moscow is particularly appealing when these buildings and Kalininsky Most are lit up at night.

ARBAT REGION

Bound by the Moscow River on both sides, the region includes the area south of Novy Arbat ulitsa and north of the Garden Ring.

Vozdvizhenka Ulitsa & Novy Arbat Ulitsa (Map 2)

Vozdvizhenka ulitsa, running west from the Kremlin, and Novy Arbat ulitsa, its continuation to the Moscow River, form the start of the road west to Smolensk.

The 'Moorish Castle' studded with seashells, was built in 1899 for an eccentric merchant named Arseny Morozov, who was inspired by a real one in Spain. The inside is sumptuous and equally over the top. It's now the **House of Friendship with Peoples of Foreign Countries** (ul Vozdvizkenka 16), which is not normally open to the public, but sometimes exhibitions are held here. Morozov's mother, who lived next door, apparently declared of her son's home, 'Until now, only I knew you were mad; now everyone will'.

Novy Arbat ulitsa, which begins beyond the Boulevard Ring, was created in the 1960s, with four matching ministry highrises. At the corner of Novy Arbat and Povarskaya ulitsa the 24-storey high-rise overwhelms the small **Church of St Simeon the Stylite** (Tserkov Simeona Stolpnika), built in the middle of the 17th century.

The **Mikhail Lermontov House-Museum** (☎ 291 5298; Malaya Molchanovka ul 2; open 2pm-5pm Wed & Fri, 11am-3pm Thur, Sat & Sun), north off Novy Arbat ulitsa, displays the background of the 19th-century author of *A Hero of Our Time*, as well as many poems.

Ulitsa Arbat

Ulitsa Arbat is a 1.25km pedestrian mall which stretches from Arbatskaya ploshchad (metro: Arbatskaya) on the Boulevard Ring to Smolenskaya ploshchad (metro: Smolenskaya) on the Garden Ring.

Moscow's most famous street is something of an art market, complete with instant-portrait painters, soapbox poets and jugglers (and some pickpockets). The Arbat is an interesting walk. It is dotted with old, pastel-coloured, merchant houses and tourist-oriented shops and cafés.

Until the 1960s, ulitsa Arbat was Moscow's main westward artery. Then a swathe was bulldozed through streets to its north to create the present Novy Arbat ulitsa, taking

Arbat, My Arbat

Arbat, my Arbat,
You are my calling
You are my happiness and my misfortune.
Bulat Okudjava

For Moscow's beloved bard Bulat Okudjava, the Arbat was not only home, it was inspiration. Although he spent his university years in Georgia dabbling in harmless verse, it was only upon his return to Moscow – to his cherished Arbat – that his poetry adopted the freethinking character for which it is known.

He gradually made the transition from poet to songwriter: 'Once I had the desire to accompany one of my satirical verses with music. I only knew three cords; now, 27 years later, I know seven cords, then I knew three. I sang, my friends liked it, and I liked it…gradually a scandal began. The compositors hated me. The singers detested me. The guitarists were terrified by me. And that is how it went on, until a very well-known poet of ours announced: Calm down, these are not songs. This is just another way of presenting poetry.'

And so a new form of art was born. The 1960s were heady times – in Moscow as elsewhere – and Okudjava inspired a whole movement of liberal-thinking poets to take their ideas to the streets. Vladimir Vysotsky and others – some more political than others – all followed in Okudjava's footsteps. The bards' iconoclastic lyrics and simple melodies drew enthusiastic crowds all around Moscow.

Today's Arbat – full of tacky souvenir stands and overpriced cafés – bears little resemblance to the hallowed haunt of Okudjava's youth, but its memory lives on in bards, buskers, painters and poets who still perform for strolling crowds on summer evenings.

out the old Arbatskaya ploshchad, a monastery and half a dozen churches. Ulitsa Arbat itself lay like a severed limb until restored as a pedestrian precinct in the 1980s.

The evocative names of nearby lanes such as Khlebny (Bread), Skatertny (Tablecloth), Serebryany (Silver), and Plotnikov (Carpenters') and that of the peaceful quarter south of the Arbat, called Staraya Konyushennaya (Old Stables), identify the area as an old settlement of court attendants. These were displaced by artists and aristocrats.

At Spasopeskosky pereulok, one of the side lanes, there is the 17th-century **Church of the Saviour in Peski** *(Tserkov Spasa na Peskakh; Map 2)*. At the far end of the lane is the elegant **Spaso House** *(Map 2)*, the residence of the US ambassador. Near ulitsa Arbat's eastern end is the **Wall of Peace** *(Stena Mira; Map 2)*, composed of hundreds of individually painted tiles on a theme of international friendship.

In a side street stands the refreshingly bizarre **Melnikov House** *(Dom Melnikova; Map 4; Krivoarbatsky per 10)*. This concoction of brick, plaster and diamond-shaped windows was built in 1927 by Konstantin Melnikov, the great constructivist architect who was denounced in the 1930s, but respected around the world. Melnikov continued to live in the house, one of the few privately owned houses in the USSR, until his death in 1974.

The statue at the corner of Plotnikov pereulok is of **Bulat Okudjava** *(Map 4)*, a 1960s cult poet, singer and songwriter, much of whose work was dedicated to the Arbat, where he lived at No 43.

At the western end of the street is the **Pushkin Arbat House-Museum** *(Map 4; ☎ 241 4212; ul Arbat 53; admission RR25; open 11am-6pm Tues-Sun)*, a house where the Pushkins lived after they married. The street ends with one of Stalin's 'Seven Sisters', the **Foreign Affairs Ministry** *(Ministerstvo innostrannykh del; Map 4)*. This is the only one of the seven buildings whose original design did not have the tower at the top. After Stalin saw the drawings and asked about the tower it was immediately added. Unlike the others it is a mere decoration put on top of the building (see the boxed text

Yuri Luzhkov, Christopher Columbus & Princess Diana

Zarub Tsereteli is nothing if not controversial. As the chief architect of the Okhotny Ryad shopping mall and the massive Cathedral of Christ the Saviour, he has been criticised for being too ostentatious, too gaudy, too overbearing and just plain too much.

The most despised of Tsereteli's masterpieces is the gargantuan statue of Peter the Great, which now stands in front of the Krasny Oktyabr chocolate factory. At 94.5m (that's twice the size of the *Statue of Liberty* without her pedestal), Peter towers over the city. Questions of taste aside, Muscovites were sceptical of the whole idea: why pay tribute to Peter the Great, who loathed Moscow, and even moved the capital to St Petersburg? Some radicals even attempted – however unsuccessfully – to blow the thing up. Today a 24-hour guard stands watch.

Mixed reactions are nothing new to Zarub Tsereteli. An earlier sculpture of Christopher Columbus has been rejected by five North American cities for reasons of cost, size and aesthetics. Some believe that the Peter the Great statue is actually a reincarnation of homeless Chris. Despite his critics, who launched a 'Stop Tsereteli' website, this favourite artist of Moscow Mayor Yuri Luzhkov does not stop.

In 2001, he unveiled a 2m bronze statue of Princess Diana, in honour of her 40th birthday. The Princess of Wales – decked out in a ruffled gown and tiara – was supposed to appear in an unnamed Moscow museum, but she seems to have skipped town.

Tsereteli's latest subject, in 2002, was Mayor Luzhkov himself. This 3m bronze has a tennis racket in hand and a ball at his feet. Tsereteli said that he hopes it will be mounted in one of Moscow's parks, where the mayor can inspire Muscovites to adopt a more active and sporty lifestyle.

'Stalin's Seven Sisters' in the Facts about Moscow chapter).

[Continued on page 111]

The Kremlin

Title page: The Kremlin is home to the Ivan the Great Bell Tower, which has 329 steps and was for a long time the tallest structure in Moscow (Christina Dameyer)

Top: Lenin's Tomb, the Kremlin wall and the neoclassical Senate building

Middle: The Tsar Cannon, cast in 1586, has never been in shot, Kremlin

Bottom: The oldest area within the Kremlin is Sobornaya ploshchad (Cathedral Square) which has six buildings including three enormous cathedrals, the work of Italian architects during the late 15th and 16th centuries

The apex of Russian political power, the Kremlin is not only the kernel of Moscow but also the whole country. From here Ivan the Terrible and Stalin orchestrated their terrors, Napoleon watched Moscow burn, Lenin fashioned the dictatorship of the proletariat, Khrushchev fought the Cold War, Gorbachev unleashed perestroika (literally, 'restructuring'), and Yeltsin concocted the New Russia.

Today the white, blue and red Russian flag flies over the Kremlin, the Soviet red flag having been hauled down on 25 December 1991.

In what was, for decades, a den of militant atheism, it may come as a surprise that the Kremlin's chief glories – the bases from which most of its famous gold domes rise – are cathedrals. The Kremlin was once the centre of Russia's Church as well as State.

The Kremlin occupies a roughly triangular plot of land covering little Borovitsky Hill on the north bank of the Moscow River, probably first settled in the 11th century. Today, it's enclosed by high walls 2.25km long, with Red Square outside the east wall. The best views of the Kremlin are from Sofiyskaya naberezhnaya, across the river, and the upper floors of Hotel Rossiya.

History

A kremlin is a town's fortified stronghold, and the first low wall around Moscow was built in the 1150s. At that time the Kremlin grounds only took up a hectare at the southwestern corner of the present Kremlin. By 1271, the town had a wooden church, a two-storey wooden house of Prince Daniil and various household buildings, barns, warehouses, cellars and stables.

Moscow continued to gain political power in the early 14th century, when Tver fell to the Golden Horde, and Moscow purchased a license (yarlyk) to become the major northern tax collector for the nomadic raiders.

The Kremlin grew with the importance of Moscow's princes and in the 1320s became the headquarters of the Russian Church, which shifted from Vladimir. During the reign of Dmitry Donskoy in the 1360s, the 'White Stone Kremlin' – which had limestone walls – was built with almost the same boundaries as today.

This version lasted until the 1475–1516 rebuilding launched by Ivan the Great. Ivan married the Byzantine princess, Sofia Paleologue, who had found refuge in Italy after the fall of Constantinople. This politically beneficial marriage strengthened Moscow's ties with Western Europe. Ivan the Great's ambition was to equal the fallen Constantinople – in grandeur, political power, achievements and architecture – and to become the third Rome; he brought stonemasons and architects from Italy to commence the project. During the reign of Ivan, the Kremlin gained new walls, three great cathedrals, and other structures, most of which still stand.

Although Peter the Great shifted the capital to St Petersburg, the tsars still showed up here for coronations and other celebrations. That

THE KREMLIN

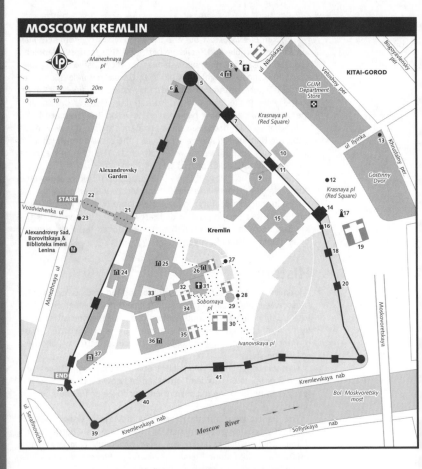

MOSCOW KREMLIN

Manezhnaya pl

KITAI-GOROD

0 10 20m
0 10 20yd

ul Nikolskaya

Bogoyavlensky per

Vetoshny per

GUM Department Store

Krasnaya pl (Red Square)

ul Ilyinka

Khrustalny per

Gostinny Dvor

Alexandrovsky Garden

Krasnaya pl (Red Square)

START

Vozdvizhenka ul

Alexandrovsy Sad, Borovitskaya & Biblioteka imeni Lenina

Kremlin

Manezhnaya ul

Sobornaya pl

Ivanovskaya pl

Moskvoretskaya

END

Kremlevskaya nab

Bol Moskvoretsky most

Kremlevskaya nab

ul Serafimovicha

Moscow River

Sofiyskaya nab

today's Kremlin is still standing is, nonetheless, thanks to several twists of fate. Catherine the Great had plans drawn up for a new classical Kremlin in the 1770s, but she ran out of money before its construction. And Napoleon blew up parts of the Kremlin before his retreat in 1812, but the timely arrival of Russian troops prevented its total destruction. The citadel wouldn't be breached again until the Bolsheviks stormed the place in November 1917.

The Great Kremlin Palace, Terem Palace and the Armoury let tourists in free before 1918. In 1918, when the Russian capital was shifted from St Petersburg after more than 200 years, the Kremlin grounds were closed to visitors. Its cathedrals and churches were only reopened for tourists in 1955.

MOSCOW KREMLIN

A Visit

Before entering the **Kremlin** (☎ 203 0349; W www.kremlin.museum.ru; adult/student RR200/100; open 10am-6pm Fri-Wed) deposit any bags you have at the left-luggage office (RR60 per bag, open 9am to 6.30pm), beneath the Kutafya Tower, just north of the main ticket office.

The main ticket office, in the Aleksandrovsky Garden just off Manezhnaya ploshchad (metro: Aleksandrovsky Sad, Borovitskaya or Biblioteka imeni Lenina), closes at 4.30pm. The ticket covers entry to all buildings, except the Armoury and Diamond Fund Exhibition (see that entry later in this special section); it's a good idea to buy tickets for these two here as well, to avoid having to queue up again once you're inside the Kremlin. A photography permit is RR50. There's also an entrance at the southern Borovistkiye Gate, mainly used by those heading straight to the Armoury. Visitors wearing shorts will be refused entry.

Seeing all the sights inside the Kremlin will require at least a half-day and probably longer. Inside the grounds, police blow whistles to stop you straying into out-of-bounds areas, which include the government buildings. You may want to bring some refreshments along as no food is sold on the Kremlin grounds. Toilets are at the south side of the Patriarch's Palace, behind the Church of the Deposition of the Robe. Cleanliness is not guaranteed.

Tours

Numerous freelance guides tout their services near the Kutafya Tower; prices (anything from US$10 to US$20 per hour) and quality vary widely. Dom Patriarshy (see the boxed text 'Want a Guide for a Day?' in the Things to See & Do chapter) offers regular tours of the main sights and occasionally runs tours of the off-limits Great Kremlin Palace.

The following buildings are listed in the order of the walking tour shown on the Moscow Kremlin map. The route begins at Kutafya Tower.

Government Buildings

The **Kutafya Tower** (Kutafya bashnya), which forms the main visitors' entrance today, stands away from the Kremlin's west wall, at the end of a ramp over the Alexandrovsky Garden. The ramp was once a bridge over the Neglinnaya River, which used to be part of the Kremlin's defences; it has flowed underground, beneath the Alexandrovsky Garden, since the early 19th century. The Kutafya Tower is the last survivor of a number of outer bridge towers that once stood on this side of the Kremlin.

From the Kutafya Tower, walk up the ramp and pass through the Kremlin walls beneath the 1495 **Trinity Gate Tower** (Troitskaya bashnya), the tallest of the Kremlin's towers. Right below your feet were the cells for prisoners in the 16th century. On your way to Sobornaya ploshchad you pass the following buildings that are closed to visitors.

The lane to the right (south), immediately inside the Trinity Gate Tower, passes the 17th-century **Poteshny Palace** (Poteshny Dvorets) where Stalin later lived. Poteshny Palace was built by Tsar Alexey Mikhailovich and housed the first Russian theatre. Here Tsar Alexey enjoyed various comedy performances; however, in keeping with conservative Russian Orthodox tradition, after the show he would go to the *banya* (Russian bathhouse), then attend a church service to repent his sins.

The bombastic marble, glass and concrete **Kremlin Palace of Congresses** (Kremlyovksy Dvorets Syezdov), built in 1960–61 for Communist Party congresses, is also a concert and ballet auditorium which holds 6000 people. North of the Kremlin Palace of Congresses is the 18th-century **Arsenal**, commissioned by Peter the Great to house workshops and depots for guns and weaponry. An unrealised plan at the end of the 19th century was to open a museum of the Napoleonic Wars. Now housing the Kremlin Guard, the building is ringed with 800 captured Napoleonic cannons.

The ultimate seat of power in the modern Kremlin, the offices of the president of Russia, are in the yellow, triangular former **Senate** building, a fine 18th-century neoclassical edifice, east of the Arsenal. Built in 1785 by architect Matvei Kazakov, it was noted for its huge cupola. In the 16th and 17th centuries this area was where the *boyars* (Russian nobles) lived. Next to the Senate is the 1930s' **Supreme Soviet** (Verkhovny Soviet) building.

Patriarch's Palace

The first building open to visitors that you reach, just past the Kremlin Palace of Congresses, is the Patriarch's Palace (Patriarshy Dvorets). It was mostly built in the mid-17th century for Patriarch Nikon, who ordered a return to the early Moscow style, thus sparking the Orthodox break with the Old Believers. The palace contains a **Museum of 17th-century Russian Applied Art & Life**, which houses church vestments, icons, illuminated books etc. It also incorporates the five-domed **Church of the Twelve Apostles** (Tserkov Dvenadtsati Apostolov), which Nikon had built as a new patriarch's chapel.

The large **Hall of the Cross** (Krestovaya Palata) was once the patriarch's official reception hall. From the 18th century the room was used to produce *miro*, a holy oil used during church services, which contains over 30 herbal components; the oven and huge pans from the production process are on display. The Hall of the Cross was once the largest room in Russia without supporting columns.

Now quiet, the palace at its prime was a busy place. Apart from the Patriarch's living quarters it had huge kitchens, warehouses and cellars stocked with food, workshops, a school for the high-born children, offices for scribes, dormitories for those waiting to be baptised, stables and carriage houses.

Pass through the arches of Patriarch's Palace into Sobornaya ploshchad (Cathedral Square), the heart of the Kremlin.

Assumption Cathedral

On the northern side of Sobornaya ploshchad, with five golden helmet domes and four semicircular gables facing the square, is the Assumption Cathedral (Uspensky sobor), the focal church of prerevolutionary Russia and the burial place of most of the heads of the Russian Orthodox Church from the 1320s to 1700. If you have limited time in the Kremlin, come straight here.

In 1470, Russian architects Krivtsov and Myshkin were commissioned by Ivan the Great to replace the old dilapidated cathedral which was previously here from 1326. As soon as the ceiling was put up, one of the walls collapsed. During Soviet times, history books said this calamity was the result of bad workmanship, but today revisionist history indicates that a bad earthquake caused the collapse. Either way, Krivtsov and Myshkin lost their job, and Italian architect Aristotle Fioravanti was given the next shot. After the foundation was completed, he toured Novgorod, Suzdal and Vladimir to acquaint himself with Russian architecture. His design is a more spacious version of the Assumption Cathedral at Vladimir, with a Renaissance twist.

In 1812, French troops used the cathedral as a stable; they looted 295kg of gold and over five tonnes of silver from here, but much of it was recovered. The church closed in 1918. According to some accounts, in 1941, when the Nazis were on the outskirts of Moscow, Stalin secretly ordered a service in the Assumption Cathedral to protect the city from the enemy. The cathedral was officially returned to the Church in 1989, but it still operates as a museum.

A striking 1660s' fresco of the Virgin Mary faces Sobornaya ploshchad, above the door once used for royal processions. The visitors entrance is at the western end.

Interior

The interior of the Assumption Cathedral is unusually bright and spacious, full of warm golds, reds and blues. The west wall features a scene of the Apocalypse, a favourite theme of the Russian Church in the Middle Ages. The pillars have pictures of martyrs on them, as martyrs are considered to be the pillars of faith. Above the southern gates there are frescoes of Yelena and Constantine, who brought Christianity to Greece and the south of Russia. The space above the northern gate is taken by Olga and Vladimir, who brought Christianity to the north.

Most of the existing murals on the cathedral walls were painted on a gilt base in the 1640s, with the exception of three grouped together on the south wall: *The Apocalypse (Apokalipsis), The Life of Metropolitan Pyotr (Zhitie Mitropolita Petra)* and *All Creatures Rejoice in Thee (O tebe raduetsya)*. These are attributed to Dionysius and his followers, the cathedral's original 15th-century mural painters. The tombs of many of the leaders of the Russian Church (metropolitans up to 1590, patriarchs from 1590 to 1700) are against the north, west and south walls.

Near the south wall is a tent-roofed, wooden throne made in 1551 for Ivan the Terrible, known as the **Throne of Monomakh**. Its carved scenes highlight the career of 12th-century Grand Prince Vladimir Monomakh of Kiev. Near the west wall there is a shrine with holy relics of Patriarch Hermogen who was starved to death during the Time of Troubles in 1612.

The **iconostasis** dates from 1652, but its lowest level contains some older icons. The 1340s *Saviour with the Angry Eye (Spas yaroe oko)* is second from the right. On the left of the central door is the *Virgin of Vladimir (Vladimirskaya Bogomater)*, an early 15th-century Rublyov school copy of Russia's most revered image, the *Vladimir Icon of the Mother of God (Vladimirskaya Ikona Bogomateri)*. The 12th-century original, now in the Tretyakov Gallery, stood in the Assumption Cathedral from the 1480s to 1930. One of the oldest Russian icons, the 12th-century red-clothed *St George (Svyatoy Georgy)* from Novgorod, is positioned by the north wall.

The original icons of the lower, local tier are symbols of victory brought from Vladimir, Smolensk, Veliky Ustyug and other places. The south door was brought from the Nativity of the Virgin Cathedral in Suzdal.

Church of the Deposition of the Robe

This delicate single-domed church (Tserkov Rizpolozhenia), beside the west door of the Assumption Cathedral, was built between 1484 and 1486 in exclusively Russian style. It was the private chapel of the heads of the Church, who tended to be highly suspicious of such people as Italian architects.

Originally an open gallery or porch surrounded the church; it was later removed and the church was connected with the palace for the convenience of the tsars. The interior walls, ceilings and pillars are covered with 17th-century frescoes. It houses an exhibition of 15th- to 17th-century woodcarvings.

Ivan the Great Bell Tower

With its two golden domes rising above the eastern side of Sobornaya ploshchad, the **Ivan the Great Bell Tower** (Kolokolnya Ivana Veliko-go) is the Kremlin's tallest structure – a landmark visible from 30km away. Before the 20th century it was forbidden to build any higher in Moscow.

Its history dates back to the Church of Ioann Lestvichnik under the Bells, built on this site in 1329 by Ivan I. In 1505, the Italian Marco Bono designed a new belfry, originally with only two octagonal tiers beneath a drum and a dome.

In 1600, Boris Godunov raised it to 81m, a public works project designed to employ the thousands of people who had come to Moscow during a famine.

The building's central section, with guilded single dome and a 65-tonne bell, dates from between 1532 and 1542. The tent-roofed annexe, next to the belfry, was commissioned by Patriarch Filaret in 1642 and bears his name. Exhibitions from the Kremlin collections are shown on the ground level.

Exit Sobornaya ploshchad on the northern side to the east of Patri-arch's Palace.

Tsar Cannon

North of the bell tower is the 40-tonne **Tsar Cannon** (Tsar-pushka). It was cast in 1586 by the blacksmith Ivan Chokhov for Fyodor I, whose portrait is on the barrel. Shot has never sullied its 89cm bore – certainly not the cannonballs beside it, which are too big even for this ele-phantine firearm.

Tsar Bell

Beside (not inside) the bell tower stands the world's biggest bell (Tsar-kolokol), a 202-tonne monster that has never rung. An earlier version, weighing 130 tonnes, fell from its belfry during a fire in 1701 and shattered. Using these remains, the current Tsar Bell was cast in the 1730s for Empress Anna Ivanovna. The bell was cooling off in the foundry casting pit in 1737 when it came into contact with water, causing an 11-tonne chunk to chip off.

After 100 years, the architect Monferrand took the damaged bell out of the pit and put it on a pedestal. The bas-reliefs of Empress Anna and Tsar Alexey, as well as some icons, were etched on its sides.

Cross south through the pleasant park of Ivanovskaya ploshchad, a good place for a break on a nice day. The views south over Moscow are spectacular. Return to Sobornaya ploshchad at your leisure.

Archangel Cathedral

Back on Soborny ploshchad, the Archangel Cathedral (Arkhangelsky sobor) at the square's southeastern corner was, for centuries, the coronation, wedding and burial church of tsars.

It was built by Ivan Kalita in 1333 to commemorate the end of the great famine, and dedicated to Archangel Michael, guardian of the Moscow princes.

By the early 16th century it fell into disrepair and was rebuilt between 1505 and 1508 by the Italian architect Alevisio Novi. Like the Assumption Cathedral, it is five-domed and essentially Byzantine-Russian in style. However, the exterior has many Venetian Renaissance features – notably the distinctive scallop shell gables and porticoes.

The tombs of all Muscovy's rulers from the 1320s to the 1690s are here, bar one (the absentee is Boris Godunov, whose body was taken out of the grave by the order of a False Dmitry and buried at Sergiev Posad in 1606).

The bodies are buried underground, beneath the 17th-century sarcophagi and 19th-century copper covers. Tsarevich Dmitry, a son of Ivan the Terrible who died mysteriously in 1591, lies beneath a painted stone canopy.

It was Dmitry's death that sparked the appearance of a string of impersonators, known as False Dmitrys, during the Time of Troubles. Ivan's own tomb is out of sight behind the iconostasis, along with those of his other sons: Ivan (whom he killed), and Fyodor (who succeeded him). From Peter the Great onwards, emperors and empresses were buried in St Petersburg; the exception was Peter II, who died in Moscow in 1730 and is here. The 17th-century murals were uncovered during restorations in the 1950s. The south wall depicts many of those buried here; on the pillars are some of their predecessors, including Andrey Bogolyubsky, Prince Daniil and his father, Alexander Nevsky.

ARCHANGEL CATHEDRAL

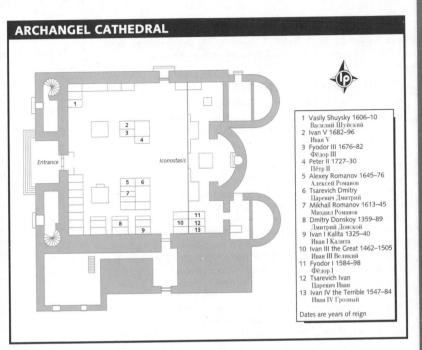

1 Vasily Shuysky 1606–10
  Василий Шуйский
2 Ivan V 1682–96
  Иван V
3 Fyodor III 1676–82
  Фёдор III
4 Peter II 1727–30
  Пётр II
5 Alexey Romanov 1645–76
  Алексей Романов
6 Tsarevich Dmitry
  Царевич Дмитрий
7 Mikhail Romanov 1613–45
  Михаил Романов
8 Dmitry Donskoy 1359–89
  Дмитрий Донской
9 Ivan I Kalita 1325–40
  Иван I Калита
10 Ivan III the Great 1462–1505
   Иван III Великий
11 Fyodor I 1584–98
   Фёдор I
12 Tsarevich Ivan
   Царевич Иван
13 Ivan IV the Terrible 1547–84
   Иван IV Грозный

Dates are years of reign

Entrance

Iconostasis

Hall of Facets

Named for its Italian Renaissance stone facing, the Hall of Facets (Granovitaya palata) was designed and built by Marco Ruffo and Pietro Solario between 1487 and 1491 during the reign of Ivan III. Its upper floor housed the tsar's throne room, scene of banquets and ceremonies.

Access to the Hall of Facets was via an outside staircase from the square below. During the Streltsky Rebellion of 1682, several of Peter the Great's relatives were tossed down the exterior **Red Staircase**, so called because it ran red with their blood. (It's no wonder that Peter hated Moscow and decided to start afresh with a new capital in St Petersburg.) Stalin destroyed the staircase, but it was rebuilt in 1994.

The namesake hall is 500 sq metres with a supporting pillar in the centre. The walls are decorated with gorgeous murals of biblical and historical themes, although none is original. Unfortunately, the entire building is closed to the public.

Terem Palace

The 16th- and 17th-century Terem Palace (Teremnoy Dvorets) is the most splendid of the Kremlin palaces. A stone palace built by Vasily III, the living quarters include a dining room, living room, study, bedroom and small chapel. Unfortunately, the palace is closed to the public, but you can glimpse its cluster of 11 golden domes and chequered roof behind and above the Church of the Deposition of the Robe.

Annunciation Cathedral

The Annunciation Cathedral (Blagoveshchensky sobor), at the south-west corner of Sobornaya ploshchad, contains the celebrated icons of master painter Theophanes the Greek. They have a timeless beauty that appeals even to those usually left cold by icons.

Vasily I built the first wooden church on this site in 1397. Between 1484 and 1489, Ivan III had the Annunciation Cathedral rebuilt to serve as the royal family's private chapel. Originally the cathedral had just three domes and an open gallery round three sides. Ivan the Terrible, whose tastes were more elaborate, added six more domes and chapels at each corner, enclosed the gallery and gilded the roof.

Under Orthodox law, Ivan's fourth marriage disqualified him from entering the church proper, so he had the southern arm of the gallery converted into the **Archangel Gabriel Chapel** (Pridel Arkhangela Gavriila), from which he could watch services through a grille. The chapel has a colourful iconostasis, dating from its consecration in 1564, and an exhibition of icons.

Many of the murals in the gallery date from the 1560s. Among them are the *Capture of Jericho* in the porch, *Jonah and the Whale* in the northern arm of the gallery, and the *Tree of Jesus* on its ceiling. Other murals feature ancient philosophers Aristotle, Plutarch, Plato, Socrates and others holding scrolls with their own wise words. Socrates' scroll reads: 'No harm will ever come to a good man. Our soul is immortal. After death the good shall be rewarded and the evil punished.' Plato announces: 'We must hope God shall send us a heavenly Teacher and a Guide.'

The small central part of the cathedral has a lovely jasper floor. The 16th-century frescoes include Russian princes on the north pillar and Byzantine emperors on the south, both with Apocalypse scenes above them. But the chapel's real treasure is the iconostasis, where restorers in the 1920s uncovered early 15th-century icons by three of the greatest medieval Russian artists.

Theophanes likely painted the six icons at the right-hand end of the deesis row, the biggest of the six tiers of the iconostasis. From left to right, these are the *Virgin Mary, Christ Enthroned, St John the Baptist,* the *Archangel Gabriel*, the *Apostle Paul* and *St John Chrysostom*. Theophanes was a master at portraying visible pathos in the facial expressions of his subjects, setting these icons apart from most others.

The third icon from the left, *Archangel Michael*, is ascribed to Andrey Rublyov, who may also have painted the adjacent *St Peter*. Rublyov is also reckoned to be the artist of the first, second, sixth, seventh and probably the third and fifth icons from the left of the festival row, above the deesis row. The seven at the right-hand end are attributed to Prokhor of Gorodets.

Exit Sobornaya ploshchad to the south and walk west along the Great Kremlin Palace.

Great Kremlin Palace

Housing the Armoury and much more, the 700-room Great Kremlin Palace (Bolshoy Kremlyovsky Dvorets) was built from 1838 to 1849 by Konstantin Thon as an imperial residence. It is now an official residence of the Russian president, used for state visits and receptions. However, unlike Russian emperors, the president doesn't have living quarters here.

The palace incorporates some of the earlier buildings such as the Hall of Facets, Terem Palace and several chapels. Although vast, the building has never received great praise, being criticised as barrack-like and pretentious. Several ceremonial halls are named for saints, including St George, St Vladimir, St Andrew, St Catherine and St Alexander. St George's Hall is mainly used for state awards ceremonies, while major international treaties are signed in St Vladimir's Hall. To save you the trouble, the Great Kremlin Palace is closed for tourists, except those on a state visit. From time to time, Dom Patriarshy Tours take tourists here (see the boxed text 'Want a Guide for a Day?' in the Things to See & Do chapter).

Armoury

In the southwestern corner of the Kremlin, the **Armoury** *(Oruzheynaya palata; adult/student RR300/175)* is a numbingly opulent collection of treasures accumulated over centuries by the Russian State and Church. Your ticket will specify a time of entry.

History

The Armoury dates back to 1511, when it was founded under Vasily III to manufacture and store weapons, imperial arms and regalia for the royal court. Later it also produced jewellery, icon frames and embroidery.

During the reign of Peter the Great, all craftsmen, goldsmiths and silversmiths were sent to St Petersburg and the armoury became a mere museum storing the royal treasures. A fire in 1737 destroyed many of the items. In the early 19th century, new premises were built for the collection. Much of it, however, never made it back from Nizhny Novgorod, where it was sent for safekeeping during Napoleon's invasion in 1812.

Still another building to house the collection was completed in 1851, but it was later demolished to make way for the dreadful Palace of Congresses. Which is why the Armoury is now housed in the Great Kremlin Palace.

Despite the disasters befallen this collection throughout the centuries, the Armoury still contains plenty of treasures for ogling, and remains a highlight of a visit to the Kremlin.

The Collection

The collection is in nine rooms, Nos 1 to 5 upstairs, Nos 6 to 9 downstairs. Don't miss the opportunity to check your bag at the entrance. The rooms contain the following:

Room 1: This room is stuffed to the gills with various gold and silver objects that lose a bit of their lustre after you've seen your eighth coronation sceptre and ninth ceremonial bowl

Room 2: The star attractions are the 14 renowned Fabergé eggs, which were given as Easter gifts by the tsar and tsarina from 1884 until the Romanov house of cards collapsed. The eggs are exquisite works of precious metals and jewels. Each opens to reveal amazingly detailed miniature objects – most famously a clockwork trans-Siberian train made of gold, with a platinum locomotive and ruby headlamp – talk about your limited edition collectables!

Rooms 3 & 4: Armour, weapons and more armour and more weapons fill these two smaller rooms

Room 5: Here you will find all those gifts proffered by visiting ambassadors over the years. Each piece of gold or silver is yet another reason why the average peasant trying to coax some life out of a mouldy seed might get

Towers of Power

The present Kremlin walls were built between 1485 and 1495, replacing the limestone walls from the 14th century. The walls are 6m to 17m tall, depending on the landscape, and 2m to 5m thick. They stretch for 2235m. Originally, a 32m-wide moat encircled the northern end of the Kremlin, connecting the Moscow and Neglinnaya Rivers.

The 20 distinctive towers were built mostly between 1485 and 1500, with tent roofs added in the 17th century. Originally, the towers had lookout posts and were equipped for heavy fighting. Most were designed by Italian masons. The more interesting towers are on the eastern and southern sides (starting at the northern corner and going clockwise):

Corner Arsenal Tower (Arsenalnaya bashnya) The stronghold of the Kremlin fortification with walls 4m thick. A well in the basement to provide water during sieges still survives today.

St Nicholas Tower (Nikolskaya bashnya) Previously a gated, defensive tower on the northeastern flank. Through this gate, Dmitry Pozharsky and Kozma Minin (as depicted in the statue in front of St Basil's Cathedral) led a civilian army and drove out the Polish occupiers.

Senate Tower (Senatskaya bashnya) Originally a nameless, gateless tower, and finally aptly named after the construction of the Senate in the 18th century

Saviour Gate Tower (Spasskaya bashnya) The Kremlin's 'official' exit onto Red Square. This gate – considered sacred – was used for processions in tsarist days. The two white-stone plaques above the gate commemorate the tower's construction. Between the tower's double walls, a staircase links five of its 10 levels. The current clock was installed in the Saviour Gate Tower in the 1850s. Hauling 3m hands and weighing 25 tonnes, the clock takes up three of the tower's levels. Its melodic chime sounds every 15 minutes across Red Square and across the country (on the radio).

a little miffed. Ignoring the plight of the masses, you can enjoy the skill of the craftspeople who made these items.

Descend the grand staircase by room 1.

Room 6: Here are plenty more reasons to revolt. Thrones and royal regalia fill the room – the joint coronation throne of boy tsars Peter (the Great) and his half-brother Ivan V, with a secret compartment from which Regent Sofia would prompt them; the coronation dresses of 18th-century empresses (Empress Elizabeth, we're told, had 15,000 other dresses).

Room 7: This room has two of the main pieces of the collection – the jewel-studded, sable-trimmed, gold Cap of Monomakh, worn for coronations for two centuries until 1682; and the 800-diamond throne of Tsar Alexey

Room 8: Only the best royal harnesses and equestrian gear are preserved here

Room 9: Centuries worth of royal carriages and sledges line the aisles in this huge room. The once-glittering gold leafing has faded and the wood has shrunk revealing gaps in the decoration, one of which surely would have kept a village of potential revolutionaries fed for several years. Look for the sleigh in which Elizabeth rode from St Petersburg to Moscow for her coronation, pulled by 23 horses at a time – about 800 in all for the trip.

Towers of Power

Tsar Tower A later addition (1680), which sits atop the Kremlin wall. Legend has it that Ivan the Terrible watched executions and other Red Square activities from the old wooden tower that previously stood on this site.

Alarm Tower (Nabatnaya bashnya) Housed the Spassky alarm bell, which was used to warn of enemy attacks and to spur popular uprisings. After quashing one uprising, Catherine the Great was so outraged that she had the clapper removed from the bell so it could sound no more. The bell remained mute in the tower for 30 years before it was finally removed.

Konstantin & Yelena Tower (Konstantino-Yeleninskaya bashnya) Served to protect the settlements outside the city, complete with firing platforms and drawbridge over the moat. During the 17th century this tower was used as a prison, earning it the nickname 'torture tower'.

Moskvoretskaya Tower The round tower at the southeastern corner

Petrovskaya Tower

First & Second Nameless Towers Both destroyed in 1771 because they interfered with the construction of the Kremlin Palace, but rebuilt after its completion

Secrets Tower (Taynitskaya bashnya) The first tower built (1485), and named for a secret passageway down to the river

Annunciation Tower (Blagoveshchenskaya bashnya) Named for the miracle-working icon on the facade. In 1633, the so-called Laundry Gate was constructed nearby for Kremlin washerwomen to go down to the Moscow River, but it was later bricked up.

Water Tower (Vodovzvodnaya bashnya) A circular tower erected at the point of confluence of the Moscow and Neglinnaya Rivers. From 1633, a water lift in this tower pumped water to a reservoir and supplied a system of underground piping for the Kremlin.

Diamond Fund Exhibition

If the Armoury hasn't sated your diamond lust, there are more in the separate **Diamond Fund Exhibition** (*Vystavka almaznogo fonda; adult/student RR300/175; closed for lunch 1pm-2pm*) in the same building. The collection, mainly of precious stones and jewellery garnered by tsars and empresses, includes such weighty beasts as the 190-carat diamond given to Catherine the Great by her lover Grigory Orlov. The displays of unmounted diamonds are stunning, revealing the real beauty of the gems. In contrast, the jewellery is so extravagant it is almost tacky. There are almost no signs – even in Russian – as the locals are only allowed in as part of a guided tour. No tours are offered in other languages, which is to your advantage, since you do not have to wait as the Russian visitors do.

Exit the Kremlin through Borovitskaya Gate Tower and stroll back to the starting point through Alexandrovsky Garden.

Alexandrovsky Garden

The first public park in Moscow, Alexandrovsky Garden (Alexandrovsky Sad) sits along the Kremlin's western wall. Colourful flower beds and impressive Kremlin views make it a favourite strolling spot for Muscovites and tourists alike. Back in the 17th century, the Neglinnaya River ran through the present gardens, with dams and mills along the banks. When the river was diverted underground, the garden was founded, in 1821, by architect Osip Bove. Enter through the original gates at the northern end.

The **Tomb of the Unknown Soldier** (Mogila neizvestnogo soldata) at its north end is a kind of national pilgrimage spot, where newlyweds bring flowers and have their pictures taken. The tomb contains the remains of one soldier who died in December 1941 at Km 41 of Leningradskoe shosse – the nearest the Nazis came to Moscow. The inscription reads: 'Your name is unknown, your deeds immortal.' There's an eternal flame, and other inscriptions listing the Soviet hero cities of WWII and honouring 'those who fell for the motherland' between 1941 and 1945. The changing of the guard happens every hour. South of the tomb, a row of red urns contains the earth from the 'hero cities', cities that withstood the heaviest fighting during WWII.

Farther south, the obelisk was originally a monument to commemorate the House of Romanovs. In 1918, it had a dramatic change in mission when it was redesignated the **Monument to Revolutionary Thinkers**, in honour of those responsible for the spread of communism in Russia.

[Continued from page 96]

Pushkin Fine Arts Museum (Map 4)

Moscow's premier foreign art museum is just a skip from the southwestern corner of the Kremlin. The Pushkin Fine Arts Museum (☎ 203 7412; ul Volkhonka 12; metro: Kropotkinskaya; foreigner adult/student RR160/60, audio guide RR100; open 10am-6pm Tues-Sun) is famous for its impressionist and postimpressionist paintings, but also has a broad selection of European works from the Renaissance onward, mostly appropriated from private collections after the revolution. There is an amazing (read: mind-numbing) array of statues through the ages.

In 1993 the Pushkin admitted that it held the gold of ancient Troy, found by the archaeologist Heinrich Schliemann in the 19th century; then in 1995 it unveiled a stash of 63 works by the likes of Degas, Renoir, Goya, El Greco and Tintoretto that had been thought lost for 50 years (see the boxed text 'Pushkin Fine Arts Museum').

Keep an eye open for any special exhibitions at the Pushkin. In recent years the museum (like the Hermitage in St Petersburg)

PUSHKIN FINE ARTS MUSEUM

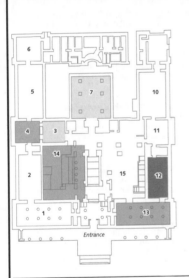
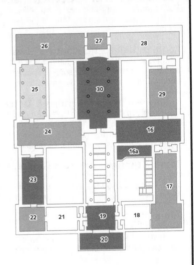

1 The Art of Ancient Egypt
2 The Art of Ancient Civilisations
3 Hellenistic, Coptic & Byzantine Art
4 Italian Art of the 13th-15th Centuries
5 Italy, Germany & Netherlands; Art of the 15th-16th Centuries
6 Italy, Germany & Netherlands; Art of the 15th-16th Centuries
7 Antique Art; Greece, Rome & the Northern Black Sea Region
10 17th-Century Dutch Art
11 Flemish & Spanish Art of the 17th Century
12 Italian Art of the 17th-18th Centuries
13 French Art of the 17th-18th Centuries
14 Greek Courtyard; Plaster Casts
15 Italian Courtyard; Plaster Casts
16 Art of the Aegean World & Ancient Greece; Plaster Casts

16a Art of the Aegean World & Ancient Greece; Plaster Casts
17 Art of the 20th Century
18 Postimpressionism. Cézanne & Gaugin
19 Exhibition Halls
20 Exhibition Halls
21 European Art in the Last Third of the 19th Century
22 French Impressionists
23 European Art in the First Half of the 19th Century
24 Greek Art of the Late Classical & Hellenistic Periods
25 The Art of Ancient Rome; Plaster Casts
26 European Art of the Middle Ages
27 European Art of the Middle Ages
28 Italian Renaissance Sculpture; Plaster Casts
29 The Sculpture of Michelangelo; Plaster Casts
30 Exhibition Hall

has revealed some fabulous art hoards kept secret since they were seized by the Red Army from Germany at the end of WWII. The museum is also making an effort to mount some ambitious temporary exhibitions from its vast legitimate holdings.

Around the Pushkin Fine Arts Museum (Map 4)

Next door to the Pushkin Fine Arts Museum there's the **Museum of Private Collections** (☎ 203 1546; ul Volkhonka 14; admission RR40; open noon-7pm Wed-Sun). This shows art collections donated by private individuals, many of whom amassed works during the Soviet era. The collectors/donors are featured, as well as the art.

Along the lane between the Pushkin and Private Collections museums is **Rerikh Museum** (☎ 203 6419; Maly Znamensky per 3/5; admission RR50; open noon-7pm Wed-Sun). Nikolay Rerikh (known internationally as Nicholas Roerich) was a mystical Russian artist of the late 19th and early

---

Pushkin Fine Arts Museum

Descriptions are provided in numerical order, although you might not visit the rooms in that order.

Rooms 1–2 (Art of Ancient Civilisations)
They contain a surprisingly excellent collection, complete with ancient Egyptian weapons, jewellery, ritual items and tombstones. Most of the items were excavated from burial sites, including two haunting mummies.

Room 3 (Hellenistic, Coptic & Byzantine Art)
Features a collection of Egyptian Fayum portraits, or death masks. The gold background and laurel wreaths are symbolic of the subject's posthumous glory. Other items are also religious in nature, including Coptic textiles and Byzantine icons.

Rooms 4–6 (Italian, German & Dutch Art of the 13th–16th Centuries)
This exhibition demonstrates the transition from the Middle Ages to the Renaissance. The Italian art, dating from the 13th to 15th centuries, includes paintings, woodcarvings, altarpieces and triptychs. The representations from the later centuries elevate the natural world, as opposed to the divine world. Artists place increasing importance on accuracy in their depictions.

Room 7 (Antique Art from Greece, Rome & the Northern Black Sea)
Houses the impressive exhibit *Treasures of Troy*, which is actually from the excavation of a settlement dating to 2500 BC. A German archaeologist donated the collection to the city of Berlin, from where it was appropriated by the Soviets in 1945.

Rooms 10–13 (European Art of the 17th Century)
Shows off the Golden Age of painting in Europe. The highlights include the dramatic Rembrandts in Room 10, especially his moving *Portrait of an Old Woman*; Rubens' vivid *Bacchanalia* in Room 11; and rich collections of Italian and French pieces in Rooms 12 and 13.

Room 14 (Greek Courtyard)
This bright, open room near the main staircase presents ancient Greek sculpture, especially models of monuments from the Acropolis

Room 15 (Italian Courtyard)
This is a reproduction of the courtyard of the 14th-century Palazzo del Podesta in Florence. The room exhibits plaster casts of German and Italian medieval and Renaissance sculpture. Three sculptures of David (by Donatello, Verrocchio and Michelangelo) are the highlights.

Room 16 (Art of the Aegean World and Ancient Greece)
Includes copies of ancient masks, weapons and sculpture

20th centuries, who now has an international following.

He spent a lot of time in the Altay mountains of Siberia, Central Asia and India painting some distinctive landscapes and mythological scenes.

The lopsided church beside the Pushkin is **St Antipy-by-the-Carriagehouse** (Tserkov Antipia na kolymazhnom dvore; ul Kolymazhnaya 8). It was supposedly commissioned by Malyuta Skuratov, the psychopath who ran the secret police for Ivan the Terrible.

Nearby, the gargantuan **Cathedral of Christ the Saviour** (Khram Khrista Spasitelya; ☎ 201 3847; open 10am-5pm daily) is a dream come true for Moscow mayor Yuri Luzhkov. It sits on the site of an earlier and similar church of the same name, built in 1839–83 to commemorate Russia's victory over Napoleon. This predecessor was destroyed during Stalin's orgy of explosive secularism. He planned to replace it with a 315m-high 'Palace of Soviets' – including a 100m statue of Lenin – but the project never got off the

Pushkin Fine Arts Museum

Room 17 (Art of the 20th Century)
Exhibits several of the most famous paintings by Matisse, such as *Goldfish*; some lesser-known pieces by Picasso; a few exquisite, primitive paintings by Rousseau; and other examples from Miro, Kandinsky and Chagall. The rich collection of 20th-century art continues to grow, with recent additions by Arp and others.

Room 18 (Postimpressionism: Cezanne & Gaugin)
They make strange bedfellows, representing the two extremes of late-19th-century art. Cezanne's still lifes and Gaugin's primitive scenes are well represented.

Rooms 19–20 (Special Exhibition Halls)
Often a highlight of a visit to the Pushkin, depending upon what's on show

Rooms 21–22 (European Art in the Late 19th Century)
These rooms are reason enough to visit the Pushkin. Room 21 contains several pieces by Van Gogh, including the scorching *Red Vineyards* and the tragic *Prison Courtyard*, painted in the last year of his life. An extensive collection of French impressionist works, based on the collection of two well-known Moscow art patrons, Sergei Shchukin and Ivan Morozov, is in Room 22. It includes representative paintings by Manet, Monet and Renoir, and sculptures from Rodin's *Gates of Hell* and *Monument to the Townspeople of Calais*.

Room 23 (European Art in the Early 19th Century)
Features a wide variety of classical portraits, as well as examples of Romantic artists such as Delacroix and Gericault

Room 24 (Greek Art of the Late Classical & Hellenistic Periods)
Features Greek gods in sensuous poses and Hellenistic humans with emotional expressions

Room 25 (Art of Ancient Rome)
This is home to more plaster casts, these decked out in togas. The room is distinctively Roman, complete with Corinthian columns and decorated ceilings.

Rooms 26–27 (European Art of the Middle Ages)
Contains, again, mostly replicas of early Christian, Byzantine and Western European medieval art. The primitivism of some of the Byzantine and Romanesque examples is appealing.

Room 28 (Italian Renaissance Sculpture)
Features more plaster casts of Donatello, among others

Room 29 (Sculptures of Michelangelo)
What more need be said? No, they are not originals.

ground, literally. Instead, for 50 years the site served the important purpose of the world's largest swimming pool.

This time around, the church was completed at an estimated cost of US$350 million in just two years, in time for Moscow's 850th birthday in 1997.

Much of the work was done by Luzhkov's favourite architect, Zarub Tsereteli (see the boxed text 'Yury Luzhkov, Christopher Columbus & Princess Diana?' later in this chapter).

It has aroused many passionate reactions from Muscovites, ranging from pious devotion to abject horror.

If they are missing their swimming pool, however, Muscovites should at least be grateful they can admire the shiny domes of a church instead of the shiny dome of Lenin's head.

A couple of streets farther back is the **Ministry of Defence** (Ministerstvo Oborony; Map 2; ul Znamenka) which is Russia's answer to the Pentagon.

Prechistenka Ulitsa & Beyond (Map 4)

Prechistenka ulitsa, which heads southwest from Kropotkinskaya metro, is virtually a museum of classical mansions, most of which date from the empire-style rebuilding after the great fire of 1812 (see the Grand Houses Tour in the Moscow Walks special section).

The **Pushkin Literary Museum** (☎ 201 3256; Prechistenka ul 12; admission RR25; open 11am-6pm Tues, Wed & Fri-Sun, 2pm-7pm Thur) is devoted to the poet's life and work.

Across the street, you'll find the location of the **Tolstoy Museum** (☎ 202 2190; Prechistenka ul 11; adult/ student RR100/50; open 11am-6pm Tues-Sun) which contains a collection of the writer's manuscripts, letters and sketches.

The **Russian Academy of Art** (Prechistenka ul 19-21) has an exhibition hall.

KHAMOVNIKI REGION

This region is surrounded on three sides by the Moscow River, as it dips down south and loops back up to the north. Its northern boundary is the Garden Ring.

Across the busy Garden Ring from the end of Prechistenka ulitsa, is the shady **Skver Devichego Polya** (Maiden's Field; Map 4) park, with its brooding Tolstoy statue. The interesting **Tolstoy Estate-Museum** (Map 4; ☎ 246 9444; ul Lva Tolstogo 21) was the writer's winter home in the 1880s and '90s. It's neither particularly big nor especially opulent, but fitting for junior nobility, which Tolstoy was.

Both Rachmaninov and Rimsky-Korsakov played the piano in the upstairs reception room; Tolstoy's training weights and his bicycle repose outside his study. Refurbished in 2002, the house has explanatory notices in English.

At the southern end of ulitsa Lva Tolstogo, the beautiful **Church of St Nicholas of the Weavers** (Tserkov Nikoli v Khamovnikakh; Map 4) vies with St Basil's Cathedral as the most colourful in Moscow.

Commissioned by the Moscow weavers' guild in 1676, it indeed looks like a great, jolly, green and orange tapestry. Inside you'll discover some equally rich frescoes and icons.

Novodevichy Convent (Map 4)

A cluster of sparkling domes behind turreted walls on the Moscow River, Novodevichy Convent (Novodevichy monastyr; ☎ 246 8526; admission RR30; open 10am-5pm Wed-Mon) is rich with history and treasures. The adjacent Novodevichy Cemetery is Moscow's most prestigious resting place, after the Kremlin wall, with many famous tombs. The name 'Novodevichy' (New Maidens) probably originates from a market, once held in the locality, where Tatars bought Russian girls to sell to Muslim harems.

Trolleybus Nos 5 and 15 come here down Prechistenka ulitsa and ulitsa Bolshaya Pirogovskaya from Kropotkinskaya metro station. Sportivnaya metro is 500m to the south.

Convent It was founded in 1524 to celebrate the taking of Smolensk from Lithuania, an important step in Moscow's conquest of the old Kyivan Rus lands. From early on, noblewomen would retire here, some willingly, some not. Novodevichy was rebuilt by Peter

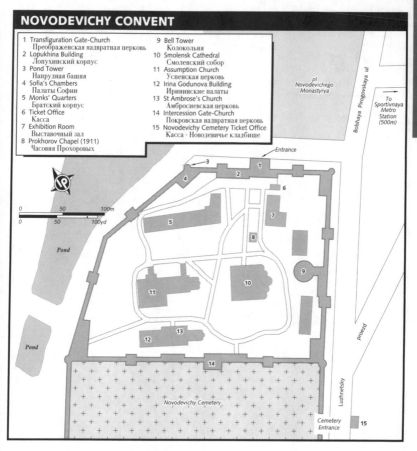

NOVODEVICHY CONVENT

1 Transfiguration Gate-Church
  Преображенская надвратная церковь
2 Lopukhina Building
  Лопухинский корпус
3 Pond Tower
  Напрудная башня
4 Sofia's Chambers
  Палаты Софии
5 Monks' Quarters
  Братский корпус
6 Ticket Office
  Касса
7 Exhibition Room
  Выставочный зал
8 Prokhorov Chapel (1911)
  Часовня Прохоровых

9 Bell Tower
  Колокольня
10 Smolensk Cathedral
  Смоленский собор
11 Assumption Church
  Успенская церковь
12 Irina Godunova Building
  Иринcинские палаты
13 St Ambrose's Church
  Амбросиевская церковь
14 Intercession Gate-Church
  Покровская надвратная церковь
15 Novodevichy Cemetery Ticket Office
  Касса - Новодевичье кладбище

the Great's half-sister Sofia, who used it as a second residence when she ruled Russia as regent in the 1680s. By this time the convent was a major landowner: it had 36 villages and 10,000 serfs around Russia.

When Peter, aged 17, deposed Sofia in 1689, he confined her to Novodevichy, and in 1698 she was imprisoned here for life after being implicated in the Streltsy rebellion. It's said Peter had some of her supporters hanged outside her window to remind her not to meddle. Sofia was joined in her retirement by Yevdokia Lopukhina, Peter's first wife, whom he considered a nag.

You enter the convent through the red and white, Moscow baroque **Transfiguration Gate-Church** (Preobrazhenskaya nadvratnaya tserkov), built in the north wall between 1687 and 1689. The first building on the left contains a room for temporary exhibitions.

Yevdokia Lopukhina lived in the **Lopukhina Building** (Lopukhinsky korpus) against the north wall and Sofia, probably, in chambers which adjoin the **Pond Tower** (Naprudnaya bashnya).

The oldest and dominant building in the grounds is the white **Smolensk Cathedral**

NOVODEVICHY CEMETERY

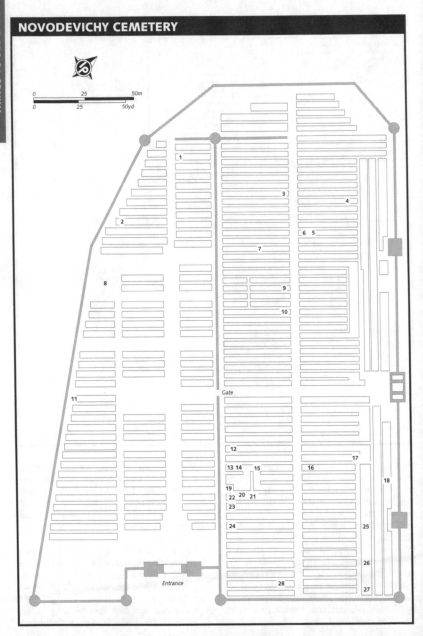

Gate

Entrance

NOVODEVICHY CEMETERY

1. Nikita Khrushchev (1894–1971), Soviet First Secretary & Premier 1957–64
   Никита Хрущёв
2. David Oystrakh (1908–74), Violinist
   Давид Ойстрах
3. Fyodor Chaliapin (1873–1938), Singer
   Фёдор Шаляпин
4. Sergey Prokofiev (1891–1953), Composer
   Сергей Прокофьев
5. Nikolay Rubinstein (1835–85), Pianist & Conductor
   Николай Рубинштейн
6. Alex&r Scriabin (1872–1915), Composer
   Александр Скрябин
7. Sergey Eisenstein (1898–1948), Film Director
   Сергей Уйсенштейн
8. Andrey Tupolev (1888–1972), Aircraft Designer
   Андрей Туполев
9. Pyotr Kropotkin (1842–1921), Anarchist
   Пётр Кропоткин
10. Andrey Gromyko (1909–89), Soviet Foreign Minister 1957–85
    Андрей Громыко

11. Raisa Gorbachev (1932–99)
    Раиса Горбачева
12. Nikolay Gogol (1809–52), Writer
    Николай Гоголь
13. Anton Chekhov (1860–1904), Writer
    Антон Чехов
14. Olga Knipper-Chekhova (1868–1959), Actor & Wife of Anton Chekhov
    Ольга Книппер-Чехова
15. Vladimir Nemirovich Danchenko (1858–1943), Co-Founder of Moscow Art Theatre
    Владимир Немирович Данченко
16. Pavel & Sergey Tretyakov (1832–98, 1834–92), Founders of Tretyakov Gallery
    Павел и Сергей Третьяков
17. Vladimir Mayakovsky (1893–1930), Poet
    Владимир Маяковский
18. Alex&ra Kollontay (1872–1952), Writer & Diplomat
    Александра Коллонтай
19. Konstantin Stanislavsky (1863–1938), Theatre

Director & Co-Founder of Moscow Art Theatre
Константин Станиславский
20. Mikhail Bulgakov (1891–1940), Writer
    Михаил Булгаков
21. Valentin Serov (1865–1911), Artist
    Валентин Серов
22. Maria Yermolova (1853–1928), Actor
    Мария Ермолова
23. Isaak Levitan (1860–1900), Artist
    Исаак Левитан
24. Mikhail Nesterov (1862–1942), Artist
    Михаил Нестеров
25. Alexey Shchusev (1873–1949), Architect
    Алексей Щусев
26. Vyacheslav Molotov (1890–1986), Soviet Foreign Minister 1939–49, 1953–56
    Вячеслав Молотов
27. Nadezhda Allilueva (1901–32), Stalin's Second Wife
    Надежда Аллилуева
28. Dmitry Shostakovich (1906–75), Composer
    Дмитрий Шостакович

(Smolensky sobor; admission RR60), modelled on the Assumption Cathedral in the Kremlin in 1524–25. Its beautifully proportioned domes were added in the 17th century. The walls of the sumptuous interior are covered in 16th-century frescoes and there's a huge iconostasis donated by Sofia, with contemporary icons as well as some from the time of Boris Godunov.

The **tombs** of Sofia, a couple of her sisters, and Yevdokia Lopukhina are all in the south nave.

The **bell tower** against the convent's east wall was completed in 1690 and is generally regarded as Moscow's finest. The red and white **Assumption Church** (Uspenskaya tserkov) and its refectory date from 1685 to 1687. The 16th-century **St Ambrose's Church** (Ambrosievskaya tserkov) is adjoined by another refectory and the **Irina Godunova Building**

(Irinskie palaty), where Boris Godunov's sister lived.

Cemetery The Novodevichy Cemetery (Novodevichiye kladbishche; admission RR30; open 9am-6pm daily) is home to the tombs of Khrushchev, Chekhov, Gogol, Mayakovsky, Stanislavsky, Prokofiev, Eisenstein, Gromyko and a mixed bag of many other Russian and Soviet notables.

In Soviet times, Novodevichy Cemetery was used for some very eminent people – notably Khrushchev – whom the authorities judged unsuitable for the Kremlin wall. The intertwined white and black blocks round Khrushchev's bust were intended by sculptor Ernst Neizvestny to represent Khrushchev's good and bad sides.

The tombstone of Nadezhda Allilueva, who was Stalin's second wife, is surrounded by unbreakable glass to prevent vandalism; apparently, her nose was once broken off. Allilueva committed suicide in 1932.

A recent addition is Raisa Gorbacheva, who was the sophisticated and visible wife of the last Soviet premier. Raisa died of leukaemia in 1999.

Tickets to the cemetery are sold at a kiosk across the street from the entrance on Luzhnetsky proezd, the continuation of ulitsa Bolshaya Pirogovskaya. If you would like to investigate this place in depth, buy the Russian map on sale at the kiosk, which pinpoints nearly 200 graves.

Luzhniki (Outer South Moscow Map)

The area within the river bend southwest of Novodevichy contains a group of sporting stadiums collectively known as Luzhniki ('Marshes', what the area used to be). The main 80,000 capacity Luzhniki Stadium was the chief venue for the 1980 Olympics, and had a huge renovation in the late 1990s. Coincidentally, the contract for the new seats went to a company controlled by the mayor's wife.

ZAMOSKVORECHIE

Zamoskvorechie ('Beyond-Moscow-River') stretches south from opposite the Kremlin, inside a big river loop. In this part of the city you'll find Moscow's most famous park, its premier gallery of Russian art, and the current headquarters of the Russian Orthodox Church.

The Vodootvodny (Drainage) Canal slices across the top of the Zamoskvorechie, preventing spring floods in the city centre and creating a sliver of island opposite the Kremlin. South was the direction from which Tatars used to attack, so Moscow's defensive forces were stationed in the Zamoskvorechie, along with quarters devoted to servicing the royal court. After the Tatar threat abated, more and more merchants moved to the area from the noisy and crowded Kitai Gorod. The secluded life of Zamoskvorechie was described by Alexander Ostrovsky in many of his plays, *The Storm* (Groza) being the most famous one.

The **Alexei Ostrovsky House-Museum** (Dom-muzey Alexeya Ostrovskog; Map 4; ☎ 953 8684; ul Bolshaya Ordynka 9; admission RR30; open noon-5.30pm Tues-Sun) is devoted to his life, the Maly Theatre he founded and Zamoskvorechie. where he lived and loved. It has beautiful paintings with views of old Moscow.

Zamoskvorechie once boasted the biggest number of churches in Moscow. Merchants usually built them to secure luck in business. Only at the end of the 18th century were merchants joined by nobles, then by 19th-century factory owners and their workers. Little damaged by Stalin, it's still a varied, intriguing area.

From almost any place here you can see the giant Peter the Great sculpture. For more on this modern monolith, see the boxed text 'Yury Luzhkov, Christopher Columbus & Princess Diana?' on page 96.

Behind the statue, the **Krasny Oktyabr Confectionery** (Red October; Map 4; ☎ 296 3552; Bersenevskaya nab 6; tours by appointment only) is Moscow's oldest and most celebrated candy maker.

The factory contains an interesting museum about the history of the factory and the candy-production process – it's not Willy Wonka but it does include some samples! Tours must be ordered well in advance – don't be afraid to play your 'foreigner' card to book.

Gorky Park (Map 4)

Stretching almost 3km along the river upstream of Krymsky Most, Gorky Park is full of that sometimes rare species, the happy Russian. Officially the Park of Culture (Park Kultury imeni A M Gorkogo; ☎ 237 1266; ul Krymsky Val; admission RR25; open 10am-sundown), named after Maxim Gorky, it's the original Soviet culture park.

Part ornamental park, part funfair, it is a good place to escape the hubbub of the city. In winter the ponds freeze and the paths are flooded to make a giant skating rink – you can rent skates if you take along some ID.

But that's not all. Gorky Park also has a small Western amusement park with two Western roller coasters and almost a dozen other terror-inducing attractions (aside from the *Peter the Great* statue).

Space buffs can shed a tear for the *Buran*, the Soviet space shuttle which never carried anyone into space. Most of the rides cost about RR10 to RR20.

The park has a number of snack bars and, behind the amusement park, a 2000-seat German beer hall. The park's main entrance is 500m from either Park Kultury or Oktyabrskaya metro.

Around Gorky Park (Map 4)

The big block opposite Gorky Park's main entrance houses the **Central House of Artists** (*Tsentralny dom khudozhnika; ☎ 238 9634; adult/student RR220/110; open 11am-7pm Tues-Sun*), which puts on good contemporary art shows. Behind it, there's the **New Tretyakov Gallery** (*Novaya Tretyakovskaya galereya; ☎ 238 1378; adult/student RR220/110; open 10am-7pm Tues-Sun*) with an excellent collection of 20th-century Russian art. Much more than just heroic images of muscle-bound men wielding scythes and busty women milking cows (although there's that too), the collection features innovative work by Malevich, Kandinsky and others. A busy art market is in the nearby arcade.

Behind the complex is the wonderful and moody **Sculptures Park** (*Park Skulptur*), a collection of Soviet statues – Stalin, Dzerzhinsky, some Lenins and Brezhnevs – put out to pasture here when they were ripped from their pedestals in the wave of anti-Soviet feeling after 1991. These discredited icons have now been joined by contemporary work, including an eerie bust of Stalin surrounded by heads representing millions of purge victims.

Nearby there is the finest of all Zamoskvorechie churches, **St John the Warrior** (*Tserkov Ivana voina; ul Bolshaya Yakimanka*), with its colourful, tiled domes. Said to have been partly designed by Peter the Great in thanks for his 1709 victory over Sweden at Poltava, it mixes Moscow and European baroque styles.

It's a working church but often locked; the big, 17th-century iconostasis is reputedly a masterpiece.

Tretyakov Gallery (Map 4)

The State Tretyakov Gallery (*Gosudarstvennaya Tretyakovskaya galereya; ☎ 951 1362; Lavrushinsky per 10; adult/student RR220/110, audio tour RR120; open 10am-6.30pm Tues-Sun*) is nothing short of spectacular, with the world's best collection of Russian icons and an outstanding collection of other prerevolutionary Russian art, particularly the 19th-century Peredvizhniki (see Architecture under Arts in the Facts about Moscow chapter).

The collection is based on that of 19th-century industrialist brothers Pavel and Sergey Tretyakov; Pavel was a patron of the Peredvizhniki. The original part of the building was created in the likeness of an old *boyar* (high-ranking noble) castle by Viktor Vasnetsov between 1900 and 1905.

Much of the Tretyakov's collection of religious art was confiscated from churches during the Soviet era. Now that the Church wants its icons back, the Tretyakov has had to battle to keep its most precious treasures. For the moment at least, it has fended off the pressure by also restoring the **Church of St Nicholas** within its grounds. About 200 icons are displayed there, and the building functions as both church and museum.

Visiting The 62 rooms are numbered, and progress in chronological order from rooms 1 to 54; the next eight rooms hold icons and jewellery. See the boxed text 'Tretyakov Gallery' for a detailed listing and map of the collections.

The entrance to the gallery is through a lovely courtyard; show up early to beat the queues. Thanks to a lavish renovation during the early 1990s, the entire gallery is accessible to wheelchairs.

Ulitsa Bolshaya Ordynka & Ulitsa Pyatnitskaya (Map 4)

The atmosphere of 19th-century Moscow lives on in the low buildings, old courtyards and clusters of onion domes along narrow ulitsa Bolshaya Ordynka, which runs 2km down the middle of Zamoskvorechie to Serpukhovskaya ploshchad. Ulitsa Pyatnitskaya is roughly parallel, 200m to the east.

Tretyakov Gallery

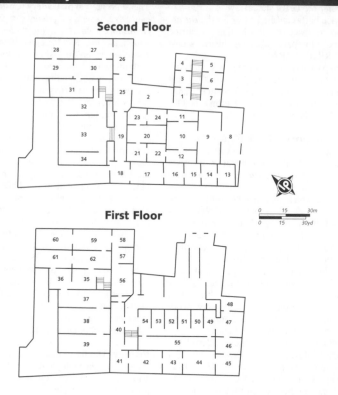

Second Floor

First Floor

The listings progress chronologically beginning on the 2nd floor, in Room 1; there are only a couple of twists and turns in the layout (see map).

Second Floor, Rooms 1–7

Contain 18th-century painting and sculpture, including **1** portraits such as Nikitin's *Portrait of Anna Petrovna* and a larger one of her by Caravaggio; **2** sculptures, mainly by Shubin, with others including Martos' *Portrait of NV Panina* and *Tombstone for SS Volkonskaya*, Rastrelli's *Portrait of an Unknown Man* and Kozlovsky's very sweet *Cupid with an Arrow*; **3** Rokotov on the left wall, with the right wall dominated by Antropov's enormous *Portrait of Peter III*; **4** paintings from graduates of the Russian Academy of Arts (which accepted children of nobility and serfs for its 15-year course which began at age five), including Shibanov's *Celebration of a Wedding Agreement* and Argunov's *Portrait of a Woman in a Russian Dress*; **5** mainly Levitsky, including *Portrait of the Artist's Daughter* and *Portrait of PA Demidov*; **6** landscapes and portraits, including the enormous *Actaeon* by Martos, Shchedrin's *Stone Bridge in Gatchina*, Alekseev's *View of the Palace Embankment from the Peter & Paul Fortress* and *View of the Roman Colosseum* by Matveev; **7** Borovikovsky's wonderful *Portrait of MI Lopukhina* and *Portrait of the Princesses Gagarin*.

Tretyakov Gallery

Rooms 8–15

Hold 19th-century painting and sculpture such as **8** Kiprensky and contemporaries, including his mega-famous *Portrait of AS Pushkin*, his *Newspaper Readers in Naples*, and what may be the artist's self-portrait; **9** mostly Bryullov, including *Equestrian* and *Self-portrait*; **10** Ivanov, dominated by his *Christ's Appearance to the People* and preliminary character sketches for this piece; **11** more work by graduates of the Academy of Arts, including Shternberg's *October Feast Day in Rome* and Solnitsev's *Peasant Family before Dinner*; **12** more Ivanov, including *Man Looking Upwards* and *Two Heads in Turbans...*; **13** mostly Tropinin's exquisite work, such as *The Lace Maker*, *The Guitarist* and the moving *Peasant Whittling a Crutch*; **14** Venetsianov's school, including his own masterpieces *Ploughing in Spring* and *Harvesting in Summer*; **15** Fedotov's amusing and ironic *Aristocrat's Breakfast*, *The Major's Proposal* and *The Fresh Cavalier – An Official on the Morning after Receiving an Award*, as well as work by his contemporaries, such as Sorokin's moving *Spanish Beggar Girl*.

Room 16

Contains realist paintings from the 1850s and 1860s, including the first paintings bought by Tretyakov in 1856 from the artists: Khudyakov's *Skirmish with Finnish Smugglers* and Shilder's *Temptation*, as well as Pukirev's discomfiting *The Unequal Marriage*. In Flavitsky's *Princess Tarakanova*, she is depicted during a flood, imprisoned in the Peter and Paul Fortress' dungeons for pretending to be the daughter of Tsaritsa Elizabeth Petrovna.

Rooms 17–22

Feature more 19th-century artists, such as **17** Perov, dominated by his *Dispute over Faith* and featuring his *Portrait of Dostoevsky*; **18** Savrasov, including *Country Road*, and Vasilev, including *The Thaw* and *After the Rain*; **19** landscapes such as Bogolyubov's fantastic *Horse Rides on the Neva* and Ayvazovsky's grim *The Black Sea*; and **20** Kramskoy's work such as *Unknown Lady*, *Christ in the Wilderness* and portraits of *Tolstoy* and *Nekrasov*; **21** Kuindzhi including his *Moonlit Night on the Dnepr* and *On the Island of Valaam*; **22** Makovsky's *Children Running from the Approaching Storm* and Bakalovich's *The Maecenas' Waiting Room*, while the centrepiece is Brodski's *Cupid in a Shell*.

Rooms 23–24

Among the museum's highlights, featuring work by the Peredvizhniki: **23** Myasoedov's profound piece *The Zemstvo Having Lunch* and Zhuravlyov's *Merchant's Funeral Banquet*; **24** Yaroshenko's *There Is Life Everywhere* and *General Staff Meeting in Fili*, Boddanov-Belsky's charming *Counting Out Loud* and Makovsky's *The Party*.

Rooms 25–27

Hold more 19th-century paintings and sculptures including **25** Shishkin's *Morning in a Pine Forest* and *Rye*; **26** Vasnetsov's *Knights*, *Alenushka*, *Telegram from the War*, *Tsarevich Ivan on a Grey Wolf* and *The Flying Carpet*; **27** Vereshchagin's brutal *Apotheosis of War*, and his panoramic *Shipka-Sheynovo: Skobolev near Shipka*, in which the artist placed himself on the darker horse behind the general and next to the flag-bearer.

Room 28

Features Surikov and is another highlight, especially *Morning of the Execution of the Streltsy*. The giant *Boyarina Morozova* depicts an Old Believer being dragged off to prison.

Rooms 29–30

Show off some incredible pieces by Repin, including *Dragonfly*, *Portrait of Turgenev* and the fantabulous *Religious Procession Through Kursk*. *Ivan the Terrible and His Son* is a devastating rendition of the historical tragedy. Unfortunately, his most famous work *The Volga Boatmen* is no longer here, but in the Russian Museum in St Petersburg.

THINGS TO SEE & DO

Tretyakov Gallery

Room 31
Features Ge, including *Peter the Great Interrogating the Tsarevich*. The painting tells the story of Tsarevich Alexei, who was raised by his mother, Peter's estranged first wife. Hateful of Peter's reforms, Alexei became a reactionary leader who was eventually sentenced to death for treason.

Rooms 32–33
Contain paintings by Vrubel, including *The Swan Princess*, *Pan*, *Portrait of MI Artsybusheva* and *Seated Demon*. These pieces were inspired by Mikhail Lermontov's poem *The Demon*.

Room 34
Highlights Nesterov, a deeply religious man who sought to reconcile his faith with the Art Nouveau style of his time. *The Hermit* was Nesterov's first major success when it was shown in 1890.

Room 35, Ground Floor
Displays Polenov's lovely *Courtyard in Moscow*, which depicts the 19th-century Arbat, and the closer view of his *Grandmother's Garden*.

Rooms 36–39
Contain late-19th- and early-20th-century works, including **36** examples of 1880s and 1890s realism, such as Stepanov's *Cranes Are Flying* and Kuznetsov's portraits of *Tchaikovsky* and *Chekhov*; **37** mainly Levitan landscapes, including *March* and *The Evening Bells Ringing*; **38** work by members of the Union of Russian Artists, such as Grabar's technicolour *February Azure*, Rerikh's *Visitors from Overseas* and Malyavin's loud *Whirlwind*; **39** Korovin, including *Portrait of ND Chichagov*, *The Northern Idyll* and *Winter in Lapplandia*, and Serov, including *Girl with Peaches*, *Mika Morozov* and *By the Window*.

Rooms 40–41
Display works from the early-20th-century 'World of Art' neoclassical movement, with examples such as Serebryakova's *At the Dressing Table*.

Rooms 42–48
Contain more early-20th-century art, including **46** examples from the avante-garde 'Blue Rose' movement, featuring Sapunov's still lifes and – go figure – floral paintings; **47** neoclassical sculpture by Konenkov; and **48** more examples from the 'Blue Rose' movement, this time featuring Saryan and Kuznetsov.

Rooms 49–54
Display lithographs, sketches and watercolours by dozens of artists that span the 18th to 20th centuries.

Room 55
Contains artistic jewellery.

The many churches located here make up a wonderful scrapbook of Muscovite architectural styles. The name 'Ordynka' comes from *orda* (horde); until the 16th century this was the start of the road to the Golden Horde's capital on the Volga, where the Tatar ambassadors lived.

Other sources maintain that the street received its name from the 'ordyntsy' who lived in this area in the 15th century. 'Ordyntsy' were the people taken hostage by

Tatars then bought by wealthy Russians to work as servants.

If you head south from Maly Moskvoretsky Most, the first lane on the right contains the tall **Resurrection Church in Kadashi**, which is a restoration centre for some other churches.

Its rich, late 17th-century decoration is a fine example of Moscow baroque. The tall and elegant belfry earned the nickname 'the candle'.

Tretyakov Gallery

Rooms 56–62
Contain one of the world's richest collections of icons and religious art; **56** is the Pre-Mongolian room, containing 12th- and 13th-century icons such as *Ustyug Annunciation* and *St Nicholas*, both brought to Moscow by Ivan the Terrible.

Room 57
Houses Russia's most revered icon, the Vladimir Icon of the Mother of God (Vladimirskaya ikona Bozhiey Materi). An image of the Virgin and infant Christ, it is credited with saving Moscow from Timur (Tamerlane), among many other wonders, and is considered the ultimate protector of Mother Russia. It resided in Kiev, Vladimir and Moscow during each city's stint as Russian capital. Probably painted by a 12th-century Byzantine, it reached Kiev from Constantinople around 1130. Andrey Bogolyubov secretly moved the icon to Vladimir's Assumption Cathedral in 1155; then it stood in the Moscow Kremlin's Assumption Cathedral from the 1480s to 1930. Patriarch Alexey was allowed to borrow it from the Tretyakov for one day in 1993 to pray to it for an avoidance of bloodshed at the White House. His prayers failed.

Room 58
Contains examples from the Novgorod and Pskov schools, such as the ubiquitous 15th-century *The Miracle of St George and the Dragon*, a favourite subject in Russian art. This victory is seen as a symbol of good triumphing over evil and appears on the emblem of old Muscovy. Other examples include the *Last Judgment*, *The Miracle of SS Florus & Laurus* and *Entombment*, all 15th-century works.

Room 59
Displays the late-14th-century *Virgin of the Don* by Theophanes the Greek, which supposedly brought Dmitry Donskoy victory over the Tatars at the Battle of Kulikovo in 1380.

Room 60
Contains Andrey Rublyov's early-15th-century *Holy Trinity* (Svyataya Troitsa), from the Trinity Monastery of St Sergius, Sergiev Posad. It is widely regarded as the best example of Russian iconography. It depicts the Old Testament Trinity – three angels who appeared to Abraham in an episode from Genesis and are seen as a prefiguration of the New Testament Trinity. On the rear wall of this room, the Deesis Row of an iconostasis features (centre) *The Saviour*, (left of centre) *The Virgin Mother*, (right of centre) *John the Baptist*, (left) *Archangel Michael* and (right) *Archangel Gabriel*. These works were painted by Rublyov and Daniil Chyorny in Moscow in 1408.

Room 61
Contains later iconography such as Dionysius and Simon Ushakov.

The small, white **SS Mikhail and Fyodor Church** *(Chernigovsky per)*, dating from the late 17th century, has two rows of spade gables and five domes on a thin tower. The larger **St John the Baptist Church**, from the same period, houses an exhibition of unusual Russian glassware. St John's **bell tower**, a Zamoskvorechie landmark which fronts ulitsa Pyatnitskaya, was added in 1753.

The empress-style **Virgin of Consolation of All Sorrows Church** *(ul Bolshaya Ordynka 20)*, dates mostly from between 1828 and 1833. Klimentovsky pereulok leads to **St Clement's Church** *(ul Pyatnitskaya 26)*, built between 1742 and 1774, a rare Moscow example of the true baroque style liked by Empress Elizabeth.

The blue and white **Church of St Nicholas in Pyzhi** *(ul Bolshaya Ordynka 27A)*, a working church, is a typical five-domed, mid-17th-century church, with spade gables and thin onion domes. **SS Martha and Mary**

Convent *(ul Bolshaya Ordynka 34A)*, with its pretty, single-domed Intercession Church, now houses church restoration offices. The church and gates were built between 1908 and 1912 in neo-Russian style. At the beginning of the 20th century, the convent was famous for charity work; it has recently reopened. The church opens only for services, but the interior frescoes are worth a visit.

The operating **St Catherine Church** *(ul Bolshaya Ordynka 60/2)* was built in 1767 to celebrate the enthronement of Catherine II. The ceiling has some remains of murals by 18th-century artist Dmitry Levitsky.

Around Paveletskaya Ploshchad (Map 5)

This wide square on the Garden Ring is dominated by the **Paveletsky Station** *(Paveletsky Vokzal)* terminus for trains to the Volga region. The finest loco in the neighbourhood, however, stands idle in an air-conditioned pavilion just east of the station. It is the **Lenin Funeral Train** *(Traurny proezd V I Lenina; open 10am-6pm Mon-Fri)* which brought Lenin's body to Moscow from Gorki Leninskie, where he died, in January 1924. The old steam engine is in beautiful condition.

The **Bakhrushin Theatre Museum** *(Teatralny muzey Bakhrushina; Map 5; ☎ 953 4470; ul Bakhrushina 31/12; admission RR30; open noon-6pm Wed-Mon)*, Russia's foremost stage museum, is on the north side of Paveletskaya ploshchad. Founded in 1894, collections cover Russian drama, ballet and opera with model stage sets, photos and original costumes, including Nijinsky's ballet shoes.

Danilovsky Monastery (Outer South Moscow Map)

The headquarters of the Russian Orthodox Church is situated behind white fortress walls, just a five-minute walk east of the Tulskaya metro. The Danilovsky Monastery *(Danilovsky Monastyr; ☎ 955 6757; Danilovsky Val; admission free; open 7am-7pm daily)* was built during the late 13th century by Daniil, who was the first Prince of Moscow, as an outer city defence. It was repeatedly altered over the years, including serving as both a factory and detention centre in Soviet times.

It was restored in time to replace Sergiev Posad as the Church's spiritual and administrative centre and the official residence of the Patriarch during the Russian Orthodoxy's millennium celebrations in 1988. Today, it radiates an air of purpose befitting the Church's role in modern Russia.

On holy days this place seethes with worshippers murmuring prayers, lighting candles and ladling holy water into jugs at the tiny chapel inside the gates. Enter beneath the pink **St Simeon Stylite Gate-Church** on the north wall.

The monastery's oldest and busiest church is the **Church of the Holy Fathers of the Seven Ecumenical Councils** where worship is held continuously from 10am to 5pm daily. Founded in the 17th century and rebuilt repeatedly, the church contains several chapels on two floors: the main one upstairs is flanked by side chapels to St Daniil (on the northern side) and SS Boris and Gleb (south). On the ground level, the small main chapel is dedicated to the Protecting Veil, and the northern one to the prophet Daniil.

The yellow and neoclassical **Trinity Cathedral**, built in the 1830s, is an austere counterpart to the other buildings.

West of the cathedral are the patriarchate's External Affairs Department and, at the far end of the grounds, the **Patriarch's Official Residence**. Against the north wall in this part of the monastery there's a 13th-century Armenian carved-stone cross or *khachkar*, a gift from the Armenian Church.

The church guesthouse in the southern part of the monastery grounds has been turned into the elegant Hotel Danilovsky (see the Places to Stay chapter).

Donskoy Monastery (Outer South Moscow Map)

The youngest of Moscow's fortified monasteries *(Donskoy monastyr; ☎ 952 1646)* was founded in 1591 and was built to house the *Virgin of the Don* icon (now in the Tretyakov Gallery). This revered icon is credited with victory in the 1380 battle of Kulikovo; it's also said that in 1591 the Tatar Khan Giri retreated without a fight after the icon showered him with burning arrows in a dream.

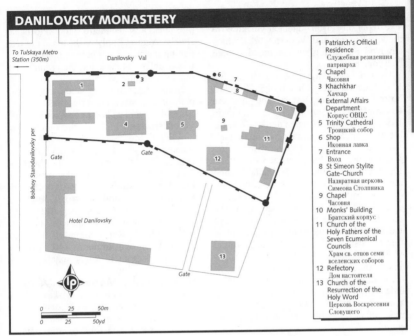

DANILOVSKY MONASTERY

To Tulskaya Metro Station (350m)

Danilovsky Val

Bolshoy Starodanilovsky per

Gate

Gate

Gate

Gate

Hotel Danilovsky

0 25 50m
0 25 50yd

1 Patriarch's Official Residence
  Служебная резиденция патриарха
2 Chapel
  Часовня
3 Khachkhar
  Хачхар
4 External Affairs Department
  Корпус ОВЦС
5 Trinity Cathedral
  Троицкий собор
6 Shop
  Иконная лавка
7 Entrance
  Вход
8 St Simeon Stylite Gate-Church
  Надвратная церковь Симеона Столпника
9 Chapel
  Часовня
10 Monks' Building
  Братский корпус
11 Church of the Holy Fathers of the Seven Ecumenical Councils
  Храм св. отцов семи вселенских соборов
12 Refectory
  Дом настоятеля
13 Church of the Resurrection of the Holy Word
  Церковь Воскресения Словущего

Most of the monastery is surrounded by a brick wall with 12 towers and was built between 1684 and 1733 under Regent Sofia and Peter the Great. From 1918 to 1927 it was the Russian Orthodox Church headquarters, then it was closed as a monastery, falling into neglect despite being used as an architecture museum.

Restored in 1990 and 1991, it's now back in Church hands.

The **Virgin of Tikhvin Church** over the north gate, built in 1713 and 1714, is one of the last examples of Moscow baroque. In the centre of the grounds is the large, brick **New Cathedral**, built between 1684 and 1693; just to its south is the smaller **Old Cathedral**, dating from 1591 to 1593.

When burials in central Moscow were banned after a plague in 1771, the Donskoy Monastery became a graveyard for the nobility, and it is littered with elaborate tombs and chapels. At ulitsa Donskaya, leading north from the monastery, there is the

Church of the Deposition of the Robe *(Map 4)*, built in 1701.

The Donskoy Monastery is a five-minute walk from Shabolovskaya metro. Go south along ulitsa Shabolovka, then take the first street west, 1-oy Donskoy proezd.

ZAYAUZIE
Around Taganskaya Ploshchad (Map 5)

Taganskaya ploshchad on the Garden Ring is a monster intersection – loud, dusty and crowded. But it's the hub of Zayauzie, the area south of the little Yauza River, and the territory of the 17th-century blacksmiths guild. Later it became an Old Believers' quarter. The square's character disappeared with a reconstruction in the 1970s and '80s, but traces remain in the streets that radiate from it.

The great block is the **Taganka Theatre** *(cnr Taganskaya pl & Verkhnyaya Radishchevskaya ul)*, famous during the Soviet era for director Yury Lyubimov's vaguely subversive repertoire, from updated Chekhov to modern Russian and Western works, which annoyed Soviet authorities and delighted everyone else.

Behind Taganskaya metro is the sombre 1712 **Taganka Gates Church of St Nicholas**. More fetching is the **Potters' Church of the Assumption** (*ul Goncharnaya 29*), built in 1654, with its star-spangled domes. Note the tile work under the 'extra' refectory dome.

Ulitsa Goncharnaya leads north to two impressive classical mansions at Nos 12 and 16, and to the **Church of St Nikita Beyond the Yauza**, which has 15th-century foundations, 16th-century walls, 17th-century chapels and an 18th-century bell tower. The church is dwarfed by the **Kotelnicheskaya apartment block**, one of the Stalinist Gothic 'Seven Sisters' skyscrapers built around 1950. See the boxed text 'Stalin's Seven Sisters' in the Facts about Moscow chapter. To the east, above the Yauza, there's the huge **Batashyov Palace** (*Yauzskaya ul 9-11*). Now a hospital, this industrialist's manor house was built in 1802 with lion gates and its own church.

The **Foreign Literature Library** (☎ *915 3636; ul Nikoloyamskaya 1*) is home to several international libraries and cultural centres, including the **American Cultural Center Library** (☎ *915 3669; open 10am-8pm Mon-Fri*), the **French Cultural Centre** (☎ *915 3669; open 1pm-6pm Mon-Fri*), and the **British Council Resource Centre** (☎ *915 3511; open 10am-8pm Mon-Fri*). Take your passport.

Northeast of Taganskaya, you can't miss the grand **Cathedral of St Martin the Confessor** (*ul Bolshaya Kommunisticheskaya 15*), built in 1792 in shameless imitation of St Paul's Cathedral in London. Though it was badly neglected during the Soviet period, it's now open and being renovated. This whole neighbourhood has a look of abandoned grace.

Andronikov Monastery & Andrey Rublyov Museum (Map 5)

The fortified 1360 Andronikov Monastery (*Spaso-Andronikov monastyr; Andronyevskaya pl*), on the banks of the Yauza, is just

over a kilometre northeast of Taganskaya ploshchad near the metro station Ploshchad Ilyicha. Andrey Rublyov, the master of icon painting, was a monk here in the 15th century. Rublyov is buried in the grounds; no-one knows quite where.

In the centre of the grounds, topped by a posy of *kokoshnik* (colourful tiles and brick patterning) gables, is the compact **Saviour's Cathedral**, built in 1427, the oldest stone building in Moscow. To the left is the combined rectory and 17th-century, Moscow baroque **Church of the Archangel Michael**. To the right, in the old monks' quarters, is the **Andrey Rublyov Museum of Early Russian Culture and Art** (☎ *278 1467; Andronyevskaya pl 10; admission RR60; open 11am-6pm Thur-Tues*), an icon museum with nothing by Rublyov himself. There are a few strong and luminous 14th- to 16th-century works interestingly juxtaposed.

Novospassky Monastery (Map 5)

One kilometre south of Taganskaya ploshchad there's yet another of Moscow's fort-monasteries.

The **New Monastery of the Saviour** (*Novopassky Monastir;* ☎ *276 9570; Verkhny Novospassky proezd; metro: Proletarskaya; admission free; open 7am-7pm Mon-Sat, 8am-7pm Sun*) dates from the 15th century, when it was relocated from inside the Kremlin. Under restoration for 30 years, it became a working monastery again in the early 1990s.

The centrepiece is the **Transfiguration Cathedral**, built by the imperial Romanov family in the 1640s in imitation of the Kremlin's Assumption Cathedral.

Frescoes depict the history of Christianity in Russia; the Romanov family tree, which goes as far back as the Viking Prince Rurik, climbs one wall.

To the left is the 1675 **Intercession Church**, which is joined to the refectory and bakery buildings. Under the river bank, beneath one of the monastery towers, is the site of a mass grave for thousands of Stalin's victims.

Across the road south of Novospassky is the sumptuous **Krutitskoe Podvorye** (*ecclesiastical residence; admission free; open 10am-6pm Wed-Mon*). It was used by the Moscow metropolitans from the 16th century, when they lost their place in the Kremlin after the founding of the Russian patriarchate. At the northern end of the grounds is the brick **Assumption Cathedral** and an extraordinary Moscow baroque **gate tower**, with friezes in unexpected yellows and blues.

Rogozhskoe Cemetery & Old Believers' Community

One of Russia's most atmospheric religious centres is the **Old Believers' community** *(Staroobryadcheskaya Obshchina; admission free; open 9am-6pm Tues-Sun)*, located at Rogozhskoe, some 3km east of Taganskaya ploshchad.

The Old Believers split from the main Russian Orthodox Church in 1653 when they refused to accept certain reforms. They have maintained old forms of worship and customs ever since.

In the late 18th century, during a brief period free of persecution, rich Old Believer merchants set up what is, perhaps, the most important Old Believers' community, around their **Rogozhskoe Cemetery** (Rogozhskoe kladbishche). The place remains an island of old Russia to this day, with dark, mysterious churches.

Take trolleybus No 16 or 26, or bus No 51, east from Taganskaya ploshchad along ulitsa Taganskaya and ulitsa Nizhnegorodskaya; get off after crossing a railway. Rogozhskoe's tall, green-domed 20th-century **bell tower** is clearly visible to the north (left). The yellow classical-style **Intercession Church** contains one of Moscow's finest collections of icons, all dating from before 1653. The oldest is the 14th-century *Spas yaroe oko* (Saviour with the Angry Eye), protected under glass near the south door.

The icons in the Deesis row (the biggest row) of the iconostasis are supposed to represent the Rublyov school, while the seventh, *The Saviour*, is attributed to Andrey Rublyov himself.

The **Church of St Nicholas** is a picturesque entry to the cemetery containing family tombs of Old Believer merchants from the Morozov, Ryabushinsksy and Soldatenkov families.

CHISTYE PRUDY (MAP 3)

This area encompasses the streets off Chistoprudny bulvar, between ulitsas Myasnitskaya and Pokrovka, to the northeast of the Kremlin.

In the late 17th century the area was known for its butchers (Myasnitskaya means butchers); logically, the area's ponds were filthy.

Peter the Great gave this area to his pal, Alexander Menshikov, who launched a bit of a PR campaign, renaming it Clean Ponds (Chistye Prudy). Apparently, he did actually have them cleaned first.

The area boasts the first Moscow post office, which was founded in 1783 in one of the houses of the former Menshikov estate. Hidden behind the post office is the famous **Menshikov Tower** (Menshikova bashnya), built in 1704–06 by the order of Menshikov at his newly founded estate.

The tower was originally 3m taller than the Ivan the Great bell tower in the Kremlin and was one of Moscow's first baroque buildings.

A 1723 thunderstorm saw it hit by lightning and seriously damaged by fire.

Trouble plagued the owner as well. Menshikov fell from grace after Peter the Great's death and was exiled to Siberia. The tower was neglected for several decades and when finally repaired in the 1780s, it lost much of its height and elegance. Today, it houses the working **Church of Archangel Gabriel**.

Chistoprudny bulvar affords a pleasant stroll. The pond has paddle boats in summer and ice skating in winter.

Pick a café and (depending on the season) sip a beer or a coffee while watching boats or skaters go by.

Komsomolskaya Ploshchad

From Chistye Prudy, prospekt Akademika Sakharova goes northeast to Komsomolskaya ploshchad, Moscow's transportation hub. Three main railway stations – and the diverse and dubious crowds that go along with that – make this one of the busiest and hairiest centres. In one square, the three stations capture Moscow's architectural diversity.

Leningrad Station (Leningradsky vokzal) on the northern side of the square, with its tall clock tower, is Moscow's oldest, built in 1851. It is very similar to its opposite number at the far end of the line, the Moscow Station in St Petersburg.

Yaroslavl Station (Yaroslavsky vokzal) next door, the start of the Trans-Siberian Railway, is a 1902–04 Art Nouveau fantasy by Fyodor Shekhtel.

Kazan Station (Kazansky vokzal), built between 1912 and 1926 on the southern side of the square, serves Central Asia and western Siberia. It's a retrospective of seven building styles going back to a 16th-century Tatar tower in Kazan. The style of architect Alexey Shchusev transformed over the years, and his later work includes Lenin's mausoleum.

The 26-storey 'wedding cake' west of Komsomolskaya ploshchad is **Hotel Leningradskaya** (Gostinitsa Leningradskaya). Another of Stalin's 'Seven Sisters' is now home to the **Agriculture Ministry** (Ministerstvo selskogo khozyaystva), 600m south on the Garden Ring (see the boxed text 'Stalin's Seven Sisters' in the Facts about Moscow chapter).

Kursk Station (Kursky vokzal), a further 1.5km south, is Moscow's biggest, with trains to eastern Ukraine, Crimea and the Caucasus.

Andrei Sakharov Museum

Southeast of Chistye Prudy, not far from Kursk Station, a two-storey house in a small park contains the Andrei Sakharov Museum (Muzey AD Sakharova; Map 3; ☎ 923 4115; Zemlyanoy Val 57; admission free; open 11am-7pm Wed-Sun).

Watch for a piece of genuine Berlin Wall in front of the building. The displays cover the life of the nuclear-physicist-turned-human-rights advocate. They detail the years of repression in Russia and provide a history of the dissident movement. Temporary expositions cover current human rights' issues. There are signs in English and audio guides are planned.

Yelokhovsky Cathedral

Spartakovskaya ulitsa, near Baumanskaya metro, is the unlikely address of Moscow's senior Orthodox cathedral. This role was given to the **Church of the Epiphany in Yelokhovo** (Tserkov Bogoyavleniya v Yelokhove; Map 3; Spartakovskaya ul 15) in 1943. (The Patriarch had been evicted from the Kremlin's Assumption Cathedral in 1918.) The Patriarch leads important services here today.

Built between 1837 and 1845 with five domes in a Russian eclectic style, the cathedral is full of gilt, icons and old women polishing, lighting candles, kneeling, crossing themselves, or kissing the floor. In the northern part of the cathedral is the tomb of St Nicholas the Miracle Worker (Svyatoy Nikolay Ugodnik).

A shrine in front of the right side of the iconostasis contains the remains of St Alexey, a 14th-century metropolitan.

MOSCOW OUTSKIRTS

Armed Forces Museum (Map 2)

The Armed Forces Museum (☎ 281 4877; ul Sovietskoy Armii 2; admission RR20; open 10am-4.30pm Wed-Sun) contains the history of Soviet and Russian forces since 1917. Among the highlights are parts of the American U-2 spy plane brought down over Siberia in 1960, as well as many tanks, planes, guns etc. Take trolleybus No 69 (or walk) 1.25km west from the Novoslobodskaya metro.

Sokolniki Park (Outer North Moscow Map)

This park (Park Sokolniki) is twice the size of Gorky Park, with a lot of sports facilities. In winter you can ice-skate or cross-country ski here and rent the gear on the spot. The 400m walk to the main entrance from the Sokolniki metro passes the attractive 1913 **Resurrection Church** (Tserkov Voskreseniya).

All-Russia Exhibition Centre (VDNKh; Outer North Moscow Map)

No other place sums up the rise and fall of the Soviet dream quite so well as the All-Russia Exhibition Centre (Vserossiysky Vystavochny Tsentr, VVTs). The old initials by which it's still commonly known, VDNKh, tell half the story: they stand for Vystavka Dostizheny

Sculptor at play in Sculptures Park, home to disgraced Soviet 'heroes'

St Basil's Cathedral, Red Square

Composition at Sculptures Park, representing the millions who were victims of Stalin

Central hall of Mayakovskaya metro station, grand-prize winner at the 1938 World's Fair in New York

CHRISTINA DAMEYER

Marshall Zhukov statue, Red Square

JONATHAN SMITH

Vernisazh market, Izmaylovsky Park

SIMON RICHMOND

Quirky sign of Pelmeshka restaurant in the Kuznetsky Most area

Narodnogo Khozyaystva SSSR – USSR Economic Achievements Exhibition.

Originally created in the 1930s, VDNKh was expanded in the 1950s and '60s to impress upon one and all the success of the Soviet economic system. Two kilometres long and 1km wide, it comprises wide pedestrian avenues and grandiose pavilions, glorifying all the aspects of socialist construction from education and health to agriculture, technology and science. The pavilions represent a huge variety of architectural styles, symbolic of the contributions from diverse ethnic and artistic movements to the common goal. You'll find the kitschest of socialist realism, the most inspiring socialist optimism and – now – the tackiest of capitalist consumerism.

VDNKh was an early casualty when those in power finally admitted that the Soviet economy had become a disaster – funds were cut off by 1990. Today, the VVTs is a commercial centre, its pavilions given over to sales of the very imported goods which were supposed to be inferior. Much of the merchandise on sale is low-priced clothing and the like from China. The domed Cosmos (Space) pavilion towards the far end became a wholesaler for TV sets and VCRs.

Although you may not want to do your shopping here, VDHKh does host international trade exhibitions. For tourists, it is a fascinating visit to see the remnants of socialism's achievements (see the boxed text 'In Memory of Soviet Economic Achievement: VDNKh' later in this chapter). The main entrance, 500m from prospekt Mira, is approached by its own imposing avenues from Hotel Kosmos or VDNKh metro.

The soaring 100m titanium obelisk beside VDNKh metro is a monument to Soviet space flight. In its base there's the **Cosmonautics Museum** (Muzey kosmonavtiki; ☎ 283 7914; admission RR30; open 10am-7pm Tues-Sun), featuring a series of displays from the glory days of the Soviet space programme.

Ostankino (Outer North Moscow Map)

The pink and white **Ostankino Palace** (Ostankinsky dvorets), a wooden mansion with a stucco exterior made to resemble stone, was built in the 1790s as the summer pad of Count Nikolai Sheremetev, probably Russia's richest aristocrat of the time. Its lavish interior, with hand-painted wallpaper and intricate parquet floors, houses the count's art treasures.

The centrepiece is the oval-shaped theatre-ballroom built for the Sheremetevs' troupe of 250 serf actors. In 1801, Count Nikolai married one of the troupe, Praskovia Zhemchugova, and the two retired to Ostankino to avoid court gossip.

Only the **Italian Pavilion** (☎ 286 6288; admission RR40; open 10am-6pm Wed-Sun May 18-1 Oct) is open for visits. There are limited hours and the pavilion is closed on days when it rains or the humidity is over 80%. The five-domed **Trinity Church** (Troitskaya tserkov), outside the palace, dates from the 1680s.

The former palace gardens, to the west, are now the pleasant Ostankino Park, with woods, a lake and a funfair.

After a fire in the late 1990s, the 540m **Ostankino TV Tower** is no longer open to the public, but it still provides a distinctive landmark for the area.

To reach the Ostankino, walk west from VDNKh metro across the car parks to pick up either tram No 7 or 11, or trolleybus No 13, 36, 69 or 73 west along ulitsa Akademika Korolyova.

Petrovsky Palace (Outer North Moscow Map)

Leningradsky prospekt, which slices north-west through the suburbs towards Sheremetevo airports and St Petersburg, is a fairly uninspiring avenue. The oddest sight along it, just north of Dinamo stadium, is the **Petrovsky Road-Palace** (Petrovsky dvorets), one of the many staging posts Catherine the Great built for her trips between St Petersburg and Moscow. This one was also Napoleon's headquarters after Moscow burned down. It is a fantastic blend of pseudo-Gothic, Moorish and traditional Russian styles. For about 50 years it housed the Air Force Engineering Academy and it is now being restored to house (yet another) luxury hotel.

OUTER NORTH MOSCOW

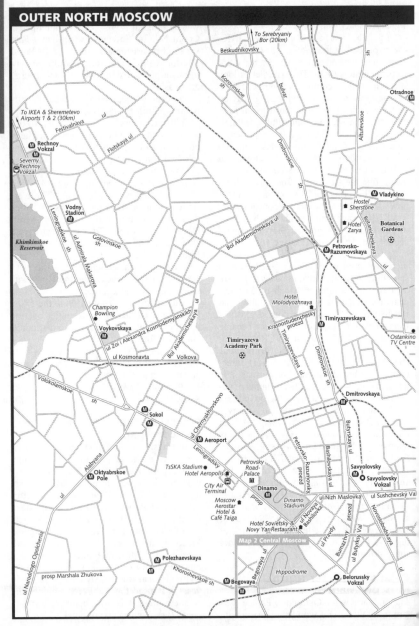

To Serebryaniy
Bor (20km)

Beskudnikovsky

Korovinskoe
sh

Dmitrovskoe
sh

bulvar

Otradnoe
Ⓜ

Altufevskoe
sh

To IKEA & Sheremetevo
Airports 1 & 2 (30km)

Festivalnaya

ul

Flotskaya ul

Ⓜ Rechnoy
Vokzal

Severny
Rechnoy
Vokzal

Ⓜ Vadykino

Hostel
Sherstone

Hotel
Zarya

Botanical
Gardens
✿

Ⓜ Vodny
Stadion

Golovinskoe
sh

ul Admirala Makarova

Leningradskoe

Bol Akademicheskaya ul

Ⓜ Petrovsko-
Razumovskaya

Botanicheskaya

Khimkinskoe
Reservoir

Hotel
Molodyozhnaya

Champion
Bowling

Ⓜ Voykovskaya

ul Zoi i Alexandra Kosmodemyanskikh

Bol Akademicheskaya

Krasnostudencheskyy
proezd

Ⓜ Timiryazevskaya

Ostankino
TV Centre

ul Kosmonavta Volkova

Timiryazeva
Academy Park
✿

Timiryazevskaya ul

Dmitrovskoe sh

Volokolamskoe
sh

Ⓜ Dmitrovskaya

ul Chernyakhovskovo

Ⓜ Sokol

Leningradsky

Ⓜ Aeroport

TsSKA Stadium
Hotel Aeropolis

City Air
Terminal

Moscow
Aerostar
Hotel &
Café Taiga

Petrovsky
Road-
Palace

prosp

Ⓜ Dinamo

Dinamo
Stadium

Petrovsko-
Razumovsky
proezd

Bashilovskaya ul

Butyrskaya ul

Ⓜ Savyolovsky

Savyolovsky
Vokzal

ul Nizh Maslovka

ul Sushchevsky Val

Novoslobodskaya

Alabyana

Ⓜ Oktyabrskoe
Pole

ul

ul Narodnogo Opolchenia

prosp Marshala Zhukova

Ⓜ Polezhaevskaya

Khoroshevskoe sh

Hotel Sovietsky &
Novy Yar Restaurant

ul Novaya
Bashilovka

Map 2 Central Moscow

Begovaya

ul Pravdy

Burmazhny
proezd

ul Butyrsky Val

Hippodrome

Ⓜ Begovaya

Belorussky
Vokzal

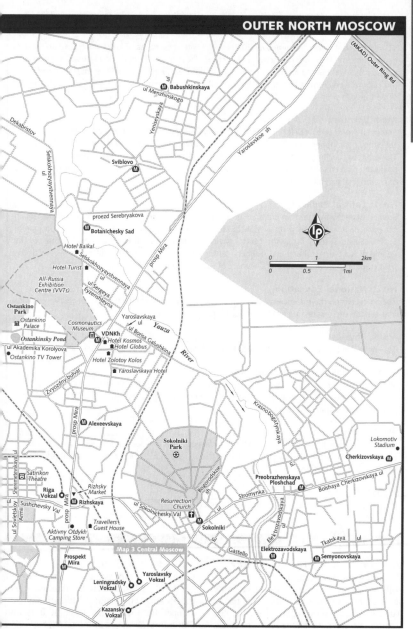

OUTER NORTH MOSCOW

(MKAD) Outer Ring Rd

ul Menzhinskogo

Ⓜ Babushkinskaya

Yenyeyskaya

Yaroslavskoe sh

Dekabristov

Selskokhozyaystvennaya ul

Sviblovo

proezd Serebryakova

Ⓜ Botanichesky Sad

Hotel Baikal
Selskokhozyaystvennaya ul

Hotel Turist

prosp Mira

All-Russia
Exhibition
Centre (VVTs)

ul Sergeya
Eyzenshteyna

Ostankino
Park

Ostankino
Palace

Cosmonautics
Museum

Yaroslavskaya
ul

ul Borsa Galushkina

Yauza River

Ostankinsky Pond

Ⓜ VDNKh

ul Akademika Korolyova

Ⓜ Hotel Kosmos
Hotel Globus

Ostankino TV Tower

Hotel Zolotoy Kolos

Yaroslavskaya Hotel

Zvyozdny bulvar

Krasnobogatyrskaya

prosp Mira

Ⓜ Alexeevskaya

Sokolniki
Park
✿

Lokomotiv
Stadium

Cherkizovskaya Ⓜ

Sheremetevskaya ul

Satirikon
Theatre

Rizhsky
Market

Preobrazhenskaya
Ploshchad

Ⓜ

Bolshaya Cherkizovskaya ul

ul Sovietskoy
Armii

Riga
Vokzal

Ⓜ Rizhskaya

prosp Mira

Sushchevsky Val

Boyorodskoe sh

Resurrection
Church

Stromynka

Elektrozavodskaya ul

Aktivny Otdykh
Camping Store

Travellers'
Guest House

ul Sokolnichesky Val

✝ Ⓜ

Sokolniki

Tkatskaya ul

Map 3 Central Moscow

Prospekt
Mira

Ⓜ

Gastello

Elektrozavodskaya Ⓜ

Ⓜ Semyonovskaya

Leningradsky
Vokzal

Yaroslavsky
Vokzal

Kazansky
Vokzal

0   1   2km
0   0.5   1mi

In Memory of Soviet Economic Achievement: VDNKh

VDNKh is a vast place, covering over 200 hectares with socialist realist kitsch – gargantuan statues, flamboyant fountains and distinctive architecture. These days, the attraction is less the exhibitions themselves – although you may happen upon a business or cultural event of interest – and more the elaborate environs, a curious vestige of Soviet paradise gone awry. Some of the highlights include the following:

Main Entrance

The main entrance to VDNKh is about 500m from prospekt Mira, but you can't miss the massive columned gate topped with Orlov's unmistakable statue of the *Tractor Driver and Collective Farmer*. These happy, healthy, hard-working youths hoisting a golden sheaf of wheat overhead have become the emblem of VDNKh. This symbol of economic achievement was erected for the opening of the original exhibition centre in 1939.

No 1: Central Pavilion

Framed perfectly by the main entrance gate, the central pavilion is the most prominent pavilion in the park. Built in 1954 by architects Shchuko and Stolyarova, it looks like a mini version of one of Stalin's 'Seven Sisters'. Today the central pavilion houses the Dom Narodov Rossii (House of the People of Russia), a cultural and business centre where visitors can acquaint themselves with the politics, education and creative endeavours of Russia's various cultures.

No 2: National Education

The so-called 'northern Caucasus' pavilion employs Caucasian architectural elements like columns and windows to create an elegant, spacious, open-air courtyard.

No 5: Physics

The incredible tiled and colonnaded facade of this pavilion evokes images of Central Asia.

Friendship of the People Fountain

VDNKh has more than 20 fountains, the most spectacular being this bronze and granite socialist-realist masterpiece. A huge granite chalice is surrounded by girls from the 15 formerly Soviet republics, all in national costume.

No 68: Armenia

This pavilion was built in 1954 in a bold, neoclassical style to house the pavilion on coal mining. Having burnt out in that forum, the pavilion will soon reopen focusing on products (and food) from the Republic of Armenia.

No 67: Karelia

Built in 1965, the entire pavilion – from architecture to exhibit – is entirely devoted to the Republic of Karelia.

Victory Park & Around (Outer West Moscow Map)

Following a vicious but inconclusive battle at Borodino (see the Excursions chapter) in August 1812, Moscow's defenders retreated along what are now Kutuzovsky prospekt and ulitsa Arbat, pursued by Napoleon's Grand Army. Today, about 3km west of Kalininsky Most and Hotel Ukraina (where the Russian commander Mikhail Kutuzov stopped for a war council), is the **Borodino Panorama** (*Muzey-panorama Borodinskaya*

In Memory of Soviet Economic Achievement: VDNKh

No 8: Young Naturalists

Built for the young florists, gardeners and vintners of the Soviet Union, this pavilion has a fairy-tale air, created by its colonnaded courtyard, its tall, transparent cupola and its semicircular orangery.

No 11: Metallurgy

It is not so beautiful to look at, but this pavilion holds a permanent exhibit on Russia's metallurgical industry.

No 66: Culture

One of the original pavilions built in 1939 by the architect Polupanov, this elegant pavilion now houses an impressive art gallery. Exhibits include traditional and modern art, including semiprecious stones, pottery and clothing.

Stone Flower Fountain

Another granite and bronze fountain, this one features fish and birds and a fantastical flower created by the colourful reflections. It was designed by the beloved children's writer, Pavel Bazhov.

No 58: Agriculture

It is no coincidence that the agriculture pavilion holds such a prominent location and extravagant building in the USSR Exhibition of Economic Achievements. The golden sculptures and the 42m cupola demonstrate the importance attributed to Soviet agricultural production.

No 32: Cosmos

Once the pride of the Soviet Union, the Cosmos pavilion now houses an electronics warehouse. However, Yuri Gagarin's formidable *Vostok* launcher still stands out front. The other aircrafts on display – a Tupolev Tu-54 and a Yakovlev Yak-42 – are open for boarding.

No 55: Electrification

Lenin's slogan 'Socialism is Soviet power plus electrification' still adorns this retro-futuristic pavilion, which was built in 1963.

Pavilions 36–44

This cluster of pavilions around the ponds in the back of the park were devoted mainly to exhibits on breeding and raising all manner of living creature, such as **37** birds, **38** fish, **42–43** horses, **44** rabbits and other furry creatures, **47** pigs, and **48** sheep. Besides the zoo-like artistic elements, there is not much to look at.

No 28: Beekeeping

Beekeeping specialists provide detailed information and exhibits on the development and maintenance of apiaries. Buy all the supplies you need and don't miss the fresh honey for sale!

bitva; ☎ 148 1927; Kutuzovsky pr 38; admission RR60; open 10am-5pm Sat-Thur), a pavilion with a giant 360° painting of the Borodino battle. Standing inside this tableau of bloodshed – as many as 100,000 were killed in 15 hours – is an impressive, if ide-

alised, way to visualise the event. See if you can spot Napoleon on his white horse.

The **Triumphal Arch**, farther out, celebrates Napoleon's eventual defeat. It was demolished at its original site in front of the Belorusskaya Station during the 1930s and

OUTER WEST MOSCOW

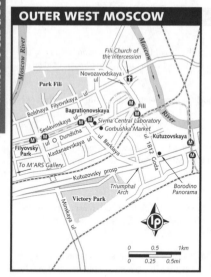

reconstructed here in a fit of post-WWII public spirit.

From here it is a short distance west to **Victory Park** (Park Pobedy), a huge memorial complex celebrating the Great Patriotic War. The park includes endless fountains, a memorial mosque, synagogue and church, and some typically kitsch Tsereteli-designed monuments. (For details about the Memorial Synagogue, see the boxed text 'Judaism in Moscow' earlier in this chapter.) The dominant monument is a 142m obelisk, 10cm for each day of the war. The **Museum of the Great Patriotic War** (☎ 142 4185; ul Bratiev Fonchenko 10; admission RR10; open 10am-5pm Tues-Sun), located within the park, has exhibits on the many Heroes of the Soviet Union. A series of audiovisual presentations, photograph and map displays, and a huge diorama give good coverage to different aspects of the war years.

Approximately 1.5km north of the Borodino Panorama, in the neighbourhood of Fili, you will discover the 1690s **Church of the Intercession** (admission RR50; open 11am-5.30pm Thur-Tues), a beautiful red-brick, Moscow baroque confection in otherwise dreary surroundings. From the Fili metro, walk some 500m north on Novozavodskaya ulitsa – it's impossible to miss.

Sparrow Hills (Outer South Moscow Map)

The best view over Moscow is from Universitetskaya ploshchad on the Sparrow Hills (Vorobyovy Gory), just across the river bend from Luzhniki. From this location most of the city spreads out before you. In the park, a ski jump runs down to the river. Take trolleybus No 7 from Kievskaya or Leninsky Prospekt metro.

Immediately behind Universitetskaya ploshchad rises the 36-storey Stalinist main spire of **Moscow University** (Moskovsky gosudarstvenny universitet), another 'Seven Sister' visible from most places in the city, thanks to its elevated site. It was built by convict labour between 1949 and 1953. Bus Nos 1, 113 and 119 travel between the back of the main building and Universitet metro.

Kolomenskoe Museum-Reserve (Outer South Moscow Map)

Kolomenskoe (Muzey-zapovednik Kolomenskoe; ☎ 115 2309; metro: Kolomenskaya; admission to grounds free, to museums RR120; grounds open 10am-9pm daily, museums open 10am-5pm daily) is an ancient royal country seat and Unesco World Heritage site, set amid 4 sq km of parkland on a bluff above a bend in the Moscow River. It is the best excursion to the outer suburbs. Lots of festivals are held here during the year and it's well worth checking to see if anything is happening during your visit.

From ulitsa Shtatnaya Sloboda, enter via the 17th-century **Saviour Gate** (Spasskaya vorota), built in the time of Tsar Alexey, at the rear of the grounds.

Inside the gate, to the left of the main path, the **Kazan Church** (Kazanskaya tserkov), also built by Alexey, faces the site of his great wooden palace demolished in 1768 by Catherine the Great. Ahead, the white, tent-roofed 17th-century **front gate and clock tower** mark the edge of the old inner palace precinct. A golden double-headed eagle, symbol of the Romanov dynasty, tops the gate.

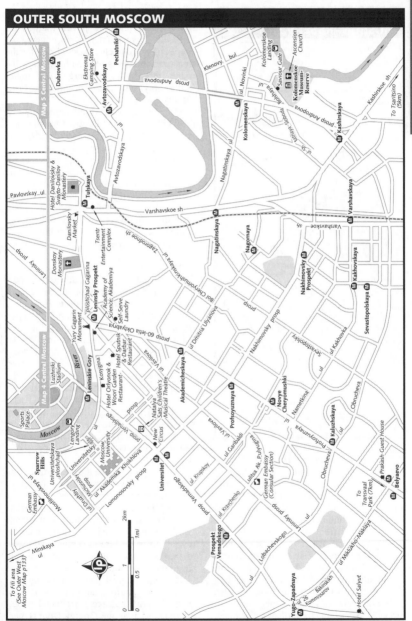

OUTER SOUTH MOSCOW

KOLOMENSKOE MUSEUM-RESERVE

1 Saviour Gate	6 Museum
2 Kazan Church	7 Front Gate & Clock Tower
3 Peter the Great's Cabin	8 Pavilion
4 Cossack Fort Watch Tower	9 Ascension Church
5 Nikolo-Karelsky	10 St George's Bell Tower
Monastery Gate Tower	11 St John the Baptist Church

The adjacent buildings house an interesting **museum** with a bit of everything: a model of Alexey's wooden palace, material on rebellions associated with Kolomenskoe, and Russian crafts from clocks and tiles to woodcarving and metalwork.

Outside the front gate, overlooking the river, rises Kolomenskoe's loveliest structure, the tall, almost rocket-like **Ascension Church** (Voznesenskaya tserkov), which is as quintessentially Russian as St Basil's Cathedral. The Ascension Church was built between 1530 and 1532 for Grand Prince Vasily III, probably to celebrate the birth of his heir Ivan

the Terrible. It was an important development in Russian architecture, paving the way for St Basil's 25 years later by reproducing the shapes of wooden churches in brick for the first time. Immediately south of it are the round 16th-century **St George's Bell Tower** (Kolokolnya Georgia) and another 17th-century tower.

Some 300m farther south across a gully, the white **St John the Baptist Church** (Tserkov Ianna Predtechi) was built for Ivan the Terrible in the 1540s or 1550s.

It has four corner chapels, which make it a stylistic 'quarter-way house' between the Ascension Church and St Basil's. Some old **wooden buildings** from elsewhere have been collected in the old palace area, among them the cabin where Peter the Great lived while supervising ship and fort building at Arkhangelsk in the 1700s.

Tsaritsino

On a wooded hill in far southeast Moscow is situated the eerie shell of the exotic summer home, the **Tsaritsino Palace** (Tsaritsinsky Dvorets; ☎ 921 0139; admission RR30; open 11am-5pm Wed-Fri, 10am-6pm Sat & Sun), that Catherine the Great began in 1775 but never finished. She allowed architect Vasily Bazhenov to work for 10 years, then sacked him, apparently because he had included a twin palace for her out-of-favour son Paul. She hired another architect, Matvey Kazakov, but then gave up altogether as money was diverted to wars against Turkey. What stands is mostly Bazhenov's fantasy combination of old Russian, Gothic, classical and Arabic styles.

From the centre take the green metro line south to Orekhovo station and turn west towards the park.

The English-style wooded park stretches all the way south to the **Upper Tsaritsinsky Pond** (Verkhny Tsaritsinsky prud), which has rowing boats for hire in summer, and west to the Tsaritsino Palace complex. Straight ahead on the far side of the causeway is the Gothic **Figurny most** (Patterned Bridge).

Up to the right from here is the impressive shell of the **main palace**, surrounded by outbuildings such as the **Operny Dom** (Opera

House), where occasional concerts are held. The large, square **Khlebny Dom** (Kitchen) is to the northeast. An English-style wooded **park** stretches to the south. Also worthy of a look is the **Bolshoy most** (Big Bridge), which spans a ravine 200m north of the Figurny most.

Kuskovo (Outer East Moscow Map)

When Count Pyotr Sheremetev married Varvara Cherkassakava in 1743, their joint property amounted to 1200 villages and 200,000 serfs. They turned their country estate at Kuskovo, 12km east of the Kremlin, into a mini Versailles, with elegant buildings scattered around formal gardens, as well as an informal park. It's a pleasant trip out from central Moscow.

The wooden main mansion, **Kuskovo Mansion** (Usadba Kuskovo; ☎ 370 0160; ul Yunosti 2; admission RR10-100 for each exhibit; open 10am-6pm Wed-Sun), was built in the 1770s and overlooks a lake where the count staged mock sea battles to entertain Moscow society. To the south, across the lake, is the informal park. North of the mansion, in the formal grounds, are an **orangery** which now houses an exhibition of 18th- to 20th-century Russian ceramics; an **open-air theatre** where the Sheremetevs' troupe of serf actors performed twice weekly; a pondside **grotto** with exotic 'sea caverns'; a **Dutch house**, glazed inside with Delft tiles; an **Italian villa**; a **hermitage** for private parties; and a **church** with a wooden bell tower.

Bus Nos 133 and 208 from Ryazansky Prospekt metro go to the main entrance. Buildings are closed when humidity exceeds 80% or when it's very cold, which counts out much of the winter.

Izmaylovo (Outer East Moscow Map)

Izmaylovo is best known for its extensive art and craft market (see the Shopping chapter), which is held every weekend. After shopping, however, Izmaylovsky Park and the crumbling royal estate are a nice place for a picnic or for some more serious outdoor activity.

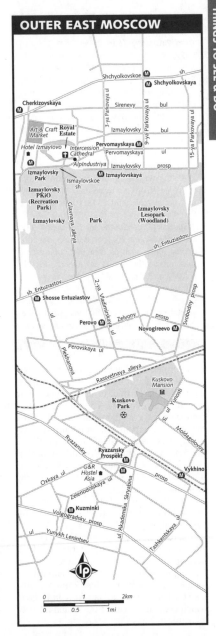

OUTER EAST MOSCOW

THINGS TO SEE & DO

Want a Guide for a Day?

Dom Patriarshy Tours (Map 2; ☎/fax 795 0927; e alanskaya@co.ru; Vspolny per 6, Moscow school No 1239) provides unique English-language tours on just about any specialised subject that might interest you. Some of the tours also provide access to otherwise closed museums. Day tours range from US$8 to US$20 per person. Look for the monthly schedule of tours at Western hotels and American restaurants.

Its spin-off, **Capital Tours** (Map 6; ☎ 232 2442; W www.capitaltours.ru; Gostiny Dvor, ul Ilyinka 4), offers a twice-daily Moscow city tour (adults/children US$18/10) as well as a Kremlin/Armoury tour (US$30/20).

Sputnik (Outer South Moscow map; ☎ 939 8310; ul Kosygina 15) specialises in more outdoorsy tours, such as camping, fishing and spas outside the city. Prices average RR300 per day, including meals.

Intourist (Map 3; ☎ 956 8844; Milyutinskiy per 13/1) runs several mainstream tours geared for large groups that visit places like the Kremlin and Pushkin Fine Arts Museum.

A former royal hunting preserve 10km east of the Kremlin, **Izmaylovsky Park** is the nearest large tract of undeveloped land to central Moscow. Its 15 sq km contain a recreation park at the western end, and a much larger expanse of woodland (Izmaylovsky Lesopark) east of Glavnaya alleya, the road which cuts north-south across the park. Trails wind around this park, making it a good place to escape the city for hiking or biking.

From Izmaylovsky Park metro, head south (away from the giant Hotel Izmaylovo) for the recreation park.

The **royal estate** is on a small, moated island. Tsar Alexey had an experimental farm here in the 17th century, where Western farming methods and cottage industries were sampled. It was on the **Silver Pond** here that his son Peter learnt to sail in a little boat, which came to be called the Grandfather of the Russian Navy.

The beautiful, five-domed 1679 **Intercession Cathedral** (Pokrovsky sobor) is an early example of Moscow baroque style made of red brick with white stone carvings. The nearby triple-arched, tent-roofed **Ceremonial Gates** (1682) and the squat brick **bridge tower** (1671) are the only other original buildings remaining from a huge estate that Tsar Alexey built in the late 17th century.

The estate saw several decades of total neglect before it was decided to build **Invalidny Dom** (Invalids House) to take care of war veterans of 1812.

Konstantin Thon was commissioned for the project and built several two- and three-storey buildings on the site. These included residential buildings, workshops, a bathhouse and other premises for household needs. The iron gate and the fountain also date to the 19th century.

The area is quite well kept and pleasant to visit any time of year. The island complex is now a part of the State History Museum and the bridge tower now contains an exhibition hall.

RIVER TRIPS

For new perspectives on Moscow neighbourhoods, fine views of the Kremlin, or just good old-fashioned transportation, a boat ride on the Moscow River is one of the city's highlights. The main route runs between the Kiev Station landing (Map 4) and the Novospassky Most landings (Map 5) near Novospassky Monastery, 1km west of Proletarskaya metro.

There are six intermediate stops: at the foot of Sparrow Hills (Outer South Moscow map); Frunzenskaya near the southern end of Frunzenskaya naberezhnaya; Gorky Park (Map 4); Krimean Most; Bolshoy Kamenny Most opposite the Kremlin (Map 6); and Ustinsky Most near Hotel Rossiya and Red Square (Map 5).

The boats seat about 200 people; most Muscovites are actually going somewhere, not just out to enjoy the ride. These boats are operated by the **Capital Shipping Company** (☎ 277 3902; tickets weekend/weekday RR140/70) and run from late April to early October. Check at the landings for the limited weekday schedules; on weekends

Space Tourism, Russian-style

Ever fancied flying into space, or at twice the speed of sound? In Russia such things can be arranged – at a price. In April 2001, American billionaire Dennis Tito made history as the first paying customer of the Russian Space Agency when he forked out a cool US$20 million to take a shot at space travel.

After several months of training at Star City, Zvezdny Gorodok, 30km from Moscow, Tito joined cosmonauts Talgat Musabayev and Yuri Baturin on board a Russian Soyuz spacecraft to pay a week-long visit to the International Space Station. The visit, initially opposed by NASA, was considered a success and in April 2002 another millionaire – South African Mark Shuttleworth – followed in Tito's space boots.

Not everyone has US$20 million to spare, so the Russian aerospace company Sub-Orbital Corporation is working together with the US-based Space Adventures (which arranged the Tito and Shuttleworth jaunts) on its C-21 shuttle, designed to take one pilot and two passengers on brief trips into space. For around US$100,000 passengers will zoom 100km up where they will leave the atmosphere for about five minutes, experiencing weightlessness and the blackness of space. The round trip will take about an hour and according to reports between 100 and 250 people have already put deposits on tickets for flights, which are hoped to start in 2005.

If you can't wait that long for a space flight then, for US$12,595, Space Adventures can arrange for you to co-pilot a MiG-25 'Foxbat'. These fighter jets can fly at over 3000km/h, more than twice the speed of sound, to an altitude of 24,000m, the outer limit of the atmosphere, from where you can see the earth curve. The flights take off from the formerly top-secret Zhukovsky Air Base, an hour's drive southeast of Moscow. Zhukovsky is the testing ground for all of Russia's newest aircraft and home to the Gromov Flight Research Institute, one of the country's largest centres for aviation research and testing.

For your money you get two nights at one of Moscow's premier hotels (includes breakfast), transfers between airport, hotel and Zhukovsky Air Base, English-speaking guide, a flight suit, model of the plane, flight instruction, training and medical check. If you can't quite afford the MiG-25 experience, fear not, since Space Adventures offers a range of flight programmes (including one to experience zero gravity) in other military aircraft. The cheapest is US$3395 for a chance to fly the L-39, the standard Russian Air Force trainer with a maximum speed of 780km/h.

For full details, contact **Space Adventures** (☎ 888-85-SPACE in USA, ☎ 703-524-7172 outside USA; ⓦ www.spaceadventures.com; 4350 Fairfax Dr, Arlington, Virginia 22203).

Simon Richmond

they run as often as every 20 minutes in either direction.

BANYA

What better way to cope with Moscow than to have it steamed, washed and beaten out of you? There are traditional banyas (Russian baths) all over town (see the boxed text 'Steaming – the Joys of Banya' earlier in this chapter).

The oldest, and a work of art themselves, are **Sandunovskiye Baths** (Map 2; ☎ 925 4631; Neglinnaya ul 14; 2-person banya RR1000/1300 per hr without/with pool; open 8am-10pm Wed-Mon). The Gothic Room has rich wood carving and the main shower room has an almost aristocratic, Roman feel to it. If you are not shy, general admission to shared facilities is cheaper.

For a less historic, more 'New Russian' experience, try the **Sauna at Chistye Prudy** (Map 3; ☎ 923 5854; Krivokolenny per 14/2; open 24hr). The facility has a jacuzzi and billiards, in addition to its Finnish sauna.

WINTER SPORTS

There's no shortage of winter in Moscow, so take advantage of it. You can rent ice skates and see where all those great Russian figure skaters come from at **Gorky Park** (Map 4; ☎ 237 1266). Bring your passport. The winter skating rink at **Chistyie Prudy**

(Map 3) is also pleasant, but you have to bring your own skates.

Izmaylovsky Park *(Outer East Moscow map; ☎ 166 8690)* has both ski and skate rental. Take bus No 7 or 131 from Izmaylovsky Park metro station and get off at the third stop.

WATER SPORTS

Public pools are difficult places to take the plunge if you are a foreigner, because they all insist on a Russian doctor's certificate proving your good health before they'll let you in. However, **Chaika Swimming Pool** *(Chaika Bassein; Map 4; ☎ 246 1344; Turchaninov per 1/3; admission RR150 per hr; open 7am-10pm Mon-Sat, 8am-7pm Sun)* will provide a check-up, complete with health certificate, for RR100 on the spot.

Transvaal Park *(☎ 785 0202; ul Golubinskaya 16; open 10am-11pm Sun-Thur, 10am-2am Fri-Sat; RR300 per 3hr)*, a gigantic entertainment complex and water park, is reminiscent of 1980s Cleveland. Opened in Moscow in 2002, the main feature is an Olympic pool and water slides. Additional attractions include a nightclub, bowling alley, roller rink and fitness centre.

On hot summer days you can join much of the city and head to the beaches at **Serebryaniy Bor**, a series of lakes and channels on the Moscow River 20km north of the city (a key detail since nothing from Moscow has yet *flushed* into the water). There are areas that are unofficially dedicated to families, gays, nudists and even disco dancers. Take the metro to Sokol and then ride trolleybus No 65 to the end of the line.

LANGUAGE COURSES

The *Moscow Times* carries lots of small ads from tutors and colleges offering short-term Russian-language lessons. Many will teach you their Russian in return for you sharing your English. For a more formal experience, try one of the following organisations:

Lingua Service Worldwide (☎ 800-394 5327, 631-424 0777, fax 631-271 3441; ⓦ www.linguaserviceworldwide.com/russia .htm) 75 Prospect Street, Suite 4, Huntington, NY 11743, USA

Russian Language Study Centre (☎/fax 095-939 0980; ⓦ www.studyrussian.com) Moscow State University (MGU)

Language Liason (☎ 800-284 4448, 973-898 1416, fax 973-898 1710; ⓦ www.languagelia son.com) 4 Burnham Pkwy, Morristown, NJ 07960 USA

Inter-university Canada (ⓦ www.interuniver sity.com) MGU

School of Russian & Asian Studies (☎ 800-55 RUSSIA, ☎/fax 617-269 2659; ⓦ www.sras .com)

Russian Village (ⓦ www.rusvillage.com)

Center for Russian Language & Culture (☎ 095-939 1463; ⓦ www.ruslanguage.ru) MGU

Places to Stay

Moscow is not a cheap place to stay. During the 1990s investment was limited to the luxury properties, of which there is no shortage. The sort of small and simple hotels that are found elsewhere in Europe are rare and when they do exist, they are overpriced and undermaintained.

Mid-range and budget hotels are primarily Soviet-era properties that have weathered the transition to a market economy with varying measures of grace. Many are huge labyrinths (like the Hotel Rossiya) that lack any charm; however, with a bit of spirit, a stay in these places can be part of the Russian adventure.

Some places to stay outside the centre can be good-value options. Access to the city is directly proportionate to access to the metro. You may not be able to afford to stay right near Red Square or on the Arbat, but try to stay near a metro station and you'll be able to reach these places easily enough.

Moscow has no central homestay agency. However, you can arrange to stay in private homes before you arrive by booking from abroad – see Homestays later in this chapter for a list of agencies.

Most of the mid-range and all of the top-end hotels accept credit cards, but be warned that many hotels – especially the less expensive options – have dual pricing and you will pay more than your Russian or Kazakh counterpart. Prices quoted in this chapter are for foreign visitors.

Some cheaper hotels may also charge a 'reservation fee' (as much as 50%) for the first night's stay (even if you don't make an advance reservation). Prices listed include the 20% value-added tax (VAT), but not the 5% sales tax, which is charged mainly at luxury hotels.

PLACES TO STAY – BUDGET
Camping
There are no camping grounds around Moscow, but take heart – staying at many of the cheaper hotels is much like camping!

Guesthouses
Galina's Flat *(Map 3;* ☎ *921 6038;* ⓔ *galinas .flat@mtu-net.ru; ul Chaplygina 8/35; dorm beds/singles/doubles US$8/15/20)* is just that – a private flat with a few extra rooms that Galina rents out. She has a total of six beds (but apparently she can make arrangements with her neighbours if her place is full). Kitchen and Internet facilities are available at this hospitable place.

G&R Hostel Asia *(Outer East Moscow map;* ☎ *378 0001, fax 378 2866;* Ⓦ *www.hostels.ru; Hotel Asia, Zelenodolskaya ul 2/3; dorm beds/singles/doubles with breakfast US$16/ 30/44),* on the top floors of an old hotel, is one of the best budget options. The management is clued up and runs a travel agency that can book train tickets and the like. Leave Ryazansky Prospekt metro from the end of the train and look for the tallest building around – that's the hostel.

Hostel Sherstone *(Outer North Moscow map;* ☎*/fax 797 8075;* Ⓦ *www.sherstone .ru; Gostinichny pr 8/1; dorm beds/singles/ doubles US$14/25/40)* is a branch of the G&R. Services include visa support, free transfers from the train station and discounts for Hostelling International card holders. It is a 10-minute walk from Vladykino metro.

Art Hostel *(Map 2; hostel* ☎ *251 2837, central reservations* ☎ *812-275 1513, fax 275 4581;* Ⓦ *www.arthostel.net; 3-ya Tverskaya-Yamskaya ul 58/5; dorm beds/singles/ doubles with breakfast US$15/20/30; curfew 1am)* has a prime location, two minutes' walk from Belorusskaya metro, in a student hostel run by kindly *babushkas*. Rooms are well furnished and facilities include a modern kitchen with microwave and washing machine. The catch is that the hostel is only open 15 December to 1 March and 1 July to 10 September (when prices are about US$5 higher per person). The entrance is on pereulok Aleksandra Nevskogo, the third door on the left.

Travellers Guest House *(Outer North Moscow map;* ☎ *951 4059, fax 280 7686;*

e tgh@glasnet.ru; ul Bolshaya Pereyaslavskaya 50, floor 10; dorm beds US$18, rooms with private/shared bathroom US$48/55) calls itself Moscow's 'first and only' budget accommodation. Perhaps the first, but no longer the only, this lacklustre place is a 10-minute walk north of Prospekt Mira metro. Rooms and shared toilets are basic, but clean, and there's almost always space. Infinity Travel Agency, which is affiliated with this place, offers all kinds of useful services.

Prakash Guest House (Outer South Moscow map; ☎ 334 8201; fax 334 2598; Profsoyuznaya ul 83/1; dorm beds/doubles US$18/50), run by an Indian team, is just a minute's walk north of Belyaevo metro. Private rooms come with breakfast, TV and phone. Some pairs of rooms share a bathroom and toilet. Use entrance two on the south side of the building; there are no signs.

Hotels

Hotels in the cheapest price range are grey places that were poor relations even in Soviet times. Note that the following prices are subject to fluctuation.

Centre For the money, you can't beat the location of **Hotel Tsentralnaya** (Map 2; ☎ 229 8957, fax 292 1221; Tverskaya ul 10; singles/doubles RR1150/1750). Unfortunately, these prices win you pretty crumby rooms and often surly service.

Hotel Minsk (Map 2; ☎ 299 1213, fax 299 0362; Tverskaya ul 22; singles/doubles RR700/1050) is plagued by the same symptoms: shabby rooms, half-hearted service, prime location. The ticket office in the lobby is useful for train and air tickets.

North The shortest of Stalin's 'Seven Sisters' is **Hotel Leningradskaya** (Map 3; ☎ 975 1815, fax 975 1802; Kalanchevskaya ul 21/40; singles/doubles from RR900/1600). Arriving at this looming skyscraper in the dead of night is likely to strike fear into you, but in daylight this showpiece Soviet hotel retains much of its grand 1950s' style and is worth considering as a base for a couple of nights.

Hotel Zarya (Outer North Moscow map; ☎/fax 482 2458; ul Gostinichnaya 4/9; singles/

doubles from RR700/800) is a large complex of short brick buildings set among the tree-lined streets near Petrovsko-Razumovskaya metro. Rooms are nothing special, but the place has a cosy atmosphere. There are nicer rooms for RR1500/2500, but they're probably not worth it.

Hotel Zolotoy Kolos (Outer North Moscow map; ☎ 217 4355, fax 286 2703; ul Yaroslavskaya 15; rooms with bathroom from RR600) is an adequate hotel near VDNKh. Rooms have phone and TV.

Yaroslavskaya Hotel (Outer North Moscow map; ☎ 247 2501, fax 247 2500; W www.moscowhotels.ru; ul Yaroslavskaya 8/1; singles/doubles from RR690/1100) is a similar option just down the road. Both of these places are frequently used by Russian business travellers visiting the Exhibition Centre, so reservations are recommended.

Hotel Turist (Outer North Moscow map; ☎ 187 7045, fax 187 7596; W www.alean.ru/tourist; singles/doubles/triples with breakfast from RR800/930/1500) is a friendly hotel complex a short walk from Botanichesky Sad metro. The brick buildings and the leafy setting near the Botanical Gardens lend this place a pleasant atmosphere, although rooms are what you'd expect for the price.

Hotel Baikal (Outer North Moscow map; ☎ 189 7529; Selskokhozyaistvennaya ul 15/1; singles/doubles RR500/1000 or RR950/1900) is opposite Hotel Turist, both geographically and aesthetically. Apparently the price variations reflect different quality levels in the rooms, but *only* guests are allowed to enter the rooms, so we may never know the difference.

Hotel Molodyozhnaya (Outer North Moscow map; ☎ 977 3155, 977 2330, fax 210 4311; Dmitrovskoe sh 27; singles/doubles with breakfast RR950/1160), a towering blue block, was built for student and youth tourists in the Soviet era (its name means 'youth'). Rooms are on the small side, but are clean. The Molodyozhnaya has a variety of average cafés, bars and restaurants. Walk 400m north from metro Timiryazevskaya.

East Built specifically for the 1980 Olympics, **Hotel Izmaylovo** (Outer East Moscow *map; Izmaylovskoe sh 71)* has 8000 beds, which apparently makes it Europe's biggest hotel. It's divided into five blocks, with the facilities managed by a thicket of organisations, some more upstanding than others. However, the atmosphere is brighter than other budget hotels and it's right outside the Izmaylovsky Park metro. The rooms are decent; all have bathroom, TV and phone.

Korpus Beta *(☎/fax 792 9898; singles/ doubles from RR660/792)* is the cheapest (and sketchiest) option.

Korpus Alfa *(☎ 166 0163, fax 166 0060; singles/doubles from RR1115/1490)* and **Korpus Vega** *(☎ 956 0640, fax 956 2850; singles/ doubles RR1000/1500)* are one step up.

Korpus Gamma *(☎ 166 3736, fax 166 7758; singles/doubles RR1880/2080)* and **Korpus Delta** *(☎ 166 4127, fax 737 7000; singles/ doubles with breakfast RR1880/2080)*, sharing the building closest to the market, have slightly snazzier rooms. All the towers have restaurants, cafés and other services.

South A seedy option is **Hotel Kievskaya** *(Map 4; ☎ 240 1444, fax 240 5388; Kievskaya ul 2; singles/doubles with bathroom RR740/ 820)*, near Kiev station (Kievsky vokzal) with all its bustle and bedlam. Reception staff may try to deter you by warning their clientele is not quite respectable – beware of theft. All rooms have phone, TV and fridge.

Hotel Varshava *(Map 4; ☎ 238 7701, fax 238 4101; Leninsky pr 2; singles/doubles US$50/100)* is not far from Gorky Park and convenient to Zamoskovrechie. Rooms are Soviet standard with basic amenities.

Hotel Yunost *(Map 4; ☎ 242 4861, fax 242 0284; ul Khamovnichesky val 34; singles/ doubles RR1350/1500)* has adequate rooms, but it's not too convenient for the price. The closest metro stations are Frunzenskaya and Sportivnaya.

Hotel Salyut *(Outer South Moscow map; ☎ 234 9292, fax 234 9363; Leninsky pr 158; singles/doubles with breakfast RR800/1300)* is about 15km southwest of the centre. It's not a bad place, although with 2000 beds service may be a tad impersonal. Prices decrease after the first night. The hotel has a

service bureau, several eateries and a sauna with a tiny pool and massage room. From Yugo-Zapadnaya metro, take bus No 227, 250, 281 or 502 two stops south along prospekt Vernadskogo.

Hotel Sputnik *(Outer South Moscow map; ☎ 930 2287, fax 930 6383; W www.hotel -sputnik.ru; Leninsky pr 38; singles/doubles with breakfast RR1170/1677)* is another 1970s' tower with basic rooms. Leninsky Prospekt metro is a 15-minute walk, or take bus No 111 or trolleybus No 4, 33, 62 or 84. Credit cards are accepted.

PLACES TO STAY – MID-RANGE

Twenty years ago, these hotels were the best Moscow had to offer. Their prices have been kept in check, and service standards have improved a bit, thanks to competition from the wave of superior top-end hotels. This is the category where prices vary the widest, even within the facility. Prices also tend to fluctuate with no warning.

Centre

Hotel Moskva *(Map 2; ☎ 960 2020, fax 960 5938; Okhotny ryad 2; singles/doubles RR1600/2500)* occupies the block between Manezhnaya ploshchad and Teatralnaya ploshchad. Here you can feel like a member of the Politburo as this was the accommodation of choice for visiting Communist Party apparatchiks. The atmosphere is appropriately sombre, but the rooms are tolerable and some have marvellous views of the Kremlin. Rumours are flying that this place will soon go the way of its former neighbour, the Intourist Hotel (now closed and soon-to-be-demolished).

Hotel Rossiya *(Map 2; ☎ 232 6046, 232 6248; ul Varvarka 6; singles/doubles from RR1500/1600)* has – literally – thousands of rooms (some are better than others, and you'll pay more for them). The Rossiya gets a bad rap because it's just so big and ugly, but some swear by the place for its unbeatable location and reasonable prices. Plus, you can't see how ugly it is if you're inside.

Hotel Belgrad *(Map 4; ☎ 248 2841, fax 248 2896; Smolenskaya ul 8; singles/doubles RR1500/1950)* offers poky but functional rooms. The location is noisy, but convenient to the western end of ulitsa Arbat.

Hotel Pekin *(Map 2; ☎ 209 2215, fax 200 1420; ⓦ hotelpekin.ringnet.ru; Bolshaya Sadovaya ul 5/1; doubles from US$62)* is better than it looks, with its cheesy Oriental decor and noisy casino. However, staff are helpful, rooms are comfortable and location is convenient – good value for money.

Hotel Sverchkov *(Map 3; ☎ 925 4978; per Sverchkov 8; rooms with breakfast from RR2500)*, on a quiet lane near Chistye Prudy, is a tiny 11-room hotel in a graceful 18th-century building. Rooms are pretty run-down, but the place is kind of homy.

East-West Hotel *(Map 2; ☎ 290 0404, fax 291 4606; ⓦ www.col.ru/east-west; Tverskoy bul 14/4; singles/doubles with breakfast from US$100/130)* is a kitsch, but rather charming, small hotel on one of central Moscow's most pleasant streets. It has a quiet, secure courtyard and a sauna for warming up in winter.

Kazakh Embassy Hotel *(Map 3; ☎ 208 0994; Chistoprudny bul 3; singles/doubles with breakfast US$102/120)* caters – as you might guess – to guests and workers of the nearby Kazakh embassy. However, others can stay in this interesting, modern building; the rooms and location are good value.

Hotel Budapest *(Map 2; ☎ 923 2356, fax 921 1266; ⓦ www.hotel-budapest.ru; Petrovskie linii 2/18; singles/doubles with breakfast US$105/147)* is the top pick in the mid-range. This elegant, central hotel has friendly management and 125 stylish rooms.

Arbat Hotel *(Map 4; ☎ 244 7628, fax 244 0093; ⓔ hotelarbat@hotmail.com; Plotnikov per 12; singles/doubles with breakfast US$120/135)* has a prime location on a quiet street just off the Arbat. This comfortable, 105-room hotel has a decent restaurant and a lovely courtyard.

North

Hotel Volga *(Map 3; ☎ 280 7729, fax 232 3240; ⓔ volgahc@dol.ru; Dokuchaev per 2; rooms with breakfast from US$60)* is a hotel complex run by Moscow's government. Most of the rooms are actually suites, with several rooms and a kitchen. The singles are

clean and share a bathroom. The Volga is a 10-minute walk from the Sukharevskaya metro station.

Hotel Kosmos *(Outer North Moscow map; ☎ 234 1000, fax 215 8880; ⓦ www.hotel-cosmos.ru; pr Mira 150; singles/doubles with breakfast from US$90)* is another Soviet monster, with 3500 beds. It is 8km from the Kremlin, but just across the road from the VDNKh metro station. This gargantuan establishment houses a whole host of – ahem – services.

Hotel Globus *(Outer North Moscow map; ☎ 286 4189; ul Yaroslavksaya 17; suites RR4500)*, just around the corner from the Hotel Kosmos, provides two-room suites with kitchen and bathroom that comfortably house two or three people. The facility is sufficiently modern, with a sauna and pool. Cheaper and unrenovated suites are available from RR1000, but make sure you take a look first.

Sheremetyevo-2 *(☎ 578 5753/4, fax 753 8091; Sheremetyevo-2 airport; rooms from RR2000)*, near the airport of the same name, is a good option if you are crashing between flights. It's a 10-minute walk, or you can avail yourself of the free shuttle to the Novotel, and walk across the street.

Hotel Aeropolis *(Outer North Moscow map; ☎ 151 0442, fax 151 7543; Leningradsky pr 37, korpus 5; singles/doubles with breakfast US$60/70)* is the former Aeroflot Hotel. Rooms are decent and clean. Unless you are going to/from the City Air Terminal (Aerovokzal), the location is not so convenient, as it requires a ride on a trolleybus or tram from either Dinamo or Aeroport metro station. Credit cards are accepted.

West

Hotel Ukraina *(Map 2; ☎ 243 3030, fax 956 2078; Kutuzovsky pr 2/1; singles/doubles RR2100/2500)* faces the White House across the Moscow River. This giant hotel, popular with tour groups, echoes Stalinist pomp with its hallways and old-fashioned, stately rooms, many with terrific views.

Hotel Mir *(Map 2; ☎ 290 9504, fax 252 0140; Bolshoy Devyatinsky per 9; singles/doubles US$105/145)* is close to the White

House. Once only the top-ranking officials from the far-flung Soviet empire stayed inside its futuristic walls. Today, guests are more likely to be politicians from the scattered Russian republics, looking for political influence. Standards are fairly high, with prices to match.

South
Hotel Danilovsky (*Outer South Moscow map*; ☎ 954 0503; e hotdanil@cityline.ru; *singles/doubles US$110/130*), Moscow's holiest hotel (in a good way), is on monastery grounds. The setting is complete with 18th-century churches and well-maintained gardens and is exquisite. The location of the monastery doesn't have much to offer, but the hotel itself is comfortable and has its own restaurant.

Hotel Orlyonok (*Outer South Moscow map*; ☎ 939 8888, fax 939 8646; e hotel@orlenok.ru; *ul Kosygina 15; rooms from US$90*) is in a pleasant part of the city, 6km southwest of the Kremlin. The hotel has been recently renovated, but the casino still attracts prostitutes and gamers. There are several authentic Korean restaurants on the ground floor. Transport is inconvenient: from Leninsky Prospekt metro it's either a 20-minute walk or a ride on trolleybus No 7.

Outer North
Hotel Sovietsky (*Outer North Moscow map*; ☎ 960 2000, fax 250 8003; e hotelsov@cnt.ru; *Leningradsky pr 32/2; singles/doubles with breakfast US$74/79*), a good example of Stalin Empire style from 1952, is one of the most atmospheric places to stay. Rooms with a mix of Stalin-era decor come with satellite TV, minibar, hairdryer and unhurried service. From 20 December to 31 January the rates are cut by 50%. The hotel adjoins the famous **Novy Yar** restaurant (see the Places to Eat chapter) that dates from 1910. The hotel is between Belorusskaya and Dinamo metro stations along the green line, a 15-minute walk from either.

Outer West
Hotel Alexandr Blok (*Map 2*; ☎ 255 9278, fax 255 9284; *near Krasnopresnenskaya nab 12; singles/doubles RR2160*) is actually the cruise ship *Alexandr Blok* moored on the Moscow River. It has been bobbing here for several years. The tiny rooms (cabins) are clean and have bathroom and TV. There's a Greek restaurant and a bar/café (breakfast is RR75), although it's hard to think of a good reason to stay here; public transport is bad and it's a 1km walk from ulitsa 1905 Goda metro.

PLACES TO STAY – TOP END
The top-end hotels in Moscow provide international-standard comfort and service. Most are managed by Western hotel chains catering mainly to business people. Expect

Mamontov's Metropol

The Hotel Metropol, among Moscow's finest examples of Art Nouveau architecture, is another contribution by famed philanthropist and patron of the arts, Savva Mamontov. The decorative panel on the hotel's central facade, facing Teatralny proezd, is based on a sketch by the artist Vrubel. It depicts the legend of the *Princess of Dreams*, in which a troubadour falls in love with a kind and beautiful princess and travels across the seas to find her. He falls ill during the voyage and is near death when he finds his love. The princess embraces him, but he dies in her arms. Naturally, the princess renounces her worldly life. The ceramic panels were made at the pottery workshop at Mamontov's Abramtsevo estate (see Abramtsevo under the Northeast – the Golden Ring in the Excursions chapter).

The ceramic work on the side of the hotel facing Teatralnaya ploshchad is by the artist Golovin. The script is a quote from Nietzsche: 'Again the same story: when you build a house you notice that you have learned something.'

During the Soviet era, these wise words were replaced with something more appropriate for the time: 'Only the dictatorship of the proletariat can liberate mankind from the oppression of capitalism.' Lenin, of course.

satellite TV, international direct dial (IDD) phones, air-con, minibars and room service in very comfortable modern rooms, as well as a range of expensive restaurants, shops, bars and services. Many hotels have health clubs or exercise rooms with pool, sauna, massage and the like.

Centre

Hotel Sretenskaya (Map 2; ☎ 933 5544, fax 933 5545; W hotel-sretenskaya.ru; ul Sretenka 15; singles/doubles from US$160/180) is a newer hotel, unusual for its relatively small size and friendly atmosphere. A fine restaurant, fitness centre and business centre are on the premises, and the 'Winter Garden' atrium is particularly welcoming. Discounts are available on weekends.

Hotel Savoy (Map 2; ☎ 929 8500/8558, fax 230 2186; ul Rozhdestvenka 3; singles/doubles from US$180/230) was the first of Moscow's new-wave luxury hotels when it reopened in 1989. The gilt, murals and chandeliers maintain the atmosphere of prerevolutionary privilege. There are just 86 rooms and suites, and the tariff includes bufet breakfast. The hotel is an Intourist-Finnair joint venture.

Hotel National (Map 2; ☎ 258 7000, fax 258 7100; e hotel@national.ru; Okhotny ryad 14/1; old-wing rooms US$300-450, new-wing rooms US$350-390) occupies the choicest location, facing the Kremlin across Manezhnaya ploshchad, at the foot of Tverskaya ulitsa. Built in 1903, its chandeliers and frescoed ceilings survived the revolution and, after a careful renovation, it is one of the best hotels. Many of the rooms in the old wing are museum-like, and the hotel publishes a guide to its antiques. Rooms in the old wing are actually slightly smaller than the standard rooms in the new wing, but warrant the higher tariff, as some of the views of Red Square are spectacular.

Hotel Metropol (Map 2; ☎ 927 6000, fax 927 6010; e moscow@interconti.com; Teatralny proezd 1/4; rooms US$360), another classic that's been reborn, has a choice position across from the Bolshoi Theatre. The rooms have high ceilings and furniture that recalls the early 1900s, when the hotel was in its prime. Fittings in the public areas are lavish, and the main restaurant has a famous stained-glass ceiling.

Hotel Baltschug Kempinski (Map 4; ☎ 230 6500, fax 230 6502; W www.kempinskimoscow.com; ul Balchug 1; singles/doubles from US$320/350) is on the Moscow River, opposite the Kremlin, and commands spectacular views. First built in 1898, it has 234 high-ceilinged rooms filled with state-of-the-art facilities; it also boasts a swimming pool. The breakfast bufet has food to match the views.

Hotel Marco Polo Presnya (Map 2; ☎ 244 3631, fax 956 5637; Spiridonyevsky per 9; singles/doubles with breakfast US$215/245), a small hotel, is in the quiet Patriarch's Pond area, 2km northwest of the Kremlin.

Marriott Grand Hotel (Map 2; ☎ 937 0000, fax 937 0001; W www.marriott.com; Tverskaya ul 26; singles/doubles US$295/305) has a large atrium and rooftop patio with excellent views. The bufet breakfast, included in the price, is lavish. President Bush (Dubya) stayed here when he visited in 2002, so security must be okay.

North

Olympic Penta Hotel (Map 2; ☎ 931 9000, fax 931 9076; W www.renaissancehotels.com/mowrn; Olimpiysky pr 18/1; singles/doubles with tax US$268), a 500-room place, is 4km north of the Kremlin and was built for the 1980 Olympics, as was the enormous indoor Olympic Sports Complex across the road. It was upgraded with Lufthansa's help around 1990 and is now German-run. Thanks to its athletic origins, the hotel boasts probably the best hotel fitness club in Moscow, with a 22m pool its guests can enjoy free of charge.

Marriott Tverskaya Hotel (Map 2; ☎ 258 3000, fax 258 3099; W www.marriott.com; 1-ya Tverskaya-Yamskaya ul 34; singles/doubles from US$285) is in a renovated and elegant Art Nouveau building about 3km north of the Kremlin, near Belorusskaya metro. Its rooms are large and well equipped. This hotel is not quite as bustling as its corporate cousins, which is an attraction to harried business travellers who just want a quiet room.

Sheraton Palace Hotel *(Map 2; ☎ 931 9700, fax 931 9708; W www.sheraton.com; ul 1-ya Tverskaya-Yamskaya 19; singles/doubles with breakfast from US$354)* is in a smart modern style, with 221 rooms and suites, and some top-class restaurants. Overseas travel agencies, including Intourist branches, can often book you in for significantly less than the quoted rate.

Moscow Aerostar Hotel *(Outer North Moscow map; ☎ 213 9000, fax 213 9001; W www.aerostar.ru; Leningradsky pr 37; singles/doubles from US$190)* is fairly conveniently placed 6km from the Kremlin on the road from the Sheremetevo-2 airport. Originally built for the 1980 US Olympic team, it sat mothballed for years after the US boycotted the event. One of Moscow's first foreign-run luxury hotels, it is now falling behind more centrally located competition. As a result, the place runs some good promotions. The 343 rooms have connections to the in-house Internet access.

Katerina Iris Congress Hotel *(☎ 933 0401; W www.katerina.msk.ru/iris/eng; Korovinskoe sh 10; singles/doubles US$198/208)*, about 15km from the centre, is convenient for Sheremetevo airport if nothing else. Built next to an eye surgery clinic, the building has an upright half-oval shape in keeping with the eye theme. The 195-room hotel, recently taken over by Swedish management, is stylish, with a bright atrium. It runs a free hourly shuttle bus to/from the city centre between 7.30am and midnight.

Novotel *(☎ 926 5900, fax 926 5903; W www .novotel-moscow.ru; singles/doubles weekends from US$160/180, weekdays US$230/ 260)* at Sheremetevo-2 airport is a good place to stay if you are stuck between flights; otherwise, it's a long trek to the centre, even with the free shuttle bus. Discounts abound here.

West

Radisson Slavyanskaya Hotel *(Map 4; ☎ 941 8020, fax 240 6915; W www.radisson.com; Berezhkovskaya nab 2; singles/doubles from US$180/210)*, a bright and modern place, is 3.5km west of the Kremlin by Kiev Station. It's almost a village in itself, with 430 rooms, a large business centre, its own shopping mall, a host of cafés and restaurants, a big pool and the American House of Cinema. If you do venture out of the hotel (not that you need to), you can walk across the modern, glass pedestrian bridge and over to the Arbat.

Golden Ring Swiss Diamond Hotel *(Map 4; ☎ 725 0100, fax 725 0101; W www.hotel -goldenring.ru; Smolenskaya ul 5; singles/ doubles US$240/264)* is close to the Foreign Affairs Ministry, the White House and the river, and has numerous amenities, including very modern rooms. Security is tight throughout. Discounts are available if you book via the Internet.

Hotel Mezhdunarodnaya-1 *(Map 2; ☎ 258 2122, fax 253 2400; Krasnoprenenskaya nab 12; singles/doubles with breakfast US$250/ 325)*, the city's longest-serving top-end hotel, is a business-oriented place on the Moscow River, 3.5km west of the Kremlin. Known as 'the Mezh', it was built in 1980 with the World Trade Centre which adjoins it. The style is mid-1970s modern; the 300-odd rooms are comfortable, but not huge, and the restaurants, bars and shops are numerous. The **Mezhdunarodnaya-2** at the north end of the complex is a more expensive apartment hotel. Owing to their prices, both hotels are within the top-end price range, but their service leaves much to be desired. Furthermore, the 1km walk from Ulitsa 1905 Goda metro is inconvenient.

East

Hotel Katerina *(Map 5; ☎ 933 0401; W www .katerina.msk.ru/eng/; Shlyuzovaya nab 6; singles/doubles with breakfast US$165/205)* is the self-proclaimed 'Swedish corner of Moscow', and comes the closest to being an intimate European-style hotel. The small lobby has a comfy fireplace where you'll be served a glass of wine, and the neighbourhood itself is quiet and leafy.

HOMESTAYS

In Moscow it's possible to find a room in a private flat which is shared with the owners. One of the good points about this type of accommodation – which is often referred to as either 'bed and breakfast' (B&B) or 'homestay' – is that it will enable you to glimpse how Russians really live. Typically you get a two-bed room, use of a bathroom, and possibly cooking facilities. Most flats that take in guests are clean and respectable, though they're rarely large!

Moscow has organisations specifically geared to accommodate foreign visitors in private flats at around US$20 or US$30 per person, normally with English-speaking hosts, with breakfast included and other services such as excursions and extra meals available.

Booking Homestays

You can contact many Russian homestay agents from overseas (if you do, check that they can provide visa support too), but you can also book through many travel agencies in your own country.

One reliable Russian organisation is the St Petersburg-based **Host Families Association** (HOFA; ☎/fax 812-275 19 92; ℮ alexei@ hofak.hop.stu.neva.ru), which can provide places with English-speaking families in Moscow from around US$25/40 for singles/ doubles including breakfast. This association charges US$30 to US$50 for a visa invitation and registration.

In Australia, Eastern European Travel Bureau, Russian Gateway Tours and Passport Travel can all book rooms in Russia – see Organised Tours in the Getting There & Away chapter for contact details. In the UK, try **Interchange** (☎ 020-8681 3612, fax 8760 0031) which offers homestays in Moscow for £43 a night.

In the USA, **Russian Home Travel** (toll-free ☎ 800-861 9335, ℮ russiahome@aol.com) offers homestay service for US$30/50 for singles/doubles, as well as visa support, event tickets, train tickets, transportation etc.

Some of these companies also offer more expensive packages, including excursions and all meals. There are also discounts for longer stays. It's worth knowing that your host family generally gets a small fraction of the price you pay the agent.

LONG-TERM RENTALS

The classified advertising section of the *Moscow Times* or ⓦ www.expat.ru are your best sources for information on long-term rentals and agencies. The entire real estate market is quite volatile, and companies come and go frequently. Better yet, if you are moving for a corporate job, get your company to make the services of its Moscow relocation agency available to you.

Places to Eat

FOOD
Seventy years of mistreatment by the Soviets has given Russian cuisine a bad rap. Today, many restaurants in Moscow allow the diner to experience Russian food as it is meant to be – exquisite *haute-russe* masterpieces once served at fancy feasts and extravagant balls, as well as the tasty and filling meals that have for centuries been prepared in peasant kitchens with garden ingredients.

By contrast, food in Soviet-style restaurants tends to be bland, overcooked or pickled, heavy on meat and potatoes and light on anything fresh. The difference is also evident in the prices; Moscow is one of the most expensive cities in the world for a good restaurant meal. Affordable, tasty meals are not easy – but not impossible – to come by. When venturing out into the culinary unknown, trust your nose; if a place smells like old cabbage or old socks, don't be afraid to give it a miss.

When you tire of borscht (beetroot soup) and beef stroganoff in Moscow, you will be able to find excellent European, American and Asian cuisine. Many of these restaurants have foreign chefs, foreign management, foreign standards, and foreign price levels to match. Cuisine from former Soviet republics – including Armenia, Uzbekistan and Ukraine – is also popular and can be delicious. Moscow is the best place outside the Caucasus to sample spicy Georgian delicacies (see the boxed text 'Table Scraps from Heaven' later in this chapter).

In Soviet days, eating out meant either a cheap meal at the local cafeteria, or for special occasions, nearly identical food at a cheesy hotel restaurant. Perhaps the current situation in Moscow is a reaction to this dreary sameness. These days, the theme restaurants are all the rage. From the Uzbek restaurant with the live camel out front, to the French restaurant with the Gothic cathedral interior, restaurateurs are going all out to ensure that their patrons' dining experience is at least interesting.

Stolovaya & Bufet
A *stolovaya* is like a cafeteria – the common person's eatery. It tends to be dreary but cheap (you can often fill up for under US$1) with a small and less-than-mouthwatering choice of cutlet, fish or meatballs, soup, boiled vegetables, bread, tea and coffee. Slide your tray along the counter and the staff will ladle out what you point at. They have poetic names such as Stolovaya No 32. Some are decent, some very grotty.

A *bufet* is similar to a stolovaya. It's a snack bar (usually in a hotel) selling cheap cold meats, boiled eggs, salads, bread, and pastries etc.

Kiosks
Around parks and markets, on streets and near train and bus stations there are cheap, stand-up places selling snacks and drinks. They're usually a poor introduction to their respective specialities, which might include *bliny* (crepes), *buterbrody* (open-face sandwiches), *pirozhki* (deep-fried meat or vegie turnovers), *sosiski* (hot dogs) or *shashlik* (meat kebab), but they're handy and cheap, and the food is usually edible.

Ordering & Paying
Restaurants that attract foreign customers often have English-language menus. Your server is unlikely to speak English, unless you're in a hotel, an expensive top-end restaurant or an American restaurant. Otherwise you're left to your own devices.

If a waiter – or your food – is taking an eternity to appear, ponder on a word Russia has given to the universal vocabulary of eating. After the victory over Napoleon in the 19th century, impatient Russian soldiers in Paris cafés would bang their tables and shout '*bystro, bystro!*' (quickly, quickly!), from which came the word 'bistro'.

When you're done you'll then have to chase up the bill *(schyot)*. If there's a service charge – noted on the menu by the words за обслуживание (for service) – there's no need to tip unless the service has been exceptional. Ten percent of the bill is generous.

Meals

Breakfast (*zavtrak*) in hotels can range from a large help-yourself bufet to bread, butter, jam, tea and a boiled egg, or nothing at all. Other breakfast favourites include bliny and *kasha* (porridge).

Russians have a preference for a fairly heavy early-afternoon meal *(obied)* and a lighter evening meal *(uzhyn)*. Dining out is usually a special occasion, so if you have Russian companions, you can expect them to go all out at either meal.

Meals (and menus) are divided into various courses such as *zakuski* (appetisers), often grouped into either hot or cold; first courses (usually soups); second courses (or mains), also called hot courses; and desserts.

Appetisers A typical Russian meal starts with a few zakuski, which are often the most interesting items on the menu. The fancier zakuski rival main courses for price.

Russia is famous for its caviar *(ikra)*, the snack of tsars and New Russians. Caviar in Russia is no longer the bargain it once was, due to declining sturgeon populations (see the boxed text 'Roe to Ruin') and the good

---

Roe to Ruin

Caviar. The very word evokes glamorous lifestyles, exotic travels and glittering festivities. Yet the world's source of this luxury item, the sturgeon, is in grave danger. Sturgeon have survived since the days dinosaurs roamed the Earth. The question now is whether these 'living fossils' can survive the relentless fishing pressure, pollution and habitat destruction that have brought many species of sturgeon to the brink of extinction.

Sturgeon are indeed remarkable fish. Clad in bony plates and equipped with broad snouts, some species of sturgeon live to be more than 100 years old and can grow up to 1125kg and 4.5m in length. Like humans, many sturgeon species reproduce relatively late in life; some do not reach sexual maturity until the ages of 15 to 25. A single sturgeon can produce hundreds of kilos of roe, though the very largest fish are extremely rare today, following decades of overfishing. In the Caspian Sea, the cradle of world caviar production, sturgeon are in crisis. Of greatest concern is the endangered beluga sturgeon, source of coveted beluga caviar, whose numbers have declined more than 90% in the past 20 years. Sturgeon face six major problems:

Overharvesting: Fish eggs, or roe, are collected from female sturgeon after they have been caught and killed. The global caviar market has placed a premium on sturgeon, prompting overfishing and poaching.

Illegal trade: Illegal trade of sturgeon and caviar exacerbates conservation problems. Political turmoil in sturgeon-producing countries like Russia has resulted in a flourishing black-market trade.

Life-history characteristics: Sturgeon reproduce more slowly than other fish and therefore are unable to recover quickly. In fact, depleted sturgeon populations may take up to a century or more to recover.

Lack of effective management: Many sturgeon and paddlefish migrate through the waters of different states and countries. This often results in a patchwork of catch levels, fishing seasons, size limits and other management measures.

Loss of habitat: Sturgeon migrate up rivers to spawn. Dam construction and diversion of river water for irrigation and other purposes have nearly eliminated spawning runs on many large river systems used by sturgeon.

Pollution: Pollutants from urban and agricultural runoff and industrial discharges have been linked to significant reproductive and other abnormalities in sturgeon, and to large fish kills

Excerpt from *Roe to Ruin*,
W www.caviaremptor.org

old market economy. However, it is still cheaper than in the West, and one of the most delicious Russian traditions.

The best is black (sturgeon) caviar *(ikra chyornaya* or *zirnistaya)*. Much cheaper and saltier is red (salmon) caviar *(ikra krasnaya* or *ketovaya)*. Russians spread it on buttered bread or bliny and wash it down with a slug of vodka or a toast of champagne. Vegetarians can try ersatz caviar made entirely from aubergine (eggplant) or other vegetables.

Most restaurant menus offer a truly mind-boggling array of salads *(salat)*, including standards such as vegetable salad *(ovoshnoy salat)*, which contains tomatoes and cucumbers, or capital salad *(stolichny salat)*, with beef, potatoes and eggs in mayonnaise. Even if you read Russian, the salads are usually not identifiable by their often nonsensical names.

First & Second Courses Rich soups may well be the pinnacle of Slavic cooking. There are dozens of varieties, often served with a dollop of sour cream. Most are made from meat stock. The most common soups include borscht, *shchi* (cabbage soup), *okroshka* (cucumber soup with a *kvas* – a beer-like drink – base), and *solyanka* (a tasty meat soup with salty vegetables and hint of lemon).

The second course can be poultry *(ptitsa)*, meat *(myaso)* or fish *(ryba)*, which might be prepared in a few different ways (see Food, in the Language chapter, for details). Don't forget to order a *garnir* (side dish) or you will just get a hunk of meat on the plate. Options here are usually limited to potatoes *(kartoshki)*, rice *(ris)* or undefined vegetables *(ovoshchi)*. Bread is usually served with every meal. The Russian black bread – a vitamin-rich sour rye – is delicious and uniquely Russian.

Perhaps most Russians are exhausted or drunk by dessert time, since this is the least imaginative course. The most common options are ice cream *(morozhenoe)*, super sweet cake *(tort)* or chocolate *(shokolat)*.

Vegetarian Food

Russia is rough on a vegetarian: vegetables are often boiled to death, tasty soups are usually made from meat stock and salads often contain beef or ham.

If you're vegetarian, say so, early and often. You'll see a lot of cabbage, cucumber and tomato salads. Russian dumplings *(pelmeni)* are usually filled with meat. However, they may also come with potatoes, cabbage or mushrooms. Zakuski include many meatless offerings such as eggs, salted fish and mushrooms. Most restaurants will offer one vegetable side dish, but it may be the ubiquitous cabbage coleslaw.

Note that potatoes *(kartoshki* or *kartofil)* – of which there are no shortage – aren't filed under 'vegetable' in the Russian mind.

DRINKS

'Drinking is the joy of the Rus. We cannot live without it.' With these words Vladimir of Kiev, father of the Russian state, is said to have rejected abstinent Islam on his people's behalf in the 10th century.

Who wouldn't want to bend their minds during those long, cold, dark winters? Russians sometimes drink vodka in moderation, but more often it's tipped down in swift shots (with a beer) with the aim of getting legless.

The *average* Russian drinks more than 12L of pure alcohol a year – equivalent to over a bottle of vodka a week – and men drink much more than women.

Alcohol

You can buy alcohol almost everywhere in Moscow: kiosks, shops, bars, restaurants – you name it. Both foreign and Russian brands are common, but be very cautious about purchasing spirits from kiosks. There is no shortage of counterfeit spirits, which are bad and cheap and can make you ill. Only buy screw-top bottles and always check that the seal is not broken. Taste carefully any liquor you've bought at a kiosk to make sure it has not been diluted or tampered with. Err on the side of caution.

Vodka This is distilled from wheat, rye or occasionally potatoes. The word comes from *voda* (water), and means something like 'a wee drop'. Its flavour (if any) comes from any additions after distillation.

Just Say 'Nyet'

Refusing a drink could be among the greatest challenges you may face in Russia. Russians usually continue to insist until they win you over. And beware – they do not stop at one! If you empty your glass once, it will be re-filled. The good news is that after the first few shots, your companions will no longer be so concerned that you are drinking too.

If you do not dare to attempt to keep up, a few tricks might help you survive Russian hospitality:

• Participate in the toast, raise your glass, but do not feel the need to drain it
• Spill. Discreetly.
• You risk making your hosts extremely uncomfortable, but if all else fails, claim to be an alcoholic: 'Ya alkogolik' for men or 'Ya alkogolichka' for women

In Moscow, the Kristall distillery is considered to be the finest. Yuri Dolgoruki is the top of the line, while Zolotoe Koltso (Golden Ring) and Moskovskaya are also high-quality vodkas. Another favourite of the 'Vodkaphiles' Club' is the Klassik. Its unique bottle is an authentic replica of a 300-year-old traditional style.

Another name gaining popularity is Smirnovskaya vodka, distilled in Chernogolovka, a small town not far from Moscow. Smirnovskaya, a distant relative of Smirnoff vodka, comes in various flavours: red pepper *(pertsovka)*, lemon *(limonnaya)*, orange *(apelsinovaya)*, cranberry *(klyukva)* and even toasted bread *(sukharnichek)*.

Vodka bottles have become a form of art in themselves, with all manner of shapes, colours and themes. Most supermarkets carry a healthy supply (see Supermarkets under Self-Catering later in this chapter), and they make excellent souvenirs.

Beer For the imbiber, beer *(pivo)* is one of the best things to come out of Russia. The old traditional breweries with their foul-smelling product that went 'off' after three days (if it had ever been on) are vanishing.

In their place are old traditional breweries that have learned new ways (such as how to brew tasty beer) and a number of joint ventures with Western brewers.

The market leader is Baltika, a Scandinavian joint-venture with Russian management, based in St Petersburg. It makes no less than nine excellent brews, fittingly labelled '1' through '9'. Just about every brewing style is represented and it's worth drinking your way through the range to find a favourite.

Where Baltika used to be the only drinkable Russian brew, other regional brands are becoming increasingly popular, including Sibirskaya Corona, Stepan Razin and Klinskoe. Each brand offers both *temnoe* (dark) and *svetloe* (light) beers.

Champagne, Wine & Brandy Russian champagne *(shampanskoe)* comes in very dry *(bryut)*, dry *(sukhoe)*, semidry *(polusukhoye)*, semisweet *(poluslatkaye)* and sweet *(slatkaye)*. Anything above dry is sweet enough to turn your mouth inside out. The best brand is the Soviet classic *Sovietskaya shampanskoe*, which costs about RR300 in a restaurant and RR150 in a supermarket, kiosk or liquor store. Most other wine comes from outside the Commonwealth of Independent States (CIS) – Eastern European brands are the cheapest – though you can find Georgian, Moldovan and Crimean wine.

Brandy is popular and it's all called *konyak*, though local varieties certainly aren't Cognac. The best non-Western konyak in Russia is Armenian, and anything classified five-star is usually fine.

Kvas This is fermented rye-bread water, which is mildly alcoholic, tastes not unlike ginger beer, and is both cool and refreshing in summer.

In the olden days it was dispensed on the street from big, wheeled tanks. Patrons would bring their own bottles or plastic bags and fill up. Or one could down a quick refresher for a few kopeks.

The kvas truck is a rare sight these days, but this cool tasty treat is still available from kiosks, Russkoe Bistro fast-food outlets and other restaurants.

Nonalcoholic Drinks

Water & Mineral Water Tap water in Moscow is potable; however, most people drink bottled water.

Tea & Coffee The traditional Russian tea-making method is to brew an extremely strong pot, pour small shots of it into glasses and fill the glasses with hot water from the samovar (an urn with an inner tube filled with hot charcoal).

The pot is kept warm on top of the samovar. Modern samovars have electric elements, like a kettle, instead of the charcoal tube. Tea is often served with sugar, although using jam instead of sugar is also quite common.

Coffee is traditionally thick, dark and served in tiny cups, perhaps with sugar. Milk or cream is rarely available for coffee. Instant coffee is becoming more common, as is powdered milk. Almost any café, restaurant or bufet, and some bakery shops, will offer tea, coffee or both.

These days, Moscow is not too far behind Seattle if you know where to look: trendy cafés selling fancy cappuccinos and imported beans are popping up all over town (see Cafés later in this chapter). Prices in these happening spots usually rival their Western counterparts.

Other Drinks Fruit juice *(sok)* and some Western-brand sodas are widely available in

A Gift to Young Housewives

The most popular cookbook in 19th-century Russia was called *A Gift to Young Housewives*, a collection of favourite recipes and household management tips which turned into a best-seller. Elena Molokhovets, a housewife herself, was dedicated to her 10 children, to the Orthodox Church, and to her inexperienced 'female compatriots' who might need assistance keeping their homes running smoothly.

This book was reprinted 28 times between 1861 and 1914, and Molokhovets added new recipes and helpful hints to each new edition. The last edition included literally thousands of recipes, as well as pointers on how to organise an efficient kitchen, how to set a proper table and how to clean a cast-iron pot: 'To clean a burned pan, strew five kopeks' worth of chloride of lime into the pot, fill with water, and boil this liquid until the pot is bleached white...then strain into a bottle. After yellowed linen is washed it may be soaked in this water for fifteen minutes or longer until it whitens.'

Molokhovets received an enormously positive response from her readers, who credited her with no less than preserving their family life. The popular perception of the time was that a wife's primary responsibility was to keep her family together, and keeping her husband well fed seemed to be the key. As one reader wrote, 'a good kitchen is...not an object of luxury. It is a token of the health and well-being of the family, upon which all the remaining conditions of life depend.' Molokhovets included some of these letters in later editions as testimony to her work.

The classic cookbook was never reprinted during the Soviet period. The details of sumptuous dishes and fine table settings – let alone questions of etiquette and style – would certainly have been considered petty and bourgeois by the Soviet regime. Yet copies of this ancient tome survived, passed down from mother to daughter like a family heirloom. Today, the book reads not only as a cookbook, but also as a lesson in history and sociology.

At the end of the 20th century, Molokhovets' 'gift' was bestowed upon the modern world, when Joyce Toomre, a culinary historian, translated and reprinted this historical masterpiece. The 1992 version, *Classic Russian Cooking: Elena Molokhovets' A Gift to Young Housewives*, includes Toomre's detailed analysis of mealtimes, menus, ingredients, cooking techniques etc. The hundreds of pages of recipes range from instructions for making wheat starch, to details on stringing an eel by its eyes before frying. (As Toomre notes, some are included purely for historical value.)

restaurants, kiosks and stores. *Napitok* and *limonad* are fruity, fizzy drinks best avoided.

Milk is common and is sold cheaply in supermarkets, but it is often not pasteurised and tends to spoil. A yogurt-like sour milk *(kefir)*, often served as a breakfast drink, is one of the few reliable sources of calcium. To adapt the wise words of Mary Poppins – just a spoonful of sugar helps the kefir go down.

DINING OUT
You can get any kind of meal you want in Moscow, so long as you're willing to pay for it. Sticker shock is common at Moscow restaurants, where prices are geared to free-spending New Russians and flush expats rather than the average person. The situation is improving, however, and many new affordable places are opening too.

Unfortunately, the places to eat that are geared to the masses typically embody the old motto: 'you get what you pay for'. Times are a-changin', however. Muscovites are eating out in droves, and restaurants, cafés and kiosks are opening up left and right to cater to them.

Some restaurants set their menu prices in *uslovie yedenitsiy*, or standard units, which is equivalent to US dollars (although you will have to pay in roubles calculated at the exchange rate of the day). Prices below are quoted in roubles or dollars, depending on the individual restaurant. More and more places are beginning to accept credit cards. Still, if it means paying or doing dishes, you may want to check first.

Most places are open from noon to midnight daily, often with later hours on weekends. Discounts of up to 25% are often available before 5pm. Alternatively, many places offer a 'business lunch' special for a fixed price. This is a great way to sample some of the pricier restaurants around town.

CAFETERIAS
Moo-Moo *(Map 4; ☎ 241 1364; ul Arbat 45/23; • Map 4; ☎ 245 78 20; Komsomolsky pr 26; meal RR150; open 10am-11pm daily)* offers an easy serve-yourself approach to Russian standards such as borscht, pelmeni

and violently-coloured desserts. Dig that spotted-cow decor.

Drova *(Map 3; ☎ 925 2725; Myasnitskaya ul 24; lunch RR150, all-you-can-eat bufet RR300; open 24hr)* has self-serve food ranging from solyanka to sushi, to sweet-and-sour pork. The place is both popular and cheap.

Pelmeshka *(Map 2; ☎ 292 8392; Kuznetsky Most 4/3; meal RR100; open 11am-midnight daily)*, clean and modern, serves pelmeni, the most filling of Russian favourites.

Soup *(Map 2; ☎ 251 1383; 1-aya Brest-skaya ul 62; meal RR250; open noon-midnight daily)* takes this most appetising element of Russian food to new heights, offering 12 hot and six cold varieties on any given day.

Kafeterii *(Map 2; Kamergersky per 5/7; meal RR100; open 10am-10pm daily)* is a scene from Moscow in 1980, and decidedly out of place on this trendy pedestrian street. Tea and vodka are probably the top sellers at this tiny place, but you can also get whatever salad or main course is on offer for the day. Come here for an authentic Soviet 'dining experience'.

RESTAURANTS
Places in this category are listed by cuisine and in roughly ascending order of price.

Russian
Yolki-Palki *(Map 4; ☎ 953 9130; Klimentovsky per 14 • Map 2; ☎ 291 6888; Novy Arbat ul 11; meal RR150, salad bar RR120; open 11am-midnight daily)* are two of many outlets for this excellent country-cottage-style Russian chain, specialising in simple, traditional dishes. The beer is cheap and there's a blessed salad bar. These places are all over town.

Annyushka *(Map 3; Chistoprudny bul; cover RR20, mains RR150-200; open 2pm-midnight daily)* is actually a tram car that circles the Chistye Prudy. Patrons can get on at several stops along the way, the easiest being at the island at the intersection of Chisto-prudny bulvar and Myasnitskaya ulitsa. Food is simple – obviously, they prepare it on a streetcar – but the bar is fully stocked. It's a fun concept, but karaoke is uncalled-for in such close quarters.

Kafe Karetny Dvor (*Map 2;* ☎ *291 6376; Povarskaya ul 52; meal RR300; open noon-midnight daily*) offers a wide range of Russian and Georgian dishes, all reasonably priced. The interior is cheerful and relaxed, or enjoy the courtyard if the weather is fine.

Kafe Margarita (*Map 2;* ☎ *299 6534; Malaya Bronnaya ul 28; business lunch RR160, mains RR280; open noon-midnight daily*) is right across the street from Patriarch's Ponds and popular with a well-read young crowd. The place is very lively in the evenings, when folk bands play.

Spets-Bufet No 7 (*Map 4;* ☎ *959 3135; ul Serafimovicha 2; meal RR300; open noon-6am daily*) is located in the basement of a once-prestigious apartment block that was home to many Communist Party apparatchiks. This 'Special Buffet' re-creates the forum where the big-wigs may have eaten. Decked out with propaganda posters and potted plants, the food is decidedly mediocre (thus making the establishment quite authentic).

Kitezh (*Map 2;* ☎ *209 6685, fax 924 8448; ul Petrovka 23/10; dinner RR600; open noon-midnight daily*) is named after a legendary town which – as a defence mechanism – could magically disappear from the sight of an enemy at the sound of a bell. This welcoming place re-creates a 17th-century interior in the basement of a building near the Petrovsky monastery. The Russian standards are tasty and reasonably priced.

Samovar (*Map 2;* ☎ *921 4688; Myasnitskaya ul 13; business lunch RR250, mains RR300-500; open noon-midnight daily*) has a menu heavy with delicious renditions of classics such as pelmeni and bliny. Or not-so-classics, like fish in champagne sauce.

New Vasyuki (*Map 4;* ☎ *201 3888; Starokonyushenny per 2, korpus 2; dinner US$15; open noon-midnight daily*), which takes its name from the novel *Twelve Chairs*, is a mixture of several styles of kitsch. Food is reliably good, and the place specialises in lamb barbecues and pig roasts. Try to ignore the cheesy band and the wall o' video behind.

Krasnaya Ploshchad, Dom 1 (*Moscow Kremlin map;* ☎ *292 1196; Krasnaya pl 1; dinner without alcohol US$30; open noon-midnight daily*) is located in the State History Museum. Appropriately, the chef is something of a historian, and he successfully re-creates the cuisine that was enjoyed by the tsars.

The 90-year-old restaurant **Novy Yar** (*Outer North Moscow map;* ☎ *960 2004; Leningradsky pr 32/2; mains RR500-700; open 10am till last guest leaves daily*) is another historical site. It once was a favourite among Moscow's elite, which includes the opera singer Fyodor Shaliapin and the merchant Savva Morozov.

When money is no object try **TsDL** (*Map 2;* ☎ *291 15 15; Povarskaya ul 50; meal US$50; open noon-midnight daily*) offering grand decor and expensive Russian cuisine. The acronym stands for Tsentralny Dom Literatov, or Central House of Writers, the historic building which houses this modern restaurant. Also here is the less expensive and quite atmospheric **Zapisky Okhotnika** (Hunter's Sketches). The name refers both to the graffiti-clad walls in the dining room and its extraordinary stuffed menagerie (the present owners being hunters).

The queen mother of *haute-russe* dining is **Café Pushkin** (*Map 2;* ☎ *229 5590; Tverskoy bul 26A; meal US$50; 1st floor open 24hr, 2nd floor open noon-midnight daily*), with an exquisite blend of Russian and French cuisine. Service and food are done to perfection. The lovely 19th-century building has created a different atmosphere on each floor, including a richly decorated library and a pleasant rooftop café.

Ukrainian

With several branches around the city, **Taras Bulba** (*Map 2;* ☎ *200 6082; ul Petrovka 30/7; meal RR600; open noon-midnight daily*) is the Ukrainian version of Yolki-Palki. There's no salad bar, but the food is good and the atmosphere homy.

In case you did not think Moscow's theme dining was over the top, **Shinook** (*Map 2;* ☎ *255 0204; ul 1905 goda 2; meal US$30; open 24hr*) has re-created a Ukrainian peasant farm near the city centre. Servers wear colourfully embroidered shirts and speak

Table Scraps from Heaven

According to Georgian legend, God took a supper break while creating the world. He became so involved with his meal that he inadvertently tripped over the high peaks of the Caucasus, spilling his food onto the land below. The land blessed by Heaven's table scraps was Georgia.

Darra Goldstein, from *The Georgian Feast*

Moscow is the best place outside the Caucasus to sample the rich, spicy cuisine of the former Soviet republic of Georgia. This fertile region – wedged between East and West – has long been the beneficiary (and victim) of merchants and raiders passing through. These influences are evident in Georgian cooking, which shows glimpses of Mediterranean and Middle Eastern flavours.

The truly Georgian elements – the differences – are what make this cuisine so delectable. Most notably, many meat and vegetable dishes use ground walnuts or walnut oil as an integral ingredient, yielding a distinctive rich, nutty flavour. Also characteristic is the mix of spices, *khmeli-suneli*, which combines coriander, garlic, chillis, pepper and savoury with a saffron substitute made from dried marigold petals.

Georgian chefs love to prepare their food over an open flame, and grilled meat is certainly among the most beloved items on any Georgian menu. Traditionally, however, meat was reserved for special occasions, and daily meals revolved around vegetables and greens. The fertile Georgian soil yields green beans, tomatoes, eggplants, mushrooms and garlic, all of which make their delicious way to the table. Herbs such as cilantro, dill, parsley and scallions are often served fresh, with no preparation or sauce, as a palette-cleansing counterpoint to the other rich dishes. Fruits such as grapes and pomegranates show up not only as dessert, but also as tart complements to roasted meats.

Here are a few tried-and-true Georgian favourites to get you started when faced with an incomprehensible menu:

Lavash – flat bread used to wrap cheese, tomatoes, herbs or meat
Khachi puri – rich, cheesy bread, made with sour or salty cheese and served hot
Mkhali – a vegetable puree with herbs and walnuts, most often made with beets or spinach
Kharcho – thick, spicy beef soup made from stale bread soaked in yoghurt
Chikhirtmi – lemony, chicken soup
Shilaplavi – rice pilaf, often with potatoes
Chakhokhbili – slow-cooked chicken with herbs and vegetables
Buglama – beef or veal stew with tomatoes, dill and garlic
Tolmas – vegetables (often tomatoes, eggplant or grape leaves) stuffed with beef
Basturma – marinated, grilled meat, usually beef or lamb
Khinkali – dumplings stuffed with lamb or a mixture of beef and pork
Pakhlava – a walnut pastry similar to baklava, but made with sour-cream dough

Wines

Wine is a crucial part of any Georgian meal. At all but the most informal occasions, Georgians call on a *tamada*, or toastmaster, to ensure that glasses are raised and drinks topped throughout the meal.

Georgian vintners utilise a process that is different from their European and New World counterparts. The grapes are fermented together with skins and stems, then stored in clay jugs, resulting in a flavour specific to the Caucasus. Noteworthy Georgian wines include:

Mukuzani – a rather tannic red, which is the best known and oldest Georgian wine
Saperavi – a dark, full-bodied red produced from grapes of the same name
Kindzmarauli – a sickeningly sweet, blood red wine which, appropriately enough, was the favourite of Stalin
Tsinandali – pale and fruity, the most popular Georgian white

with Ukrainian accents (probably lost on most tourists). The house speciality is *vareniki* (the Ukrainian version of pelmeni). As you dine, you can look out the window at a cheerful babushka while she tends the farmyard animals (very well taken care of, we're assured).

Caucasian & Central Asian

The food from the southern Soviet states is very popular in Moscow – probably because it's usually spicy and the wines are cheap.

The Georgian restaurant **Mama Zoya** *(Map 4; ☎ 201 7743; Sechenovsky per 8; meal RR200 • Map 4; ☎ 242 85 50; Frunzenskaya nab 16; open noon-11pm daily)* has two branches, the latter on a boat, where fleet-footed dancers and musicians accompany the shashlik and *khachi puri*.

Guriya *(Map 4; ☎ 246 0378; Komsomolsky pr 7/3; dinner RR300-400; open 7am-11am, noon-2.30pm, 5.30pm-10.30pm daily)* is another popular (read: cheap) Georgian place. They do the Georgian standards right, and beer is inexpensive.

Kishmish *(Map 2; ☎ 291 2010; Novy Arbat ul 28 • Map 2; ☎ 202 1083; Barrikadnaya ul 8; meal RR300; open 11am-midnight daily)* has simple spicy standards like shashlik and *plov* (rice with mutton bits, also known as *pilaf*) at the cheapest prices you'll find. The salad bar (RR170) is chock-full of Uzbek goodies.

Dioskuriya *(Map 2; ☎ 290 6908; Merzlyakovsky per 2; meal RR350; open noon-midnight daily)* is in a small house just off of Novy Arbat ulitsa. The Georgian food is delicious and the music – a trio of a capella vocalists – even better.

Vostochny Kvartal *(Map 4; ☎ 241 3803; ul Arbat 42/24; meal RR500; open noon-midnight daily)* is a modern Uzbek place with a chic interior and tasty rice plov. This is one of the best-value places on the Arbat.

Noev Kovcheg *(Map 3; ☎ 917 0717; Maly Ivanovsky per 9; meal without cognac RR750; open noon-midnight daily)*, or 'Noah's Ark', is a top-notch Armenian joint, complete with many varieties of shashlik, many more varieties of cognac and an Armenian orchestra every night.

Tiflis *(Map 4; ☎ 290 2897; ul Ostozhenka 32; meal with wine RR1000; open noon-midnight daily)* is housed in a traditional, grand Georgian house with airy balconies and indoor courtyards. Don't miss the Tiflis wine, produced in Georgia at the restaurateur's winery.

Beloye Solntse Pustyni *(Map 2; ☎ 209 7525; Neglinnaya ul 29/14; dinner RR1800; open noon-3am daily)*, which means 'The White Sun of the Desert', is a comically atmospheric place where can you eat excellent Uzbek food beside dancing sturgeon or a mannequin holding a machine gun. The decor is drawn from a classic Soviet film of the same name.

North American

You might expect beer or hockey, but no, the Canadians have brought to Moscow none other than the **Canadian Bagel** *(Map 2; ☎ 299 9701; Tverskaya ul 27; meal RR100; open 24hr)*. Bagels are fresh and delicious, just like in Canada, and the decor is more elegant than you would expect. Salads, sandwiches and soups are also available.

Vremya Yest *(Map 2; ☎ 250 9764; Lesnaya ul 1/2; meal RR300; open noon-5am daily)* specialises in beer, including a unique cocktail, *'pivovar'*, which mixes vodka with beer. The food is also pretty good (and cheap), especially the soups and salads.

Of the two locations of **The Starlite Diner** *(Map 2; ☎ 290 9638; Bolshaya Sadovaya ul 16 • Map 4; ☎ 959 8919; ul Korovy val 9, stroyeniye A; open 24hr)*, the original on the Garden Ring is the best in the warmer months as it has a wonderful, leafy outdoor seating area. Year-round (and around the clock), however, you can't beat this ersatz American diner's thick and creamy milkshakes (US$5), cheese fries (US$3) and chicken chilli (US$5).

American Bar & Grill 1 & 2 *(Map 2; ☎ 250 9525; 1-ya Tverskaya-Yamskaya ul 2/1; open 24hr • Map 5; ☎ 912 3615; Zemlyanoy val 59; open 24hr)* are both known for good breakfasts (US$8), large lunches, excellent steaks (US$15) and renowned vegetarian lasagne (US$11). The location on the bank of the Yauza River has an outdoor summer garden.

In both cases, the bar area hops at night (see the Entertainment chapter).

City Grill *(Map 2; ☎ 299 5519; ul Sadovaya-Triumfalnaya 2/30; meal US$10; open noon-2am daily)* offers surprisingly good value. Vegetarians can choose from a variety of sandwiches and salads. Nonvegetarians love the pork chops and the mashed potatoes (US$10).

Mexican

For top-notch Mexican food, try **Hola Mexico** *(Map 2; ☎ 925 8251; Pushechnaya ul 7/5; business lunch RR180, mains RR300; open noon-5am daily)*. The band gets a little loud, but after a few margaritas, you probably won't care.

Pancho Villa *(Map 4; ☎ 241 9835; ul Arbat; meal RR500; open 24hr)* claims to be Moscow's first (and best) Mexican restaurant. Not using any superlatives, we can vouch that its sidewalk café right on the Arbat is an ideal place to sip margaritas and pretend to be in Mexico.

La Cantina *(Map 2; ☎ 292 5388; Tverskaya ul 5; starters US$6, mains US$15-18; open noon-midnight daily)*, a lively bar and restaurant serving an appetising Tex-Mex menu, is always busy. Starters include nachos, guacamole and corn chips, or chilli con carne, and mains include fajitas, spare ribs, chicken and enchiladas. There's live music every night starting at 8.30pm.

Santa Fe *(Map 2; ☎ 256 1487; ul Mantulinskaya 5/1; dinner US$20, margaritas US$6; open noon-2am daily)* is where raucous, tequila-fuelled crowds wolf down huge plates of pretty authentic Mexican standards. The margaritas are tops.

Japanese

It's Sushi *(Map 2; ☎ 299 4236; Triumfalnaya pl 4/31; dinner RR300; open noon-11pm daily)* is the cheapest, although least atmospheric, place to join in Moscow's ongoing sushi craze. The sushi is fresh and affordable, with some good vegetarian options. It's located in the lobby of the Tchaikovsky Concert Hall.

Yakitoria *(Map 2; ☎ 250 5385; 1-ya Tverskaya-Yamskaya ul 1/29; open 11am-*6am • Map 2; ☎ 290 4311; Novy Arbat ul 10; sushi RR60-150 each; open noon-6am daily)* is a great place for sushi and other Japanese fare. Try the miso soup (RR80).

Another option is **Sushi Vesla** *(Map 2; ☎ 937 0521; ul Nikolskaya 25; sushi RR100-200 each; open noon-1am Sun-Thurs, noon-3am Fri-Sat)*, a hip fast-food Japanese café in the basement of the Nautilus building (enter from Teatralnaya proezd). Dishes are colour-coded to specify price; at the end of the meal the server clears the empty plates and uses them to calculate the bill.

Chinese

Pekinskaya Utka *(Map 2; ☎ 755 8401; Tverskaya ul 24; dinner RR500; open noon-midnight daily)* – that's 'Peking duck' to you and me – is a good-value Chinese restaurant with a nondescript but modern interior. The house special costs RR555 for two; a wide selection of vegetarian and other mains is available for about RR250.

Shyolk *(Map 2; ☎ 251 4134; 1-ya Tverskaya-Yamskaya ul 29/1; meal RR600; open 11am-5am daily)*, or 'Silk', is a more chic, but not too expensive, Chinese place. The 'Fire Bowl' comes highly recommended for those with a tough tongue.

Five Spices *(Map 4; ☎ 203 1283; Sivtsev Vrazhek 3/18; business lunch US$10, dinner US$30; open noon-midnight daily)* is a long-time favourite for spicy Chinese and Indian. The Russian-novel-like menu includes lots of vegetarian options.

Indian

Darbar *(Outer South Moscow map; ☎ 938 8228; 38 Leninsky pr; dinner without alcohol RR600; open noon-midnight daily)* is filled with Indian families enjoying spicy Indian cuisine, so you can tell it's on the mark. The samosas, curries, and dhal all get raves. Our only complaint was a loud Indian orchestra. Darbar is off the lobby of Hotel Sputnik.

Restoran Tandoor *(Map 2; ☎ 299 4593; Tverskaya ul 30/2; dinner US$20-25; open noon-11pm daily)* is a fine Indian restaurant that's a branch of the one of the same name in St Petersburg. The interior features colourful carpets and exotic sculptures, creating an enticing atmosphere. Food is authentic, spicy and delicious, with lots of vegetarian options.

Asian

On one of the trendiest streets in Moscow, **Tibet Kitchen** (Map 2; ☎ 923 2422; Kamergersky per 5/6; mains RR300; open noon-midnight daily) is a basement place with a cosy interior that will whisk you away to Lhasa.

Woori Garden (Outer South Moscow map; ☎ 939 8864; ul Kosygina 15; meal RR300; open noon-midnight daily) is one of several Korean restaurants in the Hotel Orlyonok, which might also be called Little Korea. The place is out of the way, but good value for a unique, authentic food experience.

Krasny (Map 4; ☎ 202 5649; Prechistenka ul 30; mains RR400-600, Mongolian barbecue RR800; open noon-midnight daily) has all kinds of Asian food, but the speciality is Mongolian barbecue (Shanaga), where you choose your own ingredients and fill your plate; the chefs then stir-fry it for you. When in doubt, stick with the recommended combinations.

Italian

Patio Pizza (Map 4; ☎ 201 56 26; ul Volkhonka 13A; pizza from RR200) also has branches all over town, but this branch across from the Pushkin Fine Arts Museum is considered the best. The pizzas come hot from wood ovens and the salad bar is huge. Patio Pizza has been joined in recent years by **Patio Pasta**, which serves the obvious cuisine.

Pizza Express (Map 4; ☎ 937 8261; Smolenskaya pl 3; breakfast US$5, pizza US$8; open 8.30am-midnight Mon-Fri, 11am-midnight Sat-Sun), legendary in London for cheap gourmet pizza, has turned its hand to Moscow. Come here in the evening for tasty pizza and live jazz, or in the morning for filling breakfast specials. Vegetarians take note – the rare, fresh green salad has been spotted here.

Verona (Map 5; ☎ 276 4150; Vorontsovskaya ul 32/36; mains RR150; café open 9am-11pm, restaurant open 7.30pm-11pm daily) is worth the trek out of the centre for affordable Italian food, and not just pizza. Save room for a cannoli and a cappuccino.

Cicco Pizza (Map 2; ☎ 229 7361; Kamergersky per 5/7; meal RR500; open noon-midnight daily) has delicious thin-crust pizza with all kinds of traditional and exotic toppings (none of which are canned peas), as well as salads and pastas. In summer you can dine at the outdoor café.

European

If you need your vitamins, **Jugannath** (Map 2; ☎ 928 3580, Kuznetsky Most 11; mains RR150; open 10am-11pm daily) is a funky, vegetarian café, restaurant and store. Service is slow but sublime, and the food is worth the wait.

Cheap and cheery, **Soleil Express** (Map 2; ☎ 725 6474; Sadovaya-Samotechnaya ul 24/27; meal RR100; open 8.30am-11pm daily) will provide fresh sandwiches, salads and cheap coffee.

Tram (Map 2; ☎ 299 0770; Malaya Dmitrovka ul 6; business lunch US$3, dinner US$8; open 24hr) is a cosy basement bistro under the Lenkom Theatre. Artists and actors frequent this place for its cheap food and eclectic atmosphere. Many of the appetising dishes are named after plays, and you can watch Tom & Jerry cartoons or Charlie Chaplin films while you wait.

Look In! (Map 2; ☎ 292 6295; Bolshaya Dmitrovka ul 9; meal RR350; open noon-midnight daily) is a play on the Russian word luk, which means onion. It refers to the restaurant's multiple layers (dine on one of three levels), or maybe to the tasty onion soup. Either way, this place is pleasant enough for the money.

York (Map 2; ☎ 208 2229; Trubnaya ul 20/2; fish & chips RR360, Guinness RR170; open noon-midnight daily) is an English restaurant upstairs and an English pub downstairs. If you're not eating, engage in a game of backgammon.

Tinkoff (Map 2; ☎ 777 3300; Protochny per 11; beer RR120, meal RR600; open noon-2am daily) is Moscow's first branch of the St Petersburg microbrewery, featuring live sports on TV, lagers and pilsners on tap, and (yikes!) a metre-long sausage on the menu.

Mekhana Bansko (Map 4; ☎ 244 7387; Smolenskaya pl 9/1; business lunch RR200, dinner RR500; open noon-11pm Sun-Thurs,

PLACES TO EAT

noon-2am Fri-Sat) is a colourful Bulgarian restaurant with large tasty portions, cheap Bulgarian wines and loud folk music.

Mesto Vstrechi *(Map 2; ☎ 229 2373; Maly Gnezdnikovsky per 9/8/7; meal RR600; open noon-5am daily)* means 'Meeting Place', which aptly describes this club/restaurant, which attracts a constant stream of regulars. The food gets mixed reviews, but the menu has a few favourites.

Le Kolon *(Map 2; ☎ 923 1701; cnr Neglinnaya ul & Kuznetsky Most; meal RR900; open noon till last guest leaves daily)* is a classy French restaurant that is not as expensive as some of its competition. The atmosphere is romantic and the food up to par.

Scandinavia *(Map 2; ☎ 200 4986; Maly Palashevsky per 7; meal US$50; open noon-midnight daily)* wins plaudits for its skilled kitchen, which turns out everything from expensive steaks to ambitious Modern European and fusion fare. The inside is dark and woodsy; in warm weather the patio is a good leafy alternative.

Le Duc *(Map 2; ☎ 255 0390; ul 1905 goda 2; meal from US$80; open noon till last guest leaves daily)* is one in a row of fancy theme restaurants along this stretch of ulitsa 1905 goda. This one re-creates the interior of a Gothic cathedral, while serving diners exquisite French food and wine.

Brunch

Sunday brunch at the luxury hotels is an institution for many expats and wealthy Russians. You can while away the hours gorging yourself on an orgy of international cuisines.

Cafe Taiga *(Outer North Moscow map; ☎ 213 9000; Leningradsky pr 37, korpus 9; brunch US$30)*, in the Moscow Aerostar Hotel, has an excellent brunch, with more Asian selections than many others.

Hotel Baltschug Kempinski *(Map 4; ☎ 230 6500; ul Balchug 1; brunch US$30)* has the best view and, like the others, it includes champagne in its price.

CAFÉS

Moscow's booming café scene is beginning to make long-running imports like **DeliFrance** *(Map 2; lobby of the Tchaikovsky Concert Hall,*

Triumfalnaya pl 4) look decidedly old hat. Still, pastries and coffee just like home make this a great place for breakfast.

Café Gotty *(Map 2; ☎ 755 8402; Tverskaya ul 24; meal RR300; open 24hr)*, around the corner, has a sort of nondescript interior, but it offers a good selection of salads and sandwiches. The menu, complete with colour photos, makes for easy ordering.

Coffee Bean *(Map 3; ☎ 923 9793; ul Pokrovka 18; open 8am-10pm • Map 2; ☎ 788 6357; Tverskaya ul 10; open 8am-11pm)* is a classic coffee bar: high ceilings, newspapers lying around, nice mugs of Joe (RR500), but no smoking.

Zen Coffee *(Map 2; ☎ 234 1784; Lesnaya ul 1/2; open 9am-11pm daily • Map 2; ☎ 292 5114; Kamergersky per 6; open 9am-11pm daily)* also has several outlets: the first of these modern, pleasant cafés is opposite Belarusskaya Vokzal; the second is on the popular pedestrian boulevard leading off from Tverskaya to Kuznetsky Most.

PirOGI *(Map 4; ☎ 951 7596; ul Pyatnitskaya 29/8; open 24hr)* is a low-key, bohemian place, serving coffee, beers and even books, which you can buy, or just peruse while you have a drink.

Donna Klara *(Map 2; ☎ 290 6974; Malaya Bronnaya ul 21/13; meal RR400; open 10am-midnight daily)*, specialising in flaky pastries and dark coffee, is a great place for breakfast.

Shokoladnitsa *(Map 2; ☎ 107 1935; ul Putechnaya 7/5; breakfast RR100, coffees RR30; open 24hr)* is the place to go for bliny, especially if you like chocolate sauce.

Museum *(Map 2; ☎ 251 6444; 1-ya Tverskaya-Yamskaya ul 11; meal without drinks RR300; open noon-2am Sun-Wed, noon-6am Thurs-Sat)* is an ultra-progressive café, where bored-looking patrons dressed in black sip expensive drinks and smoke cigarettes. The name refers to the minimalist, white walls and glass-and-plastic decor. Food is surprisingly inexpensive.

Oranzhevy Galstuk *(Map 2; ☎ 229 1952; Kamergersky per 5; snacks & drinks RR600)* is the trendiest café on this trendy lane. Appetisers and salads are scrumptious, beer is cold and people-watching is tops. At night this place is a happening club with live music.

FAST FOOD

McDonald's has many locations; you'll pass four between central Moscow and Sheremetevo-2. The original branch *(Map 2; Bolshaya Bronnaya ul 29)* is the most famous. Prices are similar to the West, so the real allure lies with two things: familiar fare and clean toilets.

Fighting for some prime retail space with McDonald's is **Russkoe Bistro**, an equally omnipresent local chain endorsed (and, coincidentally, co-owned) by Mayor Luzhkov. It serves cheap, traditional goodies such as pirozhki and bliny.

Rostik's *(Map 2; ☎ 251 4950; ul Pervaya Tverskaya-Yamskaya 2/1; open 9am-9pm daily; meal RR100)* is another fast-food chain which serves very American food (burgers, fried chicken etc). There is another location on the second floor of **GUM** *(Map 2; Red Square; open 9am-9pm daily; meal RR100)*. Both have clean toilets.

There's a handy, but pricey, **food court** in the basement of the Okhotny Ryad shopping mall *(Map 2)*.

SELF-CATERING

If you want to eat like a Muscovite, you'll buy your food, take it home and cook it there. While this may not be feasible if you're staying in a hotel, Russian food markets can be entertaining and, if nothing else, you can buy the ingredients for a good picnic.

Speciality Stores

Magazin Chai-Kofe *(Tea-Coffee Store; Map 3; ☎ 925 4656; Myasnitskaya ul 19; open 8am-8pm Mon-Fri, 9am-7pm Sat)* is one of the only places you can get top-quality coffee beans in Moscow. It always stocks around 10 brands of coffee beans priced between US$12 and US$17 per kilogram and will grind them for free. There is also a decent selection of teas and sweets. The store was built in 1896 in the style of a Chinese pagoda and is also worth a visit for its interior. The exterior has, unfortunately, been hidden by scaffolding for years.

Supermarkets

Sedmoy Kontinent Supermarkets *(Seventh Continent; open 24hr)* carry mainly local brands but also some Western ones. Central locations (with the names as seen on the exteriors) are **Okhotny Ryad Gastronom** *(Map 2; ☎ 292 2248, ul Okhotny ryad 2)*; **Gastronom Seventh Continent** *(Map 4; ☎ 959 0342, ul Serafimovicha 2)*; **Smolensky Gastronom** *(Map 4; ☎ 241 3581, ul Arbat 54/2)*; and **Tsentralny Gastronom** *(Map 2; ☎ 928 9577, ul Bolshaya Lubyanka 12/1)*.

Kalinka Stockmann Supermarket *(Map 4; Smolensky Passage, Karmanitsky pr; open 10am-10pm daily)*, a one-time Scandinavian haven in Moscow, has a foreign goods supermarket in the basement.

If you are desperate for home, try **Global USA Supermarkets** *(Map 2; ☎ 229 8786; Tverskaya ul 6; open 9am-midnight daily • Map 4; ☎ 245 5657; ul Usachyova 35; metro: Sportivnaya; open 8am-10pm daily)*, which have loads of imported products.

Sadko Foodland Supermarkets *(Map 2; ☎ 256 2213; Krasnopresnenkaya nab 14 • Map 4; ☎ 243 6659; ul Bolshaya Dorogomilovskaya 16; both open 10am-10pm daily)* are good for European brands.

Yeliseev Grocery Store *(Map 2; Tverskaya ul 14; open 8am-9pm Mon-Sat, 10am-6pm Sun)* is an old-school Soviet market, set in a luxurious prerevolutionary decor. It is an atmospheric place to shop or to just look around. However, large-scale food shopping is not so convenient, as you can't pick up the products yourself.

Markets

Moscow's food markets *(rynky)* are full of interest, as well as fruit, vegetables, cheese, honey and meat. Many of the traders and their goods are from southern CIS republics. Take your own bag. Prices are good if you bargain a bit – and keep an eye on the quality of the items that are being popped into your bag.

The most central markets are **Danilovsky Market** *(Outer South Moscow map; Mytnaya ul 74; metro: Tulskaya)*; **Rizhsky Market** *(Outer North Moscow map; pr Mira 94-96; metro: Rizhskaya)*; and **Dorogomilovsky Market** *(Map 4; ul Mozhaysky val 10)* which has an overflow section along Kievskaya ulitsa to Kiev Station.

PLACES TO EAT

Entertainment

With its lively club scene and crowded cultural calendar, this cosmopolitan city offers high-brow, low-brow and everything in between. The key to finding out what's on is the comprehensive weekly entertainment section in Thursday's *Moscow Times*. For a laugh, you can also try *Exile* (which refers specifically to listings in the low-brow category, to say the least).

The classical performing arts remain an incredible bargain in Moscow. Highly acclaimed, professional artists stage productions in a number of elegant theatres around the city, and tickets in prime seats are often only a few dollars. Of course, the Bolshoi is Moscow's most famous theatre. Other venues, however, host productions of comparable quality – tickets are a fraction of the price and the theatres themselves are often

in better shape. See the boxed text 'Tickets? Anyone for Tickets?'.

Unfortunately for summer visitors, most theatres are closed between late June and early September.

CLASSICAL MUSIC

Tchaikovsky Concert Hall *(Map 2; ☎ 299 0378; Triumfalnaya pl 4/31)* is the largest concert venue in Moscow. It seats over 1600 people and is the home of the famous State Symphony Orchestra (Gosudarstvenny Akademichesky Simfonichesky Orkestr).

Moscow Tchaikovsky Conservatoire *(Map 2; ☎ 229 8183; Bolshaya Nikitskaya ul 13)* is the country's largest music school and has two venues: the Great Hall (Bolshoy Zal) and the Small Hall (Maly Zal). Every four years, hundreds of musicians gather at the

---

Tickets? Anyone for Tickets?

Tickets for most Moscow concerts and stage and sports events are easy enough to come by, though, as happens anywhere in the world, a few very popular events sell out early.

The best and cheapest way to get tickets for an event is simple – go to the ticket office at the venue itself. Most are open for advance or same-day sales every day from 10am to 7pm. You can usually choose your seat, and typical face-value prices for classical music and theatre are RR60 to RR300, depending on your seats.

Alternatively, ticket kiosks on the street or in the metro stations sell tickets for concerts, circuses, theatres, shows and sports events, at close to their face value. The street kiosks are marked *teatralnaya kassa* or just *teatr* (театральная касса or театр). Often the tickets that are available are displayed in the window. Locations of some useful kiosks are Manezhnaya ploshchad, ploshchad Revolyutsii near the metro exit, the west side of Teatralnaya ploshchad, ulitsa Petrovka opposite the Bolshoi Theatre, Tverskaya ulitsa opposite Hotel National, Pushkinskaya ploshchad near the corner of Malaya Dmitrovka ulitsa, and outside Prospekt Mira circle line metro station.

Service bureaus and concierges in hotels sell tickets for a few main events, and sometimes have tickets when other outlets have none. But they often charge hefty commissions on what are usually cheap face values.

Tickets for the Bolshoi, the circuses and a few other events are harder to come by, although they are often available from scalpers at the venue itself about 30 minutes to an hour before the performance. The easiest way to get tickets to the Bolshoi is to go there on the day of the performance and buy them from a tout. Expect to pay upwards of US$40. Exercise caution, so that you don't buy tickets for a show that was, say, last year!

Almost all evening theatre, concert and circus performances start at 7pm.

Conservatoire to compete for the titles of top pianist, singer, cellist and violinist at the prestigious International Tchaikovsky Competition. The next competition will be held in summer 2006.

Founded in 1990 by Mikhail Pletnev, the **Russian National Orchestra** (☎ 128 1920; W www.rno.ru; ul Garibaldi 19) has since become Russia's premier classical music organisation. Privately financed, it has been accused, and rightly so, of cherry-picking the best musicians from older state-supported orchestras. The RNO has several highly acclaimed recordings of Russian classics, such as Rachmaninov's *Second Symphony* and Prokofiev's *Cinderella*. In recent years, the RNO has been summering in California,

among its many other foreign tours. When it's in Moscow, the Orchestra plays in the Great Hall of the Moscow Tchaikovsky Conservatory.

OPERA & BALLET
Bolshoi

The Bolshoi Theatre (Map 2; ☎ 292 0050; W www.bolshoi.ru; Teatralnaya pl 1) is still one of the most romantic places in Moscow. The atmosphere in the glittering, six-tier auditorium is electric. Both the ballet and the opera companies, with several hundred artists between them, perform a range of Russian and foreign works.

Since the Soviet collapse (and even before) the Bolshoi has been marred by politics,

Useful Theatre Words & Phrases

theatre	teatr	театр
opera and ballet theatre	teatr opery i baleta	театр оперы и балета
drama theatre	dramaticheskiy teatr	драматический театр
concert hall	kontsertnyy zal	концертный зал
circus	tsirk	цирк
cinema	kinoteatr, kino	кинотеатр, кино
Have you got tickets for...?	u vas bilety (bil-YET-i) na...?	У вас билеты на...?
Extra tickets?	Lishnie bilety?	Лишние билеты?
cheap tickets	deshyovye bilety	дешёвые билеты
best tickets	luchshchie bilety	лучшие билеты
stalls, lowest tier of seating	amfiteatr, parter, kresla	амфитеатр, партер, кресла
dress circle (one tier up from stalls)	bel-etazh	бель-этаж
box	lozha	ложа
balcony	balkon	балкон
first tier (eg, of balcony)	pervyy yarus	первый (1-й) ярус
second tier	vtoroy (fta-ROY) yarus	второй (2-ой) ярус
third tier	tretiy yarus	третий (3-й) ярус
row	ryad (ryat)	ряд
inconvenient place (eg, obstructed view)	neudobnoe mesto (nye-oo-DOHB-nah-yeh MYEST-ah)	неудобное место
matinee	utrenniy kontsert	утренний концерт
cloakroom	garderob (gar-di-ROP)	гардероб
guest stars	gastroli	гастроли
Swan Lake	Lebedinoe ozero	Лебединое озеро
Sleeping Beauty	Spyachkaya krasavitsa	Спячкая красавица
The Nutcracker	Shchelkunchik	Щелкунчик

scandal and frequent turnover. Yet the show must go on; and it does. At the time of research, the Bolshoi was looking forward to an exciting season, including fresh productions of Russian classic operas, as well as visits by foreign opera and ballet companies. A second, smaller stage at the theatre is scheduled to open in early 2003. Closure of the theatre for renovations – long talked about but never materialised – has been put off for at least another year.

Other Companies

The Bolshoi does not have a monopoly on ballet and opera in Moscow. Leading dancers also appear with the Kremlin Ballet and the Moscow Classical Ballet Theatre, both of which perform in the **Kremlin Palace of Congresses** (Moscow Kremlin map; ☎ 928 5232; Vozdvizhenka ul 1).

In addition, there is the **Stanislavsky & Nemirovich-Danchenko Musical Theatre** (Map 2; ☎ 229 0649; W www.stanislavsky.ru; Bolshaya Dmitrovka ul 17), another opera and ballet theatre with a similar classical repertoire and high-quality performances.

Nemirovich-Danchenko founded his Musical Theatre in the early 20th century. In 1939 he incorporated the theatre with the dance company Art Ballet, headed by former Bolshoi star Victoria Krieger, who employed many of the same theatre techniques. See the boxed text 'Stanislavsky's Methods' for more details.

THEATRE

Moscow has around 40 professional and many amateur theatres (the number changes every season. A wide range of plays (contemporary and classic, Russian and foreign) is staged at most of them, with most performances in Russian. Some of the best drama can be seen at the venues listed here.

Chekhov Art Theatre (Map 2; ☎ 229 8760; W www.art-theatre.ru; Kamergersky per 3) is also known as MKhAT, where method acting was founded over 100 years ago (see the boxed text 'Stanislavsky's Methods'). Watch for English-language versions of Russian classics performed here by the American Studio (☎ 292 0941).

Lenkom Theatre (Map 2; ☎ 299 0708, ul Malaya Dmitrovka 6) is widely believed to have the strongest acting troupe in the country. The repertoire is diverse, but tickets are hard to come by.

Maly Theatre (Map 2; ☎ 923 2621, Teatralnaya pl 1/6) is a lovely theatre founded in 1824. Mainly 19th-century works are performed, and often they were premiered here.

Pushkin Drama Theatre (Map 2; ☎ 203 4221, 290 4658; W www.pushkin.theatre.ru; Tverskoy bul 23) provides classic Russian drama and new material as well.

Satirikon Theatre (Outer North Moscow map; ☎ 289 7836, 289 7885; Sheremetyevskaya ul 8) boasts one of Moscow's most talented theatre producers, Konstantin Raikin, as well as a whole host of big-name directors. The Satirikon earned a reputation in the early 1990s with its outrageously expensive production of the *Three Penny Opera*; it has since broken its own record for expenditure with *Chantecler*, which featured ducks, cockerels and hens dancing on stage. From Rizhskaya metro take any trolleybus to the Kinoteatr Gavana stop and just follow the crowds.

Sovremennik Theatre (Map 3; ☎ 921 1790, 921 6473; Chistoprudny bul 19A) runs superb Russian classics. Watch for regular productions of Chekhov's *The Cherry Orchard*.

Tabakov Theatre (Map 3; ☎ 928 9685, ul Chaplygina 1A) is named after its present director, Oleg Tabakov, a famous actor who is also the current director of MKhAT. Rumour has it that this theatre will soon move out of its snug basement quarters to a locale more befitting a prominent company.

Taganka Theatre (Map 5; ☎ 915 1015, 915 1217; Zemlyanoy val 76/12) was once famous for its rebellious director Yuri Lyubimov, even more unruly actor Vladimir Vysotsky and a troupe to match. The theatre has suffered financially in recent years, but continues to put on a good show.

Children's Theatres

Cultural instruction starts at a young age in Moscow, with many companies and performances geared specifically toward kids. Performances are almost always in Russian

Stanislavsky's Methods

In 1898, over an 18-hour restaurant lunch, actor-director Konstantin Stanislavsky and playwright-director Vladimir Nemirovich-Danchenko founded the Moscow Art Academic Theatre as the forum for method acting. The theatre is known by its Russian initials MKhAT, short for Moskovsky Khudozhestvenny Akademichesky Teatr.

More than just another stage, the Art Theatre adopted a 'realist' approach, which stressed truthful portrayal of characters and society, teamwork by the cast (not relying on stars), and respect for the writer. 'We declared war on all the conventionalities of the theatre…in the acting, the properties, the scenery, or the interpretation of the play', Stanislavsky wrote.

This treatment of *The Seagull* rescued playwright Anton Chekhov from despair after the play had flopped in St Petersburg. *Uncle Vanya*, *Three Sisters* and *The Cherry Orchard* all premiered in the MKhAT. Gorky's *The Lower Depths* was another success. In short, the theatre revolutionised Russian drama.

Method acting's influence in Western theatre has been enormous. Today in the USA, Stanislavsky's theories are the primary source of study for many actors, including such greats as Stella Adler, Marlon Brando, Sanford Meisner, Lee Strasberg, Harold Clurman, and Gregory Peck.

MKhAT, now technically called the Chekhov Moscow Art Theatre, still stages regular performances of Chekhov, among others.

but, especially with the puppet theatres, the language is universal. Daily performances are usually in the afternoons.

Obraztsov Puppet Theatre & Museum *(Map 2; ☎ 299 3310, 299 5563; ul Sadovaya-Samotyochnaya 3)* runs colourful Russian folk tales and adapted classical plays. Kids can get up-close and personal with the incredible puppets at the museum.

Kuklachev Cat Theatre *(☎ 249 2907; Kutuzovsky pr 25)* features acrobatic cats doing all kinds of stunts to the audience's delight. Director Yuri Kuklachev says: 'We do not use the word '*train*' here because it implies forcing an animal to do something; and you cannot force cats to do anything they don't want to. We *play* with the cats.'

Durov Animal Theatre *(Map 2; ☎ 971 3047; ul Durova 4)* stages shows with animals, including its most popular '*Railway for Mice*'.

Moscow Puppet Theatre *(☎ 261 2197; ul Spartakovskaya 26)* runs lots of Russian folk tales suitable for the very young.

Young Spectator's Theatre *(Teatr Yunogo Zritelya; Map 2; ☎ 299 5360; Mamonovsky per 10)* runs plays for children over 13, but *Storm*, by Ostrovsky, is highly recommended for adults as well.

Natalya Sats Children's Musical Theatre *(Outer South Moscow map; ☎ 930 9021; pr Vernadskogo 5)* is highly educational, with musical plays for children and short lectures before the performance.

CIRCUS

Moscow has two separate circuses, which put on glittering shows for Muscovites of all ages. The first half of the show is usually a modern mix of dance, cabaret and rock music before animals and acrobats assert themselves. Both circuses perform at 7pm Wednesday to Sunday, with additional daytime shows on weekends.

New Circus *(Outer South Moscow map; ☎ 930 2815; pr Vernadskogo 7)*, with 3400 seats, is near Moscow University and has the strongest reputation, especially for its animal acts and clowns.

Old (Nikulin) Circus at Tsvetnoy bulvar *(Map 2; ☎ 200 6889; Tsvetnoy bul 13)*, more central than the New Circus, is in a modernised 19th-century building and produces shows around a central theme.

EXHIBITIONS

There is always a fascinating variety of short-term art, historical, cultural and other exhibitions around Moscow and many museums have special sections for temporary exhibitions. Other good shows can be found in the city's numerous art galleries, which are listed in the *Moscow Times*.

M'ARS Gallery (☎ 146 2029; Malaya Filyovskaya ul 32; open noon-8pm Tue-Sat, noon-6pm Sun) was founded by artists who were banned in the Soviet era and usually has some good new works on display. It is west of the centre near Pionerskaya metro.

Guelman Gallery (Map 4; ☎ 238 2783, 238 8492; ul Malaya Polyanka 7/7, stroyenie 5; open noon-6pm Tue-Sat) is worth checking for modern Russian art. Exhibits range from simple graphics to elaborate sculpture, but the shows are generally fresh and interesting.

BARS & CLUBS

The club scene is more volatile in Moscow than elsewhere. Tastes are fickle, the DJ decamps, or the owner closes shop and retires to Monaco, one step ahead of the tax authorities. That said, clubbers and pubbers should be able to find any type of entertainment venue during their stay in Moscow. Most of the places below serve food.

Come summer, outdoor beer tents and shashlik stands pop up all over the city. One of the most pleasant places to head is the **Hermitage Gardens** (Map 2; metro: Pushkinskaya/Tverskaya), where you can dress and look how you want to – unlike at some of Moscow's trendier clubs where 'face control' rules are arbitrarily supervised by thuggish bouncers.

Kitaysky Lyotchik Dzhao-Da (Chinese Pilot; Map 2; ☎ 924 5611; W www.jao-da.ru; Lubyansky proezd 25; cover RR150; open 10am-8pm Mon-Fri, noon-10pm Sat-Sun, live music from 10.30pm), in a basement close by Kitai Gorod metro, is one of the best and most relaxed club/restaurants, often with live music.

Proekt OGI (Map 3; ☎ 229 5489; W proekt .ogi.ru; Potapovsky per 8/12; admission RR50-80; open 8am-11pm daily) is a vaguely hippy, but still hip, place for student types. Enter through the unmarked door in the corner of the courtyard. There's live music most nights.

Krizis Zhanra (Crisis of Genre; Map 4; ☎ 241 1928; W www.krisis.narod.ru; Bolshoy Vlasyevsky per 4/22; open 11am-midnight daily) is another bohemian place, with decent Georgian fare and cool, live music.

Kult (Map 5; ☎ 917 5706; ul Yauzskaya 5; open noon-midnight Sun-Wed, noon-6am Thurs-Sat) is a hang-out for arty types, complete with a gallery with exhibitions by local artists. It hosts live jazz during the week and DJs on weekends.

Both **Bunker** (Map 2; ☎ 200 1506; Tverskaya ul 12; admission varies; open 24hr) and its successor **B2** (Map 2; ☎ 209 9918; Bolshaya Sadovaya ul 8; cover RR100; open 24hr) have cheap food and drinks, and live music almost every night.

Sixteen Tons (Map 2; ☎ 253 5300; W www .16tons.ru; ul Presnensky val 6; admission RR100-200; open 11am-6am daily) has a brassy English pub/restaurant downstairs, with an excellent house-brewed bitter. Upstairs, the club gets some of the best local and foreign bands that play in Moscow.

Rhythm & Blues (Map 2; ☎ 203 6008, 203 6556; Starovagonkovsky per 19/2; admission RR50-100; open noon-midnight) is a reasonably priced music venue which pays tribute – both in musical terms and decoratively – to good old fashioned rock 'n' roll. The prices are surprisingly reasonable for its prime location off the Arbat (RR150 for a pitcher of beer).

Propaganda (Map 2; ☎ 924 5732; W www .propagandamoscow.com; Bolshoy Zlatoustinsky per 7) is happening, especially on Thursday, when DJs spin a cool mix for the beautiful people to dance to.

Voodoo Lounge (Map 2; ☎ 253 2323; W www.voodoolounge.ru; Sredny Tishinsky per 5/7; open 6pm-6am, closed Monday in winter) is another hot spot for dancing. The exotic international theme includes salsa lessons on Tuesday nights and an Arabian-style chill-out room.

Expat Club (Map 2; ☎ 298 5414; W www .expatclub.ru; Pevchesky per 4; open noon-6am daily) attracts decent bands on weekends, and shows sports and movies on other nights. Apparently, membership is free but 'subject to approval'.

Garage (Map 2; ☎ 209 1848; Tverskaya ul 16/2; open 24hr) is a funky Soviet-theme underground bar on Pushkinskaya ploshchad, with an old BMW machine protruding over the bar. After 3am, anything goes. There's no cover charge, but strict 'face control'.

Hungry Duck (Map 2; ☎ 923 6158; Pushechnaya ul 9/6; admission varies; open noon-6am daily) is an infamous bar, often described as the wildest in Europe. Its reputation is that most people lose most of their clothes by midnight, with every woman dancing on the bar. This may have something to do with the policy of free drinks for women till 11pm on some nights.

As for expat bars, you can't go far wrong at either **American Bar & Grill** (see the Places to Eat chapter) or **Rosie O'Grady's** (Map 4; ☎ 203 9087, ul Znamenka 9/12; open noon-1am daily), both of which are pretty self-explanatory.

Doug & Marty's-Moscow (Map 3; ☎ 917 0150; W www.dougandmartys.com; Zemlyanoy val 26; open noon-9am daily), across from the Kurskaya metro, is the latest incarnation of what used to be Chesterfields. Sports on the big screen and great happy hour specials (especially Wednesday nights) keep this place packed with expats. Food is 50% cheaper before 9pm.

Akademiya (Outer South Moscow map; ☎ 938 5775; Academy of Sciences, Leninsky pr 32A), on the 22nd floor, boasts a magnificent view of the city. This retro bar is popularly known as 'The Brains', after the surreal metallic structure that tops the building.

Besedka (Map 2; ☎ 200 5763; 1-ya Tverskaya Yamskaya ul 7; concerts 7pm daily) calls itself a 'Bard Café' and is a one-of-a-kind place. Not exactly music, but more than poetry, the stuff of bards lives on in Russian intellectual circles (see the boxed text 'Arbat, my Arbat' in the Things to See & Do chapter), and here.

Gay & Lesbian Venues

Elf Café (Map 3; ☎ 917 2014; Zemlyanoi val 13/1; open 11am-midnight Mon-Thurs, 11am-3am Fri-Sun), near Kurskaya metro, is a tiny gay bar with an even tinier dance floor, lending it a cosy feel.

Samovolka (Map 3; ☎ 261 78 44; ul Novaya Basmannaya 9; open 10pm-6am daily), meaning 'AWOL', connotes freedom, sex and booze to Russian military men. Decor at this gay club near Komsomolskaya metro follows the military theme and male staff sport fatigues (at least at the start of the night).

Three Monkeys (Map 5; ☎ 953 0909, 951 1563; Sadovnicheskaya ul 71/2; 6pm-6am daily; admission free with RR50 minimum) attracts poor student types, and whomever poor student types attract. Saturday night is 'dyke night' until midnight.

Ryby and **Sad** are both crowded basement places next door to each other on Maly Gnezdnikovsky pereulok. Sad opened during 2002 and is more upmarket. The once-popular Chameleon (later it was known as Barracks) is being boycotted by Moscow's gay community due to several recent reported incidents of homophobic violence.

Jazz & Blues

BB King (Map 2; ☎ 299 8206; Sadovaya-Samotechnaya ul 4/2; noon-2am daily) is the best venue for live jazz and blues. Concerts and jam sessions go into the wee hours.

Club Forte (Map 2; ☎ 202 8833; Bolshaya Bronnaya ul 18; admission Thur-Sat RR300; concert 9pm) is known for the band Arsenal, which plays here on Friday nights. The jazzy, kind-of-intellectual atmosphere is fun, though the music is bland. Book ahead.

Le Club (Map 5; ☎ 915 1042; Verkhnyaya Radishchevskaya ul 21; admission free before 9pm, RR200-300 after 9pm; open noon-midnight Sun-Thurs, noon till last customer leaves Fri & Sat) is a cosy bohemian place, where a local artsy crowd and business types listen to solid jazz. Igor Butman's Big Band plays every Monday. The place serves food and wine, and concerts usually start at 9pm.

BOWLING & BOOZE

Cosmic Bowling (Map 4; ☎ 246 3666; ul Lva Tolstogo 18; bowling RR600/hr; open noon-5am daily) is the place to head if you fancy a spot of high-tech bowling (it has several psychedelic fluorescent lanes) or pool.

Champion Bowling (Outer North Moscow map; ☎ 747 5000; W www.champion.ru;

ENTERTAINMENT

Leningradskoe sh 16; open 5pm-6am Mon-Fri, noon-6am Sat-Sun) is a huge complex featuring bowling, billiards, karaoke, sushi, big screen TVs and more. Trek out to metro Voikovskaya.

CINEMAS

American House of Cinema *(Map 4; ☎ 941 8747; Berezhkovskaya nab 2)*, inside the Radisson Slavyanskaya Hotel, shows major Hollywood movies in English.

Other theatres that occasionally run current release films in English are **Dome Theatre** *(Map 2; ☎ 931 9873; Olympiisky pr 18/1)* in Olympic Penta Hotel, and **Sportland Movie Restaurant** *(Map 2; ☎ 291 2041; Novy Arbat ul 21)*. All of these places are pretty random about subtitles and dubbing, so call in advance to confirm what's on.

Other theatres showing films in Russian include **35MM** *(Map 3; ☎ 917 5496; ul Pokrovka 47)*, **Kodak Kinomir** *(Map 2; ☎ 209 4359, 200 3563; Nastasinsky per 2)*, **Pushkinsky Cinema** *(Map 2; ☎ 229 2111, Pushkinskaya pl 2)*, **Museum Cinema** *(Map 2; ☎ 255 2896, 255 9095; Druzhinnikovskaya ul 15)*, and **Illuzion Cinema** *(Map 5; ☎ 915 4353, 915 4339; Kotelnicheskaya nab 1/15)* in one of Stalin's 'Seven Sisters'.

SPECTATOR SPORTS

Russia's premier football league, Vysshaya Liga, has five teams in Moscow: Spartak, Lokomotiv, TsCKA, Torpedo and Dinamo. Each has a loyal following. You can often buy tickets immediately before the games which are played at the venues listed here.

Dinamo Stadium *(Outer North Moscow map; ☎ 212 3132; Leningradsky pr 36; metro: Dinamo)* seats 51,000 people and hosts namesake Dinamo.

Luzhniki Stadium *(Outer South Moscow map; ☎ 201 1164; Luzhnetskaya nab 24; metro: Sportivnaya)* gleams from its rebuilding, with 80,000 new seats. It hosts the Torpedo and Spartak teams.

Lokomotiv Stadium *(Outer Moscow Map; ☎ 161 4283; Bolshaya Cherkizovskaya ul 125; metro: Cherkizovskaya)* hosts Lokomotiv and seats 30,000. It was reconstructed in 2002.

Moscow's main entrant in the top ice hockey league (Super Liga) is **Dinamo**, which plays at the stadium of the same name.

Since the days of Olympic glory, men's basketball trails football and ice hockey as a distant third in popularity.

TsCKA *(Outer North Moscow map; ☎ 213 2288; Leningradsky pr 39A; metro: Aeroport)*, a top Moscow team, does well in the European league but all too often serves as a retirement home for North America's NBA, which poaches the best players. In contrast, some of the best play and games come from the TsCKA women's team, which plays from September to May.

Shopping

Back in the old days, the only place to buy a tin of caviar or a painted box was at an elite Beriozka store. Entry was restricted to foreigners and people with foreign currency, every store carried the same dull stuff and prices were high. The only other options were the sad selection at the State Department Store, or the notorious black market. Russia has come a long way – one no longer need defy the law to bring home a decent, affordable souvenir, and basic toiletries are no longer luxuries.

That said, shopping is not among Russia's main attractions. Foreign goods cost the same as (if not more than) they do at home. If the item seems like a steal, then it's probably a bargain-basement counterfeit. Local items are often of low quality, although this situation is improving.

The selection of souvenir-type items is always changing and growing, as craftsmen unleash long-dormant creativity and collectors uncover long-hidden treasures. Local items you may want to purchase include caviar, vodka, linens, traditional crafts and Soviet paraphernalia. Many markets carry antique items, such as old stamps, books and posters, as well as some furniture and household items. Concerning antiques and anything else more than 25 years old, see Customs in the Facts for the Visitor chapter for details on export restrictions.

WHAT TO BUY
Food & Drink
Exotic foods and drinks are among the most interesting and affordable items by which to remember Russia. Most characteristic are vodka and caviar, *zakuski* (appetisers) of the tsar's court and the Soviet politburo. Caviar is not as cheap as it used to be (see the boxed text 'Roe to Ruin' in the Places to Eat chapter), but it is still widely available in food stores and at farmers markets.

Vodka can cost as much or as little as you are willing to pay. Be careful of cheap brands, however, especially when purchasing from

kiosks or small stores. The market is flooded with cheap counterfeits, some of which can be downright dangerous. You will be safe if you stick to the major food outlets listed in the Places to Eat chapter. You will also find a wide variety of decorative bottles, some with historical or regional themes. Vodka connoisseurs admire the design and shape of the bottles almost as much as the fiery brew itself.

Specialities from the former Soviet republics, such as Armenian cognac or Georgian wine, are also unusual treats for the gourmand. While not Russian per se, they are certainly more available and affordable in Moscow than in most other parts of the world.

The Russian sweet tooth is notorious (a fact that's evidenced by the profusion of gold teeth). Russians adore confections and chocolate, and, without fail, prefer locally produced treats over any old Belgian or Swiss chocolate. Never mind that the major Russian confectionaries are largely owned by Cadbury or Nestle, Russian chocolate is a matter of national pride. (Keep this in mind when buying chocolate for Russian friends.) Super-sweet Russian candy is perhaps an acquired taste, but it can be a fun souvenir for the sweet tooth in your life. Many companies produce beautiful pieces with fancy wrapping and colourful boxes in honour of local events, holidays or historical places. The Krasny Oktyabr candy factory on the banks of the Moscow River is widely considered the best confectioner around.

All of these items are available at any of the food stores listed in the Self-Catering section of the Places to Eat chapter. The most atmospheric place to do your food shopping is the historic **Yeliseev Grocery Store** *(Map 2; ☎ 229 5562; Tverskaya ul 14).*

Linens
Russia's cool, moist summers and fertile soil are ideal for producing flax, the fibre

used to manufacture linen. This elegant, durable fabric is respectfully known in Russia as 'His Majesty Linen'.

Some manufacturers claim that archaeologists have excavated linen pieces that have held up for over 1000 years. High-quality linen products such as tablecloths, napkins, bed covers and even clothing are still manufactured in Russia – and prices are lower than their Western counterparts.

Vologda Linen *(Moscow Kremlin map; ☎ 232 9463; Gostinny Dvor, ul Ilyinka 4; open 10am-8pm daily)* has fine clothes and linens produced according to traditional Russian methods. The stuff is beautiful and reasonably priced.

Arts, Crafts & Antiques

The speciality of Russian craftsmen is painted wooden knick-knacks. It starts with the traditional *matrioshkas* (sets of painted wooden dolls within dolls) and takes off from there (see the boxed text 'How Matrioshka Got Her Start'). Traditional wooden dishes and utensils are painted in decorative, floral patterns. This style, which is called Khokhloma, is named for its village of origin, north of Nizhny Novgorod. Wooden spoons are the most common, but bowls, cups, napkin rings and salt and pepper dishes are also easy to find. Now that artists

are free to create as they please, styles and patterns are more diverse, but the trend is still decidedly traditional.

Chess is extremely popular in Russia. These days, chess sets in all varieties of size and style are for sale. Owing to the shading and texture of materials used, the boards are often works of art in themselves. Pieces can be elaborately detailed, often based on some historical theme (eg, the Russians versus the Tatars).

Painted lacquer boxes – known as *Palekh* boxes – are usually black with a colourfully detailed scene. Prices are directly proportionate to the detail and skill with which they are painted.

The best selection of these items is at the Vernisazh market at Izmaylovsky Park (see Arts & Crafts Markets later in this chapter).

Nobody leaves Russia without forming a decisive opinion about Gzhel porcelain, the curly white pieces with cobalt blue floral design. Gzhel is a village situated 50km southeast of Moscow, known since the 14th century for its pottery. In 1972, the Gzhel Association set up porcelain workshops in the area and created its distinctive design, which now identifies all of its pieces, including its tableware, vases, miniatures, toys and more. All the pieces are hand-painted, making each one unique. And now Gzhel's

---

The Secret of Surviving Russian Winter

Pavlovsky-Posad woollen shawls are warm enough even for Russian weather and their vivid floral designs are bright enough even for bleak winter monotony. No wonder these shawls and headscarves have been popular with Russian women for over 100 years! Pavlovsky-Posad scarves and shawls originated from the textile industry in the Bogorodsk area. In 1812, a merchant opened a yarn-processing factory in a nearby village; eventually the factory began dying scarves, and by the end of that century it was producing scarves on a mass basis.

The patterns combine elements of Western and Oriental art. The traditional design is a red, yellow and blue floral design with green leaves on a black, green or brown background. The fabric is produced by a unique technology using 100% single-thread merino wool, which makes the fabric very thin and smooth.

The shawls are a good bargain; the most expensive ones with silk fringes that are 1.5m by 1.5m cost around RR500. The smallest headscarves, 88cm by 88cm, cost about RR150. For care, dry cleaning is recommended.

The original items should be thin, not bulky, and have a clear floral print, but you probably won't find many fakes.

'fine, folk art' comes in all forms, from traditional vodka sets to New Russian novelty items. Love it or hate it, nothing says 'Russia' like a Gzhel teapot. These pieces are available at department stores such as TsUM or at the gallery at VDNKh (see Where to Shop later in this chapter), or at **Gzhel Factory Shop** (Map 2; ☎ 299 2953; Sadovaya-Samotechnaya ul 12/2).

Soviet Paraphernalia

The Soviet Union is gone, but not forgotten. Old-timers continue to dig out of closets and basements all manner of stuff bearing the hammer and sickle, including military jackets and hats, flasks, *shapkas* (fur hats), pins, watches, flags etc. There is a lot of it and nobody wants it anymore, so you can find this stuff cheaply. Again, the best place is the Vernisazh market.

CDs, DVDs & Videos

The Russian government is not exactly strict about copyright laws, which makes pirated CDs, DVDs and videos a great bargain. The selection is usually vast, but random, with prices as low as RR100 to RR200 per disc/tape.

Most markets will have at least one stall dedicated to music, video and games, and you will also find stalls and kiosks in many underground passages and metro entrances. For the widest selection, **Gorbushka market** (Outer West Moscow map) is the market to try for CDs (and the like) of dubious origin. The best time to go is Saturday morning. Follow the crowds out of Bagrationovskaya metro station.

WHERE TO SHOP

For details of Moscow's food markets, see Self-Catering in the Places to Eat chapter.

Shopping Streets

Novy Arbat is the Moscow equivalent of London's Oxford Street or an American suburban mall, in that it's the place for mid-range shops. It's also equally unattractive. The streets around Kuznetsky Most just east of the Bolshoi and those around GUM are home to the most upmarket shops.

Shopping Malls

GUM (Gosudarstvenny Univermag; Map 2; ☎ 921 3211; open 8.30am-8.30pm Mon-Sat, 11am-7pm Sun), on the eastern side of Red Square, has made the transition to a market economy in fine form. It's buffed up and the 19th-century building is a sight in itself. Although often called a 'department store', this is a misnomer, as it is really a huge collection of individual shops spread over several floors.

Okhotny Ryad shopping mall (Map 2; ☎ 737 8409; Manezhnaya pl; open 10am-10pm daily) is a zillion-dollar mall built in the 1990s. Although it was originally filled with expensive boutiques and no people, times have changed, and the stores now cater to all income levels and are usually packed. There's a big, crowded food court on the ground floor.

Deep in Okhotny Ryad shopping mall, **La Casa de Cuba** (☎ 737 8409) offers an extensive range of Cuban cigars.

Department Stores

TsUM (Map 2; ☎ 292 1157; ul Petrovka 2; open 9am-8pm Mon-Sat, 9am-6pm Sun) is a real department store, stocking everything from perfume to clothes, and electronics to sporting goods.

Detsky Mir (Children's World; Map 2; ☎ 238 0096; open 9am-8pm Mon-Sat) was the premier toy store during Soviet times. It now has a fun mix of imported and Russian-produced toys. It also has well-stocked departments for sporting goods, homewares and other toys for adults.

Univermag Moskovsky (Map 3; Moskovsky Department Store; ☎ 207 9007; Komsomolskaya pl 6; open 8.30am-8.30pm Mon-Sat, 11am-7pm Sun) is handily next to three train stations and definitely doesn't have a sophisticated exterior. However, its contents have considerably improved over the last five years and goods are reasonably priced. The place has several inexpensive eateries and a currency exchange.

IKEA (☎ 737 5301) is the cheap and cheerful Swedish furniture giant. The enormous store is in Khimky, on the M10 near the turn for Sheremetevo-2 airport.

Arts & Crafts Markets

The weekend **Vernisazh market** at Izmaylovsky Park *(Outer East Moscow map)* is a sprawling area packed with art and handmade crafts. You'll find Moscow's biggest original range of matrioshkas, Palekh and Khokhloma ware, and dozens of artists selling their own work. There are also rugs from the Caucasus and Central Asia, some very attractive pottery, antique samovars, handmade clothes, jewellery, fur hats, chess sets, toys, Soviet posters and much more.

Quality is mostly high and many of the items are truly original. Prices can be reasonable, but you have to bargain for them. The market is two minutes' walk from Izmaylovksy Park metro; follow the crowds past the big hotel complex outside the station.

Many other artists set up their stalls on ulitsa Krymsky Val opposite the entrance to Gorky Park *(Map 4)*, particularly on Saturday and Sunday. The art here is a mite less commercial than at Izmaylovksy Park, and there are only a few crafts.

How Matrioshka Got Her Start

Rare is the tourist that leaves Russia without a sample of the most Russian of all souvenirs, the matrioshka. The hand-painted, wooden, nesting doll which so symbolises Russia is not, as you might imagine, an ancient craft developed and perfected by generations of peasant families. Rather, the concept was adapted from a traditional Japanese toy.

In the 19th century, Russian artists were eager to embrace cultural styles which would unite traditional and modern elements and contribute to the growing sense of national identity at that time (see Arts in the Facts about Moscow chapter). Savva Mamontov, a celebrated patron of the arts, established art studios at his Abramtsevo estate where artists could do just that. Toys were considered a particularly creative form of folk art, and Savva's brother Anatoly set up a workshop to revive and develop folk peasant toys. In this workshop, Mamontov had a collection of toys from around the world, including a Japanese nesting doll depicting the Buddhist sage Fukuruma. Inspired by this prototype, the toy maker Vassily Zviozdochkin and the artist Sergei Maliutin created the earliest Russian nesting dolls, identified by Slavic features and peasant dress.

During this time, the names Matryona and Matryosha were popular female names. Derived from the word for 'mother', the names conjured up images of a healthy, portly woman with plenty of children. Thus the diminutive of the name was applied to the nesting dolls, symbolic of motherhood, fertility and Mother Russia.

At the beginning of the 20th century, large-scale production of the Russian matrioshka began at the toy centre at Sergiev Posad. Here, artists developed a unique, realistic style of painting the dolls, depicting colourful village life, patriotic historical figures and beloved literary characters.

The new Bolshevik regime began cracking down on this creative outlet as early as 1923. An act was passed which banned the exhibition and sale of any matrioshkas, which were not consistent with the regime's artistic or ideological goals. The ban included such controversial figures as tailors, bakers and any entrepreneurial types; Gypsies (Roma), Jews and other ethnic groups; fantastical figures like mermaids and goblins; and so on. Eventually, the matrioshka's diversity and creativity diminished, and she adopted one predictable female image. Factory production began in the 1930s, and this 'art' was nearly lost.

The 1990s saw a revival of the author's matrioshka (pieces designed and painted by individuals). Production returned to artists and craftsmen, who are free to paint whom and how they wish. As a result, modern-day matrioshkas take on every imaginable character and style.

Once again (this time due to market forces), artists often get inspiration for this Russian craft from foreign sources. From Warner Brothers to the brothers Bush, from Red Sox to Red Wings, from the Simpsons to Star Wars, many Western popular cultural images are depicted on the dolls these days.

Souvenir & Antique Shops

VDNKh Culture Pavilion *(Outer North Moscow map;* ☎ *181 9481; VDNKh Pavilion No 66)* houses an art salon which features well-known and typically Russian products, such as Gzhel porcelain, Pavlovsky-Posad scarves, Palekh boxes and more.

Inostrannye Knigi *(Foreign Books; Map 2;* ☎ *290 4082; Malaya Nikitskaya ul 16; open 10am-7pm Mon-Sat)* is a place you should visit, not so much for the books, but also for used furniture, crockery, silverware and clothing – some of it quite old. It's like a garage sale and, unlike other places, you're allowed to paw through stuff.

Salon Moskovskogo Fonda Kultury *(Moscow Culture Foundation Salon; Map 4;* ☎ *951 3302; ul Pyatnitskaya 16; open 10am-8pm Mon-Sat)* is one of the most authentic places to buy Russian arts and crafts. There are also many antiques, but watch those export rules!

Novikh Russkikh Mir *(World of New Russians; Map 2;* ☎ *241 0081;* Ⓦ *www.newrussian.net; ul Arbat 36; open 10am-9pm)* has a wide range of overpriced but amusing gifts of mostly traditional Russian items with a New Russian theme (eg, the Gzhel mobile phone).

Magazin-Salon Bolshoi Teatr *(Bolshoi Theatre Store; Map 2;* ☎ *292 0494; ul Petrovka 3; open 10am-8pm Mon-Sat)* carries mainly dance costumes and equipment. Some of the stuff – such as its masks, boas and costume jewellery – might make fun souvenirs, or you can buy an old-fashioned Bolshoi Theatre T-shirt.

Bookshops

Dom Knigi *(Map 2;* ☎ *290 4507;* Ⓦ *www.mdk-arbat.ru; Novy Arbat ul 8; open 10am-8pm daily)* is among the largest bookshops in Moscow. The huge selection includes reference books, souvenir and travel books, and a decent selection of English-language novels.

Anglia British Bookshop *(Map 2;* ☎ *203 5802; Khlebny per 2/3; open 10am-7pm Mon-Sat, 10am-5pm Sun)* has Moscow's best selection of books in English, including titles from Lonely Planet. Another option is **Angliskaya Kniga po Kuznetskom** *(English Book on Kuznetsky; Map 2;* ☎ *928 2021; Kuznetsky Most 18/7; open 10am-7pm Mon-Fri, 10am-6pm Sat)*.

Torgovy Dom Biblio-Globus *(Map 2;* ☎ *928 3567; Myasnitskaya ul 6)* is a Russian bookshop with a variety of reference and souvenir

Clean the World of Capitalist Debris!

The most intriguing Soviet paraphernalia – both historically and artistically – are the old propaganda posters that touted the goals and denounced the enemies of the day. Their bold colours and even bolder messages provide a fascinating insight to Soviet culture.

Although printed in vast quantities, original Soviet posters are quite rare today. Most of them were posted, as they were meant to be, and eventually destroyed from wear and tear. The most rare posters feature political characters such as Trotsky or Kirov, who later fell out of favour with the regime. In true Soviet style, all evidence of these people was systematically destroyed.

Work by the most celebrated poster artists, such as Rodchenko, Lissitsky and Klutsis, might sell for as much as US$100,000. More recent posters – especially post-WWII – are available for a few hundred dollars or less, depending on their size and condition. Pick your favourite cause – abstinence, literacy, feminism, the military, anticapitalism etc – and soak up the propaganda. A few collectors with incredible collections hang out in the northwest corner of the Vernisazh market.

Now the old propaganda posters are also being reproduced and sold in bookshops. Interestingly, these are being marketed – not to tourists, as they are all in Russian – but to curious (younger) and nostalgic (older) Russians. Contemporary Moscow society regards public campaigns to stamp out capitalism and to build communism a peculiar novelty. Reproductions are available for a few hundred roubles.

books on language, art and history. There's also a good selection of maps and travel guides.

Film Processing

Focus Photoshop *(Map 2; Tverskaya ul 4; open 8am-8pm daily)* is conveniently located and well stocked with photographic equipment, slide film, camcorder tapes and other items to help you record your Russian visit. Developing facilities are reliable.

Sivma Central Laboratory *(Outer West Moscow map; ☎ 145 6855; Bagrationovsky proezd 7; open 9am-8pm Mon-Sat, 10am-6pm Sun)*, for professional film development, is one of the very few places where you can get slide film processed in 90 minutes for under US$3 – without scratching. It's in a long, grey building a five-minute walk from the Bagrationovskaya metro station.

Camping Gear

AlpIndustriya *(Outer East Moscow map; ☎ 165 9481; Izmailovskaya pl 1)* stocks a wide variety of basic camping equipment, including the city's largest selection of tents and sleeping bags.

Ekstremal *(Outer South Moscow map; ☎ 926 8923; ul Saikina 1/2)* sells mostly high-end gear, including lots of imported brands.

Aktivny Otdykh *(Outer North Moscow map; ☎ 281 1078; 74 pr Mira)* has a smaller selection of gear, but prices are competitive and the location is more central. This place features mostly Russian brands, which are fine for mild weather.

Excursions

The region around Moscow is, in many ways, the heartland of Russia, with a subtly changing landscape crossed by winding rivers and dotted by peasant villages, the typical provincial scene immortalised by so many artists and writers. The towns and villages are an equally typical mixture of the ancient and picturesque, the modern and drab.

As soon as you leave Moscow, the contrasts between the fast-paced, modern capital and the slower, old-fashioned (and often poorer), provincial world become apparent. Even one trip out of the big city will provide a glimpse of the life that the majority of Russians lead.

This chapter covers places within about 300km of Moscow. Most are a feasible day trip from the capital, but some of the more distant places are easier with an overnight (or longer) stop. The 'Golden Ring' of historic towns and villages northeast of Moscow is well worth a few days of your time.

GETTING THERE & AWAY

Local tour agencies such as Dom Patriarshy Tours organise excursions to most of these destinations. See the boxed text 'Want a Guide for a Day?' in the Things to See & Do chapter. However, you can save loads of money (if not time) by travelling independently if you have language skills or courage (both are not necessary). The region around Moscow is accustomed to receiving tourists and not impossible to navigate.

Suburban Train

Many places in this chapter can be reached by suburban trains from Moscow. This is among the easiest, if not the quickest, form of Russian transport to use: find the suburban ticket hall (пригородный зал, *prigorodny zal*) at the appropriate Moscow station, check the timetable for a train going where you want, buy your ticket and you're off. All carriages are the same class and no advance bookings

Getting Back to Nature

At least 30% of Russians – including many Muscovites – own a small country home, or dacha. Often little more than a wooden hut, these retreats offer Russians refuge from city life. They don't usually have electricity or running water, but they always have a fertile spot that's far away – at least psychologically – from the city. On weekends from May to September, Moscow begins to empty out early on Friday as people head to the country.

The dacha's most remarkable feature is its garden, which is usually bursting with flowering fruit trees and vegie plants. Families today still grow all manner of vegetables and fruits, which get sold at the market or canned for the winter. Throughout the winter, city dwellers can enjoy strawberry *kompot* (canned, syrupy fruit) or pickled mushrooms, and fondly recall their time in the countryside.

After playing in the dirt, the next stop is undoubtedly the *banya*. While bathhouses exist in the city, the countryside banya experience cannot be replicated. Crowding into the tiny, wooden hothouse; receiving a beating with fragrant *veniki* (birch branches) straight from the forest; cooling down with a dip in the pond or – more extreme – a roll in the snow…now *that's* getting back to nature.

Nothing piques hunger like the Russian banya, and what better way to enjoy the fruits of one's labour than with a hearty meal. Dacha cuisine evokes the peasant's kitchen: tasty soups that are the highlight of Russian cuisine; typically Russian *kasha*, or porridge, which sates any appetite; and coarse, black Russian bread. These dishes often use ingredients straight from the garden, coop or pasture. Simple to prepare, rich in flavour and nourishing to body and soul, dacha fare is exemplary of how Russians return to their rural roots for replenishment.

or compartment reservations are needed. Buses often run the same routes and take less time than the suburban trains.

Car
The most efficient, albeit most expensive, way to visit the destinations around Moscow is by car. Renting a car in Moscow will allow you to visit more than one destination in a day, or to take a tour around the Golden Ring in a few days. Alternatively, you can often hire cars with drivers at the local bus stations. The rates are about RR10 per kilometre from Moscow, but less around the smaller towns, which may be cost effective if you are travelling in a group, or if you are on a tight schedule.

Boat
Long-distance passenger services occasionally run along the Volga River and connect Moscow with Uglich, Yaroslavl, Kostroma, Plyos and cities all the way down to Astrakhan near the Caspian Sea. Cruises booked in Moscow or abroad will also take you to these places. For details, see the Getting There & Away chapter.

Northeast – the Golden Ring
Северо-восток – Золотое Кольцо

The Golden Ring (Zolotoe Koltso) is a modern name for a loop of very old towns northeast of Moscow that preceded the present capital as the political and cultural heart of Russia. The towns' churches, monasteries, kremlins and museums make a picturesque portfolio of early Russian art, architecture and history. Some of the towns are little more than villages, providing a glimpse of peaceful country life as it is lived all over European Russia.

Visitors do run the risk of 'old Russian church' overload, so it pays to travel selectively. The most visited places are Sergiev Posad and Suzdal, as they are accessible from Moscow and artistically exquisite. Other places are less touristy and generally more run-down, which can be appealing in its own way.

Some places in the Golden Ring can be visited on day or overnight trips from Moscow. Alternatively, if you have time, devote a few days to visiting several of these ancient gems. Transport and accommodation are easy enough to find along the way. One or two-day excursions are also available from Moscow.

VLADIMIR
ВЛАДИМИР
☎ 09222 • postcode 600012 • pop 360,000

Little remains in Vladimir (178km northeast of Moscow) from its medieval heyday, when it was Russia's capital. However, what does remain – several examples of Russia's most ancient and formative architecture – is worth pausing to see en route to/from the more charming town of Suzdal.

History
Vladimir was founded by Vladimir Monomakh of Kyiv in 1108 as a fort in the Rostov-Suzdal principality, which he later gave to his son Yury Dolgoruky. Under Yury's son, Andrey Bogolyubsky (1111–1174), it became capital of the principality, and capital of all Kyivan Rus after Kyiv was sacked in 1169. Andrey and his brother Vsevolod III (1176–1212) consolidated themselves as the strongest Russian princes and brought builders and artists from as far away as Western Europe to give Vladimir a Kyiv-like splendour.

Devastated by nomadic raiders in 1238 and 1293, the city recovered each time, but its realm disintegrated into small principalities, with Moscow increasingly dominant. The head of the Russian Church resided here from 1300 to 1326, but then moved to Moscow. Worldly power finally shifted to Moscow around this time too. Even so, the rulers remained nominally Grand Princes of Vladimir until the 15th century. In the 20th century, Vladimir prospered anew on the back of textile, mechanical engineering and chemical industries.

Orientation
Vladimir's main street is ulitsa Bolshaya Moskovskaya, although it sometimes goes by its former name, ulitsa III Internatsionala. To make matters more confusing, other segments of the street go by different names, including simply ulitsa Moskovskaya, which is just west of the Golden Gate. This is where you'll find the cathedrals of the Assumption and St Dmitry, standing impressively at the top of the tree-covered slope down to the

Klyazma River, and the Golden Gate 500m west. The rail and bus stations are both on ulitsa Vokzalnaya at the bottom of the same slope 500m east. The M7 Moscow–Nizhny Novgorod road makes a loop round the northern side of the city.

Information
There's a **post and telephone office** (ul Pod-belskogo; open 8am-8pm Mon-Fri) as well as an **Internet Café** (☎ 325 257; ul Bolshaya

EXCURSIONS

History of the Golden Ring

The 'Golden Ring' is a recently coined term that evokes a heroic distant past. Located northeast of Moscow, the Golden Ring is composed of some of Russia's oldest cities, wherein occurred the events that shaped early Russian history.

Towards the end of the 9th century, Slav tribes began to migrate into the hilly forestland of the Volga headwaters. They established small farming communities along the rivers and lakes, eventually absorbing the Finno-Ugric tribes that already occupied the region. These Slav settlements made up the easternmost reaches of the Kyivan (Kievan) Rus principality and bordered the formidable Turkic Bulgar state of the Middle Volga.

Wary of his eastern rival, the Kyivan Grand Prince, Vladimir I, defeated the Bulgars in combat and secured by treaty his claim of sovereignty over these Slav tribes. Vladimir then made his son, Yaroslav, the regional potentate, responsible for collecting tribute and converting pagans among the locals. Upon his death, in 1015, Vladimir's realm was divided among his sons, ushering a prolonged period of violent sibling rivalry and fragmented power.

The victors that eventually emerged from this fratricidal competition were the descendants of Yaroslavl's son Vsevolod, who had inherited the Rostov-Suzdal principality. As a result, the locus of power in medieval Russia gradually shifted eastward. In this period, the Golden Ring towns prospered and expanded under a string of shrewd and able princes who competed against Kyiv (Kiev) in the west and battled the Bulgars in the east.

In the early 12th century, Suzdal's Vladimir Monomakh founded the fortress city of Vladimir, high above the Klyazma River. He entrusted the eastern lands to his young son, Yury Dolgoruky. In 1125, Yury took the title Grand Prince and declared Suzdal as the northern capital of Rus. In 1157, Yury's son, Andrei Bogolyubsky, moved the Grand Prince's throne to Vladimir, which grew into the dominant city-state in the region. When the Mongols paid a visit in the 13th century, Alexander Nevsky, Russia's first war hero, rebuilt Vladimir and restored the city's political status.

The heirs of Vladimir Monomakh sought to create a realm that rivalled Kyiv, the cradle of eastern Slavic civilization. Under the reign of Andre Bogolyubsky, in particular, the region experienced a building frenzy. Imposing towers, golden gates, fortified monasteries and elegant churches were constructed to match the cultural ambitions of its political rulers. Rostov, Suzdal, Vladimir and Sergiev Posad each played important parts in making the Golden Ring the spiritual centre of Russian Orthodoxy.

The heyday of the Golden Ring towns was short-lived. Marauding Mongol invaders overran their realm and forced their princes to pay them homage. With this change in regional politics, the erstwhile lesser principality of Muscovy rose in prominence through its role as the Golden Horde's chosen tribute collector. Gradually, the once proud principalities of the Golden Ring were absorbed into the expanding Muscovite state. Eventually, they were reduced in status to just another set of provincial capital towns.

Moskovskaya 51; RR30 per hour; open 8am-9pm Mon-Sat). Hotel Vladimir has an ATM in the lobby.

Assumption Cathedral

Begun in 1158, the **Assumption Cathedral** *(Uspensky sobor; admission RR30; open 1.30pm-5pm daily)* is a white-stone version of Kyiv's brick Byzantine churches. Its simple but majestic form is adorned with fine carving, innovative for the time. Extended on all sides after a fire in the 1180s, and at the same time gaining four outer domes, the cathedral has changed little since.

The cathedral used to house the *Vladimir Icon of the Mother of God* brought from Kyiv by Andrey Bogolyubsky. A national protector bestowing supreme status to its city of residence, the icon was moved to Moscow in 1390 and is now kept in the Tretyakov Gallery.

Inside the working church a few restored 12th-century murals of peacocks and some prophets holding scrolls can be deciphered about halfway up the inner wall of the outer north aisle; this was originally an outside wall. The real treasures are the *Last Judg-ment* frescoes by Andrey Rublyov and Daniil Chyorny, painted in 1408 in the central nave and inner south aisle, under the choir gallery towards the west end.

The church also contains the original coffin of Alexander Nevsky of Novgorod, the 13th-century military leader who was also Prince of Vladimir. He was buried in the former **Nativity Monastery** east of here, but his remains were moved to St Petersburg in 1724 when Peter the Great awarded him Russian hero status.

Adjoining the cathedral on the northern side are an 1810 **bell tower** and the 1862 **St George's Chapel**.

Cathedral of St Dmitry

A quick stroll east of the Assumption Cathedral is the smaller **Cathedral of St Dmitry** (Dmitrievsky sobor, 1193–97), where the art of Vladimir-Suzdal stone carving reached its pinnacle.

The church is permanently closed, but the attraction here is its exterior walls, covered in an amazing profusion of images.

The top centre of the north, south and west walls all show King David bewitching the

Art & Architecture of the Golden Ring

The majority of the Golden Ring's surviving architectural monuments date from spurts of building and rebuilding after the collapse of the Golden Horde. Most were built in the 16th and 17th centuries by the Moscow princes, the Church and a new class of rich merchants.

However, the buildings that give the region a key place in the story of Russian architecture were constructed before the Mongols came. Most important are three 12th-century buildings in and near Vladimir: the cathedrals of the Assumption and St Dmitry, and the Church of the Intercession on the Nerl. These are the vital link between the architecture of 11th-century Kyiv and that of 15th-century Moscow – early northern interpretations of Kyiv's Byzantine brick churches.

The Vladimir-Suzdal region also inherited Kyiv's Byzantine artistic traditions, though only a few fragments of 12th- and 13th-century frescoes survive in the Vladimir and Suzdal cathedrals and in the old church at Kidiksha. (Some icons also survive in Moscow and St Petersburg museums.) While still primarily Byzantine, these works employ bold colours and depict empathetic human expressions that herald later Russian developments.

This 'Vladimir-Suzdal school' came to an end with the Mongol-led invasions, and Novgorod was left to continue the development of Russian art. Art revived, prolifically, in the Golden Ring from the 15th century, but never regained its earlier pioneering role. The best examples are the realistic late-17th-century murals by Gury Nikitin of Kostroma and his followers, which adorn several Golden Ring churches.

birds and beasts with music. The Kyivian prince Vsevolod III, who had this church built as part of his palace, appears at the top left of the north wall, with a baby son on his knee and other sons kneeling on each side. Above the right-hand window of the south wall, Alexander the Great ascends into heaven, a symbol of princely might; on the west wall appear the labours of Hercules.

Across the small street, the **Vladimir Region Pre-Revolutionary History Museum** (ul Bolshaya Moskovskaya 64; admission RR30; open 10am-4pm Tues-Sun) displays many remains and reproductions of the ornamentation from the cathedrals of the Assumption and St Dmitry.

Golden Gate

Vladimir's Golden Gate (Zolotye Vorota), part defensive tower, part triumphal arch, modelled on the very similar structure in Kyiv, was built by Andrey Bogolyubsky to guard the main, western entrance to his city. Restored under Catherine the Great, the Golden Gate now houses a **military museum** (☎ 322 559; admission RR30; open 10am-4pm Wed-Mon), which includes a diorama of old Vladimir being ravaged by nomadic raiders.

Across the street to the south you can see a remnant of the old wall which protected the city.

Located near the Golden Gate, in the red-brick former Old Believers' Trinity Church (1913–16), is a **Crystal, Lacquer Miniatures & Embroidery Exhibition** (☎ 324 872; ul Moskovskaya 2; admission RR20; open 10am-4pm Wed-Mon) featuring the crafts of Gus-Khrustalny and other nearby towns.

Other Attractions

Along ulitsa Bolshaya Moskovskaya, the late 18th-century **Trading Arcades** (Torgovye ryady) continue to serve their original purpose, housing shops and cafés.

Down a narrow winding street dotted with lampposts, **St George Church** (Georgievskaya tserkov; ul Georgievskaya 2A) houses the Vladimir Theatre of Choral Music. Performances are usually held on Saturday and Sunday from September to May. The entrance is at the back of the street.

Just south of here in an old water tower on Kozlov val (part of the old ramparts), the **Old Vladimir Exhibition** (admission RR20; open 10am-4pm Tues-Sun) is interesting for its site, as well as old photographs it houses. The **Princess' Convent** (Knyagnin monastyr), off ulitsa Nekrasova, was founded by Vsevolod III's wife, Maria. It is now a convent again after spending some decades as a museum of orthodoxy and atheism. The only substantial surviving building is its 16th-century **Assumption Cathedral** (Uspensky sobor), with many well-preserved 1640s frescoes.

Places to Stay

Hotel Vladimir (☎ 323 042, fax 327 201; e tour@gtk.elcom.ru; ul Bolshaya Moskovskaya 74; singles/doubles with shared bathroom RR150/290, with private bathroom from RR700) is the most pleasant and conveniently located place to stay. Renovations are ongoing, so rooms vary widely.

Hotel Zarya (☎ 225 264, fax 225 281; Studenaya gora 36; singles/doubles from RR200/300), about 1km west of the cathedrals, is pretty run-down.

Places to Eat

Bar-Restoran Stary Gorod (☎ 325 101; ul Bolshaya Moskovskaya 41; mains RR100-200; open 11am-2am daily) is a good, inexpensive place opposite the Cathedral of St Dmitry.

Next door, **Sobornaya Ploshchad** (☎ 325 725; ul Bolshaya Moskovskaya 39; mains RR50; open 11am-midnight daily) is a more bar-like version of the same thing.

The town's best restaurant (at least where all tour groups seem to be taken) is **Zolotye Vorota** (☎ 323 116; ul Bolshaya Moskovskaya 15; meal RR250).

Shopping

Khudozhestvenny Salon (☎ 322 211; ul Bolshaya Moskovskaya 26; open 10am-7pm Mon-Fri, 10am-5pm Sat) sells antiques such as old photographs, Russian medals and Roi de Paris wall clocks at a fraction of Moscow prices. **Sapphire** (ul Gagarina 2; open 10am-7pm Mon-Sat, 10am-4pm Sun) is where you can find some high-quality silver jewellery made to old Russian designs.

EXCURSIONS

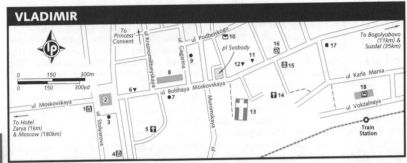

VLADIMIR

PLACES TO STAY & EAT
6   Starye Vorota
     Старые Ворота
11   Bar-Restoran Stary Gorod
     Бар-Ресторан Старый
     Город
12   Sobornaya Ploshchad
     Соборная Площадь
17   Hotel Vladimir
     Гостиница Владимир

OTHER
1   Crystal, Lacquer Miniatures &
    Embroidery Exhibition
    Выставка хрусталя
    лаковой миниатюры и
    вышивки

2   Golden Gate
    Золотые ворота
3   Old city wall
    Старая стена города
4   Old Vladimir Exhibition
    Выставка Старый
    Владимир
5   St George Church
    Георгиевская Церковь
7   Khudozhestvenny Salon
    Художественный Салон
8   Trading Arcades
    Торговые ряды
9   Sapphire
    Магазин Сапфир

10   Post & Telephone Office
     Почтамт и переговорный
     пункт
13   Assumption Cathedral
     Успенский собор
14   Cathedral of St Dmitry's
     Дмитриевский собор
15   Vladimir Region Pre-
     Revolutionary History
     Museum
     Музей истории доре
     волюционного прошлого
     Владимирского края
16   Internet Café
     Интернет-салон
18   Bus Station
     Автовокзал

Getting There & Away

From Moscow's Kursk Station, there is one afternoon express train (RR130/115 1st/2nd class, 2½ hours) and many slow suburban trains to Vladimir every day. Privately run buses also leave regularly from Kursk and Kazan stations to Vladimir (RR50, three hours). They do not run on a timetable, but leave as they fill up.

There are also buses to/from Moscow's Shchyolkovsky station, as well as Kostroma (RR120, five hours), Ivanovo (RR60, three hours) and Suzdal (RR10, one hour).

Getting Around

Trolleybus No 5 from the train and bus stations runs up to and along ulitsa Bolshaya Moskovskaya, passing Hotel Vladimir, the two main cathedrals and the town centre,

Hotel Zarya, and out to the western edge of town. Trolleybus No 1 runs from end to end of town along the same street.

BOGOLYUBOVO
БОГОЛЮБОВО
☎ 0922 • pop 3900

When Andrey Bogolyubsky was returning north from Kyiv in the late 1150s, his horses – so the story goes – stopped where Bogolyubovo now stands, 11km east of Vladimir, and wouldn't go another step. This is supposedly why Andrey made his capital in nearby Vladimir, rather than at his father's old base of Suzdal.

Whatever the legend, Andrey built a stone fortified palace that dates from 1158–65 at this strategic spot near the meeting of the Nerl and Klyazma Rivers. Nearby, in 1165, he built possibly the most perfect of all old Russian buildings, the Church of the Intercession on the Nerl.

Palace & Monastery

A tower and arch from Andrey Bogolyubsky's palace survive, amid a dilapidated but reopened 18th-century monastery, by the Vladimir–Nizhny Novgorod road in the middle of Bogolyubovo. The dominant buildings today are the monastery's 1841 **bell tower** beside the road, and its 1866 **Assumption Cathedral**. East of the cathedral, there is an arch and tower, on whose stairs – according to a chronicle – Andrey was assassinated by hostile *boyars* (nobles). The arch abuts the 18th-century **Church of the Virgin's Nativity**.

Church of the Intercession on the Nerl

To reach this famous little church (Tserkov Pokrova na Nerli), go back about 200m towards Vladimir from the monastery-palace complex and then turn into ulitsa Frunze, which winds downhill and under a railway bridge. Under the bridge, take the path to the left along the side of a small wood. The church appears across the meadows, about 1.25km from the bridge.

Its beauty lies in its simple but perfect proportions, a brilliantly chosen waterside site and sparing use of delicate carving. If it looks a mite top-heavy, it's because the original helmet dome was replaced by a cushion dome in 1803.

Legend has it that Andrey had the church built in memory of his favourite son, Izyaslav, who was killed in battle against the Bulgars. As with the Cathedral of St Dmitry in Vladimir, King David sits at the top of three facades, the birds and beasts entranced by his music. The interior has more carving, including 20 pairs of lions. If the church is closed, try asking at the house behind it.

Getting There & Away

Take trolleybus No 1 east from Vladimir and get off at Khimzavod. Go along the main road for 100m to the taxi van stop. Taxi vans operate between 7am and 10pm.

You need to get off at the second stop. Drivers from central Vladimir should head straight out east along the main road. From Suzdal, turn left when you hit Vladimir's northern bypass and go 5km.

GUS-KHRUSTALNY & MESHCHYORA NATIONAL PARK
Гус-Хрустальный и Мещёра Парк
☎ 09241 • postcode 601550 • pop 72,600

The town of Gus-Khrustalny, 180km east of Moscow and 90km south of Vladimir, is not technically a part of the Golden Ring, but it does feature a few interesting sights, including the nearby Meshchyora National Park.

Since the glass production factory was founded here in 1756, Gus-Khrustalny has been known for its high quality and widely varied glassware. If you are passing through, you might stop at the **Museum of Artistic Glass** for an overview of the crystal production and its role in the town's development.

More importantly, the town is a base from which to visit **Meshchyora National Park** (☎ 586 17), a protected area which includes over 60 lakes and rivers teeming with pike, perch and beavers. The park attracts boaters, fishers and campers, and is especially ideal for travellers who might not be carrying equipment with them. Camping equipment is available for rental, as are bicycles, rafts and motorboats. Anglers should visit Lake Beloe, the deepest of the park's lakes. The exquisite Lake Martynovo is a wide, shallow lake, often covered by lilies and other water flora.

Several buses every day go from Vladimir or from Moscow's Shchyolkovskaya Station (five hours) to Gus-Khrustalny. To get to the park, take a local bus to the village of Urshelsky.

MUROM
МУРОМ
☎ 09234 • postcode 602200 • pop 140,800

A contender for membership in the Golden Ring is lovely Murom, 137km southeast of Vladimir on the banks of the River Oka. Murom is not one of the regular stops on the Golden Ring tour, but it is an enjoyable destination if you wish to get off the beaten track.

EXCURSIONS

Founded in 862, the town's name derives from the Finno-Ugric tribe Muroma which inhabited this area. The **Murom Historical and Art Museum** (☎ *331 52;* w *www.museum.murom.ru; open 10am-5pm daily*) has an excellent exhibit on the history of this people and the archaeological findings from the area.

Locals boast that Murom is among the prettiest towns in Russia; indeed, writer Maxim Gorkii apparently agreed when he wrote, 'Whoever has not seen Murom from the Oka, has not seen Russian beauty.' The town is littered with 16th-, 17th- and 18th-century churches and monasteries, lending this peaceful place a romantic, nostalgic air. Among the oldest and best examples is the elegant **Spasso-Preobrazhensky Cathedral**, built in 1552 with financing from Ivan the Terrible's victory in Kazan. The Spassky Monastery, where it is located, is first documented in 1096, when one of Vladimir Monomakh's sons was killed in a siege there.

Several buses a day go to Murom from Vladimir (three hours), or catch a train from Moscow's Kursk station (five hours).

SUZDAL
СУЗДАЛЬ
☎ 09231 • postcode 601260 • pop 12,000
You have to pinch yourself in Suzdal, 35km north of Vladimir, to be reminded that you've not slipped back in time to ancient Russia. Such is the enchantment spun by this architecturally protected town with its profusion of old monasteries, convents and churches and intricately decorated *izbas* (wooden cottages) dotted in green fields around the meandering Kamenka River.

History
First mentioned in 1024, Suzdal was made capital of the Rostov-Suzdal principality by Yury Dolgoruky in the 12th century. When Andrey Bogolyubsky returned from Kyiv in 1157, he made Vladimir the capital, and from then on the principality was known as Vladimir-Suzdal. Set in a fertile wheat-growing area, Suzdal remained a trade centre even after the Mongol-led invasions. Eventually, it united with Nizhny Novgorod until both were annexed by Moscow in 1392.

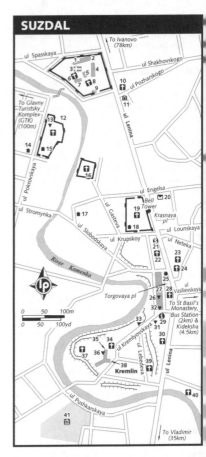

Under Muscovite rule, Suzdal became a wealthy monastic centre, with incredible development projects funded by Vasily III and Ivan the Terrible in the 16th century. In the late 17th and 18th centuries, wealthy merchants paid for 30 charming little churches, which still adorn the town.

Orientation & Information
The main street, ulitsa Lenina, runs north–south through Suzdal. The bus station is 2km east along ulitsa Vasilevskaya.

The **tourist information office** (☎ *216 00; ul Kremlyovskaya 1; open 10am-6pm*

SUZDAL

PLACES TO STAY
14 Hotel Gostevoy dom
   Kuchkova
   Гостевой Дом Кучкова
15 Izba Cabins
   Избы
17 Likhoninsky Dom
   Лихонинский Дом
18 Hotel Rizopolozhenskaya
   Гостиница
   Ризоположенская

PLACES TO EAT
13 Restoran Trapeznaya
   Ресторан Трапезная
26 Emolya
   Эмоля
31 Restoran Pogrebok
   Ресторан Погребок
32 Restoran Gostiny Dvor
   Ресторан Гостиный двор
33 Slavyansky Bar
   Славянский бар
36 Restoran Trapeznaya
   Ресторан Трапезная

**SAVIOUR MONASTERY OF ST
EUTHYMIUS**
Спасо-Евфимиевский Монастыр
1 Monastery Prison
   Тюрьма
2 Hospital & St Nicholas'
   Church
   Больничные кельи и
   Никольская церковь
3 Cathedral of the
   Transfiguration of the Saviour
   Спасо-Преображенский
   собор

4 Monks' Quarters
   Братский корпус
5 Bell Tower
   Звонница
6 Assumption Church
   Успенская церковь
7 Father Superior's
   Chambers
   Камеры Отца-игумена
8 Annunciation Gate Church
   Благовещенская
   надвратная церковь
9 Southern Gate Tower
   Южные ворота

OTHER
10 Our Lady of Smolensk
   Church
   Смоленская церковь
11 18th Century Town House
   Жилой дом XVIII в.
12 Intercession Convent
   Покровский монастырь
16 Alexandrovsky Convent
   Александровский
   монастырь
19 Monastery of the Deposition
   of the Holy Robe
   Ризоположенский
   монастырь
20 Post & Telephone
   Office
   Почтамт и переговорный
   пункт
21 Sberbank
   Сбербанк
22 St Lazarus' Church
   Лазаревская церковь

23 Virgin of All Sorrows Church
   Скорбященская церковь
24 Emperor Constantine Church
   Царевоконстантиновская
   церковь
25 Produce Market
   Рынок
27 Trading Arcades
   Торговые ряды
28 Resurrection Church
   Воскресенская церковь
29 Tourist Information Office
   Туристическое бюро
30 Predtechenskaya Church
   Предтеченская церковь
34 Nativity of the Virgin
   Cathedral
   Рождественский собор
35 Archbishop's Chambers
   Архиерейские палаты
37 St Nicholas' Church
   (Wooden)
   Никольская церковь
   (деревянная)
38 Cathedral Bell Tower
   Соборная колокольня
39 St Nicholas' Church
   Никольская церковь
40 SS Kosma & Damian Church
   Церковь Косьмы и
   Дамиана
41 Museum of Wooden
   Architecture & Peasant Life
   Музей деревянного
   зодчества и крестьянск
   ого быта

EXCURSIONS

Wed-Sun) assists with hotel reservations, transportation and excursions – that is, if it's actually open during advertised hours.

Sberbank *(ul Lenina; open 8am-4.30pm Mon-Fri)* is across from the *apteka* (pharmacy). The nearby **post and telephone office** *(Krasnaya pl)* is open 24 hours for phone calls.

Kremlin

The 1.4km-long earth rampart of Suzdal's kremlin, founded in the 11th century, today encloses a few streets of houses and a handful of churches, as well as the main cathedral group on ulitsa Kremlyovskaya.

The **Nativity of the Virgin Cathedral** (Rozhdestvensky sobor), its blue domes spangled with gold, was founded in the 1220s, but only its richly carved lower section is original white stone, the rest being 16th-century brick. The inside is sumptuous with 13th- and 17th-century frescoes and 13th-century damascene (gold on copper) west and south doors. Unfortunately, the cathedral is under restoration and is closed indefinitely.

The **Archbishop's Chambers** (Arkhiyereyskie palati) lining the south side of the cathedral yard, house the **Suzdal History Exhibition** (☎ 204 44; admission RR30; open 10am-5pm Wed-Mon). The exhibition includes the original 13th-century door from the cathedral, photos of its interior and a visit to the 18th-century **Cross Hall** (Krestovaya palata), which was used for receptions. The tent-roofed 1635 bell tower on the east side of the yard contains additional exhibits.

Just west of this group stands the 1766 wooden **St Nicholas' Church** (Nikolskaya tserkov), brought from Glatovo village near Yuriev-Polsky. Another **St Nicholas' Church** *(ul Lebedeva)*, one of Suzdal's own fine small churches, built in 1720–39, is just east of the cathedral group, with its pointed tower fronting the road.

Torgovaya Ploshchad

Suzdal's Torgovaya ploshchad (Trade Square) is dominated by the pillared **Trading Arcades** (1806–11) along its western side. Although the four churches in the immediate vicinity are closed, the five-domed 1707 **Emperor Constantine Church** (Tsarevokonstantinovskaya tserkov), over in the square's northeastern corner, is a working church with an ornate interior. Next to it is the smaller 1787 **Virgin of All Sorrows Church** (Skorbyashchenskaya tserkov).

Monastery of the Deposition of the Holy Robe

The Monastery of the Deposition of the Holy Robe (Rizopolozhensky monastyr) was founded in 1207, but the existing buildings date from the 16th to the 19th century. The monastery is now pretty dilapidated. Still, its two pyramidal entrance turrets (1688) on the south gate are exquisite. Suzdal's tallest structure, a 72m **bell tower** (1813–19), rises from the east wall. The central 16th-century **Deposition Cathedral** (Rizopolozhensky sobor) is reminiscent of the Moscow Kremlin's Archangel Cathedral, with its three helmet domes.

Alexandrovsky Convent

This little, white convent (Alexandrovsky monastyr) at the top of the river embankment stands out for its simple, quiet beauty. Reputedly founded in 1240 by Alexander Nevsky for noblewomen whose menfolk had been killed by nomadic raiders, its present **Ascension Church** (Voznesenskaya tserkov) and bell tower date from 1695.

Saviour Monastery of St Euthymius

Founded in the 14th century to protect the town's northern entrance, Suzdal's biggest monastery *(Spaso-Yevfimievsky monastyr; admission RR150, photos RR50; open 10am-6pm Tues-Sun)* grew mighty in the 16th and 17th centuries after Vasily III, Ivan the Terrible and the noble Pozharsky family funded impressive new stone buildings and big land and property acquisitions. It was girded with its great brick walls and towers during the 17th century. Enter through the **Southern Gate Tower**.

Inside, the **Annunciation Gate Church** (Blagoveshchenskaya Nadvratnaya tserkov) houses an very interesting exhibit on Dmitry Pozharsky (1578–1642), leader of the Russian army that drove the Polish invaders from Moscow in 1612.

A tall 16th- to 17th-century **bell tower** stands before the seven-domed **Cathedral of the Transfiguration of the Saviour** (Spaso-Preobrazhensky sobor). Every hour on the hour during opening times, a short concert of chimes is given on the bell tower's bells. The cathedral was built in the 1590s in 12th- to 13th-century Vladimir-Suzdal style. Inside, restoration has uncovered some bright 1689 frescoes by the school of Gury Nikitin from Kostroma. A choir of monks often performs here; the short but heavenly a cappella concerts take place once a day in summer. The **tomb** of Prince Dmitry Pozharsky is by the cathedral's east wall.

The 1525 **Assumption Church** (Uspenskaya tserkov) facing the bell tower adjoins the old **Father Superior's Chambers**, which houses a display of Russian icons. The **monks' quarters** across the compound contain a museum of artistic history.

At the north end of the complex is the old **monastery prison**, set up in 1764 for religious dissidents. It now houses a fascinating exhibit on the monastery's military history and prison life, including displays for some of the better-known prisoners who stayed here. The combined **hospital and St Nicholas' Church** (Bolnichnye kelyi i Nikolskaya tserkov, 1669) contains a rich museum of 12th- to 20th-century Russian applied art, much of it from Suzdal itself.

Across ulitsa Lenina from the southeast corner of the monastery are the 1696–1707 **Our Lady of Smolensk Church** (Smolenskaya tserkov) and Suzdal's only surviving early 18th-century **town house**.

Intercession Convent

The Intercession Convent (Pokrovsky monastyr), founded in 1364 and closed during Soviet times, is once again home to a small community of nuns. The three-domed **Intercession Cathedral** (Pokrovsky sobor) in the centre, built in 1510–18, holds regular services.

The convent was originally a place of exile for the unwanted wives of tsars, among them Solomonia Saburova, first wife of Vasily III, who was sent here in the 1520s because of her supposed infertility. The story goes that she finally became pregnant too late to avoid being divorced. A baby boy was born in Suzdal but, fearing he would be seen as a dangerous rival to any sons produced by Vasily's new wife, Yelena Glinska, Solomonia had him secretly adopted, pretended he had died and staged a mock burial. This was probably just as well for the boy, since Yelena did indeed produce a son – Ivan the Terrible.

The legend received dramatic corroboration in 1934 when researchers opened a small 16th-century tomb beside Solomonia's, in the crypt beneath the Intercession Cathedral. They found a silk and pearl shirt stuffed with rags – and no bones. The crypt is closed to visitors.

The **museum** of the convent's history was closed at the time of research.

Museum of Wooden Architecture & Peasant Life

This wooden 'model village' *(admission RR30; open 9.30am-3:30pm Wed-Mon)*, illustrating old peasant life in this region of Russia, is a short walk across the river south of the kremlin. Besides log houses, windmills, a barn and many tools and handicrafts, its highlights are the 1756 **Transfiguration Church** (Preobrazhenskaya tserkov) and the simpler 1776 **Resurrection Church** (Voskresenskaya tserkov). The building interiors are open only from May to October.

Other Suzdal Buildings

Almost every corner in Suzdal has its own little church with its own charm. Some other gems include the simple 1719 **Resurrection Church** *(Voskresenskaya tserkov; Torgovaya pl)*; the shabby but graceful 1720 **Predtechenskaya Church** *(Predtechenskaya tserkov; ul Lenina)*; and the slender multi-coloured tower of the 1667 **St Lazarus' Church** *(Lazarevskaya tserkov; Staraya ul)*. The 1725 **SS Kosma and Damian Church** (Kosmodamianovskaya tserkov) is picturesquely placed on a bend in the river. Suzdal's fifth monastery is the 17th-century **St Basil's** (Vasilevsky monastyr) on the Kideksha road. No doubt you will find your own favourite.

Kideksha

The 1152 **Church of SS Boris and Gleb** (Borisoglebskaya tserkov) situated on the Nerl River, in this quiet village 4km east of Suzdal, is the oldest in the district, built for Yury Dolgoruky, who had a small wooden palace (which has disappeared) here.

The church, rebuilt many times, has lost its original vault, roof and dome, and gained a 19th-century porch. But the church's old floor, a metre below the modern one, gives a sense of the place's age; drawings in the porch give an idea of what it may once have looked like.

A few fragments of 12th-century frescoes remain, including two figures on horseback, probably Vladimir's sons Boris and Gleb, who were killed by another son, Svyatopolk, and became the first Russian saints. The other buildings in the compound are 18th century.

Places to Stay

Hotel Rizopolozhenskaya *(☎ 205 53; ul Lenina; singles/doubles from RR250/300)* is housed in the decrepit Monastery of the Deposition. Many of the cheaper rooms at this hotel are pretty crummy; get them to show you the *luks* ones for RR600.

EXCURSIONS

Likhoninsky Dom (☎ 219 01, fax 0922-327 010; ul Slobodskaya 34; doubles RR630), the nicest place to stay, is on a quiet street near the town centre. The renovated 17th-century house has only four rooms, with a pretty garden outside. The building is unmarked except for the number 34.

If you're on a tour, it's likely you'll end up at the charmless **Glavny Turistsky Komplex** (GTK; ☎ 209 08, fax 207 66; singles/doubles with breakfast RR450/600). Contact GTK if you want to book one of the quaint izba cabins within the grounds of the **Intercession Convent**, which cost RR1360 for two people.

Hotel Gostevoy dom Kuchkova (☎ 215 07, fax 202 52; ul Pokrovskaya 35; doubles with breakfast RR1700), situated on a quiet street not far from the Pokrovsky Convent, provides eight comfortable (but overpriced) doubles.

Places to Eat

Restoran Trapeznaya (meal RR300; open 9am-10pm daily), in the Intercession Convent's Conception of St Anna Refectory Church, serves good Russian food. Ask for warming, mildly alcoholic medovukha (mead) to wash it all down. Hours are observed somewhat erratically.

Another **Restoran Trapeznaya** (☎ 217 63; mains RR100-200; open 11am-11pm daily) is in the Archbishop's Chambers in the kremlin. The food is similar, but the atmosphere more lively.

The inexpensive **Slavyansky Bar** (☎ 200 62; ul Kremlyovskaya 6; dishes about RR30; open noon-7pm Wed-Mon) serves snacks, sandwiches and salads.

Restoran Pogrebok (☎ 217 32; ul Kremlyovskaya 5; open 11am-8pm Wed-Sun) has a wider selection on the menu and slightly higher prices. The **Restoran Gostiny Dvor** (☎ 217 78; open 11am-midnight daily), at the southern end of the Trading Arcades, has a bar downstairs and restaurant upstairs.

The town's best view is from the outside tables at **Emolya** (☎ 210 11; ul Lenina 84; meal RR150; open 11am-midnight daily) at the western side of the Trading Arcades. Pop in at sunset and stay till dark for the great vistas.

There's a **produce market** at the eastern side of the Trading Arcades.

Getting There & Away

Buses run hourly to/from Vladimir (RR10, one hour). Otherwise, most of the buses originate elsewhere. Buses from Vladimir go to Ivanovo (RR60, two hours, four daily), to Yaroslavl (RR150, five hours, twice daily) and to Kostroma (RR120, 4½ hours, daily). There is one daily bus direct from Moscow's Shchyolkovsky Bus Station (RR80, 4½ hours).

Getting Around

Some buses from Vladimir continue past the bus station into the centre of Suzdal. Ask the driver to let you off at the Trading Arcades.

YURIEV-POLSKY
ЮРЬЕВ-ПОЛСКИЙ
☎ 09246 • postcode 601800 • pop 22,000

Founded by Yuri Dolgoruky in 1152, Yuriev-Polsky sits on the Kaluksha River about halfway between Vladimir and Pereslavl-Zalessky. This tiny town is not easy to reach, but it boasts an ancient and ornate stone church and a village atmosphere that harkens back to earlier centuries.

Yuriev-Polsky is still surrounded by 12th-century ramparts, which provide a lovely view of the villagers' painted wooden houses and overflowing gardens. Within them, **St George's Church** was built in 1230 by Yuri Dolgoruky's grandson Svyatoslav Vsyevolodovich (who is buried in the small chapel between the north porch and the apse). The facade is completely covered in elaborate stone carvings: soldiers and saints, birds and beasts, Bible stories and battle scenes. St George is depicted above the north porch holding a shield that displays a snow leopard, the emblem of the Vladimir-Suzdal dynasty. The Crucifixion on the same wall bears Svyatoslav's signature, although it is disputed if he himself actually carved the cross, or if it was carved to honour his victories over the Volga Bulgars. The church collapsed and was rebuilt in the 15th century, but the architect was unable to reconfigure the stones exactly as they had been. The result is some incongruous scenes in the carving.

The **Monastery of St Michael the Archangel** was also founded by Svyatoslav. The buildings date mainly from the 17th and 18th century and contain historical and natural exhibits about the area. Across the street are the 19th-century Trading Arcades.

Unless you are driving, Yuriev-Polsky is inconvenient; public transport is sporadic and the village has no accommodation facilities. Occasional buses run from Pereslavl-Zalessky (two hours) and Vladimir (two hours). The easier option is probably to hire a taxi from near the bus station.

IVANOVO
ИВАНОВО

☎ 0932 • postcode 153000 • pop 550,000

Ivanovo, some 78km north of Suzdal on the Suzdal–Kostroma road, is known for two (connected) features: its cotton textiles and its women. The town's female population, swelled by the textile mills' labour needs, apparently once heavily outnumbered its male population and Ivanovo is still known as the 'town of brides'.

Ivanovo is a drab and dreary industrial town. However, if you have to change buses here you can easily entertain yourself for an afternoon. Head to the **Art Museum** (☎ 301 641; ul Lenina 33; admission RR3; open 11am-5pm Wed-Mon), which has a decent collection of Russian works, or to the **Ivanovo Chintz Museum** (☎ 300 630; ul Baturina 11/42), which illustrates the development of the textile industry to present times. The latter is housed in an Art Nouveau mansion.

Palekh
Палех

Ivanovo is occasionally used as a base for visiting Palekh, the small village famous for icon painters and small lacquer boxes, 65km southeast on the Nizhny Novgorod road. Palekh has a **museum** (open Tues-Sun) of local icons and boxes, with – yes – a gift shop. There are also some fine, restored, 14th- to 19th-century icons in the **Raising of the Cross Church** (Krestovo-Sdvizhenskaya tserkov).

There are frequent buses from Ivanovo and one daily from Vladimir, via Suzdal.

Places to Stay

If you must spend the night in Ivanovo, **Hotel Tourist** (☎ 376 436, Naberezhnaya 9; singles/doubles 450/700) will put you up. Rooms have bathroom, TV and fridge. The hotel has an acceptable restaurant.

Getting There & Away

In Ivanovo, the train station is at the north end of ulitsa Engelsa. Trains to Ivanovo run from Moscow's Yaroslavl Station (RR100, eight hours). The bus station is several kilometres away in the south of town. Buses run frequently to/from Moscow's Shchyolkovsky Bus Station (RR180, 6½ hours), Suzdal (RR60, two hours), Vladimir (RR100, three hours) and Kostroma (RR60, two hours). There are a few buses a day to Yaroslavl (RR70, two hours).

PLYOS
ПЛЁС

☎ 09339 • pop 155555 • pop 40,000

Plyos is a tranquil town of wooden houses and hilly streets winding down to the Volga waterfront, halfway between Ivanovo and Kostroma. Though fortified from the 15th century and later a Volga trade centre, Pylos' renown now stems from its late 19th-century role as an artists' retreat. Isaak Levitan, possibly the greatest Russian landscape artist, found inspiration here in the summers of 1888–90. The playwright Chekhov commented that Plyos 'put a smile in Levitan's paintings'.

Walk along the riverfront and explore the oldest part of town, as evidenced by the ramparts of the old fort, which date from 1410. The hill is topped by the simple 1699 **Assumption Cathedral** (Uspensky sobor), one of Levitan's favourite painting subjects.

The **Levitan House Museum** (Dom-Muzey Levitana; ☎ 437 82; ul Sovietskaya 11; admission RR20; open 10am-5pm Tues-Sun), in the eastern part of the town, across the small Shokhonka River, displays works of Levitan and other artists against the background of the Volga.

You can get here by bus from Ivanovo or Kostroma, or – best – in summer by hydrofoil from Kostroma or Yaroslavl (see those cities' Getting There & Away sections).

KOSTROMA
КОСТРОМА
☎ 0942 • postcode 156000 • pop 300,000

Kostroma, situated on the Volga River some 95km north of Ivanovo, was founded in the 1150s and was once one of the Golden Ring's most important cultural and commercial centres.

Little remains from these ancient roots, however, as a fire in 1773 destroyed everything wooden, and the centre was rebuilt in Russian classical style.

The town's pride and joy is clearly the Monastery of St Ipaty (Ipatevsky monastyr), which was founded in 1332 by a Tatar ancestor of Boris Godunov before later being patronised – like Kostroma in general – by the Romanov dynasty.

Orientation
The main part of the town lies along the north bank of the Volga, with the bus and train stations, about 4km east of the centre. The Monastery of St Ipaty is west of the centre across the Kostroma River, a Volga tributary. The central square is ploshchad Susaninskaya.

Information
The **post and telephone office** (cnr uls Sovietskaya & Podipeva; open 9am-9pm daily) is east of ploshchad Susaninskaya. As part of the same complex, there are **internet facilities** (☎ 621 020; open 9am-9pm daily).

Monastery of St Ipaty
Legend has it that a Tatar prince named Chet (who later founded the house of Godunovs) was returning to Moscow in 1330 and fell ill. At this time he had a vision of the Virgin Mary and the martyr Ipaty of the Ganges, who aided his recovery. When he

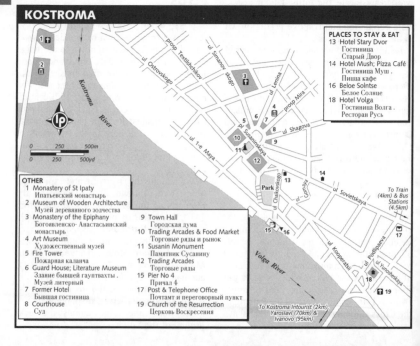

KOSTROMA

PLACES TO STAY & EAT
13 Hotel Stary Dvor
    Гостиница
    Старый Двор
14 Hotel Mush; Pizza Café
    Гостиница Муш .
    Пицца кафе
16 Beloe Solntse
    Белое Солнце
18 Hotel Volga
    Гостиница Волга
    Ресторан Русь

OTHER
1 Monastery of St Ipaty
   Ипатьевский монастырь
2 Museum of Wooden Architecture
   Музей деревянного зодчества
3 Monastery of the Epiphany
   Богоявленско· Анастасьинский
   монастырь
4 Art Museum
   Художественный музей
5 Fire Tower
   Пожарная каланча
6 Guard House; Literature Museum
   Здание бывшей гауптвахты .
   Музей литерный
7 Former Hotel
   Бывшая гостиница
8 Courthouse
   Суд
9 Town Hall
   Городская дума
10 Trading Arcades & Food Market
    Торговые ряды и рынок
11 Susanin Monument
    Памятник Сусанину
12 Trading Arcades
    Торговые ряды
15 Pier No 4
    Причал 4
17 Post & Telephone Office
    Почтамт и переговорный пункт
19 Church of the Resurrection
    Церковь Воскресения

To Train (4km) & Bus Stations (4.5km)

To Kostroma Intourist (2km), Yaroslavl (70km) & Ivanovo (95km)

EXCURSIONS

returned to Moscow he was baptised and founded the Monastery of St Ipaty to mark the occasion.

The monastery's more recent history is closely tied to the Godunov and Romanov families, fierce rivals in high-level power games before the Romanovs established their 300-year dynasty in the 17th century. In 1590, the Godunovs built the monastery's **Trinity Cathedral** (Troitsky sobor), which contains over 80 old frescoes by a school of 17th-century Kostroma painters, headed by Gury Nikitin (plus some 20th-century additions). The fresco in the southern part of the sanctuary depicts Chet Godunov's baptism by St Ipaty.

The **bell tower**, modelled after the Ivan the Great Bell Tower in Moscow, chimes concerts every hour.

In 1600, Boris Godunov, the only member of his family to become tsar, exiled Fyodor, the head of the Romanov family, to this monastery, along with his son Mikhail. Mikhail Romanov was in Kostroma when he was elected tsar in 1613, at the end of the Time of Troubles. In honour of the event, all his Romanov successors made a point of coming here to visit the monastery's red **Romanov Chambers** (Palaty Romanova), opposite the cathedral.

The monastery (☎ 312 589; admission RR30; open 9am-5pm daily May-Oct, 10am-5pm Sat-Thur Nov-Apr) is 2.5km west of the town centre. Take bus No 14 from the central ploshchad Susaninskaya and get off once you cross the river; you'll see the monastery to your right.

Museum of Wooden Architecture

Behind the monastery is an attractive outdoor museum (☎ 577 872; admission RR10, photos RR20; open 9am-5pm daily May-Oct) of northern-style wooden buildings, including peasant houses and churches (one built without nails). Most of the buildings are not open, but the grounds are pleasant for strolling, listening to the croaks of frogs and admiring the handiwork of the artists. This is a case of the museum being nearly indistinguishable from the village. The surrounding neighbourhood also consists of storybook-like houses, blossoming gardens and picturesque churches, which include a **domed wooden church** directly north of the monastery.

Town Centre

Ploshchad Susaninskaya was built as an ensemble under Catherine the Great's patronage after the 1773 fire. Clockwise around the northern side are: a 19th-century **fire tower** (still in use, and under Unesco protection) with a little museum on fire-fighting; a former military **guard house**, housing a small literature museum; an 18th-century **former hotel** for members of the royal family; the **palace** of an 1812 war hero (now a courthouse); and the **town hall**.

In the streets between there are many merchants' **town houses**. The Art Museum (☎ 514 390; pr Mira 5 & 7; admission RR30 each; open 10am-6pm Tues-Sun) includes two elaborate neo-Russian buildings. No 5 houses a portrait gallery, as well as appropriately decorated 19th-century rooms such as the White Hall (Beliy Zal). No 7, built in 1913 to celebrate 300 years of Romanov rule, contains a collection of mainly 16th- to 19th-century Russian art.

The old **Trading Arcades** on the southern side of ploshchad Susaninskaya now house a bustling **food market**. Sections of the trading rows are named for the products which were traditionally sold here (ie, Vegetable, Butter, Gingerbread). Note the road Molochny Gora (Milk Hill) which leads from the arcades down to the Volga.

The **monument** in the park between the arcades is to local hero Ivan Susanin, who guided a Polish detachment hunting for Mikhail Romanov to their deaths – and his own – in a swamp.

Churches

The **Monastery of the Epiphany** (Bogoyavlensko-Anastasinsky monastyr; ul Simanovskogo 26) is now the residence of the Archbishop of Kostroma. The large **cathedral** in this 14th- to 19th-century complex is the city's main working church. The 13th-century icon of *Our Lady of St Theodore*, on the right-hand side of the iconostasis, is supposedly the source of many miracles.

The 17th-century **Church of the Resurrection** *(Tserkov Voskresenia; ul Nizhnaya Debrya 37)* near Hotel Volga, with bright patterned exterior decoration, was partly financed with a load of gold coins mistakenly shipped from London.

Places to Stay

Hotel Stary Dvor *(☎ 316 039; ul Sovietskaya 6; rooms without/with bathroom RR150/500)* is centrally located, but otherwise rather sketchy.

Hotel Volga *(☎ 546 062, fax 546 262; ul Yunosheskaya 1; singles/doubles with breakfast RR500/700)* is 2km east of the centre just off ulitsa Podlipaeva, near the Volga bridge. The rooms are reasonably clean; some have Volga views. The restaurant is adequate.

Hotel Mush *(☎ 312 400, fax 311 045; ⓦ www.mush.com.ru; ul Sovietskaya 29; singles/doubles US$50/60)* is the best hotel in town, considering its central location and welcoming atmosphere. There is a pleasant and inexpensive pizza café downstairs.

Kostroma Intourist *(☎ 533 661, fax 532 301; ul Magistralnaya 40; singles/doubles US$49/69)* is a modern, Western-style hotel with two good restaurants. Its location, about 2km south of the Volga bridge on the road to Yaroslavl and Ivanovo, is inconvenient unless you are driving. From ulitsa Podlipaeva, in front of Hotel Volga, take bus No 10.

Buses approaching Kostroma from Yaroslavl or Ivanovo pass the Volga and the Kostroma Intourist, and the drivers may be willing to drop you off, saving you a trek back into town from the bus station.

Places to Eat

Besides the **hotel restaurants** mentioned above, food options in Kostroma are pretty limited. Of these, **Restaurant Rus** *(☎ 546 262; ul Yunosheskaya 1; meal RR250; open noon-11pm daily)* in the Hotel Volga comes highly recommended for Russian food.

Near Pier No 4, **Beloe Solntse** *(☎ 579 057; ul Lesnaya 2; cover charge RR30, mains RR300; open noon-midnight daily)* is overpriced, but the food is spicy and the decor colourful. There is live music and dancing most nights.

Getting There & Away

Train The train station is 4km east of ploshchad Susaninskaya. There are three or four daily suburban trains to/from Yaroslavl (RR200, three hours), an overnight train to/from Moscow's Yaroslavsky Station (RR680, 8½ hours) and a daily train to/from Khabarovsk in the Russian Far East.

Bus The bus station *(Kineshemskoe sh)* is 4.5km east of ploshchad Susaninskaya on the continuation of ulitsa Sovietskaya. There are buses to/from Moscow (8½ hours, six daily), Yaroslavl (two hours, eight daily), Ivanovo (two hours, eight daily), Vladimir (5½ hours, daily) via Suzdal (4½ hours) and Vologda (seven hours, daily).

Boat The best way to get between Kostroma and Yaroslavl in summer is by hydrofoil, which runs twice a day in either direction. The hydrofoils depart from the main Pier *(prichal)* No 4 to Yaroslavl (1½ hours) and downstream to Plyos (one hour). Timetables are posted at the pier. Long-distance river boats between Moscow and points down the Volga as far as Astrakhan also call at Kostroma.

Getting Around

Bus Nos 1, 2, 9, 9 Expres, 14K, 19 and others run between the bus station and the central ploshchad Susaninskaya, along the full length of ulitsa Sovietskaya. Trolleybus No 2 runs between the train station and ploshchad Susaninskaya.

YAROSLAVL
ЯРОСЛАВЛЬ

☎ 0852 • postcode 150000 • pop 680,000

Yaroslavl, 250km northeast of Moscow, is the urban counterpart to Suzdal. This is the biggest place between Moscow and Arkhangelsk, and it has a more urban feel than anywhere else in the Golden Ring. Its big-city skyline, however, is dotted with onion domes and towering spires, not smoke stacks and skyscrapers. As a result of a trade boom in the 17th-century, churches are hidden around every corner. The poet Grigoriev wrote, 'Yaroslavl is a town of unsurpassed beauty; Everywhere is the Volga and everywhere is history.' And everywhere, everywhere, there are churches.

History

In 1010, the Kyivan prince Yaroslav the Wise took an interest in a trading post called Medvezhy Ugol (Bear Corner). According to legend, Yaroslav subjugated and converted the locals by killing their sacred bear with his axe. So the town was founded, and its coat of arms bears (no pun intended) both the beast and the weapon.

Yaroslavl was the centre of an independent principality by the time the Tatars came. Developed in the 16th and 17th centuries as the Volga's first port, it grew into Russia's second-biggest city of the time, fat on trade with the Middle East and Europe. Rich merchants competed to build churches bigger than Moscow's, with elaborate decoration and bright frescoes on contemporary themes. Though the city's centrepiece is the Monastery of the Transfiguration of the Saviour, the merchant churches are what makes the city unique.

Orientation

Yaroslavl centre lies at the crux of the Volga and Kotorosl Rivers, inside the ring road, Pervomayskaya ulitsa. The centre of the ring is Sovietskaya ploshchad, from which streets radiate out to three squares: Bogoyavlenskaya ploshchad with the landmark monastery; ploshchad Volkova with the classical facade of the Volkov Theatre; and Krasnaya ploshchad near the river station.

Information

You can change money or use the ATM at **Alfa-Bank** (☎ 739 177; ul Svobody 3; open 9am-6pm Mon-Thurs, 9am-4.30pm Fri). **Sberbank** (☎ 729 518; ul Kirova 6; open 8.30am-4pm Mon-Sat) changes money and gives credit-card advances.

The **main post and telephone office** (Komsomolskaya ul 22; open 8am-8pm Mon-Sat, until 6pm Sun) also offers Internet services.

The **Internet Club** (☎ 726 850; pr Lenina 24; open 9am-11pm daily) in the Dom Kultury (House of Culture) has more facilities.

Dom Knigi (☎ 304 751; ul Kirova 18; open 10am-7pm Mon-Fri, 10am-6pm Sat) has a good selection of maps and books, as does **Rospechat** (ul Kirova 10) down the street.

Monastery of the Transfiguration of the Saviour & Around

Founded in the 12th century, the Monastery of the Transfiguration of the Saviour (Spaso-Preobrazhensky monastyr; ☎ 303 869; Bogoyavlenskaya pl 25; admission free, exhibits RR20 each; grounds open 8am-5pm, museums open 10am-5pm Tues-Sun) was one of Russia's richest and best-fortified monasteries by the 16th century.

The oldest surviving structures, dating from 1516 but heavily altered since then, are the **Holy Gate** (Svyatye vorota), near the main entrance, and the austere **Cathedral of the Transfiguration** (Preobrazhensky sobor), which is under restoration. The north section of the church used to house the monastery library.

To get a new perspective on things, climb the **bell tower** (zvonnitsa). The summit provides a panorama of the city and a close-up view of the spiky gold bulbs that top some of the monastery buildings.

Off Bogoyavlenskaya ploshchad is the vaulted, red-brick **Church of the Epiphany** (Tserkov Bogoyavlenia), which was under restoration at the time of research, but is usually open to the public. Built by a wealthy 17th-century merchant, its rich decoration includes bright exterior ceramic tiles (a Yaroslavl speciality), vibrant frescoes and a carved iconostasis.

A statue of Yaroslav the Wise stands in the centre of the square. Just past the 19th-century **Trading Arcades** (Torgovye ryady), is the **Znamenskaya Watchtower** (Znamenskaya bashnya; Pervomayskaya ul), built in 1658 on what was then the edge of the city.

Church of Elijah the Prophet

This lovely church (Tserkov Ilyi Proroka; Sovietskaya pl; admission RR25; open 10am-1pm & 2pm-6pm daily May-Sept) was built by

EXCURSIONS

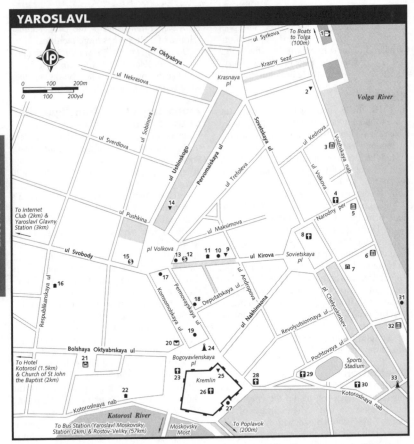

YAROSLAVL

prominent 17th-century fur dealers. It has some of the Golden Ring's brightest frescoes by the ubiquitous Gury Nikitin of Kostroma and his school, and detailed exterior tiles. The church is closed during wet spells.

River Embankments

The embankments of the Volga and Kotorosl Rivers, from the Church of Elijah the Prophet back to the Monastery of the Transfiguration of the Saviour, make an enjoyable 1.5km walk. A pedestrian promenade runs along the bank of the Volga below the level of the street, Volzhskaya naberezhnaya.

From the Church of Elijah the Prophet, head towards the river on Narodny pereulok. Here, the **Church of St Nicholas the Miracle-Worker** (Tserkov Nikoly Nadeina) was the first of Yaroslavl's stone merchant churches, built in 1622. It has a sparkling baroque iconostasis and frescoes showing the life and works of the popular St Nicholas. It's normally open as a museum.

The unique, private collection **Music & Time** (☎ 328 637; Volzhskaya nab 33A; admission RR25; open 10am-7pm Tues-Sun) is in the little house just north. John Mostoslavsky enthusiastically guides visitors through his

YAROSLAVL

EXCURSIONS

fascinating collection of clocks, musical instruments and other antiques.

South along the naberezhnaya is the old Governor's Mansion that now houses the **Yaroslavl Art Museum** (☎ 353 355; Volzhskaya nab 23; admission RR30; open 10am-5pm Tues-Sun), with 18th- to 20th-century Russian art.

On the next block, the **History of Yaroslavl Museum** (☎ 304 175; Volzhskaya nab 17; open 10am-6pm Wed-Mon) is in a lovely 19th-century merchant's house.

A new **monument** to victims of war and repression in the 20th century is in the peaceful garden. Some other surviving merchants' houses are around, such as the **Dom Matveev** (cnr Volzhskaya nab & Sovietsky per).

A little farther along the embankment are the **Volga Bastion** (Volzhskaya bashnya), built as a watchtower in the 1660s and a fine early 19th-century church.

The 17th-century former Metropolitan's Palace (Mitropolyichyi Palaty) houses the

old Yaroslavl art section of the **Art Museum** (☎ 729 287; admission RR30; open 10am-5pm Sat-Thur), with icons and other work from the 13th to 19th centuries.

In the leafy park behind the museum is a stone-slab **monument** marking the spot where Yaroslav founded the city in 1010. The park stretches right out onto the tip of land between the Volga and the Kotorosl Rivers. Above the Kotorosl, the raised embankments indicate the site of Yaroslavl's old kremlin.

The more time you spend, the more churches you will discover, most dating to the 17th century. Three more are along the naberezhnaya: Church of the Saviour-in-the-Town; Church of the Archangel Michael; and Church of Nikol Rubleny. Several more are south of the Kotorosl in the settlements of Korovniki and Tolchkovo. For more information, pick up the brochure *Yaroslavl* (available in several languages) at one of the museum gift shops.

EXCURSIONS

River Trips

Summer services from the river station on the Volga at the north end of Pervomayskaya ulitsa include a range of slow *prigorodnye* (suburban) boats to local destinations. The best trip is to **Tolga**, one hour from Yaroslavl on the Konstantinovo route, which has a convent with some delightful 17th-century buildings near the river.

Places to Stay

Hotel Kotorosl (☎ 212 415, fax 216 468; e kotorosl@yaroslavl.ru; Bolshaya Oktyabrskaya ul 87; singles/doubles RR550/800) is the best-value place to stay, within walking distance of the train station, and offering modern rooms and decent facilities.

Hotel Yuta (☎ 218 793, fax 329 786; Respublikanskaya ul 79; singles/doubles RR600/900) has decent rooms, but they charge a 50% reservation fee the first night (even if you did not make a reservation). The bar with tinted mirrors is too dark to see your food, let alone somebody you might be dining with.

Hotel Volga (☎ 731 111, fax 728 276; ul Kirova 10; doubles without/with bathroom RR600/1000) is located at the very centre on a small pedestrian street and has an elegant staircase and furnishings. The nicer rooms come with bathroom, TV, phone and refrigerator; staff are helpful.

Hotel Yubileynaya (☎ 726 565; w www.yubil.yar.ru; Kotoroslnaya nab 26; singles/doubles with breakfast from RR900/1500), more conventional than Hotel Volga, overlooks the Kotorosl River. It's the usual concrete slab, but rooms are comfortable. There's a restaurant, bar and business centre with Internet access.

Places to Eat

Café Rus (☎ 729 438; ul Kirova 8; meal RR50; open 8am-8pm daily) is perhaps the cheapest, most unpretentious place to eat in town. It's a unique blend of a Soviet eatery and Russian peasant dacha. You have to pay first, then pass the receipt to the grumbling serving lady by the counter. Ironically, the **Restaurant Rus** upstairs is perhaps the most pretentious place in town, but the food is good.

Cosy **Kafe Lira** (☎ 727 938; Volzhskaya nab 43; meal RR100; open noon-11pm daily) serves soups and salads and drinks at reasonable prices.

Café Premyera (☎ 728 601; Pervomayskaya ul; meal RR200) serves Russian food and beer in the small park behind the Volkov Theatre. The place is popular with young families and dating couples.

Spasskie Palaty (☎ 304 807; pl Bogoyavleniy 25; meal RR300; open noon-8pm daily) is popular with tourist groups for its atmospheric location inside the gates of the monastery and its tasty Russian fare.

Poplavok (☎ 303 666), situated below the naberezhnaya, is a new restaurant housed on a boat in the small harbour on the Kotorosl River. The location is ideal for summer dining and drinking.

Shopping

Russian Flax (☎ 305 670; Pervomayskaya ul 51) sells fine linen table cloths, napkins and bedclothes at remarkably low prices; you can also have stuff made to order.

Getting There & Away

Train The main station is **Yaroslavl Glavny** (ul Svobody), 3km west of the centre. The lesser **Yaroslavl Moskovsky** is near the bus station, 2km south of town. Around 20 trains a day run to/from Moscow's Yaroslavl Station (RR400, about five hours). Most of these are headed farther north (like Arkhangelsk) or east (Yekaterinburg, Novosibirsk and Vladivostok). It may be easiest to get tickets on trains that terminate at Yaroslavl.

There also are daily services to/from St Petersburg and Nizhny Novgorod. For closer destinations such as Rostov (RR120, two hours) or Kostroma (RR200, three hours), it's easiest to get suburban trains.

Bus The **bus station** (Moskovsky pr) is 2km south of the Kotorosl River, beside the Yaroslavl Moskovsky train station. One or two buses go daily to/from Moscow's Shchyolkovsky Bus Station (six hours), plus about five buses stopping in transit. Most of these stop at Pereslavl-Zalessky and Sergiev Posad. Other departures include:

Ivanovo – three hours, two or three daily
Kostroma – two hours, 10 to 11 daily
Pereslavl-Zalessky – three hours, three to four daily
Rostov-Veliky – 1½ hours, seven daily
Uglich – three hours, four daily
Vladimir – six hours, one or two daily
Vologda – five hours, two to three daily in transit

Boat In summer from the river station at the northern end of Pervomayskaya ulitsa. The hydrofoils to downstream destinations will take you to Kostroma (1½ hours) and Plyos (three hours). Tickets go on sale about 30 minutes before departure.

From about early June to early October, long-distance Volga passenger ships stop every couple of days in Yaroslavl on their way between Moscow and cities like Nizhny Novgorod, Kazan and Astrakhan. Timetables are posted at the river station, which also has an information window.

Getting Around
Tram No 3 goes along Bolshaya Ok-tyabrskaya ulitsa to the tram terminus a short walk west of Bogoyavlenskaya ploshchad (from Yaroslavl Glavny station, head 200m to the right for the stop on ulitsa Ukhtomskogo). Trolleybus No 1 runs between the station and ploshchad Volkova and Krasnaya ploshchad.

From the bus station and Yaroslavl Moskovsky train station, trolleybus No 5 or 9 from the far side of the main road outside will get you to Bogoyavlenskaya ploshchad; No 5 goes on to Krasnaya ploshchad.

UGLICH
УГЛИЧ
☎ 08532 • postcode 152610 • pop 39,000
Uglich is a quaint, shabby town on the Volga River, 90km northwest of Rostov-Veliky. A regular stop for Volga cruises, this tiny town has enough attractions to fill a morning.

Here Ivan the Terrible's son Dmitry – later to be impersonated by the string of False Dmitrys in the Time of Troubles (see Archangel Cathedral in The Kremlin special section) – was murdered in 1591, probably on Boris Godunov's orders. Within the waterside kremlin, the 15th-century **Prince's Chambers** (Knyazhyi palaty) house a historical exhibit, including the coffin which carried Dmitry's body to Moscow. The red **Church of St Dmitry on the Blood** (Tserkov Dmitria-na-krovi), with its cluster of spangled blue domes, was built in the 1690s on the spot where the body was found. Its interior is decorated with bright frescoes and the bell that tolled for Dmitry.

The five-domed **Transfiguration Cathedral** (Preobrazhensky sobor) and an **Art Museum** are also in the kremlin (☎ 536 78; admission RR20 each site; open 9am-1pm, 2pm-5pm daily).

Opposite each other, along ulitsa Karla Marxa from the kremlin, are two other fine buildings from the 1690s: the **Church of the Nativity of John the Baptist**; and the large, but badly dilapidated, **Monastery of the Resurrection**.

When you tire of Dmitry, Uglich boasts Russia's first **Vodka Museum** (☎ 235 58; ul Berggolts 9; admission RR50), a small but entertaining exhibit with samples!

If you get stuck in Uglich, you can stay at the **Hotel Uglich** (☎ 503 70; ul Yroslavskaya 50; rooms without/with bat RR130/170 per person), but be prepared for hard beds and cold showers. Buses go once or twice a day to Yaroslavl. Buses to Rostov do not run regularly, so you may have to go via Borisoglebsk. Otherwise, taxis sit outside the tiny bus station if you are short on time.

ROSTOV-VELIKY
РОСТОВ-ВЕЛИКИЙ
☎ 08536 • postcode 152100 • pop 40,000
After Suzdal, Rostov-Veliky (also known as Rostov-Yaroslavsky) is the prettiest of the Golden Ring towns – a tranquil, rustic place with a magnificent kremlin and beautiful monasteries magically sited by shimmering Lake Nero. Around 220km northeast of Moscow, it is one of Russia's oldest towns, first chronicled in 862.

Perhaps to flatter its home-grown aristocracy, Yury Dolgoruky called Rostov *Veliky* (Great) during the 12th century, while making Suzdal the capital of his Rostov-Suzdal principality. By the early 13th century, the

EXCURSIONS

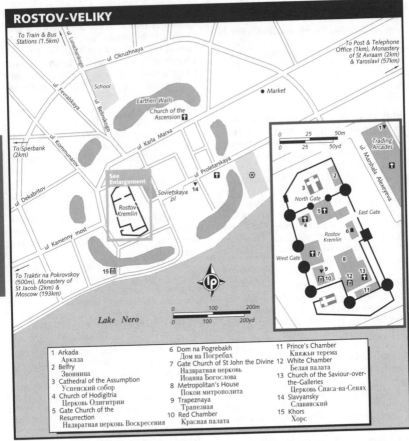

ROSTOV-VELIKY

1 Arkada
  Аркада
2 Belfry
  Звонница
3 Cathedral of the Assumption
  Успенский собор
4 Church of Hodigitria
  Церковь Одигитрии
5 Gate Church of the
  Resurrection
  Надвратная церковь Воскресения

6 Dom na Pogrebakh
  Дом на Погребах
7 Gate Church of St John the Divine
  Надвратная церковь
  Иоанна Богослова
8 Metropolitan's House
  Покои митрополита
9 Trapeznaya
  Трапезная
10 Red Chamber
  Красная палата

11 Prince's Chamber
  Княжьи терема
12 White Chamber
  Белая палата
13 Church of the Saviour-over-
  the-Galleries
  Церковь Спаса-на-Сенях
14 Slavyansky
  Славянский
15 Khors
  Хорс

Rostov region had split first from Suzdal and then into smaller pieces. The Tatars did not leave much of it standing, and in the late 1600s an ambitious Orthodox Metropolitan, Iona Sysoevich, cleared almost everything else away for a wonderful private kremlin on the shore of Lake Nero.

On the highway in from the south, look out for fairy-tale views across the lake to the kremlin and the Monastery of St Jacob.

Orientation & Information

The train and bus stations are together in the drab modern part of Rostov, 1.5km north of the kremlin. The kremlin sits on the northern shore of Lake Nero; the surrounding town consists mostly of izbas, trees and empty grassy spaces.

The main **post and telephone office** (*ul Severnaya 44*) is around 1km east of the kremlin. There's no bank but you may be able to change money at the Lion gift shop near the old Trading Arcades next to the kremlin.

Kremlin

The unashamedly photogenic **kremlin** (*☎ 317 17; admission RR100; open 10am-5pm daily*) is Rostov's main attraction. Although founded in the 12th century, nearly all the buildings here date from the 1670s and 1680s.

The **Cathedral of the Assumption** (Uspensky sobor), with its five magnificent domes, dominates the kremlin, although it is just outside its north wall. Outside service hours, you can get to the cathedral through the door in the **church shop** (ul Karla Marxa). The cathedral was here a century before the kremlin, while the **belfry** (zvonnitsa) was added in the 1680s. The belfry consists of 15 bells, each with its own name. The largest, weighing 32 tonnes, is called Sysoi. The monks play magnificent bell concerts, which can be arranged through the excursions office for RR100.

The west gate (the main entrance) and north gate are straddled by **gate churches** (Tserkov Voskreseniya and Tserkov Ioanna Bogoslova), richly decorated with 17th-century frescoes. Enter these churches from the monastery walls, which you can access from stairs next to the North Gate. Like several other buildings within the complex these are only open from 1 May to 30 September.

Between them, there's the **Church of Hodigitria** (Tserkov Odigitrii) which houses an exhibition of Orthodox Church vestments and paraphernalia.

The metropolitan's private chapel, the **Church of the Saviour-over-the-Galleries** (Tserkov Spasa-na-Senyakh), has the most beautiful interior of all, smothered in colourful frescoes. There are museums filled with icons, paintings, and enamelware, in the Metropolitan's House as well as the **White Chamber**, which was the dining hall, and **Red Chamber**, which was formerly the guesthouse.

The ticket office is in the west gate, but you can also enter through the north gate.

Monasteries & Other Buildings

The restored **Monastery of St Jacob** (Spaso-Yakovlevsky monastyr) is the fairy-tale apparition you'll see as you approach Rostov by road or rail. Although you can take bus No 1 or 2 for 1.5km west of the kremlin, it's a very pleasant walk there alongside Lake Nero. Heading east of the kremlin, bus No 1 will also bring you to the dilapidated **Monastery**

of **St Avraam** (Avraamevsky monastyr), with a cathedral dating from 1553.

Khors (☎/fax 324 83; ⓦ www.enamel.by .ru; ul Podozerka 30; admission free; open noon-10pm) is a tiny, private museum that's named after a pagan sun god. Walk towards the lake as you exit the monastery and look for a charming two-storey wooden house with a garden. The eclectic collection includes some antique household items, models of wooden churches and paintings by local artists. The two small rooms are available for rent to 'artists passing through'. The artist who runs the place also hosts workshops on enamel and Rostov artistry.

To enjoy a lovely view of the kremlin from the lake, you may be able to hire a row boat in front of Khors or further east in the park.

Places to Stay & Eat

Dom na Pogrebakh (☎ 312 44; rooms with shared bathroom from RR300), right inside the kremlin, provides clean, wood-panelled rooms that vary somewhat in size and view. A few more expensive rooms have private bathrooms.

Trapeznaya (☎ 328 71; meal RR200; open 8am-8pm daily) is a restaurant with an atmospheric location, inside the kremlin near the metropolitan's house.

Traktir na Pokrovskoy (☎ 355 74, ul Pokrovskaya; meal around RR200) is slightly more expensive than Trapeznaya, but the fare is the same.

Arkada (☎ 337 05; Sovietsky per 2/3; meal RR200; open 11am-11pm Mon-Fri, 11am-2am Sat-Sun) is a pub-like place in the Trading Arcades.

Slavyansky (☎ 322 28; Sovietskaya pl 8), 100m east of the kremlin, is a new ritzier place that gets local recommendations.

Getting There & Away

Train The fastest train option from Moscow is the Express service from Yaroslavl Station (RR100/75 1st/2nd class, three hours). Otherwise try for a ticket on one of the long-distance trains stopping at Rostov en route to Yaroslavl or beyond, or go by suburban train, changing trains halfway at Alexandrov, which takes about five hours.

Bus Services from Rostov to Yaroslavl (RR30, 70 minutes) go roughly every hour. These include direct ones and those stopping at Rostov in transit to Yaroslavl. Other transit buses go to Moscow (four to five hours, three daily) via Pereslavl-Zalessky and Sergiev Posad (RR100, four to five hours, three daily), Pereslavl-Zalessky (RR60, two hours, three daily) and Uglich (RR100, three hours, two daily).

Getting Around
Bus No 6 (RR5) runs between the train station and the centre.

PERESLAVL-ZALESSKY
ПЕРЕСЛАВЛЬ-ЗАЛЕССКИЙ
☎ 08535 • postcode 152100 • pop 45,000
On the shore of Lake Pleshcheyevo, almost halfway between Moscow and Yaroslavl, Pereslavl-Zalessky is a very popular dacha-destination for Muscovites, who enjoy the peaceful Russian village atmosphere. The southern half of the town is characterised by narrow dirt lanes lined with carved wooden izbas and blossoming gardens.

Pereslavl-Zalessky (Pereslavl Beyond the Woods) was founded in 1152 by Yury Dolgoruky. The town's claim to fame is as the birthplace of Alexander Nevsky. Its earth walls and the little Cathedral of the Transfiguration are as old as the town.

Orientation & Information
Pereslavl is pretty much a one-street town, with the bus station at the southwestern end, 2km from the centre. Apart from the kremlin area, most of the historic sights are out of the centre.

The **Yartelekom Service Centre** (☎ 215 95; ul Rostovskaya 20) has Internet and telephone facilities. Maps are available at the ticket office of the Goritsky Monastery or at Hotel Pereslavl.

Central Area
The walls of Yury Dolgoruky's **kremlin** are now a grassy ring around the central town. Inside, the simple **Cathedral of the Transfiguration of the Saviour** (Spaso-Preobrazhensky sobor), started in 1152, is one of the oldest

standing buildings in Russia. A bust of Alexander Nevsky stands in front. Three additional churches across the grassy square make for a picturesque corner: the tent-roofed **Church of Peter the Metropolitan** (Tserkov Petra mitropolita), built in 1585 and renovated in 1957, and the 18th-century twins fronting the road.

The **Trubezh River** winds 2km from the kremlin to the lake. You can follow the northern riverbank most of the way to the lake by a combination of paths and streets. The **Forty Saints' Church** (Sorokosvyatskaya tserkov) sits picturesquely on the south side of the river mouth.

Southwest of the kremlin, the **Nikolsky Women's Monastery** is undergoing massive renovation. Since its founding way back in 1350, this monastery has been on the brink of destruction – whether from Tatars, Poles or Communists – more than seems possible to survive. In 1994, four nuns from the Yaroslavl Tolga Convent came to restore the place, and today it looks marvellous. Rumour has it that the rebuilding is being bankrolled by a wealthy Muscovite businessperson, who has benefited from the nuns' blessings.

Nikitsky Monastery
Founded in 1010, this monastery (Nikitsky Monastyr; admission free; open 10am-5pm daily) received its current name only in the 12th century, after the death of the martyr St Nikita, who lived here. To punish his body for his sins, Nikita clasped his limbs in chains and spent his remaining days in an underground cell on the grounds. The handcuffs, which now hang in the monastery's main **cathedral**, are said to help cure addictions and other worldly vices. Behind the cathedral, a small chapel is being built around the dank cell where Nikita died.

Nikitsky Monastery is about 3km north of the centre on the west side of the main road. Bus Nos 1, 3 and 4 go most of the distance, or you can catch a taxi from Narodnaya ploshchad.

South Pereslavl-Zalessky
The **Goritsky Monastery** (Goritsky monastyr; ☎ 381 00; w http://museum.pereslavl.ru)

PERESLAVL-ZALESSKY

Lake Pleshcheyevo

Footbridges

Narodnaya pl.

Trubezh River

Kremlin Walls

Trubezh River

Podgornaya ul

To Botik Museum (4km)

Train Station

ul Kardovskogo

To Fyodorovsky Monastery (2km), Sergiev Posad (65km) & Moscow (125km)

To Market, Nikitsky Monastery (2km), Yaroslavl (70km) & Rostov-Veliky (125km)

Rostovskaya ul

Sovetskaya ul

0   500   1000m
0   500   1000yd

1 Hotel Pereslavl
   Гостиница Переславль
2 Yartelecom Service Centre
   Ярtelecom сервисный центр
3 Taxi Stand
   Стоянка такси
4 Zolotoe Koltso
   Золотое Кольцо
5 Cathedral of the
   Transfiguration of the Saviour
   Спасо-Преображенский собор
6 Church of Peter the Metropolitan
   Церковь Петра митрополита
7 Blinnaya
   Блинная

8 Forty Saints' Church
   Сорокосвятская церковь
9 Nikolsky Women's Monastery
   Никольский женский
   монастырь
10 Assumption Cathedral; Goritsky Monastery
   Успенский собор; Горицкий монастырь
11 Purification Church of
   Alexandr Nevsky
   Церковь Александра
   Невского Сретенского
12 Danilovsky Monastery
   Даниловский монастырь
13 Bus Station
   Автостанция

EXCURSIONS

was founded in the 14th century, though today the oldest buildings are the 17th-century gates, gate-church and belfry. From the bus station, walk about 1.2km, then turn left and it's up on the hill. The centrepiece is the baroque **Assumption Cathedral** (Uspensky sobor) with its beautiful carved iconostasis. In the refectory is a **museum** (*admission RR10 plus RR10 per exhibit; open 10am-5pm Wed-Mon*) with icons and incredible carved wooden furnishings.

Across the highway from Goritsky, there is the 1785 **Purification Church of Alexander Nevsky** (Tserkov Alexandra Nevskogo-Sretenskogo), which is a working church. To the east, on a hillock overlooking fields and dachas, is the **Danilovsky Monastery** (Danilovsky monastyr), whose tent-roofed **Trinity Cathedral** (Troitsky sobor) was built in the 1530s. Another 16th-century walled monastery is the **Fyodorovsky Monastery** (Fyodorovsky monastyr), about 2km south on the Moscow road.

Botik Museum

Lake Pleshcheyevo takes credit as one of the birthplaces of the Russian navy. It is one of the places where Peter the Great developed his obsession with the sea, studying navigation and building a flotilla of over 100 little ships by the time he was 20.

Four kilometres along the road past the Goritsky Monastery, at the south end of the lake, is the small Botik Museum (☎ 227 88; *admission RR20; open 10am-5pm Tues-Sun*). Its highlight is the sailboat *Fortuna*, the only one of Peter the Great's boats (except one in the St Petersburg Naval Museum) to survive fire and neglect.

In theory, you can reach the Botik on a tiny narrow-gauge train that rattles along its single track from the central ulitsa Kardovskogo. The ride is fun, but the train runs sporadically.

Lake Pleshcheyevo

Pereslavl sits on the edge of Pleshcheyevo National Park, which is dominated by the lake of the same name. The lake's shallow waters are popular for fishing, swimming and windsurfing. The legendary *Siny Kamen*, or 'Blue Stone', sits on the shores of Lake Pleshcheyevo. This 12-tonne boulder was apparently the target of pagan worship for many moons, and still attracts pilgrims to the lake shore.

Places to Stay & Eat
Pleshcheyevo National Park (*☎ 229 88; camping RR50*) is a pleasant place to pitch a tent. The park also operates a number of small resorts and cottages around the lake.

Hotel Pereslavl (*☎ 217 88, fax 226 87; ul Rostovskaya 27; singles/doubles with shared bathroom RR420/640, with private bathroom RR600/1080*), 400m north of the Trubezh River, was built in 1985 but is already falling apart. The rooms are what you would expect for the price. There is quite a pleasant **restaurant** downstairs where everything is under US$2.

Blinnaya (*ul Sovietskaya 10A; bliny RR15; 9am-9pm daily*) offers nothing but fresh, delicious bliny.

Zolotoe Koltso (*☎ 222 49; pl Narodnaya 11; meal RR350; open noon-midnight*) is a more stylish place with an extensive menu and live music.

Getting There & Away
Pereslavl has no mainline train station. Buses, however, go to Moscow (RR60, 2½ hours, three daily), Sergiev Posad (RR30, one hour, three daily) and Yaroslavl (RR60, three hours, two daily) via Rostov-Veliky (RR60, 1½ hours). Other buses pass through en route to Moscow, Yaroslavl and Kostroma.

Getting Around
Bus No 1 runs up and down the main street from just south of the bus station; heading out from the centre, you can catch it just north of the river. Taxis sit at Narodnaya ploshchad.

SERGIEV POSAD
СЕРГИЕВ ПОСАД
☎ 254 • postcode 141300 • pop 100,000
Sergiev Posad is the town around the Trinity Monastery of St Sergius, one of Russia's most important religious and historical landmarks. Often referred to by its Soviet name Zagorsk, Sergiev Posad is 60km from the edge of Moscow on the Yaroslavl road. If you find you have time for just one trip out of Moscow, this is the obvious choice.

The monastery was founded in about 1340 by Sergius of Radonezh (now patron saint of Russia), a monk with enough moral authority to unite the country against Tatar rule, blessing Dmitry Donskoy's army before it gave the Tatars their first beating in 1380. The monastery's status as defender of the motherland grew during the Time of Troubles; it withstood a 16-month siege when Moscow was occupied by the Poles.

As a *lavra*, or an exalted monastery, it grew enormously wealthy on the gifts of tsars, nobles and merchants all looking for divine support. Closed by the Bolsheviks, it was reopened after WWII as a museum, residence of the Patriarch and a working monastery.

The Patriarch and the administrative centre of the Church moved to the Danilovsky Monastery in Moscow in 1988, but the Trinity Monastery of St Sergius remains one of Russia's most important spiritual sites.

For its concentrated artistry and its unique role in the interrelated histories of the Russian Church and State, it is well worth a day trip from Moscow.

Orientation & Information
Prospekt Krasnoy Armii is the main street, running north–south through the town centre. The train and bus stations are on opposite corners of a wide yard to the east of prospekt Krasnoy Armii. The monastery is about 400m north.

For money exchange, **Guta Bank** (*☎ 422 28; pr Krasnoy Armii 148; open 9.30am-4.30pm Mon-Sat*) is accessible from the parking lot behind. There's a **post and telephone office** (*pr Krasnoy Armii 127A*) outside the southeast wall of the monastery.

Trinity Monastery of St Sergius
The monastery (*Troitse-Sergieva Lavra; ☎ 453 56; admission free, photos RR100; grounds*

SERGIEV POSAD

Trinity Monastery of Saint Sergius

To McDonald's (50m) & Hotel Zagorsk (100m)

prosp Krasnoy Armii

ul Mitkina

Vokzalnaya ul

prosp Krasnoy Armii

1-ya Rybnaya ul.

To Moscow (60km)

Vokzalnaya pl

Train Station

0   100   200m
0   100   200yd

PLACES TO STAY & EAT
2 Sever
   Север
3 Trapeza na Makovtse
   Трапеза на Маковце
17 Russky Dvorik Restaurant
   Русский Дворик Ресторан
18 Russky Dvorik Hotel
   Русский Дворик Гостиница

OTHER
1 Guta Bank
   Гута банк
4 Tsar's Chambers
   Царские палаты
5 Kalichya Tower
   Каличья башня
6 Bell Tower
   Колокольня
7 Grave of Boris Godunov
   Могила Бориса Годунова
8 Cathedral of the Assumption
   Успенский собор
9 Gate Church of John the Baptist
   Церковь Иоанна Предтечи
10 Chapel-at-the-Well
   Надкладезная часовня
11 Church of the Descent of the Holy Spirit
   Духовская церковь
12 Vestry
   Ризница
13 Trinity Cathedral
   Троицкий собор
14 Ticket Office
   Касса
15 Refectory Church of St Sergius
   Трапезная церковь Св Сергия
16 Post & Telephone Office
   Почтамп и переговорный пункт
19 Bus Station
   Автостанция

open 10am-6pm daily) has additional charges to visit the museums inside.

Tours of the grounds and churches (not the museums), given by English-speaking monks, cost RR550 per person. Book tours by phone or at the kiosk next to the Gate-Church of John the Baptist. Female visitors should wear headscarves, and men are required to remove hats in the churches.

Trinity Cathedral Built in the 1420s, this squat, dark yet beautiful church (Troitsky sobor) is the heart of the Trinity monastery. A memorial service for St Sergius (whose tomb stands in the southeast corner) goes on all day, every day. The icon-festooned interior, lit by oil lamps, is largely the work of the great medieval painter Andrey Rublyov and his students.

Cathedral of the Assumption This cathedral (Uspensky sobor), with its star-spangled domes, was modelled on the cathedral of the same name in the Moscow Kremlin. It was finished in 1585 with money left by Ivan the Terrible in a fit of remorse for killing his son. Services are held here in summer; otherwise, you may find it closed. Outside the west door is the **grave** of Boris Godunov, the only tsar not buried in the Moscow Kremlin or St Petersburg's SS Peter and Paul Cathedral.

Nearby, the resplendent **Chapel-at-the-Well** (Nadkladeznaya chasovnya) was built over a spring said to have appeared during the Polish siege. The five-tier, baroque bell tower took 30 years to build in the 18th century, and once had 42 bells, the largest of which weighed 65 tonnes.

Vestry Situated behind the Trinity Cathedral, the vestry (riznitsa; admission RR150; open 10am-5.30pm Tues-Sun) displays the monastery's extraordinary treasury, bulging with 600 years of donations by the rich and powerful – tapestries, jewel-encrusted vestments, solid gold chalices and more.

Refectory Church of St Sergius The huge block with the 'wallpaper' paint job and lavish interior (Trapeznaya tserkov Sv

EXCURSIONS

Sergia) was once a dining hall for pilgrims. Now it's the Assumption Cathedral's winter counterpart, with morning services in cold weather. The green building next door is the Metropolitan's Residence.

Church of the Descent of the Holy Spirit

This little 15th-century church (Dukhovskaya tserkov), with the bell tower under its dome, is a graceful imitation of Trinity Cathedral. It's used only on special occasions. It contains, among other things, the grave of the first Bishop of Alaska.

Places to Stay & Eat

Hotel Zagorsk (☎ 425 16; pr Krasnoy Armii 171; rooms from US$32) is about 500m north along the street from the monastery gate.

Russky Dvorik Hotel (☎ 753 92, fax 753 91; ul Mitkina 14/2; singles/doubles with breakfast from US$50/70) is a delightful small hotel just a short walk east of the monastery. It is decorated in rustic style but quite modern. It also has a separate **restaurant** (☎ 451 14, pr Krasnoy Armii 134; meal RR500), that gets overrun with tour groups at lunch but is otherwise quite pleasant.

The touristy restaurant **Trapeza na Makovtse** (☎ 411 01, pr Krasnoy Armii 131; mains RR400; open 9am-9pm daily) is a little pricey, but the view of the monastery walls from the outside tables is worth it.

Sever (☎ 412 20; pr Krasnoy Armii 141; meal RR120; open 10am-9pm daily) is cheaper but the food is as hit-and-miss as the Soviet-style service. There's also **McDonald's**, further up prospekt Krasnoy Armii.

Getting There & Away

Train Suburban trains run every half-hour or so to/from Moscow's Yaroslavl Station (RR30, 1½ hours); take any train bound for Sergiev Posad or Alexandrov. The fastest option is the daily Express train to Yaroslavl (RR90/60 1st/2nd class, 55 minutes).

To continue on to Rostov-Veliky (3½ hours) or Yaroslavl (five hours), you may have to change at Alexandrov to a Yaroslavl-bound suburban train.

Bus Buses to Sergiev Posad from Moscow leave from Yaroslavl Train Station every half-hour from 8.30am to 7.30pm (RR30, 70 minutes). If you are facing Komsomolsky prospekt with Yaroslavsky Station behind you, the bus stop is to your left, next to the underground passage.

Three daily buses start at Sergiev Posad and run to Pereslavl-Zalessky (RR20, 75 minutes). About nine northbound buses a

---

Big Bad Bells

After the Bolsheviks destroyed its mighty bells, the Trinity Monastery of St Sergius bell tower was silent for 72 years. Only in 2002 were the first two of the bells replaced. The *Pervnets*, or 'First Born', is 27 tonnes, and the *Blagovestnik*, or 'Evangelist', weighs 35½ tonnes. The two bells are the largest cast in Russia in 200 years.

A third bell is scheduled to be cast and raised in 2003, although the gigantic Tsar, as it will be called, faces many obstacles. The 64-tonne monster poses a technical challenge for Zil, the commissioned metallurgical plant. ZiL was selected for the job because of its track record of casting heavy bells with accurate tone, but it has never faced such a huge dong. Even more daunting is the nearly US$2.9 million price tag. Potential donors are being tempted by the prospect of having their name engraved on the bell alongside the names of the president and the Patriarch.

Besides calling the faithful to prayer and to celebrations, church bells in Russia are an evocative symbol of devastation and triumph. After battle, a victorious prince would often confiscate the bell from the main tower to force silence on the defeated. During times of war, bells were melted down so the materials could be used for cannons. But the raising of the bell raises spirits, and the chimes ring out glory. During the 1980s, monks and architects scoured abandoned churches in search of bells to place in the towers of monasteries and churches that were reopening.

day stop here in transit to Yaroslavl, Kostroma or Rybinsk; all these will take you to Pereslavl-Zalessky, Rostov-Veliky or Yaroslavl if you can get a ticket.

ABRAMTSEVO
АБРАМЦЕВО
The small Abramtsevo estate, 15km southwest of Sergiev Posad, was a seedbed for several 19th-century movements aiming to preserve patriarchal Russian religious, social and aesthetic values. In the 1840s and 1850s it was the home of Sergey Axakov, pioneer novelist of Russian realism, and a refuge for upper-class intellectuals.

In 1870 Savva Mamontov, a railway tycoon and art patron, bought Abramtsevo and turned it into an artists' colony dedicated to a renaissance of traditional Russian art and architecture, which would have a strong influence on painting, sculpture, applied art and even theatre. The list of resident painters alone is a who's who of 'neo-Russianism' – Ilya Repin, landscape artist Isaak Levitan, portraitist Valentin Serov and the quite un-Slavonic painter and ceramicist Mikhail Vrubel.

Other projects included woodworking and ceramics workshops, Mamontov's private opera (where Fyodor Chaliapin made his debut) and several buildings designed, built and decorated by group efforts.

All this is now the **Abramtsevo Estate Museum-Preserve** (☎ 254-324 70; admission RR35; open 10am-5pm Wed-Sun), which makes a good addition to a day trip to Sergiev Posad. In addition to the highlights below, there are arts and crafts exhibits in the other buildings on the grounds, which cost extra. The museum is closed the last Friday each month, and sometimes in April and October.

Main House
Several rooms have been preserved intact. Axakov's dining room and study contain paintings and sculptures of family and friends, but most of the house is devoted to the Mamontov years. The main attraction is Mamontov's dining room, featuring Repin's portraits of the patron and his wife, and

Serov's luminous *Girl with Peaches*. A striking majolica bench by Vrubel is in the garden.

Saviour Church 'Not Made by Hand'
The prettiest building in the grounds, this small church (Tserkov Spasa Nerukotvorny) seems to symbolise Mamantov's intentions. It's a carefully researched homage by half a dozen artists to 14th-century Novgorod architecture. The iconostasis is by Repin and Vasily Polenov. The tiled stove in the corner (still working) is exquisite.

Hut on Chicken Legs
This just goes to show that serious art does not have to be truly serious. The Slavophile painter Viktor Vasnetsov conjured up the fairy tale of Baba Yaga (the witch) with this playhouse with feet (although chicken legs they are not).

Convent of the Intercession
Between Abramtsevo and Sergiev Posad, in the village of Khotkovo, is the Convent of the Intercession (Pokrovsky monastyr); it was founded in 1308, though the present buildings are 18th century or later.

The parents of Sergius of Radonezh, Russia's patron saint and founder of the Trinity Monastery of St Sergius at Sergiev Posad, are buried in the convent's recently restored **Intercession Cathedral** (Pokrovsky sobor). The biggest building is the early 20th-century **St Nicholas' Cathedral** (Nikolsky sobor).

Getting There & Away
Abramtsevo and Khotkovo are just before Sergiev Posad on suburban trains from Moscow's Yaroslavl Station. Most trains heading to Sergiev Posad or Alexandrov stop at both places (but a few skip Abramtsevo, so check). There are regular buses (RR10, 20 minutes) between Abramtsevo and Sergiev Posad.

By car, turn west off the M8 Moscow–Yaroslavl highway just north of the 61km post. Signs to both Khotkovo and Abramtsevo mark the turn-off. For the Khotkovo convent, turn left just before the rail tracks in the village; for Abramtsevo, continue over the railway for a few more kilometres.

Northwest
Северо-запад

KLIN
КЛИН
Tchaikovsky lived in Klin, 90km northwest of central Moscow, from 1885 until his death in 1893. Here he wrote his *Pathetique* symphony (the Sixth), as well as the *Nutcracker* and *Sleeping Beauty*. His last residence is now a **museum** *(Dom-Muzey Chaykovskogo; ☎ 224-581 96; ul Chaykovskogo 48; admission RR60; open 10am-6pm Fri-Tues)*, kept much like it was when Tchaikovsky lived there. You can browse through the documents and personal effects, including his Becker grand piano. Occasional concerts are held here.

Getting There & Away
Klin is on the road and railway from Moscow to Tver, Novgorod and St Petersburg. Suburban trains from Moscow's Leningrad Station operate to Klin (1½ hours) throughout the day. Services between Klin and Tver – a trip of just over one hour – are frequent.

ZAVIDOVO
ЗАВИДОВО
Midway between Klin and Tver on the road to St Petersburg, the village of Zavidovo is located in a beautiful spot at the confluence of the Volga and the Shosha Rivers. On the outskirts of the village is the **Zavidovo Holiday Complex** *(☎ 937 9944; rooms from RR3900, cottage from RR6300)*, which offers all kinds of recreation activities, such as horse riding, water skiing, tennis, boating and fishing. This is one of the most popular spots for Muscovites to come for water sports.

Comfortable cottages are in various architectural styles, including Finnish cabins, Alpine chalets and Russian dachas. Suburban trains from Moscow's Leningrad Station take about two hours.

TVER
ТВЕРЬ
☎ 0822 • postcode 170000 • pop 450,000
Tver, on the Volga 150km northwest of Moscow, was the capital of an unruly ministate that was Moscow's chief rival in the 14th and 15th centuries. Its subsequent history is less fortuitous: the city was punished for rising against the Golden Horde, conquered by Ivan III, savaged by Ivan the Terrible, seized by the Poles, and completely destroyed by fire in 1763. The city experienced a sort of rebirth when Catherine the Great made it one of her rest-stops between St Petersburg and Moscow. It now looks like a little rustic St Petersburg in places.

In April 1940, Tver's NKVD headquarters hosted a murder, or murders to be precise. Over 6000 Polish POWs were shot one by one in a soundproofed room at night. They were buried in trenches near Mednoe, 20km west of Tver.

In 1990 Tver dumped its Soviet name, Kalinin (after Mikhail Kalinin, Stalin's puppet president during WWII, who was born here). Though Tver is not in the same league as some of the old Russian towns of the Golden Ring, it has just enough attractions to make it a worthwhile day trip from Moscow. You might also want to stop here for the same reason as Catherine – to rest during your journey between Moscow and St Pete.

Orientation & Information
The Volga runs roughly west–east through Tver, with the town centre on the southern side. Ulitsa Sovietskaya is the main east–west street. It intersects the north–south Tverskoy prospekt, which becomes Chaykovskogo prospekt farther south.

The train station is 4km south of the centre, at the point where Chaykovskogo prospekt turns 90° east and becomes ulitsa Kominterna. The bus station is 300m east of the train station.

The **main post and telephone office** *(ul Sovietskaya 31; open 8am-8pm Mon-Sat)* is open for international phone calls 24 hours a day. A good source of maps is the **Knigi bookshop** *(☎ 332 070; ul Tryokhsvyatskaya 28; open 10am-7pm Mon-Fri, 10am-5pm Sat & Sun)*.

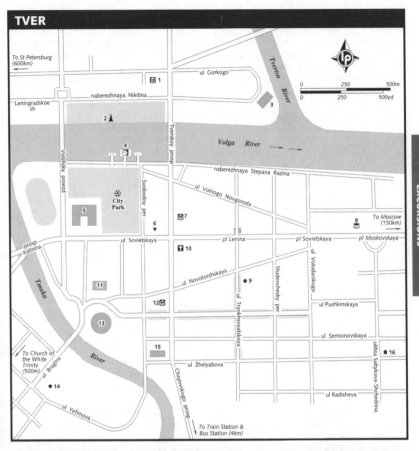

TVER

PLACES TO STAY & EAT	2 Afanasy Nikitin Statue	8 Post and Telephone Office
6 Vina Stavropolya	Памятник Афанасию	Почтамт и переговорный
Вина Ставрополья	Никитину	пункт
11 Hotel Tsentralnaya	3 River Station	9 Knigi Bookshop
Гостиница Центральная	Речной вокзал	Магазин Книги
15 Hotel Volga	4 Excursion-Boat Landings	10 Church of the Ascension
Гостиница Волга	Пристань для речных	Церковь Вознесения
16 Hotel Osnabruck	экскурсий	12 Tram Stop
Гостиница Оснабрюк	5 'Road Palace' Art Gallery	Остановка трамваев
OTHER	Путевой Дворец	13 Circus
1 Museum of Tver Life	7 Tram Stop	Цирк
Музей тверского быта	Трамвайная остановка	14 Market
		Рынок

Things to See
South of the River Classical town houses and public buildings from the late 1700s and early 1800s line **ulitsa Sovietskaya** and the riverfront **naberezhnaya Stepana Razina**. The classical **Church of the Ascension** *(Tserkov Voznesenia; cnr ul Sovietskaya & Tverskoy pr)* is nearby.

At the western end of ulitsa Sovietskaya, fronted by a statue of Mikhail Kalinin, stands the town's most imposing building – Catherine the Great's 1775 **Road Palace** (Putevoy Dvorets). It houses the Tver **Art Gallery** *(☎ 333 531; ul Sovietskaya 5; admission RR10; open 11am-5pm Wed-Sun)*, which features 18th-century interiors and furniture, as well as Russian and Western European art. The **City Park**, on the river bank behind the palace, often holds live concerts on summer weekends. In summer, Volga excursion boats sail every hour from the piers.

The quaintest part of town is the streets of old wooden houses with carved eaves and window frames, west of the market. Here is Tver's oldest building, the stately 1564 **Church of the White Trinity** *(Tserkov Beloy Troitsy; Trudolyubia per)*, where daily services are held.

North of the River There's a promenade stretching along the north bank of the Volga, providing lovely views of the old houses on the south bank. The **statue** in the park here is of Afanasy Nikitin, a local merchant who went overland to India 30 years before Vasco da Gama sailed there, and wrote a bestseller about his trip.

The **Museum of Tver Life** *(☎ 318 404; ul Gorkogo 19/14; admission RR15; open 11am-5pm Wed-Sun)* is housed in an 18th-century merchant's manor house. It exhibits arts, crafts, furniture and other domestic artefacts from several centuries.

Places to Stay & Eat
The cheap options are **Hotel Tsentralnaya** *(☎ 489 093; ul Novotorzhskaya 1; rooms from RR200)* and **Hotel Volga** *(☎ 338 100, fax 379 557; ul Zhelyabova 1; rooms from RR360)*. Both hotels are from the same dreary Soviet concrete mould.

Hotel Osnabruck *(☎ 488 433, fax 488 412; ⓔ info@hotel.tver.ru; ul Saltykova-Shchedrina 20; singles/doubles with breakfast US$60/80)* is a sort of Western-style, three-star hotel.

Apart from the **hotel restaurants**, the city has a lot of cafés in the centre, each having a standard selection of cheap salads, sandwiches and drinks.

Vina Stavropolya *(Stavropol Wines; ☎ 333 748; ul Sovietskaya 7; dishes from RR150)* features a good selection of wines from the Stavropol region in the south of Russia.

Getting There & Away
Suburban trains (RR30) take two to three hours to reach Tver (often still called Kalinin on timetables) from Moscow's Leningrad Station. Departures are approximately hourly. Most of the trains between Moscow and St Petersburg also stop at Tver. There are also buses (RR50, three hours) to/from Yaroslavl Station.

Getting Around
Tram Nos 2, 5, 6 and 11 run from the bus and train stations up Tchaikovskogo and Tverskoy prospekts to the town centre.

LAKE SELIGER
ОЗЕРО СЕЛИГЕР
About 360km from Moscow, the picturesque, island-dotted Lake Seliger has long been a popular vacation spot for intellectual and outdoorsy types. The lake's fresh waters make for excellent canoeing, fishing and swimming, while the surrounding forests attract hikers, hunters and berry pickers. Several of the lake's 160 islands are particularly attractive, whether it's for their quaint fishing villages, pristine inland waterways, or in one case, a 16th-century monastery.

The headwaters of the Volga are not far west of here. A spring near the village of Volgaverkhovye forms a tiny stream, small enough to step over. It flows for 10km before reaching Lake Sterzh, the first in a chain of Upper Volga lakes, and there picks up momentum. Humble beginnings for the mighty Volga!

Ostashkov
Осташков

☎ 08235 • postcode 172730 • pop 31,000

In its early history, this region was the subject of constant disputes between Vladimir, Muscovy and Novgorod. Legend tells the tale of one particularly devastating rampage of Klichen island by the Novgorod army at the end of the 14th century. Apparently, the only survivor of the massacre was a fisherman named Yevstashka, who rebuilt his home on a peninsula on the southern shore of the lake. Thus, the village of Ostashkov was born.

Today the pretty, old-fashioned town of Ostashkov is a good base for visiting the lakes region. The brainchild of 18th-century architect Starov, the wide streets and grand buildings are a model of town planning.

Orientation & Information Ostashkov's organised grid pattern is easy to navigate. The main street, Leninsky prospekt, leads from the lakeshore in the north into the centre, where several 17th-century buildings have been preserved.

The **post office** (Yuzhny per 7A) has a 24-hour telephone office next door. Maps are sold at **Knigi bookshop** (Leninsky pr 45). Across the road, the **Obretenie art gallery** sells souvenirs, wood carvings and paintings by local artists.

Things to See & Do The oldest buildings are along Leninsky prospekt. The 17th-century Troitsky Cathedral at the northern end houses the **Local Studies Museum** (Krayevedchesky muzey; admission RR15; open 10am-5pm daily). For an additional fee, you may be able to climb the belfry. Another stone cathedral nearby is the Voskresensky Cathedral, built in 1689, with its red and white belfry from the end of the 18th century. The town hall is from 1720.

Ostashkov is also the home of two ancient monasteries: the Zhitennoy, which was founded in 1673, and the Znamensky, which dates from 1716.

From the dock at the north end of Leninsky prospekt, **boats** run all the way up the lake from May to September.

Places to Stay & Eat A typically run-down, Soviet-style option is **Hotel Seliger** (☎ 209 52, 13 218; pr Kalinina; rooms with meal from RR500). The hot water supply is unpredictable.

There are several *turbazy* (rustic tourist cabins) around the lake where you can enjoy the great outdoors and lovely views. One option is **Sokol** (☎ 131 21; rooms with meals RR450, cottages with meals RR500 per person), a resort in a lovely forest setting 35km from Ostashkov.

Khottabych (ul Rabochaya 24; meal RR100; open until 10pm daily) is a decent place to eat with an outdoor seating area. **Ashen** (ul Zagorodnaya 26; meal RR300; open 24hr) is more lively, complete with some tasty Georgian dishes and the requisite live music.

Don't leave without sampling the local speciality, smoked eel, which you can buy at the **market** behind Hotel Seliger.

Getting There & Away If you are driving, take the Leningrad road to Torzhok, then route A111 to Ostashkov. The trip takes about four hours.

Buses run from Tver to Ostashkov (4½ hours, five daily). A slow train (RR150) to Ostashkov leaves from Leningrad Station every other day (11½ hours). In summer, a quicker overnight bus (RR100) runs from Shchyolkovsky Bus Station on weekends (8½ hours).

Stolbny Island
Столбный Остров

About 30km north of Ostashkov on Stolbny Island is the **Nilova Pustyn Monastery** (Monastyr Nilova Pustyn). In 1628, a pilgrim by the name of Nil Stelbensky received divine instructions in a dream and settled on this island. Later that century, the monastery was founded by visiting monks and pilgrims.

The monastery grounds were used as a Stalinist labour camp for a spell during the Soviet period.

The Polish prisoners killed at Tver in 1940 were held on Stolbny before they were murdered.

The magnificent **Annunciation Cathedral** (Blagoveshchensky sobor) was built in the 19th century. The belfry – being renovated at the time of research – offers a breathtaking view of the lake and the islands. Because it's an operating monastery, some restrictions apply – you are not allowed to photograph the monks or any other people on the monastery grounds. Entry to the grounds is free, but you have to receive permission from the monastery authorities to get to the belfry.

From the belfry, you can spot a few 18th-century churches around town: Petropavlovskaya cathedral (1764), the church of Nil Solbensky (1755) and the tiny Vsekhsvyatitelskaya (1701). The southern tip of the island is home to the Vozdvizhenskaya church, which was built in 1788.

If you want to stay on Stolbny, try the pension **Svetlitsa** (☎ 214 33; *rooms with meals from RR550 per person*). Boats to Stolbny Island depart from the dock in Ostashkov.

LAKE VALDAI
ОЗЕРО ВАЛДАЙ
☎ 81666

Lake Valdai is another one in the chain of peaceful and picturesque lakes located about halfway between Moscow and St Petersburg. It is surrounded by the Valdai National Park, which is composed of more than 1500 sq km of protected wilderness, including 76 lakes. This area has long been a summer retreat for the most powerful inhabitants of the Kremlin, including President Putin. There is even a luxurious guesthouse that was built for Stalin, although the paranoid dictator apparently never stayed in the dacha, which he dubbed 'a mousetrap'.

Besides hobnobbing with the powers that be, Lake Valdai is an ideal place for boating, fishing, hiking, camping and any other outdoor activity that catches your fancy.

Things to See & Do
Besides the wide range of outdoor activities around the lake, the town of Valdai, 390km from Moscow, also offers a few interesting sights (in case it rains).

Valdai was one of many towns along the Moscow–St Petersburg route, which served as a staging post. In 1770, Catherine the Great decided to build a road palace here so she would have a place to spend the night. Only the elegant **St Catherine's Church** was completed. Today, it contains a **museum** exhibiting the local speciality craft – bells for the harnesses of the troikas that transported the passengers.

The **Holy Lake Iversky Monastery**, founded in 1653, sits on a Lake Valdai island. The monastery was founded by Patriarch Nikon, who reportedly said: 'There is paradise in heaven and Valdai on earth.' Now a working monastery, this peaceful place is inhabited by a small number of monks.

You can reach the monastery by boat from Valdai or by crossing over the pontoon bridge.

Places to Stay & Eat
Valdai National Park (☎ 218 09) has camping facilities, as well as guided nature hikes.

The **Dom Otdykha Valdai** (☎ 352 91; *Roshchino; rooms with meals from RR700 per person*), long a favourite of the Soviet elite, is owned and operated by the Kremlin. In summer it is usually completely booked by Kremlin officials, but rooms are often available off-season. There are also some cottages available, among them the infamous Stalin dacha.

Other resorts around the lake offer a variety of accommodation and sports facilities. Some options include the snazzy **Goluboi Fakel** (☎ 206 99; *Black Lake; cottages from RR1200 per person*) or the cheaper **Severnoy Syaniye** (☎ 095-264 5862; *Lake Uzhin; rooms with meals from RR480 per person*).

There are a few nondescript cafés in the centre of Valdai.

Getting There & Away
A daily train (four to five hours) from Leningrad Station to Pskov stops in Valdai. Alternatively, all trains between Moscow and St Pete stop in nearby Bologoye.

Many resorts offer transportation from either station.

West
Запад

ISTRA & NEW JERUSALEM MONASTERY
ИСТРА И НОВО-ИЕРУСАЛИМСКИЙ МОНАСТЫРЬ

In the 17th century, Patriarch Nikon, whose reforms drove the Old Believers from the Orthodox Church, decided to show that Russia deserved to be the centre of Christendom by building a little Holy City right at home, complete with its own Church of the Holy Sepulchre. Thus, the grandiose **New Jerusalem Monastery** *(Novo-Iyerusalimsky Monastyr; ☎ 231-497 87; exhibits RR10-15 each, guided tour RR50; open 10am-5pm Tues-Fri, 10am-6pm Sat & Sun)* was founded in 1656 near the picturesque (now polluted) Istra River, 50km west of central Moscow. The project was nearly stillborn when the abrasive Nikon lost his job.

Unlike other Moscow monasteries, this one had no military use, though with its perimeter walls and towers it looks like a fortress. In WWII, the retreating Germans blew it to pieces, but it's gradually being reconstructed. After years as a museum, the monastery is now in Orthodox hands and attracts a steady stream of worshippers. The nearby woods are a popular picnic spot.

Monastery

In the centre of the monastery grounds is the **Cathedral of the Resurrection** (Voskresensky sobor), intended to look like Jerusalem's Church of the Holy Sepulchre. Like its prototype, it's really several churches under one roof. The huge rotunda – very ambitious in 1685 – collapsed under its own weight a few decades after it went up and had to be rebuilt. One part of the cathedral where the reconstruction is complete is the unusual underground **Church of SS Konstantin and Yelena** (Konstantino-Yeleninskaya Tserkov), entered via an interior staircase, with a belfry peeping up above the ground outside the cathedral. Nikon was buried in the cathedral, beneath the **Church of John the Baptist** (Tserkov Ioanna Predtechi).

At the rear of the grounds is the Moscow baroque **Nativity Church** (Rozhdestvenskaya tserkov), with chambers for the tsar on the left and the abbot on the right. It houses a **museum** with books, porcelain, paintings, icons, old armour and a section on the history of the monastery. Behind the monastery near the river is Nikon's former 'hermitage', a rather unmonastic three-storey affair.

Museum of Wooden Architecture

Just outside the monastery's north wall, the Moscow region's Museum of Wooden Architecture *(contact info & hours same as monastery; admission RR8)* is a collection of renovated 17th- to 19th-century buildings. They show off the traditional 'gingerbread' woodwork outside and give a glimpse of old rural life inside.

Getting There & Away

Suburban trains run about twice an hour from Moscow's Riga Station to Istra (about one hour), from where buses run to the Muzey bus stop by the monastery.

By car, leave Moscow by Leningradsky prospekt and its continuation, Volokolamskoe shosse, and continue through Dedovsk to Istra. The monastery is 2km west of the town centre.

ARKHANGELSKOE
АРХАНГЕЛЬСКОЕ

On the Moscow River, a short distance west of Moscow's outer ring road, **Arkhangelskoe** *(☎ 363 1375; admission RR35 to grounds, RR35 to exhibits; open 10am-5pm Wed-Sun)* is one of the grandest estates in the region. A grandson of Dmitry Golitsyn, a statesman under Peter the Great, started work on a palace in the 1780s but lost interest and sold it all to Prince Nikolay Yusupov, one of the richest Russians of that time (or since).

During several ambassadorships and as Director of the Imperial Museums, Yusupov accumulated a private art collection that outclassed many European museums. After a rough start – the house was pillaged by Napoleon's troops, trashed in a serfs' revolt

EXCURSIONS

EXCURSIONS

and nearly burned down – Yusupov fixed it up and filled it with his treasures. The grounds and buildings are beautiful.

The **main house** of the palace consists of a series of elegant halls that show off Yusupov's paintings, furniture, sculptures, tapestries, porcelain and glass. His paintings include an entire room devoted to the Italian master Tiepolo, and – according to one source – portraits of each of his 300 mistresses.

The multilevel, Italianate **gardens** are full of 18th-century copies of classical statues. A colonnade on the eastern side was meant to be a Yusupov family mausoleum, but was never finished.

Yusupov also organised a troupe of serf actors that eventually became one of the best known of its kind, and built them a **theatre** just west of the gardens. Predating everything else is the little white 1667 **Church of the Archangel Michael** (Arkhangelskaya Tserkov).

Getting There & Away

The estate is 22km west of central Moscow. Bus Nos 62 and 151 from Moscow's Tushkinskaya Bus Station stop at Arkhangelskoe. If you're driving, drive northwest on Leningradsky prospekt, stay to the left as it becomes Volokolamskoe shosse, then beyond the outer ring road, fork left into Ilinskoe shosse.

BORODINO
БОРОДИНО

In 1812, Napoleon invaded Russia, lured by the prospect of taking Moscow. For three months the Russians retreated, until on 26 August the two armies met in a bloody, one-day battle of attrition at the village of Borodino, 130km west of Moscow.

In 15 hours, more than one-third of each army was killed – over 100,000 soldiers in all. Europe would know nothing as terrible until WWI.

The French seemed to be the winners, as the Russians withdrew and abandoned Moscow. But Borodino was in fact the beginning of the end for Napoleon, who was soon in full, disastrous retreat.

The entire battlefield (more than 100 sq km) is now the **Borodino Field Museum-Preserve**, basically vast fields dotted with dozens of memorials marking specific divisions and generals (most erected at the battle's centenary in 1912). It includes a **museum** (☎ 238-515 46; Ⓦ www.borodino .ru; open 10am-6pm Tues-Sun), which was recently renovated in honour of the battle's 190th anniversary in 2002.

The front line was roughly along the 4km road from Borodino village to the train station. The French were to its west, the Russians to its east. Most of the monuments are close to the road. The hill-top monument about 400m in front of the museum is the **grave** of Prince Bagration, a heroic Georgian infantry general who was mortally wounded in battle.

Farther south there's a concentration of monuments around Semyonovskoe village. This was the scene of the battle's most frenzied fighting where Bagration's heroic Second Army – opposing far larger French forces – was virtually obliterated. The redoubts around Semyonovskoe changed hands eight times in the battle. Apparently, the Russian commander, Mikhail Kutuzov, deliberately sacrificed Bagration's army to save his larger First Army, opposing lighter French forces in the northern part of the battlefield.

Kutuzov's headquarters are marked by an obelisk in the village of Gorki. Another obelisk near the Shevardinsky redoubt to the southwest – paid for in 1912 with French donations – marks Napoleon's camp.

Ironically, this battle scene was re-created during WWII, when the Red Army confronted the Nazis on this very site. Memorials to this battle also dot the fields, and WWII trenches surround the monument to Bagration. Near the train station are two WWII mass graves. The **Saviour Borodino Monastery** (☎ 238-510 57; admission RR15; open 10am-5pm Tues-Sun) has a small exhibit on the WWII battle.

The rolling hills around Borodino and Semyonovskoe are largely undeveloped, due to its historic status, so facilities are extremely limited. Be sure to bring a picnic lunch.

BORODINO BATTLEFIELD

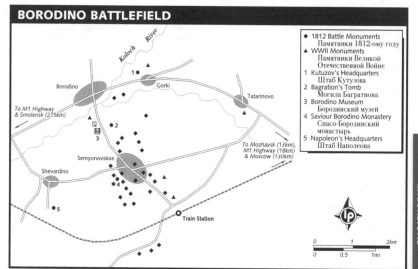

Key:
- ◆ 1812 Battle Monuments / Памятники 1812-ому году
- ▲ WWII Monuments / Памятники Великой Отечественной Войне
- 1 Kutuzov's Headquarters / Штаб Кутузова
- 2 Bagration's Tomb / Могила Багратиона
- 3 Borodino Museum / Бородинский музей
- 4 Saviour Borodino Monastery / Спасо-Бородинский монастырь
- 5 Napoleon's Headquarters / Штаб Наполеона

Getting There & Away

Suburban trains leave in the morning from Moscow's Belorusskaya Station to Borodino (RR20, two hours). A few trains return to Moscow in the evening, but be prepared to spend some time waiting. If you miss the train, you may be able to catch a bus to nearby Mozhaysk, from where there are frequent trains and buses.

Since the area is rural, visiting by car is more convenient and probably more rewarding. If driving from Moscow, stay on the M1 Minsk highway till the Mozhaysk turn-off, 95km beyond the Moscow outer ring road. It's 5km north to Mozhaysk, then 13km west to Borodino village.

PEREDELKINO
ПЕРЕДЕЛКИНО

Boris Pasternak – poet, author of *Doctor Zhivago* and winner of the 1958 Nobel Prize for literature – lived for a long time in a dacha in this now-trendy writers' colony on Moscow's southwestern outskirts, just 5km beyond the city's outer ring road. Pasternak's dacha is now a museum, the **Dom-Muzey Pasternaka** (☎ 934 5175; ul Pavlenko 3; admission RR25, guided tour RR50; open 10am-4pm Thur-Sun). The museum features the room where he died and the room where he finished *Dr Zhivago*. From the main road, turn left at the yellow brick building.

Though officially in disgrace when he died in 1960, thousands of people came to Pasternak's funeral, and even before *perestroika* (literally 'restructuring') his grave had a steady stream of visitors. Follow the main road to the hill to the cemetery; in a little pine grove towards the rear on the right-hand side, you will see the stone slab bearing Pasternak's profile. Above the graveyard sits the tiny 15th-century **Transfiguration Church** (Preobrazhenskaya Tserkov), which conducted religious services throughout the Soviet period.

Getting There & Away

Frequent suburban trains go from Moscow's Kiev Station to Peredelkino (20 minutes) on the line to Kaluga-II Station. If you're driving, take Kutuzovsky prospekt, which becomes Mozhayskoe shosse. Beyond the outer ring road, continue on the Minskoe shosse (highway M1) and at the 21km post turn left to Peredelkino.

South
Юг

GORKI LENINSKIE
ГОРКИ ЛЕНИНСКИЕ

After Lenin narrowly survived an assassination attempt in 1918, he and his family took occasional rests at the lovely 1830s manor house on this wooded estate, 32km southeast of the Kremlin.

The estate was redesigned in neoclassical style by the Art Nouveau architect Fyodor Shekhtel. Lenin spent more and more time at Gorki Leninskie after suffering strokes in 1922 and 1923. He left only once in the eight months before he died here on 21 January 1924.

Now this **museum** (☎ 548 9309; admission RR10, guided tour RR120; open 10am-4pm Wed-Mon) maintains some of the rooms as they were, and the clocks still read 6.50 (am), the time of Lenin's death. You can also see a large collection of Lenin's personal items, which were moved from his Kremlin office in 1994. There is a decent **café** on the grounds.

Getting There & Away

Bus No 439 leaves every 30 minutes for the estate from the Domodedovskaya metro station in Moscow. By car, follow the M4 Kashirskoe shosse about 8km to 11km beyond the Moscow outer ring road, then turn left to Gorki Leninskie.

MELIKHOVO
МЕЛИХОВО

The estate south of Moscow where Anton Chekhov lived from 1892 until 1899 is now open as a **museum** (Muzey A P Chekhova; ☎ 272-236 10) dedicated to the playwright. Chekhov wrote *The Seagull* and *Uncle Vanya* here. 'My estate's not much,' he wrote of Melikhova, 'but the surroundings are magnificent.' Visitors today can wander the village and peek in the 18th-century wooden **church**.

Chekhov was somewhat of a legendary figure in town, where he built three local schools and a fire station. When he was in residence, he flew a red flag above his home, notifying peasants that they could come for medical advice and treatment.

Suburban trains operate from Moscow's Kursk Station to the town of Chekhov (one hour), 12km west of Melikhovo. Occasional buses run between Chekhov and Melikhovo. By car, Melikhovo is about 7km east of the dual carriageway that parallels the old M2 Moscow–Oryol road, signposted 50km south of the Moscow outer ring road.

PRIOKSKO-TERRASNY BIOSPHERE RESERVE
ПРИОКСКО-ТЕРРАСНЫЙ ЗАПОВЕДНИК

The Priokso-Terrasny Biosphere Reserve (☎ 27-707 145; admission RR25, guided tour RR45; open 9am-4pm daily) covers 50 sq km bordering the northern flood plain of the Oka River, a tributary of the Volga. It's a meeting point of northern fir groves and marshes with typical southern meadow steppe, and its varied fauna includes a herd of European bison, brought back from near extinction since WWII.

You cannot wander freely around the reserve by yourself, so it's best to make advance arrangements for one of the informative tours.

There's a small **museum** near the office, with stuffed specimens of the reserve's fauna, typical of European Russia, including beavers, elk, deer and boar. You're unlikely to see the real thing outside, except maybe elk or deer in winter.

The reserve's pride, and the focus of most visits, is its European bison nursery (pitomnik zubrov).

Two pairs of bison, one of Europe's largest mammals (some weigh over a tonne), were brought from Poland in 1948. Now there are about 60, and more than 200 have been sent out to other parts of the country. The bison come into the nursery in greatest numbers at feeding time, which is early morning and early evening.

For this reason, it's well worthwhile considering spending the night at the **Kordon Hotel** which is situated on the grounds of the preserve.

Getting There & Away

Public transport is difficult. If you leave before 8am, you can take a suburban train from Moscow's Kursk Station to Serpukhov (two hours), then a rare bus to the village of Danki, 1km from the reserve's excursion bureau. You might also be able to negotiate a ride from the station.

If you are driving, the turn-off from the Moscow–Oryol highway is 76km south of the Moscow outer ring road. Driving from Moscow, you have to turn west and then double back under the highway. Go through Danki then turn right to the reserve. It's 5km from the highway to the excursion bureau.

TULA
ТУЛА

☎ 0872 • postcode 300000 • pop 550,000

The city of Tula, 170km south of Moscow, is a polluted industrial town on the way to Ukraine, however, it is home to a few interesting museums, and could make a worthwhile stop if you are headed south. Named for the Tulitsa River, it was first mentioned in historical documents in 1146, when the prince Svyatoslav Olgovich paid a visit. Tula lay in the path of Mongol-led armies advancing on Moscow and was constantly under siege during the 14th century. After the Mongol defeat at the 1380 Battle of Kulikov, Tula was incorporated into Muscovy and fortified.

Things to See

The **kremlin** *(pl Vosstania)* at the heart of the city was built in 1514–21 with thick limestone walls about 1km round.

Inside, the **Epiphany Cathedral** (Bogoyavlensky sobor) houses the **Weapons Museum** *(☎ 312 406; ⓦ www.arms-museum .tula.ru; admission RR20; open 10am-1pm, 2pm-4.45pm Wed-Sun)*. Gunsmithing in Tula dates to the 16th century, and the town's fate was sealed when Peter the Great founded a small arms factory in 1712. Among the conventional weapons in the museum (from muskets to kalashnikovs) are many curiosities; for example, the 'Velodog' is a pistol designed for sale to British cyclists, who might need to gun down dangerous dogs in their path!

If all those guns make you hungry, you might stop by at the **Tula Gingerbread Museum** *(Tulsky Muzey Pryanika; ☎ 777 390; ul Okyabrskaya 45; admission RR25; open 10am-2pm, 3pm-4pm Wed-Sun)* for a snack. The small museum shows the history of this local speciality and how it is made.

The **Antiquity Museum** *(☎ 361 663; pr Lenina 47; admission RR15; open 10am-5pm daily)* is an exhibit of archaeological findings from Tula.

Visitors are invited to live a day in the life of a 16th-century Tulan – to play old-fashioned games, participate in ceremonies and hang out in a log cabin.

Places to Stay & Eat

Hotel Moskva *(☎ 200 341; doubles RR900)*, outside Tula's Moskovsky Station, seems to be the only place that considers itself good enough for the foreigners. It's not really friendly, and the doubles are small.

Babushkas around town sell a tasty local speciality called *Tulsky pryanik* (glazed gingerbread with an apricot jam filling).

Getting There & Away

Suburban trains from Moscow's Kursk Station take four or five hours to Tula. You might also try to get on a long-distance train heading for Kursk or Ukraine, many of which stop at Tula. There are several daily buses from Moscow's Shchyolkovsky Bus Station (4½ hours).

YASNAYA POLYANA
ЯСНАЯ ПОЛЯНА

Located 14km south of central Tula and roughly 240km from Moscow, Yasnaya Polyana *(☎ 087-513 5425; ⓦ www.tulrci.edu.ru/ Polyana; admission RR160; open 9.30am-6pm Wed-Sun)* is the estate where the great Russian writer Count Leo Tolstoy was born and buried.

Tolstoy spent much of his life in this **house**, which is a simple place filled with many of his possessions. His nearby **grave** is unmarked, except for the bouquets of flowers left by newlyweds. In autumn, the apple trees are laden with fruit, which visitors can pick and snack on.

Getting There & Away

The new express suburban train from Moscow's Kursk Station is the easiest way to get to Yasnaya Polyana. Otherwise, you have to go to Tula then take bus No 114 to Shchekino, which stops at the the Yasnaya Polyana turn-off.

Look for the blue 'Yasnaya Polyana' sign on the main road south from central Tula. From here it's 1km west (right) to the estate entrance.

If you're driving from Moscow, it's easiest to follow Tula's western bypass all the way to its southern end and then turn back north towards Tula. The Yasnaya Polyana turn-off is about 24km from the southern end of the bypass on the road back towards central Tula.

Language

Who Speaks What?

Everyone in Moscow speaks Russian. It and most of the other languages are written in variants of the Cyrillic alphabet. Russian grammar may be daunting, but your travels will be far more interesting if you at least take the time to learn the Cyrillic alphabet, so that you can read maps and street signs.

It's quite easy to find English-speakers in Moscow; the major hotels are a good place to start. Don't expect to find much English spoken by average folk, as the language has only recently become a widely accessible subject in schools.

Before you head off, get a copy of Lonely Planet's detailed and useful *Russian phrasebook* and a small dictionary such as the *Pocket Oxford Russian Dictionary*.

RUSSIAN
Cyrillic Alphabet

The Cyrillic alphabet resembles Greek with a few additional characters. Every language that uses Cyrillic has its own slightly different variant. The alphabet table on p.??? shows the letters of the Russian alphabet and the Roman-letter equivalents used to transliterate them in this language guide.

Pronunciation

The sounds of а, о, е and я are 'weaker' when the stress in the word does not fall on them – eg, in вода, *voda* (water) the stress falls on the second syllable, so it's pronounced *vada*, with the 'a' representing both the unstressed pronunciation for о and the stressed pronunciation for a. The vowel й only follows other vowels in so-called diphthongs, eg, ой *oy*, ей *ey*. Note that Russians usually print ё without the dots, a source of confusion in pronunciation.

The 'voiced' consonants б, в, г, д, ж and з are not voiced at the end of words, eg, хлеб (bread) is pronounced *khlyep* (not *khlyeb*), or before voiceless consonants. The г in the common adjective endings его and ого is pronounced 'v'.

Soft & Hard Sign

Two letters have no sound but function by modifying other sounds. A consonant followed by the 'soft sign' ь is spoken with the tongue flat against the palate, as if followed by the faint beginnings of a 'y' – it's represented in this section by an apostrophe. The rare 'hard sign' ъ after a consonant inserts a slight pause before the next vowel.

Transliteration

There's no ideal system for rendering Cyrillic in the Roman alphabet; the more faithfully a system indicates pronunciation, the more complicated it is.

The transliteration system used in this language guide differs from that used in the rest of the book (which follows the US Library of Congress System I – good for deciphering printed words and rendering proper names); it's intended to assist you in pronouncing Russian letters and sounds, with an emphasis on practicality. Most letters are transliterated in accordance with the pronunciation guide in the Cyrillic alphabet table on the following page. A few exceptions are listed below:

е	written as **e** (except at the beginning of words, when it's written as **ye**)
ай	written as **ay**
ей	written as **ey**
ий	written as **iy**
ой	written as **oy** (when stressed), as **ay** (when unstressed)
ый	written as **y**
ж	written as **zh**
х	written as **kh**

Useful Words & Phrases

Two words you're sure to use are Здравствуйте *(zdrastvuyte)*, the universal 'hello' (but if you say it a second time in one day to the same person, they'll think you forgot you already saw them!), and Пожалуйста *(pazhalsta)*, the multipurpose word for 'please' (commonly included in all polite

The Russian Cyrillic Alphabet

Cyrillic	Roman	Pronunciation
А, а	a	as the 'a' in 'path' (in stressed syllables) as the 'a' in 'about' (in unstressed syllables)
Б, б	b	as the 'b' in 'but'
В, в	v	as the 'v' in 'van'
Г, г	g	as the 'g' in 'god'
Д, д	d	as the 'd' in 'dog'
Е, е *	e	as the 'ye' in 'yet' (in stressed syllables) as the 'yi' in 'yin' (in unstressed syllables)
Ё, ё **	yo	as the 'yo' in 'yonder'
Ж, ж	zh	as the 's' in 'measure'
З, з	z	as the 'z' in 'zoo'
И, и	i	as the 'i' in 'litre'
Й, й	y	as the 'y' in 'boy'
К, к	k	as the 'k' in 'kind'
Л, л	l	as the 'l' in 'lamp'
М, м	m	as the 'm' in 'mad'
Н, н	n	as the 'n' in 'not'
О, о	o	as the 'o' in 'more' (in stressed syllables) as the 'a' in 'path' (in unstressed syllables)
П, п	p	as the 'p' in 'pig'
Р, р	r	as the 'r' in 'rub' (rolled)
С, с	s	as the 's' in 'sing'
Т, т	t	as the 't' in 'ten'
У, у	u	as the 'u' in 'put'
Ф, ф	f	as the 'f' in 'fan'
Х, х	kh	as the 'ch' in 'Bach'
Ц, ц	ts	as the 'ts' in 'bits'
Ч, ч	ch	as the 'ch' in 'chin'
Ш, ш	sh	as the 'sh' in 'shop'
Щ, щ	shch	as 'sh-ch' in 'fresh chips'
ъ	(no symbol)	'hard sign' (see p.???)
Ы, ы	y	as the 'y' in 'busy'
ь	'	'soft sign'; (see p.???)
Э, э	e	as the 'e' in 'ten'
Ю, ю	yu	as the 'yu' in 'yule'
Я, я	ya	as the 'ya' in 'yard' (in stressed syllables) as the 'yi' in 'yin' (in unstressed syllables)

* Е, е is transliterated Ye, ye when at the beginning of a word

** Ё, ё is often printed without dots

requests), 'you're welcome', 'pardon me', 'after you' and more.

Good morning.
dobraye utra Доброе утро.
Good afternoon.
dobry den' Добрый день.
Good evening.
dobry vecher Добрый вечер.
Goodbye.
da svidaniya До свидания.
Goodbye (informal).
paka Пока.
How are you?
kak dela? Как дела?
Yes.
da Да.
No.
net Нет.

Thank you (very much).
(bal'shoye) spasiba
(Большое) спасибо.
Pardon me.
prastite/pazhalsta
Простите/Пожалуйста.
No problem/Never mind.
nichevo (literally 'nothing')
Ничего.
I like (it).
mne nravitsya
Мне нравится.
Can you help me?
pamagite pazhalsta
Помогите, пожалуйста.
May I take a photo?
***mozhna fatagrafiravat'*?**
Можно фотографировать?

Pronouns

Normally, the polite form вы (*vy*, 'you' plural) is used in conversation. The informal ты (*ty*, 'you' singular) is for talking to children, relatives and close friends.

I
ya я
you (singular informal)
ty ты
he, she, it
on, ana, ano он, она, оно

we

my   мы

you (polite plural or singular)

vy   вы

they

ani   они

Names & Introductions

In introducing yourself you can use your first name, or first and last. Russians often address each other by first name plus patronymic (a middle name based on their father's first name) – eg, Natalya Borisovna (Natalya, daughter of Boris), Pavel Niko-laevich (Pavel, son of Nikolay). This requires careful attention when someone is being introduced to you!

What's your name?

kak vas zavut?   Как вас зовут?

My name is ...

menya zavut ...   Меня зовут ...

Pleased to meet you.

ochen' priyatna   Очень приятно.

my husband

moy muzh   мой муж

my wife

maya zhina   моя жена

my boyfriend

moy paren'   мой парень

my girlfriend

maya devushka   моя девушка

Language Difficulties

I don't speak Russian.

ya ni gavaryu pa ruski

Я не говорю по-русски.

I don't understand.

ya ni panimayu

Я не понимаю.

Do you speak English?

vy gavarite pa angliyski?

Вы говорите по-английски?

Can you write it down, please?

zapishite pazhalsta

Запишите, пожалуйста

translator

perevotchik

переводчик

Countries

Where are you from?

atkuda vy?   Откуда вы?

Australia

afstraliya   Австралия

Canada

kanada   Канада

France

frantsiya   Франция

Germany

germaniya   Германия

Great Britain

velikabritaniya   Великобритания

Ireland

irlandiya   Ирландия

New Zealand

novaya zelandiya   Новая Зеландия

USA, America

se she a/amerika   США/Америка

Getting Around

How do we get to ...?

kak dabrat'sa k ...?

Как добраться к ...?

When does it leave?

kagda atpravlyaetsya?

Когда отправляется?

The usual way to get to the exit in a crowded bus is to say to anyone in the way, Вы выходите? *(vy vykhoditi?)*, 'Are you getting off?'.

bus

aftobus   автобус

taxi

taksi   такси

train

poyezt   поезд

tram

tramvay   трамвай

trolleybus

traleybus   троллейбус

fixed-route minibus

marshrutnaye   маршрутное

taksi   такси

railway station

zhileznadarozhny vagzal

железнодорожный (ж. д.) вокзал

stop (bus, tram etc)
  astanofka
  остановка
ticket, tickets
  bilet/bilety
  билет/билеты
ticket/tickets (city bus, trolleybus/tram)
  talon/talony
  талон/талоны
metro token, tokens
  zheton/zhetony
  жетон/жетоны
map
  karta
  карта
transport map
  skhema transparta
  схема транспорта

Accommodation

How much is a room?
  skol'ka stoit nomer?
  Сколько стоит номер?
Do you have a cheaper room?
  u vas est' dishevle nomer?
  У вас дешевле номер?

hotel	
gastinitsa	гостиница
room	
nomer	номер
key	
klyuch	ключ
boiling water	
kipyatok	кипяток
toilet paper	
tualetnaya bumaga	туалетная бумага
towel	
palatentse	полотенце
blanket	
adeyala	одеяло
too hot/stuffy	
zharka/dushna	жарко/душно

The ... isn't working.
  ... ne rabotaet.   ... не работает.

toilet	
tualet	туалет
tap/faucet	
kran	кран

heating	
atapleniye	отопление
light	
svet	свет
electricity	
electrichestva	электричество

Around Town

House numbers are not always in step on opposite sides of the street. Russian addresses are written back to front (country first, then postal code, city or town, street address, and name at the bottom).

Where is ...?
  gde ...?   Где ...?
I'm lost.
  ya zabludilsya/   Я заблудился/
  zabludilas' (m/f)   заблудилась.

to (on) the left	
naleva	налево
to (on) the right	
naprava	направо
straight ahead	
pryama	прямо
near	
daleko	далеко
far	
bliska	близко
north	
sever	север
south	
yuk	юг
east	
vastok	восток
west	
zapad	запад
(go) back	
nazat	назад
here, there	
tut, tam	тут, там

avenue	
praspekt	проспект (просп.)
church	
tserkof'	церковь
circus	
tsirk	цирк
lane	
pereulak	переулок (пер.)
museum	
muzey	музей

square/plaza	
ploshchat'	площадь (пл.)
street	
ulitsa	улица (ул.)
theatre	
teatr	театр
toilet	
tualet	туалет
money	
den'gi	деньги
currency exchange	
abmen valyuty	обмен валюты
bank	
bank	банк
travellers cheques	
darozhnye cheki	дорожные чеки
small change	
razmen	размен
post office	
pochta	почтамт
stamp	
marka	марка
postcard	
atkrytka	открытка
telephone	
telefon	телефон
fax	
faks	факс/телефакс
... telephone office	
... telefonyy punkt	... телефонный пункт
intercity	
mezhdugorodny	междугородный
international	
mezhdunarodny	международный

Shopping
I need ...	
mne nuzhna ...	Мне нужно ...
Do you have ...?	
u vas est'...?	У вас есть ...?
Please show me.	
pakazhiti	Покажите,
pazhalste	пожалуйста.
How much is it?	
skol'ka stoit?	Сколько стоит?
bookshop	
knizhny	книжный магазин
magazin	

Signs

Вход	**Entrance**
Выход	**Exit**
Мест Нет	**No Vacancy**
Справки	**Information**
Открыт	**Open**
Закрыт	**Closed**
Касса	**Cashier/Ticket Office**
Больница	**Hospital**
Милиция	**Police**
Туалет	**Toilet**
Мужской (М)	**Men**
Женский (Ж)	**Women**

department store	
univirsal'ny	универсальный
magazin	магазин
market	
rynak	рынок
newsstand	
gazetny kiosk	газетный киоск
pharmacy	
apteka	аптека
shop	
magazin	магазин
good/OK	
kharasho	хорошо
bad	
plokha	плохо
open/closed	
otkryta/zakryta	открыто/закрыто

Time, Days & Date
What time is it?	
katory chas?	Который час?
At what time?	
f katoram chasu?	В котором часу?
hour	
chas	час
minute	
minuta	минута
am/in the morning	
utra	утра
pm/in the afternoon	
dnya	дня
in the evening	
vechera	вечера
local time	
mesnaye vremya	местное время

Emergencies

I'm sick.
  ya bolen (m)   Я болен.
  ya bal'na (f)   Я больна.
I need a doctor.
  mne nuzhen vrach Мне нужен врач.
Help!
  na pomashch!/ На помощь!/
  pamagite!   Помогите!
Thief!
  vor!   Вор!
Fire!
  pazhar!   Пожар!
hospital
  bal'nitsa   больница
police
  militsiya   милиция

Moscow time
  maskovskaye московское время
  vremya
When?
  kagda?   Когда?
today
  sevodnya   сегодня
tomorrow
  zaftra   завтра
yesterday
  vchera   вчера
day after tomorrow
  poslezaftra   послезавтра

Monday
  panedel'nik понедельник
Tuesday
  ftornik   вторник
Wednesday
  sreda   среда
Thursday
  chetverk   четверг
Friday
  pyatnitsa   пятница
Saturday
  subota   суббота
Sunday
  vaskrisen'e воскресенье

(Centuries are written in Roman numerals.)
century, centuries
  в., вв. *(v, vv)*

year, years
  г., гг. *(g, gg)*
beginning/middle/end
  начало/середина/конец
  (nachala/seredina/kanets)
AD (literally 'our era')
  н.э. *(n.e – nasha era)*
BC (literally 'before our era')
  до н.э. *(do n.e – da nashey ery)*
10th century AD
  X в. н.э. *(disyaty vek nashey ery)*
7th century BC
  VII в. до н.э. *(syed'moy vek da nashey ery)*

Numbers

How many?
  skol'ka?   Сколько?

0	*nol'*
1	*adin*
2	*dva*
3	*tri*
4	*chetyri*
5	*pyat'*
6	*shest'*
7	*sem'*
8	*vosem'*
9	*devyat'*
10	*desyat'*
11	*adinatsat'*
12	*dvenatsat'*
13	*trinatsat'*
20	*dvatsat'*
21	*dvatsat' adin*
30	*tritsat'*
40	*sorak*
50	*pyat'desyat*
60	*shest'desyat*
70	*sem'desyat*
80	*vosimdesyat*
90	*devyanosta*
100	*sto*
200	*dvesti*
300	*trista*
400	*chetyrista*
500	*pyat'sot*
1000	*tysyacha*
10,000	*desyat' tysyach*

one million
  (adin) milion (один) миллион

FOOD

restaurant
restaran ресторан
café
kafe кафе
canteen
stalovaya столовая
snack bar
bufet буфет
buffet/smorgasbord/Swedish Table
shvetskiy stol шведский стол
take away
s saboy с собой

Types of snack shop include:

блинная *(blinaya)* serves *bliny* (pancakes with savoury or sweet fillings)

бутербродная *(buterbrodnaya)* serves little open sandwiches

закусочная *(zakusachnaya)* serves miscellaneous snacks

пельменная *(pil'mennaya)* serves *pelmeni* (meat ravioli)

пирожковая *(pirashkovaya)* serves *pirozhki* (deep-fried meat or vegetable turnovers)

чебуречная *(chiburechnaya)* serves Armenian or Georgian *chebureki* (spicy, deep-fried mutton pies)

шашлычная *(shashlychnaya)* serves *shashlyk* (charcoal-grilled meat kebab)

At the Restaurant
Ordering

Except at the fanciest restaurants (or foreign restaurants) waiters will probably not speak English.

waiter
afitsiant официант
waitress
afitsiantka официантка
menu
minyu меню
hot
garyachiy горячий
cold
khalodnyy холодный
more
yishchyo ещё

What's this?
shto eta?
Что это?
I'd like ...
ya by khatel/khatela ... (m/f)
Я бы хотел/хотела ...
May we order?
mozhna zakazat?
Можно заказать?
Please bring ...
prinisiti, pazhalsta ...
Принесите пожалуйста ...
That's all.
vsyo
Всё.
Bon appetit!
priyatnava apitita!
Приятного аппетита!
The bill/check, please.
schyot, pazhalsta
Счёт, пожалуйста.

Menu Decoder
Breakfast

If you are staying in a hotel, breakfast (завтрак, *zaftrak*) can range from a large help-yourself buffet spread to bread, butter, jam, tea and a boiled egg or nothing at all. Items you might find include:

блины *(bliny)* or блинчики *(blinchiki)* – thin pancackes, usually filled with jam, cheese or meat

каша *(kasha)* – Russian-style buckwheat porridge

сырники *(syrniki)* – fritters of cottage cheese, flour and egg

творог *(tvarog/tvorag)* – cottage cheese

кефир *(kifir)* – yogurt-like sour milk, served as a drink

яйцо *(yaytso)* – egg

всмятку *(fsmyatku)* – soft-boiled

крутое *(krutoye)* – hard-boiled

омлет *(amlet)* – omelette

яичница *(yaishnitsa)* – fried

сметана *(smitana)* – sour cream

Lunch & Dinner

Russians like a fairly heavy early-afternoon meal (обед, *ahbet*) and a lighter evening meal (ужин, *uzhyn*). Meals (and menus) are divided into courses:

закуски *(zakuski)* – appetisers, often grouped into cold *zakuski* (холодные закуски) and hot *zakuski* (горячие закуски)

первые блюда *(pervyya bluda)* – first courses, usually soups

вторые блюда *(vtariya bluda)* – second courses or 'main' dishes

горячие блюда *(garyachiya bluda)* – hot courses (same as second courses)

сладкие блюда *(sladkiya bluda)* – sweet courses or desserts

Main dishes may be further divided into:

фирменные *(firmeniye)* – house specials

национальные *(natsianalniye)* – national or ethnic dishes

порционные *(portsioniye)* – special orders

мясные *(myasniye)* – meat

рыбные *(rybniye)* – fish

птица *(ptitsa)* – poultry

овощные *(ovashniye)* – vegetable

Cooking Styles

Words you might spot on the menu are:

варёный *(varyonyy)* – boiled

жареный *(zharinyy)* – roasted or fried

отварной *(atvarnoy)* – poached or boiled

печёный *(pichyonyy)* – baked

фри *(fri)* – fried

Appetisers

The fancier appetisers (*zakuski*, закуски), rival main courses for price. A few *zakuski* worth trying are:

икра *(ikra)* – caviar

блины со сметаной *(bliny sa smitanay)* – pancakes with sour cream

грибы в сметане *(griby fsmitani)* – mushrooms baked in sour cream

рыба солёная *(ryba salyonaya)* – salted fish

семга копчёная *(syimga kapchyonaya)* – smoked salmon

салат из помидоров *(salat iz pamidorof)* – tomato salad

салат из огурцов *(salat iz agurtsof)* – cucumber salad

салат столичный *(salat stalichnyy)* – salad comprised of vegetable and beef bits, potato and egg in sour cream and mayonnaise

Soup

Rich soups may be the pinnacle of Slavic cooking. There are dozens of varieties, often served with a dollop of sour cream. Most are made from meat stock. The Russian word for soup sounds the same, суп. Among the most common soups are:

борщ *(borshch)* – beetroot with vegetables and meat

лапша *(lapsha)* – chicken noodle

окрошка *(akroshka)* – cold or hot soup made from cucumbers, sour cream, potatoes, egg, meat and *kvas* (a beer-like drink)

рассольник *(rasol'nik)* – pickled cucumber and kidney

солянка *(salyanka)* – thick meat or fish soup with salted cucumbers and other vegetables

уха *(ukha)* – fish soup with potatoes and vegetables

харчо *(kharcho)* – garlicky mutton, Caucasian-style

щи *(shchi)* – cabbage or sauerkraut (many varieties)

Poultry & Meat

Poultry (птица, *ptitsa*) is usually chicken (курица, *kuritsa* or цыплёнок, *tsyplyonak*). Meat (мясо, *myasa*) is usually:

баранина *(baranina)* – mutton

говядина *(gavyadina)* – beef

свинина *(svinina)* – pork

The list of possible dishes (and possible names) is huge, but following are some common meat and poultry dishes:

антрекот *(antrikot)* – entrecote, boned sirloin steak

бифстроганов *(bifstroganaf)* – beef stroganoff, beef slices in a rich sauce

бифштекс *(bifshteks)* – steak', usually a glorified hamburger filling

голубцы *(galuptsy)* – cabbage rolls stuffed with meat

жаркое *(zharkoye)* – meat or poultry stewed in a clay pot, usually with mushrooms, potatoes and vegetables

котлета *(katleta)* – croquette of ground meat

котлета по-жарская *(katleta pa-zharskaya)* – croquette with minced chicken

котлета по-киевски *(katleta pa-kiefski)* – chicken Kiev, fried boneless chicken breast stuffed with butter (watch out, it squirts!)

пельмени *(pil'meni)* – pelmeni or Siberian-style meat dumplings

плов *(plov)* – pilaf, rice with mutton bits, from Central Asia

цыплёнок табака *(tsyplyonak tabaka)* – chicken Tabaka, grilled chicken Caucasian-style

шашлык *(shashlyk)* – skewered and grilled mutton or other meat, adapted from Central Asia and Transcaucasia

Fish
Fish is рыба *(ryba)*.

омуль *(omul')* – omul, like salmon, from Lake Baikal

сёмга *(syomga)* – salmon

судак *(sudak)* – pike perch

форель *(farel')* – trout

осётр *(asyotr)*, осетрина *(asitrina)* or севрюга *(sivryuga)* – sturgeon

осетрина отварная *(asitrina atvarnaya)* – poached sturgeon

осетрина с грибами *(asitrina zgribami)* – sturgeon with mushrooms

Vegetables
Vegetables are овощи *(ovashchi)*; greens are зелень *(zelin')*. A garnish is гарниры *(garniry)*.

горох *(garokh)* – peas

капуста *(kapusta)* – cabbage

картошка *(kartoshka)* or картофель *(kartofil')* – potato

морковь *(markof')* – carrots

огурец *(agurets)* – cucumber

помидор *(pamidor)* – tomato

Fruit
Fruit is фрукты *(frukty)*.

абрикос *(abrikos)* – apricot

арбуз *(arbus)* – watermelon

виноград *(vinagrad)* – grapes

груша *(grusha)* – pear

дыня *(dynya)* – melon

яблоко *(yablaka)* – apple

Other Foods
On every table are stacks of bread (хлеб, *khlep*). The best is Russian 'black' bread, a vitamin-rich sour rye. Russians are mad about wild mushrooms (грибы, *griby*); in late summer and early autumn they troop into the woods with their buckets. Other items are:

рис *(ris)* – rice

сыр *(syr)* – cheese

масло *(masla)* – butter

перец *(pyerits)* – pepper

сахар *(sakhar)* – sugar

соль *(sol')* – salt

Desserts
Perhaps most Russians are exhausted or drunk by dessert time, since this is the least imaginative course.

блинчики *(blinchiki)* – pancakes with jam or other sweet filling

кисель *(kisel')* – fruit jelly (Jell-o to Yanks)

компот *(kampot)* – fruit in syrup (probably from a tin)

оладьи *(alad'l)* – fritters topped with syrup or sour cream

пирожное *(pirozhnaye)* – pastries

мороженое *(morozhenoe, marozhinaye)* – ice-cream

Vegetarian Food
Menus often have a category like vegetable

(овощные), milk (молочные), egg (яичные) and flour (мучные) dishes, but don't get your hopes up.

I'm a vegetarian.
   Я вегетарианка.   *ya vigitarianka* (f)
   Я вегетарианец.   *ya vigitarianits* (m)
I can't eat meat.
   Я не ем мясного.   *ya ni em myasnova*
without meat
   без мяса   *bez myasa*
only vegetables
   только овощи   *tol'ka ovashchi*

DRINKS
Nonalcoholic
water
   вода   *vada*
boiled water
   кипяток   *kipyatok*
mineral water
   минеральная   *mineralnaya vada*
   вода
soda water
   газированная   *gazirovanaya*
   вода   *vada*
coffee
   кофе   *kofe*
tea
   чай   *chai*
with sugar
   с сахаром   *s sakharam*

with jam
   с вареньем   *s faren'im*
milk
   молоко   *malako*
juice
   сок   *sok*
lemonade
   лимонад   *limanad*
soft drink
   безалкогольный напиток
   bezalkagol'nyy napituk

Alcoholic
alcohol
   алкоголь   *alkagol'*
vodka
   водка   *votka*
sparkling wine (Champagne-style)
   советское   *savyetskaya*
   шампанское   *shampanskaya*
red/white wine
   красное/белое   *krasnaya/belaya*
   вино   *vino*
brandy
   коньяк   *kan'ak*
beer
   пиво   *piva*
kvas (beer-like drink)
   квас   *kvas*

To your health!
   За ваше здоровье!
   za vashe zdarov'e!

Glossary

aeroport – airport
avtovokzal – bus terminal

bankomat – ATM machine
banya – Russian bathhouse, similar to a sauna
Beriozka – literally 'Birch tree'; refers to chain of Soviet stores selling souvenirs for hard currency
biblioteka – library
bilet – ticket
bliny – crepes
bolnitsa – hospital
bolshoy – big
borscht – beetroot soup
boyar – high-ranking noble
bufet – snack bar
bulvar – boulevard; sometimes abbreviated as 'bul'
Bulvarnoe Koltso – Boulevard Ring; one of Moscow's ring roads
buterbrod – open-faced sandwich

dacha – country cottage or summer house
deklaratsia – customs declaration form
devushka – young woman
duma – parliament

elektrichka – slow, suburban train

firmenny poezd – a fancy, fast train, often with a special name

GAI (Gosudarstvennaya Avtomobilnaya Inspektsia) – State Automobile Inspectorate
glasnost – openness; used in reference to the free-expression aspect of the Gorbachev reforms
gostinitsa – hotel
GUM (Gosudarstvenniy Universalny Magasin) – State Department Store, located on Red Square

ikra – caviar
izba – single-storey wooden cottage found in the countryside
izveshchenie – a notice of permission

kamera khraneniya – left-luggage
kasha – porridge
kassa – cash register or ticket office
kefir – yogurt-like sour milk
Khokhloma – region north of Nizhny Novgorod; refers to traditional style of colourfully painted kitchen utensils
khram – cathedral
kokoshniki – tiers of colourful tiles and brick patterns which are common in Russian architecture
konyak – brandy, usually Armenian
korpus – building
kremlin – fort, usually a town's foundation
kupenyy or **kupe** – 2nd class on a train; usually four-person couchettes
kvas – mildly alcoholic fermented juice

luks or **lyux** – luxury or 1st class; often refers to a sleeping car on a train

maly – small
matrioshka – painted wooden nesting dolls
mesto – place, as in seat on a train
mezhdugorodnyy – inter-city
mezhdunarodnyy – international
MID – Ministry of Foreign Affairs
MKAD (Moskovskaya Koltsovaya Avtomobilnaya Doroga) – Moscow's outer ring road delineating the city limits
monastyr – monastery
most – bridge
muzey – museum
MVD – Ministry of Internal Affairs
myagkiy – soft; refers to 1st class on a train

naberezhnaya – embankment; sometimes abbreviated as 'nab'

okroshka – cucumber soup with a kvas base
OVIR (Otdel Viz I Registratsii) – Department of Visas and Registrations, now known as PVU

Palekh – town near Ivanovo; refers to painted lacquer boxes
parilka – steam room in a *banya*

225

passazhirskiy poezd – slow, intercity passenger train
Paskha – Easter
pelmeni – dumplings filled with meat or vegetables
Peredvizhniki – literally 'Wanderers'; used in reference to a prominent 19th-century artistic movement
perekhod – cross walk, often underground
pereryv – break period, often in the middle of the day, when stores close
perestroika – literally 'restructuring'; refers to Gorbachev's economic reforms of the 1980s
pereulok – lane; sometimes abbreviated as 'per'
pirozhek – deep-fried meat or vegetable turnover
platskartnyy – 3rd class, general seating on an intercity train
ploshchad – square; sometimes abbreviated as 'pl'
prigorodny poezd – slow, suburban train
prigorodny zal – separate ticket hall for suburban trains
proezd – passage
prospekt – avenue; sometimes abbreviated as 'pr'
provodnitsa – conductor
PVU (Passport i Viza Upravlenie) – Passport and Visa Service

rastoyanie – distance in kilometres
restoran – restaurant
Rozhdestvo – Christmas, celebrated on 7 January
rynok – market

sad – garden
Sadovoe Koltso – Garden Ring; one of Moscow's ring roads
samizdat – underground publishing during the Soviet period

samovar – urn used to heat water for tea
shampanskoe – Russian sparkling wine
shapka – fur hat
shashlik – meat kebab
shatyor – tent roof, a common architectural feature
shchi – cabbage soup
shosse – highway; sometimes abbreviated as 'sh'
shtuka – piece or item; often used as a unit of sale
skoryy poezd – fast train
solyanka – salty meat-based soup with cucumber and lemon
sosiski – hot dogs
spalnyy vagon or **SV** – sleeping car
stolovaya – canteen or cafeteria

taksofon – pay phone
teatr – theatre
tramvay – tram which runs on tracks above ground, usually outside the city centre
trolleybus – electric bus
tserkov – church

ulitsa – street; sometimes abbreviated as 'ul'
uslovnye yedensitsy – standard unit; tied to the US dollar and regularly used to quote the prices in both upmarket restaurants and hotels

vagon – train carriage
val – rampart
veniki – birch branches, used for a cleansing beating in the banya
vokzal – train station

zakuski – appetisers
zheton – metal token; used for some older pay phones or left-luggage lockers
zhyostkiy – 2nd-class (hard class) on a train; usually in reference to four-person couchettes

Thanks

Many thanks to the travellers who used the last edition and wrote to us with helpful hints, useful advice and interesting anecdotes:

Nikolas Andredakis, Brent R Antonson, Katherine Bakeev, Lone Bech, Marl Allen Brown, Alister Carroll, Farid Chetouani, Terry Collins, Mrs Cook, Alain Courtois, Julie Coutureq, David de Kleine, Marcel de Vroed, Andrea Dekkers, Ian Douglas, Kim Dutkoski, Hannah Dvorak-Carbone, P Ekerot, Mary Ellis, Chris Enting, Dietmar Fischer, António Folgado, Julien & Florence Fuchs, Elvira Gabbasova, Jane Galvin, Tavis Gorman, Ed Graystone, Spencer Green, Yaniv Hamo, Anna Harmala, Terry Hart, Katrin Hoedemacker, Marie Javins, Dr Christopher Johnson, Sanjiv Kapur, Kitty Lee, Phil Lewis, Reginald Leyssens, Erik Lindqvist, Darren Lydom, Lachlan MacQuarrie, J Mak, Cathy & Kevin Marston, Andre Martino, Anu Mathur, Damian McCormack, Britta Moebius, Manja Nickel, Erin K O'Brien, Momo Ohta, Shannon O'Loughlin, Maarten Peeters, Piergiorgio Pescali, Alex Phillips, Michael Pike, Marie-Anne Poussart, Susan Renkert, Jurrian Reurings, Patti Ryan, David Salas, Richard Salveter, Joe Schill, Matthias Schmoll, Ann I Schneider, Runes Schwartz, Tim Shabarekh, Joshua Sharkey, Karl Sigiscar, Barrny Smith, D Srbovic, Timo Stewart, Lesley Sumner, Fred Thornett, David Towers, Johannes van der Heide, Dick van Mersbergen, Clem Vetters, Naomi Wall, Liz & Todd Werner, Whui Mei Yeo, Andrew Young

Lonely Planet Guides by Region

Lonely Planet is known worldwide for publishing practical, reliable and no-nonsense travel information in our guides and on our Web site. The Lonely Planet list covers just about every accessible part of the world. Currently there are 16 series: Travel guides, Shoestring guides, Condensed guides, Phrasebooks, Read This First, Healthy Travel, Walking guides, Cycling guides, Watching Wildlife guides, Pisces Diving & Snorkeling guides, City Maps, Road Atlases, Out to Eat, World Food, Journeys travel literature and Pictorials.

AFRICA Africa on a shoestring • Botswana • Cairo • Cairo City Map • Cape Town • Cape Town City Map • East Africa • Egypt • Egyptian Arabic phrasebook • Ethiopia, Eritrea & Djibouti • Ethiopian Amharic phrasebook • The Gambia & Senegal • Healthy Travel Africa • Kenya • Malawi • Morocco • Moroccan Arabic phrasebook • Mozambique • Namibia • Read This First: Africa • South Africa, Lesotho & Swaziland • Southern Africa • Southern Africa Road Atlas • Swahili phrasebook • Tanzania, Zanzibar & Pemba • Trekking in East Africa • Tunisia • Watching Wildlife East Africa • Watching Wildlife Southern Africa • West Africa • World Food Morocco • Zambia • Zimbabwe, Botswana & Namibia
Travel Literature: Mali Blues: Traveling to an African Beat • The Rainbird: A Central African Journey • Songs to an African Sunset: A Zimbabwean Story

AUSTRALIA & THE PACIFIC Aboriginal Australia & the Torres Strait Islands •Auckland • Australia • Australian phrasebook • Australia Road Atlas • Cycling Australia • Cycling New Zealand • Fiji • Fijian phrasebook • Healthy Travel Australia, NZ & the Pacific • Islands of Australia's Great Barrier Reef • Melbourne • Melbourne City Map • Micronesia • New Caledonia • New South Wales • New Zealand • Northern Territory • Outback Australia • Out to Eat – Melbourne • Out to Eat – Sydney • Papua New Guinea • Pidgin phrasebook • Queensland • Rarotonga & the Cook Islands • Samoa • Solomon Islands • South Australia • South Pacific • South Pacific phrasebook • Sydney • Sydney City Map • Sydney Condensed • Tahiti & French Polynesia • Tasmania • Tonga • Tramping in New Zealand • Vanuatu • Victoria • Walking in Australia • Watching Wildlife Australia • Western Australia
Travel Literature: Islands in the Clouds: Travels in the Highlands of New Guinea • Kiwi Tracks: A New Zealand Journey • Sean & David's Long Drive

CENTRAL AMERICA & THE CARIBBEAN Bahamas, Turks & Caicos • Baja California • Belize, Guatemala & Yucatán • Bermuda • Central America on a shoestring • Costa Rica • Costa Rica Spanish phrasebook • Cuba • Cycling Cuba • Dominican Republic & Haiti • Eastern Caribbean • Guatemala • Havana • Healthy Travel Central & South America • Jamaica • Mexico • Mexico City • Panama • Puerto Rico • Read This First: Central & South America • Virgin Islands • World Food Caribbean • World Food Mexico • Yucatán
Travel Literature: Green Dreams: Travels in Central America

EUROPE Amsterdam • Amsterdam City Map • Amsterdam Condensed • Andalucía • Athens • Austria • Baltic States phrasebook • Barcelona • Barcelona City Map • Belgium & Luxembourg • Berlin • Berlin City Map • Britain • British phrasebook • Brussels, Bruges & Antwerp • Brussels City Map • Budapest • Budapest City Map • Canary Islands • Catalunya & the Costa Brava • Central Europe • Central Europe phrasebook • Copenhagen • Corfu & the Ionians • Corsica • Crete • Crete Condensed • Croatia • Cycling Britain • Cycling France • Cyprus • Czech & Slovak Republics • Czech phrasebook • Denmark • Dublin • Dublin City Map • Dublin Condensed • Eastern Europe • Eastern Europe phrasebook • Edinburgh • Edinburgh City Map • England • Estonia, Latvia & Lithuania • Europe on a shoestring • Europe phrasebook • Finland • Florence • Florence City Map • France • Frankfurt City Map • Frankfurt Condensed • French phrasebook • Georgia, Armenia & Azerbaijan • Germany • German phrasebook • Greece • Greek Islands • Greek phrasebook • Hungary • Iceland, Greenland & the Faroe Islands • Ireland • Italian phrasebook • Italy • Kraków • Lisbon • The Loire • London • London City Map • London Condensed • Madrid • Madrid City Map • Malta • Mediterranean Europe • Milan, Turin & Genoa • Moscow • Munich • Netherlands • Normandy • Norway • Out to Eat – London • Out to Eat – Paris • Paris • Paris City Map • Paris Condensed • Poland • Polish phrasebook • Portugal • Portuguese phrasebook • Prague • Prague City Map • Provence & the Côte d'Azur • Read This First: Europe • Rhodes & the Dodecanese • Romania & Moldova • Rome • Rome City Map • Rome Condensed • Russia, Ukraine & Belarus • Russian phrasebook • Scandinavian & Baltic Europe • Scandinavian phrasebook • Scotland • Sicily • Slovenia • South-West France • Spain • Spanish phrasebook • Stockholm • St Petersburg • St Petersburg City Map • Sweden • Switzerland • Tuscany • Ukrainian phrasebook • Venice • Vienna • Wales • Walking in Britain • Walking in France • Walking in Ireland • Walking in Italy • Walking in Scotland • Walking in Spain • Walking in Switzerland • Western Europe • World Food France • World Food Greece • World Food Ireland • World Food Italy • World Food Spain **Travel Literature:** After Yugoslavia • Love and War in the Apennines • The Olive Grove: Travels in Greece • On the Shores of the Mediterranean • Round Ireland in Low Gear • A Small Place in Italy

Lonely Planet Mail Order

L onely Planet products are distributed worldwide. They are also available by mail order from Lonely Planet, so if you have difficulty finding a title please write to us. North and South American residents should write to 150 Linden St, Oakland, CA 94607, USA; European and African residents should write to 10a Spring Place, London NW5 3BH, UK; and residents of other countries to Locked Bag 1, Footscray, Victoria 3011, Australia.

INDIAN SUBCONTINENT & THE INDIAN OCEAN Bangladesh • Bengali phrasebook • Bhutan • Delhi • Goa • Healthy Travel Asia & India • Hindi & Urdu phrasebook • India • India & Bangladesh City Map • Indian Himalaya • Karakoram Highway • Kathmandu City Map • Kerala • Madagascar • Maldives • Mauritius, Réunion & Seychelles • Mumbai (Bombay) • Nepal • Nepali phrasebook • North India • Pakistan • Rajasthan • Read This First: Asia & India • South India • Sri Lanka • Sri Lanka phrasebook • Tibet • Tibetan phrasebook • Trekking in the Indian Himalaya • Trekking in the Karakoram & Hindukush • Trekking in the Nepal Himalaya • World Food India **Travel Literature**: The Age of Kali: Indian Travels and Encounters • Hello Goodnight: A Life of Goa • In Rajasthan • Maverick in Madagascar • A Season in Heaven: True Tales from the Road to Kathmandu • Shopping for Buddhas • A Short Walk in the Hindu Kush • Slowly Down the Ganges

MIDDLE EAST & CENTRAL ASIA Bahrain, Kuwait & Qatar • Central Asia • Central Asia phrasebook • Dubai • Farsi (Persian) phrasebook • Hebrew phrasebook • Iran • Israel & the Palestinian Territories • Istanbul • Istanbul City Map • Istanbul to Cairo • Istanbul to Kathmandu • Jerusalem • Jerusalem City Map • Jordan • Lebanon • Middle East • Oman & the United Arab Emirates • Syria • Turkey • Turkish phrasebook • World Food Turkey • Yemen **Travel Literature**: Black on Black: Iran Revisited • Breaking Ranks: Turbulent Travels in the Promised Land • The Gates of Damascus • Kingdom of the Film Stars: Journey into Jordan

NORTH AMERICA Alaska • Boston • Boston City Map • Boston Condensed • British Columbia • California & Nevada • California Condensed • Canada • Chicago • Chicago City Map • Chicago Condensed • Florida • Georgia & the Carolinas • Great Lakes • Hawaii • Hiking in Alaska • Hiking in the USA • Honolulu & Oahu City Map • Las Vegas • Los Angeles • Los Angeles City Map • Louisiana & the Deep South • Miami • Miami City Map • Montreal • New England • New Orleans • New Orleans City Map • New York City • New York City Map • New York City Condensed • New York, New Jersey & Pennsylvania • Oahu • Out to Eat – San Francisco • Pacific Northwest • Rocky Mountains • San Diego & Tijuana • San Francisco • San Francisco City Map • Seattle • Seattle City Map • Southwest • Texas • Toronto • USA • USA phrasebook • Vancouver • Vancouver City Map • Virginia & the Capital Region • Washington, DC • Washington, DC City Map • World Food New Orleans **Travel Literature**: Caught Inside: A Surfer's Year on the California Coast • Drive Thru America

NORTH-EAST ASIA Beijing • Beijing City Map • Cantonese phrasebook • China • Hiking in Japan • Hong Kong & Macau • Hong Kong City Map • Hong Kong Condensed • Japan • Japanese phrasebook • Korea • Korean phrasebook • Kyoto • Mandarin phrasebook • Mongolia • Mongolian phrasebook • Seoul • Shanghai • South-West China • Taiwan • Tokyo • Tokyo Condensed • World Food Hong Kong • World Food Japan **Travel Literature**: In Xanadu: A Quest • Lost Japan

SOUTH AMERICA Argentina, Uruguay & Paraguay • Bolivia • Brazil • Brazilian phrasebook • Buenos Aires • Buenos Aires City Map • Chile & Easter Island • Colombia • Ecuador & the Galapagos Islands • Healthy Travel Central & South America • Latin American Spanish phrasebook • Peru • Quechua phrasebook • Read This First: Central & South America • Rio de Janeiro • Rio de Janeiro City Map • Santiago de Chile • South America on a shoestring • Trekking in the Patagonian Andes • Venezuela **Travel Literature**: Full Circle: A South American Journey

SOUTH-EAST ASIA Bali & Lombok • Bangkok • Bangkok City Map • Burmese phrasebook • Cambodia • Cycling Vietnam, Laos & Cambodia • East Timor phrasebook • Hanoi • Healthy Travel Asia & India • Hill Tribes phrasebook • Ho Chi Minh City (Saigon) • Indonesia • Indonesian phrasebook • Indonesia's Eastern Islands • Java • Lao phrasebook • Laos • Malay phrasebook • Malaysia, Singapore & Brunei • Myanmar (Burma) • Philippines • Pilipino (Tagalog) phrasebook • Read This First: Asia & India • Singapore • Singapore City Map • South-East Asia on a shoestring • South-East Asia phrasebook • Thailand • Thailand's Islands & Beaches • Thailand, Vietnam, Laos & Cambodia Road Atlas • Thai phrasebook • Vietnam • Vietnamese phrasebook • World Food Indonesia • World Food Thailand • World Food Vietnam

ALSO AVAILABLE: Antarctica • The Arctic • The Blue Man: Tales of Travel, Love and Coffee • Brief Encounters: Stories of Love, Sex & Travel • Buddhist Stupas in Asia: The Shape of Perfection • Chasing Rickshaws • The Last Grain Race • Lonely Planet ... On the Edge: Adventurous Escapades from Around the World • Lonely Planet Unpacked • Lonely Planet Unpacked Again • Not the Only Planet: Science Fiction Travel Stories • Ports of Call: A Journey by Sea • Sacred India • Travel Photography: A Guide to Taking Better Pictures • Travel with Children • Tuvalu: Portrait of an Island Nation

LONELY PLANET

You already know that Lonely Planet produces more than this one guidebook, but you might not be aware of the other products we have on this region. Here is a selection of titles that you may want to check out as well:

St Petersburg map
ISBN 1 86450 179 0
US$5.99 • UK£3.99

St Petersburg
ISBN 1 86450 325 4
US$15.99 • UK£9.99

Russian phrasebook
ISBN 1 86450 106 5
US$7.95 • UK£4.50

Russia & Belarus
ISBN 1 74059 265 4
US$29.99 • UK£18.99

Trans-Siberian Railway
ISBN 1 86450 335 1
US$15.99 • UK£12.99

Eastern Europe phrasebook
ISBN 1 86450 227 4
US$8.99 • UK£4.99

Eastern Europe
ISBN 1 74059 289 1
US$27.99 • UK£15.99

Europe on a shoestring
ISBN 1 74059 314 6
US$24.99 • UK£14.99

Read This First: Europe
ISBN 1 86450 136 7
US$14.99 • UK£8.99

Poland
ISBN 1 74059 082 1
US$19.99 • UK£12.99

Kraków
ISBN 0 86442 698 4
US$14.95 • UK£9.99

Romania & Moldova
ISBN 1 86450 058 1
US$16.99 • UK£10.99

Available wherever books are sold

Index

Text

Bold indicates maps.

Bars & Clubs

Places to Stay

Places to Eat

Boxed Text

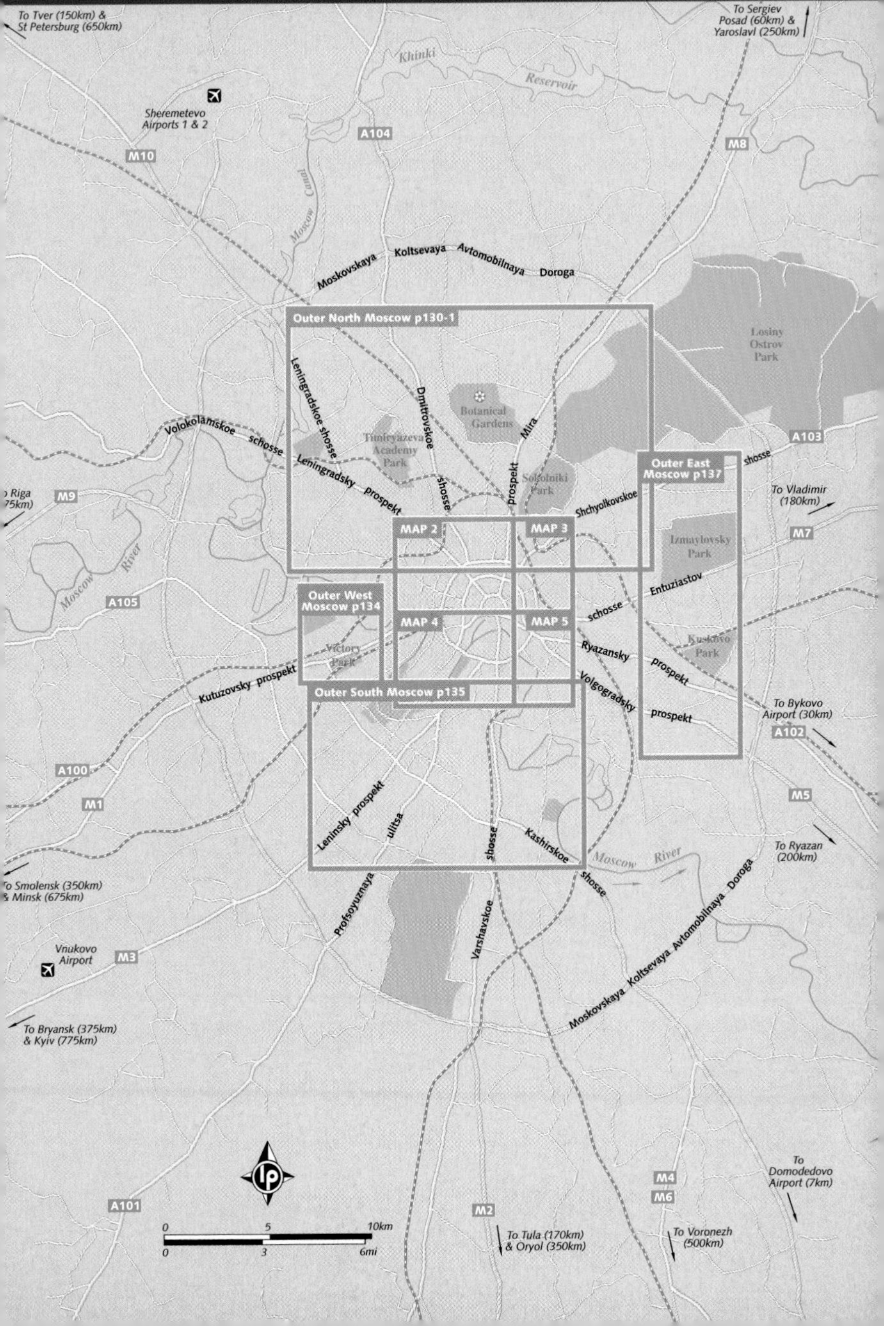

To Tver (150km) &
St Petersburg (650km)

To Sergiev
Posad (60km) &
Yaroslavl (250km)

Khinki

Reservoir

Sheremetevo
Airports 1 & 2

M10

A104

M8

Moskovskaya Koltsevaya Avtomobilnaya Doroga

Outer North Moscow p130-1

*Losiny
Ostroy
Park*

Leningradskoe schosse

Dmitrovskoe

Botanical
Gardens

Mira

A103

Timiryazevskoe
Academy
Park

prospekt

Sokolniki
Park

**Outer East
Moscow p137**

schosse

Leningradsky prospekt

schosse

Shchyolkovskoe

To Riga
(75km)

M9

*Izmaylovsky
Park*

MAP 2

MAP 3

To Vladimir
(180km)

M7

River

A105

Entuziastov

*Kuskovo
Park*

Moscow

**Outer West
Moscow p134**

MAP 4

MAP 5

schosse

prospekt

Victory
Park

Ryazansky

Kutuzovsky prospekt

Volgogradsky

prospekt

To Bykovo
Airport (30km)

A100

Outer South Moscow p135

prospekt

A102

M1

M5

Leninsky prospekt

ulitsa

Kashirskoe

To Ryazan
(200km)

Profsoyuznaya

schosse

Moscow River

To Smolensk (350km)
& Minsk (675km)

Vnukovo
Airport

M3

Varshavskoe

schosse

Moskovskaya Koltsevaya Avtomobilnaya Doroga

To Bryansk (375km)
& Kyiv (775km)

To
Domodedovo
Airport (7km)

M4

M6

A101

LP

0   5   10km
0   3   6mi

M2

To Tula (170km)
& Oryol (350km)

To Voronezh
(500km)

MAP 2 CENTRAL MOSCOW

Bolotnay
1 ❖ Botkinsky 1-y proezd
Botkinsky 2 proezd
Noveya Bashilovka ul
Begovaya alleya
Skakovaya ul
ul Pravdy ul
Leningradsky prosp
Yamskogo Polya 3-ya ul
Payatsky per
Novolesnoy

Khoroshevsky 1 proezd
ul Polikarpova
Begovaya ul

Hippodrome

Lesnoy 2-ya per
Lesnoy 4-y per
Lesnoy 3-y
ul Butyrsky val
Verkhnyaya ul

0   200   400m
0   200   400yd

Belorusskaya ❿ M Belorusskaya 3 ▼
Tverskaya
Zatava pl
5
ul Alekseandra Nevski
pereulok Aleksa Nevski
Belorussky
Vokzal
7 ▼ 8 ▼ 4 ▼
9 ▼ 10 ▼
6
3-ya Tverskaya Yamskaya
2-ya Tverskaya Yamskaya
1-ya Tverskaya Yamskaya

M Begovaya

2 ▼
Gruzinsky val
Bol Kondratevsky
Gruzinsky per
11
12 ▼
Brestskaya
13

ul Presnensky val
Elektrichesky per
Mal Tishinsky per
Sredny Tishinsky per
Tishinskaya pl
Vasilevskaya ul
ul Yuliusa Fuchika
1-ya ul

Khodynskaya ul
2-y Zemlyny per
1-y Zemlyny per
Sredny Tishinsky per
39 ▼
Bol Tishinsky per
Bol Tishinsky per
Bol Gruzinskaya ul

Bol Sadov
3 ❚

Bol
Zvenigorodsky
2-y per
Delabraskaya ul
Bol Zvenigorodsky 1-y per
ul Klimashkina
Novopresnensky per
Bol Gruzinskaya ul
Zoologichesky per
Krasna per
ul Yaroslava Gasheka
Krasna

ul Serega Makeeva
Rastorguevsky per
Gruzinskaya
Mal

ul 1905 goda
ul Presnensky val
Stolyarny per
Zoologichesky ul
Vermolayevsky per
37
Bol Patriarshy per

Ulitsa 1905
Goda
M
40 ▼
Zvenigorodskoe sh
Zvenigorodskoe sh
38 🖼
Spiridonovka
46
ul Kostikova
ul Krasnaya Presnya
45 ●

ul A Zhivova
Troitsgorny val
ul 1905 goda
Predtechensky per
Barrikadnaya ul
M Barrikadnaya
42 ▼
43 ▭
Granatny per
44 ●
Mal Nikitskaya ul

Krasnopresnenskaya M
ul Zamorenova
41 ▭
Verkhniy Predtechensky per
Druzhinnikovskaya ul
Bol Konyus kovsky per
169 ●
168 ▼
167 ▼
Bol Nikitskaya ul

ul Severyanovskaya 2-ya
Studenchesky per
ul 1905 goda
Bol Trekhgorny per
Novovagankovsky per
Srednly Troitgorny per
Mal Tipolgorny per
Rochdelskaya ul
ul Nikolaeva
Glubsky
per
Kudrinsky
per
Stanislav ul
Skateriny per
Khlebny per
Povarskaya ul
166 ●

ul Mantulinskaya
177 ▼
176
175 ♠
174 ▼
170 🏛
171 ▭
172 ●
Kompozitorskaya ul
184
Park
Krasnaya
Presnya
179 ▪
173 ●
Bol Devyatinsky per
186
185 🏣
178 ▼
Moscow River
Novy Arbat ul
Novy Arbat ul

nab Tarasa Shevchenko
Ukrainsky bul
Kutuzovsky prosp
180 ▪
Kalininsky most
Smolenskaya nab
Bol Novopesshovsky
Protochny per
Panfilovsky per
Pryamoy per
Novinsky bul
ul Voevodina
Spasopeskovskaya pl
183 🏣
181 ▭
182 ▼
per Shlomina

MAP 4

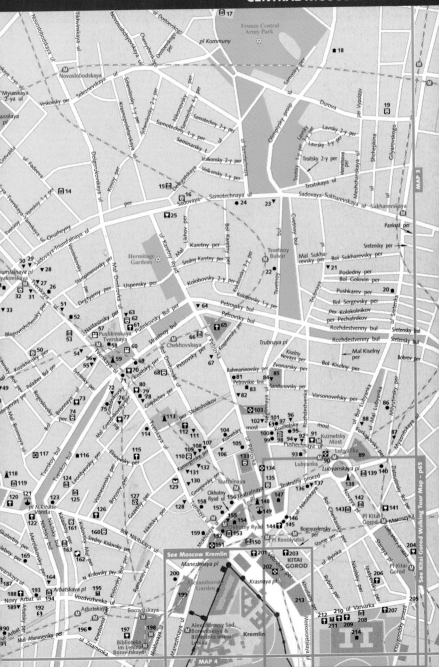

MAP 2 CENTRAL MOSCOW

PLACES TO STAY
5 Art Hostel
  Искуссвенное Общежитие
6 Marriott Tverskaya Hotel
  Гостиница Марриотт
  Тверская
11 Sheraton Palace Hotel
  Гостиница Шератон Палас
18 Hotel Olympic Penta ; Dome
  Theatre
  Гостиница Олимпик Пента
  и Кинотеатр под Куполом
20 Hotel Sretenskaya
  Гостиница Сретенская
26 Marriott Grand Hotel; AlfaBank
  Марриотт Гран Отель и
  Альфабанк
34 Pekin Hotel
  Гостиница Пекин
47 Hotel Marco Polo Presnya
  Гостиница Марко Поло Пресня
52 Hotel Minsk
  Гостиница Минск
79 Hotel Tsentralnaya
  Гостиница Центральная
83 Hotel Budapest
  Гостиница Будапешт
93 Hotel Savoy
  Гостиница Савой
116 East-West Hotel
  Гостиница Восток Запад
147 Hotel Metropol
  Гостиница Метрополь
154 Hotel Moskva
  Гостиница Москва
159 Hotel National
  Гостиница Националь
172 Hotel Mir
  Гостиница Мир
175 Hotel Mezhdunarodnaya-1
  Гостиница Международная-1
179 Hotel Alexandr Blok
  Гостиница Александр Блок
180 Hotel Ukraina
  Гостиница Украина
214 Hotel Rossiya
  Гостиница Россия

PLACES TO EAT & CAFÉS
2 Canadian Bagel
  Канадский бейгл
3 Zen Coffee; Vremya Yest
  Зен Кофе
7 Shyolk
  Шельк
8 Yakitoria
  Якитория
9 Soup
  Суп
12 Museum
  Музеум
21 York
  Йорк
23 Soleil Express
  Солейл Экспресс
27 Restoran Tandoor
  Ресторан Тандур
28 City Grill
  Сити Грилль

29 American Bar & Grill 1
  Американский бар и грилль
30 Rostik's
  Ростикс
31 Canadian Bagel
  Канадский бейгл
33 Starlite Diner
  Старлайт Дайнер
42 Kishmish (Barrikadnaya)
  Кишмиш на Баррикадной
48 Donna Klara
  Донна Клара
49 Kafe Margarita
  Кафе Маргарита
51 Pekinskaya Utka, Café Gotty
  Пекинская Утка и Кафе Готти
54 Night Flight
  Найт Флайт
55 Scandinavia
  Скандинавия
56 McDonald's
  Макдоналдс
63 Tram
  Трам
64 Taras Bulba
  Тарас Бульба
67 Kitezh
  Китеж
72 Café Pushkin
  Кафе Пушкинь
76 Mesto Vstrechi
  Место Встречи
78 Coffee Bean
  Кофе бин
82 Yakitoria
  Якитория
84 Beloye Solntse Pustyni
  Белое Солнце Пустыни
87 Samovar
  Самовар
88 Tsentralny Gastronom
  Supermarket
  Центральный Гастроном
92 Hola Mexico
  Ола Мексика
94 Shokoladnitsa
  Шоколадница
96 Jagannath; Moscow Artists'
  Union Exhibition Hall
  Джаганнат: Выставочный
  Зал Союза Художников
102 Le Kolon
  Ле Колон
106 Pelmeshka
  Пельмешка
107 Oranzhevoy Galstuk
  Оранжевой Галстук
108 Kafeteriya
  Кафетерия
109 Cicco Pizza
  Чикко Пицца
111 Look In!
  Лук-ин
128 La Cantina
  Ла Кантина
130 Global USA Supermarket
  Глобал США
131 Tibet Kitchen
  Тибетская Куня

132 Zen Coffee
  Зен Кофе
137 Sushi Vesla
  Суши Весла
155 Okhotny Ryad Gastronom
  Гастроном Оотный Ряд
164 Dioskuriya
  Диоскурия
167 Central House Writers (TsDL);
  Zapisky Okhotnika
  Ресторан Центрального
  Дом Литератов (ЦДЛ) и
  Записки Охотника
168 Kafe Karetny Dvor
  Кафе Каретный Двор
174 Shinook, Le Duc
  Шинук и Ле Дюк
177 Santa Fe
  Санта-Фэ
178 Sadko Foodland Supermarket
  Супермаркет Садко Фудлэнд
182 Tinkoff
  Тинкофф
186 Kishmish (Novy Arbat)
  Кишмиш на Новым Арбате
189 Yolki-Palki
  Ёлки-Палки

BARS & CLUBS
13 Besedka
  Беседка
25 BB King
  Б.Б. Кинг
36 B-2
  Б-2
39 Voodoo Lounge
  Вуду Лаунж
40 Sixteen Tons
  Шестнадцать Тониов
70 Garage
  Гараж
73 Club Forte
  Клуб Форте
77 Ryby; Sad
  Рыбы и Сад
80 Bunker
  Бункер
91 Hungry Duck
  Голодная Утка
141 Propaganda
  Пропаганда
197 Rhythm & Blues
  Ритм и блюз
204 Kitaysky Lyotchik Dzhao-Da
  Китайский Лётчик Джао-Да

MUSEUMS & GALLERIES
14 Glinka Museum of Musical
  Culture
  Музей Музыкальной
  Культуры имени Глинки
15 Museum of Decorative & Folk Art
  Музей декоративного и
  прикладного искусства
17 Armed Forces Museum
  Музей Вооруженных Сил
43 Chekhov House-Museum
  Дом-музей Чехова
53 Contemporary History Museum
  Музей современной истории

MAP 2 CENTRAL MOSCOW

66 Moscow Museum of
Contemporary Art
Московский музей
современного искусства
119 Gorky House-Museum
Дом-музей Горького
124 Museum of Folk Art
Музей народного искусства
125 Stanislavsky House-Museum
Дом-музей Станиславского
139 Vladimir Mayakovsky Museum
Музей Владимира
Маяковского
142 Polytechnical Museum
Политехнический музей
143 Moscow City History Museum
Музей истории города
Москвы
150 Former Central Lenin Museum
Бывший Центральный
музей В. И. Ленина
153 Archaeological Museum
Музей археологии города
Москвы
163 Museum of Oriental Art
Музей искусства народов
Востока
170 Shalyapin House-Museum
Дом -музей Шаляпина
187 Mikhail Lermontov House
Museum
Дом-музей Лермонтова
194 Gogol Memorial Rooms; Gogol
Statue
Мемориальные комнаты
Гоголя и Памятник Гоголю
208 Chambers in Zaryadie Museum
Музей Палаты в Зарядье

CHURCHES & MONASTERIES
61 Church of the Nativity of the
Virgin in Putinki
Церковь Рождества
Богородицы в Путинках
65 Upper St Peter Monastery
Высоко-Петровский
Монастырь
112 Church of SS Cosma & Damian
Церковь святых Косьмы и
Дамиана
115 Church of the Resurrection
Церковь Воскресения
120 Church of the Grand Ascension
Церковь Большого Вознесения
122 Church of Feodor Studit
Церковь Феодора Студита
126 Church of the Small Ascension
Церковь Малого Вознесения
144 Zaikonospassky Monastery
Заиконоспасский монастырь
183 Church of the Saviour in Peski
Церковь Спаса на Песках
188 Church of St Simeon the Stylite
Церковь Симеона Стольника
201 Kazan Cathedral
Казанский Собор
203 Monastery of Epiphany
Богоявленский монастырь

205 All Saints Cathedral on the
Kulishka
Храм всех святых на
Кулышках
206 Church of the Trinity in Nikitniki
Церковь Троицы в Никитниках
207 St George's Church
Церковь Св. Георгия
209 Monastery of the Sign
Знаменский монастырь
210 St Maxim the Blessed's Church
Церковь Максима Блаженного
212 St Barbara's Church
Церковь Св. Варвары

THEATRES
16 Obraztsov Puppet Theatre &
Museum
Кукольный театр имени
Сергея Образцова
19 Durov Theatre
Театр Дурова
32 Tchaikovsky Concert Hall
Концертный зал имени
Чайковского
50 Young Spectator's Theatre
Театр Юного Зрителя
62 Lenkom Theatre
Театр Ленком
68 Stanislavsky & Nemirovich-
Danchenko Musical Theatre
Музыкальный театр имени
Станиславского и
Немировича-Данченко
74 Pushkin Drama Theatre
Драматический театр
имени Пушкина
110 MKhAT (Chekhov Art Theatre)
МХАТ имени Чехова
133 Bolshoi Theatre
Большой Театр
135 Maly Theatre
Малый Драматический Театр
160 Moscow Tchaikovsky
Conservatoire
Консерватория имени
Чайковского
161 Mayakovsky Theatre
Театр имени Маяковского

OTHER
1 Botkin Hospital
Боткина Больница
4 Czech Airlines
Чешские Авиалинии
10 British Airways
Британская Авиадиния
22 Old (Nikulin) Circus at Tsvetnoy
Boulevard
Цирк Никулина на
Цветном бульваре
24 Gzhel Factory Shop
Гжель заводский магазин
35 Bulgakov's Flat
Квартира Булгакова
37 Patriarch's Ponds
Патриаршие Пруды
38 Moscow Zoo
Московский зоопарк
41 Museum Cinema
Кино Музея

44 Inostrannie Knigi
Магазин Иностранные книги
45 Patriarshy Dom Tours
Патриарший Дом Туры
46 European Medical Centre
Европейский Медицинский
Центр
57 Kodak Kinomir
Кодак Киномир
58 Izvestia
Известия
59 Pushkin Statue
Памятник Пушкину
60 Pushkinsky Cinema
Кинотеатр Пушкинский
69 Moscow News
Московские Новости
71 Yeliseev Grocery Store
Елисеевский магазин
75 LOT Polish Airlines
ЛОТ Польская авиалиния
81 Aeroflot
Аэрофлот
85 Sandunovskiye Baths
Сандуновские бани
86 Intourist
Интурист
89 Lubyanka
Лубянка
90 Detsky Mir (Children's World);
NetLand
Детский Мир и Нетлэнд
95 Angliskaya Kniga po
Kuznetsk
Английская Книга по
Кузнецком
97 Atlas Map Store
Атлас магазин
98 Internet Club
Интернет Клуб
99 Committee for Culture
Комитет Культуры
100 Turkish Airlines
Турецкая авиалиния
101 Alpha Bank
Альфабанк
103 Petrovsky Passazh
Петровский Пассаж
104 Japan Airlines; SAS; Air China
Японские Авиалинии и
Скандинавские Авиалинии
и Авиалинии Китая
105 Magazin – Salon Bolshoi Teatr
Магазин-салон Большого
Театра
113 Yury Dolgoruky Statue
Памятник Юрию Долгорукому
114 Moscow Mayor's Office
Московская Мэрия
117 Lyubovicheskaya Synagogue
Любавическая синагога
118 Statue of Alexander Blok
Памятник Александру Блоку
121 Rotunda Fountain
Фонтан Ротонда
123 ITAR-TASS
ИТАР-ТАСС

MAP 2 CENTRAL MOSCOW

JOHN S KING

The beautiful cluster of sparkling domes and turreted walls of Novodevichy Convent

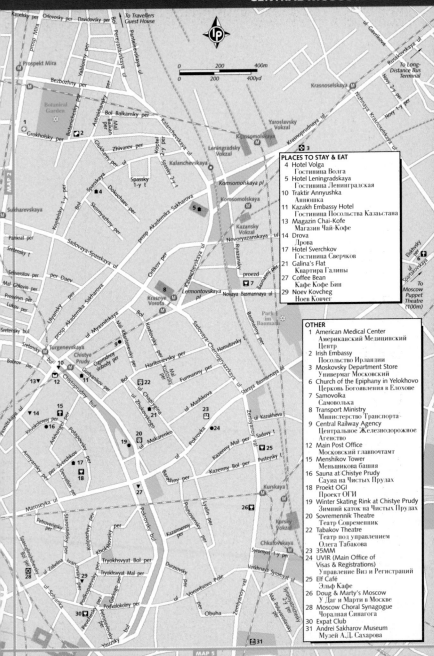

PLACES TO STAY & EAT

4 Hotel Volga
Гостиница Волга
5 Hotel Leningradskaya
Гостиница Ленинградская
10 Traktir Annyushka
Аннюшка
11 Kazakh Embassy Hotel
Гостиница Посольства Казахстана
13 Magazin Chai-Kofe
Магазин Чай-Кофе
14 Drova
Дрова
17 Hotel Sverchkov
Гостиница Сверчков
21 Galina's Flat
Квартира Галины
27 Coffee Bean
Кафе Кофе Бин
29 Noev Kovcheg
Ноев Ковчег

OTHER

1 American Medical Center
Американский Медицинский Центр
2 Irish Embassy
Посольство Ирландии
3 Moskovsky Department Store
Универмаг Московский
4 Church of the Epiphany in Yelokhovo
Церковь Богоявления в Елохове
5 Samovolka
Самоволка
7 Transport Ministry
Министерство Транспорта
9 Central Railway Agency
Центральное Железнодорожное Агенство
12 Main Post Office
Московский главпочтамт
15 Menshikov Tower
Меньшикова башня
16 Sauna at Chistye Prudy
Сауна на Чистых Прудах
18 Proekt OGI
Проект ОГИ
19 Winter Skating Rink at Chistye Prudy
Зимний каток на Чистых Прудах
20 Sovremennik Theatre
Театр Современник
22 Tabakov Theatre
Театр под управлением Олега Табакова
23 35MM
24 UVIR (Main Office of Visas & Registrations)
Управление Виз и Регистраций
25 Elf Café
Эльф Кафе
26 Doug & Marty's Moscow
У Дага и Марти в Москве
28 Moscow Choral Synagogue
Хоральная Синагога
30 Expat Club
31 Andrei Sakharov Museum
Музей А.Д. Сахарова

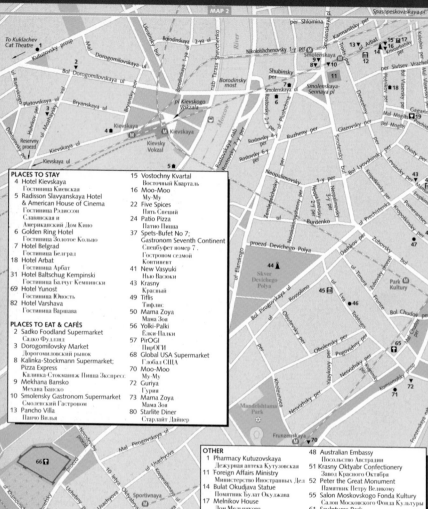

MAP 4 CENTRAL MOSCOW

MAP 2

Spasopeskovskaya pl

PLACES TO STAY
4 Hotel Kievskaya
  Гостиница Киевская
5 Radisson Slavyanskaya Hotel
  & American House of Cinema
  Гостиница Рэдиссон
  Славянская и
  Американский Дом Кино
6 Golden Ring Hotel
  Гостиница Золотое Кольцо
7 Hotel Belgrad
  Гостиница Белград
18 Hotel Arbat
  Гостиница Арбат
31 Hotel Baltschug Kempinski
  Гостиница Балчуг Кемпински
69 Hotel Yunost
  Гостиница Юность
82 Hotel Varshava
  Гостиница Варшава

PLACES TO EAT & CAFÉS
2 Sadko Foodland Supermarket
  Садко Фудлэнд
3 Dorogomilovsky Market
  Дорогомиловский рынок
8 Kalinka-Stockmann Supermarket;
  Pizza Express
  Калинка-Стокманн Пицца Экспресс
9 Mekhana Bansko
  Механа Банско
10 Smolensky Gastronom Supermarket
  Смоленский Гастроном
13 Pancho Villa
  Панчо Вилья

15 Vostochny Kvartal
  Восточный Квартал
16 Moo-Moo
  Му-Му
22 Five Spices
  Пять Специй
24 Patio Pizza
  Патио Пицца
37 Spets-Bufet No 7;
  Gastronom Seventh Continent
  Спецбуфет номер 7 .
  Гостроном седмой
  Континент
41 New Vasyuki
  Нью Васюки
43 Krasny
  Красный
49 Tiflis
  Тифлис
50 Mama Zoya
  Мама Зоя
56 Yolki-Palki
  Ёлки-Палки
57 PirOGI
  ПирОГИ
68 Global USA Supermarket
  Глобал США
70 Moo-Moo
  Му-Му
72 Guriya
  Гурия
73 Mama Zoya
  Мама Зоя
80 Starlite Diner
  Старлайт Дайнер

OTHER
1 Pharmacy Kutuzovskaya
  Дежурная аптека Кутузовская
11 Foreign Affairs Ministry
  Министерство Иностранных Дел
14 Bulat Okudjava Statue
  Помятник Булат Окуджава
17 Melnikov House
  Дом Мельникова
19 Krizis Zhanra
  Кризис Жанра
20 Canadian Embassy
  Посольство Канади
21 Delta; Sabina
  Авиалиния Делта .
  Авиалиния Сабина
29 Andrew's Consulting
  Туристическое агенство Андрея
32 Rosie O'Grady's
  Рози О'Грэди с
35 Pashkov House
  Дом Пашкова
42 Leo Tolstoy Statue
  Памятник Льву Толстому
46 Cosmic Bowling
  Космик Боулинг
47 Finnair
  Финнэр

48 Australian Embassy
  Посольство Австралии
51 Krasny Oktyabr Confectionery
  Завод Красного Октября
52 Peter the Great Monument
  Памятник Петру Великому
55 Salon Moskovskogo Fonda Kultury
  Салон Московского Фонда Культуры
61 Sculptures Park
  Парк скультптур
64 Chaika Swimming Pool
  Плавательный бассейн Чайка
67 American Express; KLM
  Голландские Королевские
  Авиалинии . Америкэн Экспресс
71 Infinity Travel
  Туристическое Агенство
  Инфинити Тревел
74 Gorky Park Amusement Park
  Парк развлечений в Парке Горького
75 Gorky Park Main Entrance
  Главный вход в Парк Горького
79 French Embassy
  Посольство Франции
81 Air France
  Эр Франс
83 Gorky Park Beer Hall
  Пивной Павильон в Парке Горького

Outer South Moscow Map p135

0 — 200 — 400m
0 — 200 — 400yd

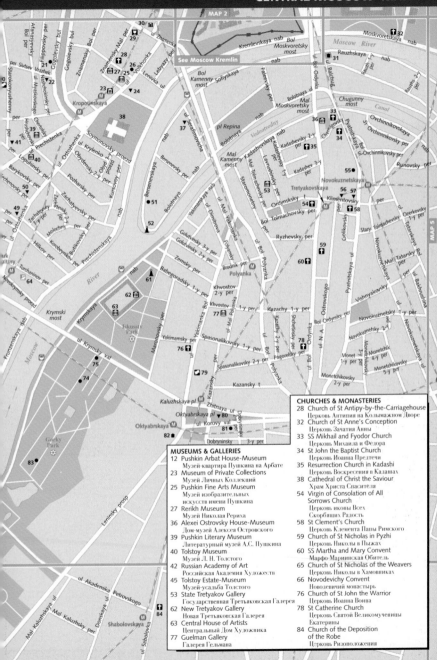

MAP 2

Kremlevskaya nab

See Moscow Kremlin

Moscow River

Moskvoretskaya nab

Rauzhskaya nab

MAP 5

CHURCHES & MONASTERIES

28 Church of St Antipy-by-the-Carriagehouse
    Церковь Антипия на Колымажном Дворе
32 Church of St Anne's Conception
    Церковь Зачатия Анны
33 SS Mikhail and Fyodor Church
    Церковь Михаила и Федора
34 St John the Baptist Church
    Церковь Иоанна Предтечи
35 Resurrection Church in Kadashi
    Церковь Воскресения в Кадашах
38 Cathedral of Christ the Saviour
    Храм Христа Спасителя
54 Virgin of Consolation of All
    Sorrows Church
    Церковь иконы Всех
    Скорбящих Радость
58 St Clement's Church
    Церковь Клемента Папы Римского
59 Church of St Nicholas in Pyzhi
    Церковь Николы в Пыжах
60 SS Martha and Mary Convent
    Марфо-Мариинская Обитель
65 Church of St Nicholas of the Weavers
    Церковь Николы в Хамовниках
66 Novodevichy Convent
    Новодевичий монастырь
76 Church of St John the Warrior
    Церковь Иоанна Воина
78 St Catherine Church
    Церковь Святой Великомученицы
    Екатерины
84 Church of the Deposition
    of the Robe
    Церковь Ризоположения

MUSEUMS & GALLERIES

12 Pushkin Arbat House-Museum
    Музей-квартира Пушкина на Арбате
23 Museum of Private Collections
    Музей Личных Коллекций
25 Pushkin Fine Arts Museum
    Музей изобразительных
    искусств имени Пушкина
27 Rerikh Museum
    Музей Николая Рериха
36 Alexei Ostrovsky House-Museum
    Дом-музей Алексея Островского
39 Pushkin Literary Museum
    Литературный музей А.С. Пушкина
40 Tolstoy Museum
    Музей Л. Н. Толстого
42 Russian Academy of Art
    Российская Академия Художеств
45 Tolstoy Estate-Museum
    Музей-усадьба Толстого
53 State Tretyakov Gallery
    Государственная Третьяковская Галерея
62 New Tretyakov Gallery
    Новая Третьяковская Галерея
63 Central House of Artists
    Центральный Дом Художника
77 Guelman Gallery
    Галерея Гельмана

MAP 5 CENTRAL MOSCOW

PLACES TO STAY & EAT
2 American Bar & Grill 2
  Американский Бар и Гриль-2
16 Verona
  Верона
21 Hotel Katerina
  Гостиница Катерина

CHURCHES & MONASTERIES
3 Andronikov Monastery & Andrey
  Rublyov Museum
  Спасо-Андроников Монастырь
  и музей Андрея Рублева
8 Church of St Nikita Beyond the Yauza
  Церковь Никиты за Яузой
10 Potters' Church of the Assumption
  Церковь Успения Богородицы
  в Гончарной Слободе
11 Taganka Gates Church of
  St Nicholas
  Церковь Николы у Таганских Ворот
13 Cathedral of St Martin
  the Confessor
  Храм Святого Мартина
  Исповедника
17 New Monastery of the Saviour
  Новоспасский монастырь

OTHER
1 Kult
  Культ
4 Foreign Literature Library
  Библиотека иностранной литературы
5 Batashyov Palace
  Дворец Баташова
6 Illuzion Cinema
  Кинотеатр Иллюзион
7 Kotelnicheskaya Apartment Block
  Многоквартирый дом на Котельнической набережной
9 Le Club
  Ле Клуб
12 Taganka Theatre
  Театр на Таганке
14 Western Union
15 Three Monkeys
  Три Обезьяны
18 Bakhrushin Theatre Museum
  Театральный музей Бахрушина
19 Lenin Funeral Train
  Траурный поезд Ленина
20 Netcity
22 Novospassky Most Boat Landing
  Пристань Новоспасский Мост
23 Krutitskoe Podvorye
  Крутицкое Подворье

Painted floral motifs on the walls of St Basil's Cathedral

JONATHAN SMITH

Tsereteli's controversial statue of Peter the Great

SIMON RICHMOND

Detail of doorway at the Archangel Cathedral

JONATHAN SMITH

The Triumphal Arch near Borodino Panorama, Kutuzovsky prospekt

A selection of matrioshkas – traditional, hand-painted, wooden, nesting dolls

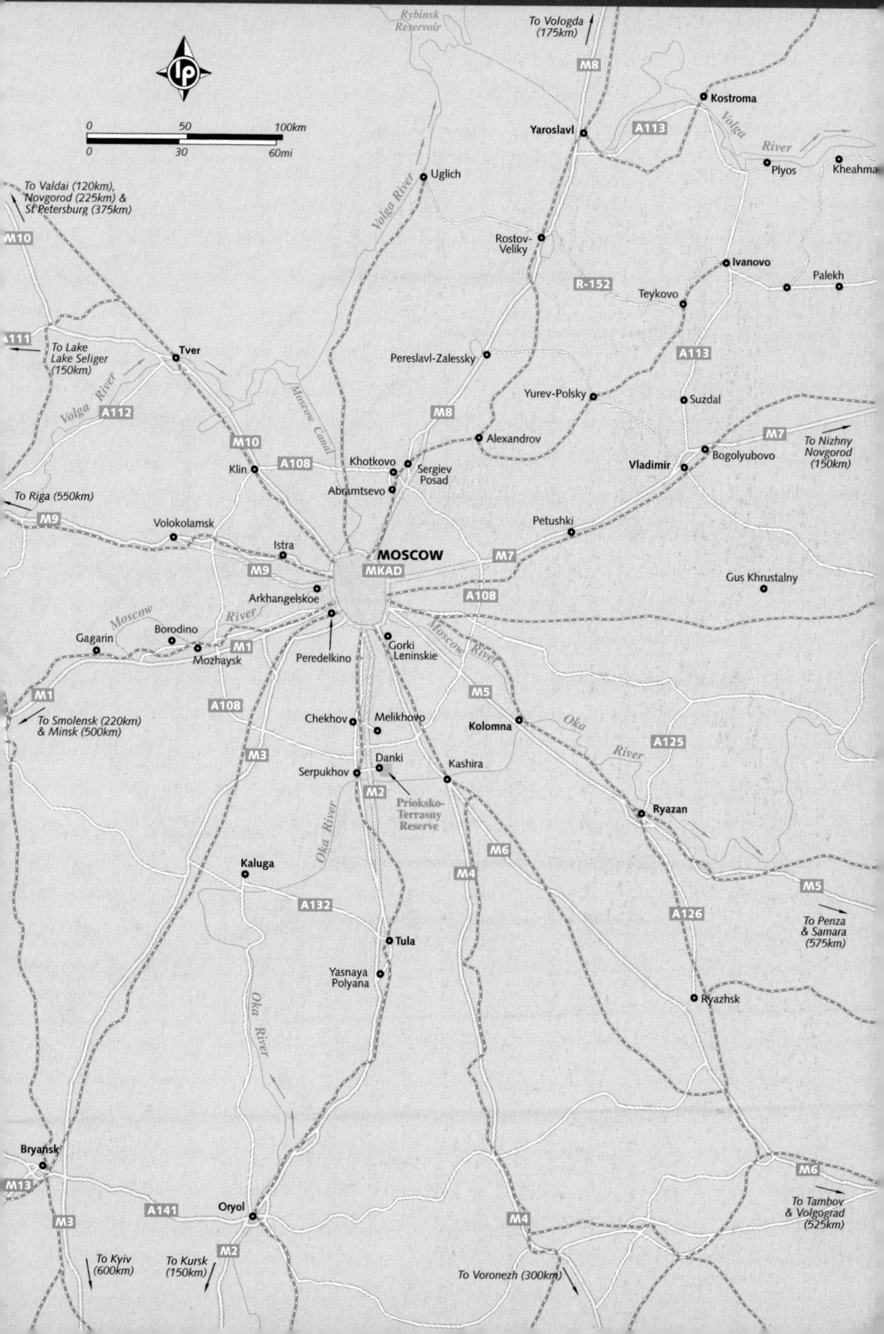

Rybinsk
Reservoir

To Vologda
(175km)

M8

Kostroma

Yaroslavl

A113

Volga River

Plyos

Kheahma

Uglich

Rostov-
Veliky

R-152

Teykovo

Ivanovo

Palekh

To Valdai (120km),
Novgorod (225km) &
St Petersburg (375km)

M10

Volga River

Tver

Pereslavl-Zalessky

Yurev-Polsky

A113

Suzdal

M7

To Lake
Lake Seliger
(150km)

111

Volga River

A112

Moscow Canal

M8

Alexandrov

Vladimir

Bogolyubovo

To Nizhny
Novgorod
(150km)

M10

A108

Khotkovo

Sergiev
Posad

Klin

To Riga (550km)

M9

Volokolamsk

Istra

Abramtsevo

Petushki

M9

MOSCOW

M7

Gus Khrustalny

MKAD

A108

Arkhangelskoe

Moscow
River

Gagarin

Borodino

M1

Peredelkino

Gorki
Leninskie

Moscow River

Mozhaysk

M1

To Smolensk (220km)
& Minsk (500km)

A108

Chekhov

Melikhovo

M5

Kolomna

Oka
River

A125

M3

Danki

Kashira

Serpukhov

M2

Ryazan

Prioksko-
Terrasny
Reserve

M6

Kaluga

M4

A126

A132

M5

Oka River

Tula

To Penza
& Samara
(575km)

Yasnaya
Polyana

Ryazhsk

Oka River

Bryansk

M6

M13

M3

A141

Oryol

M4

To Tambov
& Volgograd
(525km)

M2

To Kyiv
(600km)

To Kursk
(150km)

To Voronezh (300km)

MAP 7 MOSCOW METRO

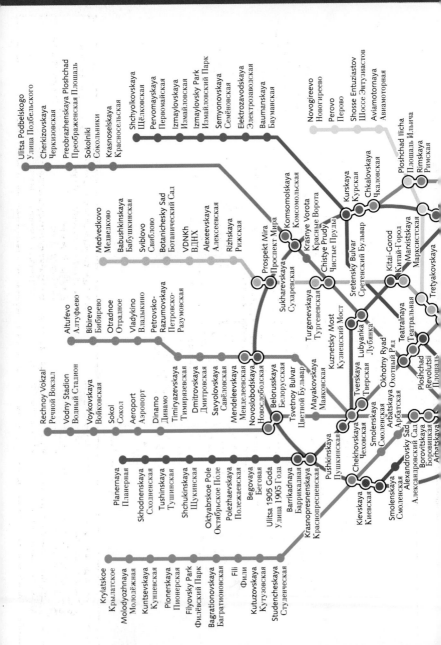